D0407830

MAJOR THEORIES OF PERSONALITY DISORDER

Major Theories of Personality Disorder

Edited by
JOHN F. CLARKIN
and
MARK F. LENZENWEGER

THE GUILFORD PRESS
New York   London

© 1996 The Guilford Press
A Division of Guilford Publications, Inc.
72 Spring Street, New York, NY 10012

Printed in the United States of America

This book is printed on acid-free paper.

Last digit is print number: 9 8 7 6 5 4 3 2 1

Library of Congress Cataloging-in-Publication Data

Major theories of personality disorder / edited by John F.
   Clarkin, Mark F. Lenzenweger.
      p. cm.
   Includes index.
   ISBN 1-57230-082-5
   1. Personality disorders. I. Clarkin, John F.
II. Lenzenweger, Mark F.
RC554.M24 1996
616.85′8—dc20   95-53935
                                                           CIP

Contributors

Aaron T. Beck, MD, Department of Psychiatry, University of Pennsylvania, Philadelphia

Lorna Smith Benjamin, PhD, Department of Psychology, University of Utah, Salt Lake City

John F. Clarkin, PhD, Department of Psychiatry, Cornell University Medical College, New York, New York

Roger D. Davis, PhD candidate, Jackson-Memorial Hospital, University of Miami, Coral Gables, Florida

Richard A. Depue, PhD, Laboratory of Neurobiology of Personality and Emotion, Department of Human Development, Cornell University, Ithaca, New York

Otto F. Kernberg, MD, Department of Psychiatry, The New York Hospital–Cornell Medical Center, White Plains; Columbia University Center for Psychoanalytic Training and Research, New York, New York

Mark F. Lenzenweger, PhD, Laboratory of Experimental Psychopathology, Cornell University, Ithaca, New York; Department of Psychiatry, Cornell University Medical College, New York, New York

Theodore Millon, PhD, DSc, Department of Psychiatry, Harvard Medical School/McLean Hospital, Belmont, Massachusetts; Department of Psychology, University of Miami, Coral Gables, Florida; Institute for Advanced Studies in Personology and Psychopathology, Miami, Florida

James L. Pretzer, PhD, Department of Psychiatry, Case Western Reserve University, Cleveland, Ohio; Cleveland Center for Cognitive Therapy, Beachwood, Ohio

Preface

Personality has long held the attention not only of psychologists and clinical psychiatrists but also theologians, philosophers, and novelists. This fascination lies in the notion that an understanding of the human personality will yield insights into the fundamental nature of humankind. Understanding personality will tell us what makes us tick, so to speak. All students of personality are reincarnations of this age-old desire to understand the motivations and wiles of the human psyche.

Since the introduction of the DSM-III in 1980 and its creation of a separate diagnostic axis (i.e., Axis II) for the personality disorders, interest in the description and classification of the personality disorders has expanded dramatically. The growing empirical research base, driven in part by the introduction of Axis II, has begun to illuminate a variety of fundamental issues in our understanding of the personality disorders. Not only have there been major developments in both the description and diagnosis of them, but advances are occurring in our understanding of the genetic, neurobiological, personologic, and psychosocial variables serving to cause and/or maintain these forms of psychopathology. Moreover, the epidemiology of personality disorders as well as their longitudinal course and development are ripe for exploration, with studies in this area getting underway in recent years.

This rapidly accumulating body of empirical data clearly indicates that the personality disorders are of great interest to research clinicians and psychopathologists, confirming the longstanding interest of the practicing clinician who has always noted the prevalence and disruptive nature of personality pathology. Clinicians know all too well that the treatment of personality disorders is difficult, and that these disorders greatly diminish the quality of life for those who suffer from them. The increase in empirical research is surely welcome; however, a profound lack of theoretical clarity about the disorders has become evident both in the research and in the clinical literature. This volume is an attempt to fill the void with an explication of a few major contemporary theories of the personality disorders. Our vision, therefore, was to assemble a number of position statements from senior theoreticians, each reflecting a distinctly different vantage point in his or her model. We were extremely fortunate to be able to call upon our outstanding colleagues in the personality disorder field, who responded enthusiastically to our idea. We believe we have assembled an exceptional group of contributors, individuals who have each thrown theoretical light on the personality disorders from their respective viewpoints of cognitive, psychodynamic, interpersonal, ecological, and biological perspectives. We have opened this volume with our own position paper that lays the groundwork for the papers that follow, highlighting a variety of historical issues in this area as well as junctures in the research approaches to personality pathology that require greater clarity. It is our firm belief that personality disorders research is just beginning to enter a second phase of development, one that will focus more closely on etiology and pathogenesis, and we argue that sound theoretical models will be essential tools in helping us map this new and exciting uncharted territory.

An effort such as this does not stand alone. It is embedded in a rich professional, clinical, and academic matrix. Therefore, we would like to take this opportunity to thank our chairman of psychiatry at the Cornell University Medical College, Dr. Jack Barchas, for his scholarly advice, administrative support, and enthusiasm in connection with this specific undertaking. His breadth of view about the human condition is inspiring and his generative support has proven essential to our research in personality disorders.

J.F.C.
White Plains, New York

M.F.L.
Ithaca, New York

Contents

1

The Personality Disorders: History, Classification, and Research Issues

MARK F. LENZENWEGER
JOHN F. CLARKIN

In the dialogue between theory and experience, theory always has the first word. It determines the form of the question and thus sets limits to the answer.
—François Jacob (1982, p. 15)

Theory without data runs the risk of ungrounded philosophizing, but data without theory leads to confusion and incomprehension. The definition of the personality disorders in DSM-III (American Psychiatric Association, 1980; and its successors) as well as their separation from other clinical syndromes (Axis I disorders) greatly enhanced the legitimacy of this class of psychopathology as an area for research. Personality disorder research has shown unprecedented and exciting expansion over the past 10 to 15 years. It is the thesis of this volume (in the spirit of the quote from François Jacob) that the time has come to articulate contrasting and competing (at times, partially overlapping) theories of personality disorder in order to stimulate intellectual clarity within the growing body of empirical data on the personality disorders. Moreover, it is our hope that the models and theories of personality pathology presented in this volume will serve not only an organizing function but, perhaps more importantly, as useful heuristics for the next wave of empirical research on the personality disorders.

BRIEF HISTORICAL OVERVIEW
OF PERSONALITY DISORDER THEORIES

One can trace the conceptualization and articulation of personality and related personality pathology in the history of psychiatry and clinical psychology and in the development of personality theory and research in the tradition of academic psychology. Whereas there was considerable interaction between psychiatry and clinical psychology, the writings and research generated by the field of academic psychology were focused mainly on normal personality and had little relationship to the clinical traditions. Our goal is not to review the history of personality theory and related personality disorder theory. Rather, our major focus is to briefly summarize the conceptualizations of those personality theorists who have ventured into the area of personality disorders or the relationship of personality to pathology. This overview is necessarily selective and makes no claim to be exhaustive. We provide references that the interested reader can pursue.

Vaillant and Perry (1985) trace the articulation in the history of clinical psychiatry of the notion that personality itself can be disordered back to work in the 19th century on "moral insanity." By 1907, Kraepelin had described four types of psychopathic personalities. The psychoanalytic study of character pathology began in 1908 with Freud's *Character and Anal Eroticism.* This was followed by Franx Alexander's distinction between neurotic character and symptom neuroses and by Reich's psychoanalytic treatment of personality disorders.

Clinical Psychology and the Assessment
of Personality Pathology

The most unique contributions of clinical psychology to the history of personality and personality pathology were the development and application of instruments for the assessment of personality pathology in clinical settings. The flowering of what became known as the "traditional" approach to personality assessment in clinical settings is exemplified in the writings of Rapaport, Gill, and Schafer (1968). Acrding to these authors, diagnostic testing of personality and ideational content was concerned with "different types of organizations of the subject's spontaneous thought processes, and attempts to infer from their course and characteristics the nature of his personality and maladjustment'' (p. 222). The focus of this traditional approach was shaped by the environment of the day, that is, by the psychiatric diagnostic system in vogue (officially and unofficially) and the predominantly psychodynamic treatment approaches.

In contrast to the full-battery traditional approach, the Minnesota Multiphasic Personality Inventory (MMPI), a self-report questionnaire, was first published in 1943 by Starke Hathaway, PhD, and J. Charnley McKinley, MD (Hathaway & McKinley, 1983), with scales measuring salient clinical syndromes of the day such as depression, hypocondriasis, schizophrenia, and others. The fact that the MMPI was called a ''personality'' test is itself a manifestation of the intertwining of concepts of clinical syndromes and personality/personality pathology. Interestingly, only two (Scale 4: Psychopathic Deviate and Scale 5: Masculinity–Femininity) of the original nine clinical scales actually assessed constructs akin to personality traits or attributes; Scale 0, developed later, was designed to assess social introversion.

In more recent times, there has been less emphasis in clinical assessment in psychiatric settings on projective tests used to assess personality defined in a global sense and more focus on the development of successors to the MMPI that have utilized advances in psychometric development and are more tied to a diagnostic system that makes a distinction between Axis I syndromes and Axis II personality pathology. Illustrative of these instruments are the Millon Clinical Multiaxial Inventory (MCMI; and its successor, the MCMI-II) and the Personality Assessment Inventory (PAI). Given the historical role and importance attached to the clinical interview procedure in psychiatry as well as the advances achieved in the design of structured interviews for the major mood disorders and psychoses (e.g., the Present State Examination [PSE] and Schedule for Affective Disorders and Schizophrenia [SADS]) through the 1970s, it was not surprising to see the careful development of semistructured interviews, for example, the Structural Clinical Interview for DSM-III-R (SCID-II; Spitzer, Williams, & Gibbon, 1987), and the Personality Disorder Examination (PDE; Loranger, 1988), that reliably assess personality disorders as described in the DSM system. Though Axis II structured interviews are primarily used in research settings, their promise for clinical work is appreciable and welcome. The interested reader is referred to Zimmerman (1994) for an excellent review of the extant interviews as well as their applications.

Other self-report personality questionnaires have been developed to capture the dimensions thought to underlie the diagnostic criteria on Axis II. This would include the work of Livesley and colleagues (e.g., Schroeder, Wormworth, & Livesley, 1994) and Clark (1993). Some would speculate that the personality disorders involve maladaptive and inflexible expressions of the basic dimensions of personality as captured in the five-factor model of personality (see Digman, 1990, or John, 1990) or the interpersonal circumplex model of personality (e.g., Wiggins & Pincus, 1989). The personality disorders on Axis II can be described in terms of the five-factor model from theoretical (Widiger, Trull, Clarkin, Sanderson, & Costa, 1994) and empirical (Schroeder et al., 1994) points of view (see below). Finally, at least one effort is under way to develop a comprehensive self-report instrument designed to capture both the putative dimensions underlying normal personality as well as those domains relevant to the assessment of DSM-IV-defined Axis II disorders (i.e., the OMNI Personality Inventory under development by A. W. Loranger).

Academic Psychology

The field of personality within the larger academic world of psychology has been a time-honored tradition that has suffered ups and downs. An examination of the reviews of the field of personality in the *Annual Review of Psychology* provides a historical sense of the academic debates in the field and significant issues that were passionately fought over in the past—for example, do traits exist? One senior observer of the field (Pervin, 1990) has enumerated the recurrent issues, some of which are relevant to and may be rethought (and fought) in the field of personality disorders: (1) definition of personality, (2) relationship of personality theory to psychology and other subdisciplines, including clinical psychology, (3) view of science, (4) views of the person, (5) the idiographic–nomothetic issue, (6) the internal–external issue (i.e., what in the person interacts with which aspect of the environment), (7) the nature–nuture issue, (8) the developmental dimension, (9) persistence and change in personality, and (10) emphasis on conscious versus unconscious processes.

Traditionally, academic personality psychologists studied nonclinical populations. They were more interested in the "normal" personality and consequently gave little attention in their theories to abnormal personality or personality pathology. For example, one of the early leaders of normative personality theory, Gordon Allport (1937) criticized Freud for suggesting a continuum of personality pathology; instead he postulated a division in personality processes between the normal personality and the neurotic personality. The tendency on the part of academic personologists to theorize about and research normative personality most probably reflects not only their substantive area of interest (i.e., normalcy), but also their training (i.e., absence of training in clinical methods and lack of exposure to psychopathological populations) and place of work (the university psychology department as opposed to the clinic and/or psychopathology laboratory). Until relatively recently, there were very few academic personologists who extended their theorizing or empirical work to the pathological personality realm; exceptions such as Henry Murray (1938) and Timothy Leary (1957) are well known. This is a theme that will reverberate throughout this volume: in what setting does the theoretician of personality disorders work, and how does that affect the resulting theory?

THE NEO-KRAEPELINIAN REVOLUTION: DSM-III AND THE BIRTH OF AXIS II

Just as the academic personologists have focused on the normative personality and its structure and development, those in the clinical area (clinical psychologists, psychopathologists, psychiatrists, psychoanalysts) have focused their attention and efforts on the pathological variations seen in human personality functioning. DSM-I (American Psychiatric Association, 1952) provided four categories of psychiatric disorder: (1) disturbances of pattern, (2) disturbances of traits, (3) disturbances of drive, control, and relationships, and (4) sociopathic disturbances. These and subsequent categories of personality disorder in DSM-II (American Psychiatric Association, 1968) were used only when the patient did not fit comfortably in other categories. The personality disorders defined on a separate axis, whether or not a symptomatic disorder was present, first appeared in DSM-III (American Psychiatric Association, 1980). The interested reader is referred to Millon (1982) for one of the best historical reviews of both the process of DSM-III's construction and its formulation of personality disorders as well as a more general prior history of personality disorders.

The advent of DSM-III and its successors, which utilize a multiaxial diagnostic system that makes a distinction between clinical syndromes (Axis I) and personality disorders (Axis II), both brought into sharp focus and encapsulated the controversy concerning the nature and role of personality/personality pathology in the history of psychiatry and the history of modern personality research. The introduction of a distinction between clinical syndromes and personality disorders as well as explicit description of personality pathology within DSM-III by no means brought about unanimity and intellectual peace. In many ways, the introduction of the formal Axis II classification scheme ushered in what would begin an exceedingly active phase of psychopathology research—namely clarification and validation of the personality disorder constructs and beginning efforts at illumination of the relationships between personality and personality disorder (see "Normal Personality and Personality Disorder," below).

Numerous examples can be cited of active productive discussion resulting from the introduction of DSM-III nomenclature: Some have argued from accumulated clinical experience that the particular disorders defined in Axis II do not adequately match clinical reality. Distinctions between hysterical and histrionic personality disorders have been neglected in Axis II (see Kernberg, Chapter 3, this volume); or the very existence of pathological masochism has been only variably recognized and fraught with debate; or clinically rich concepts of psychopathy have been given diminished attention in favor of a behaviorally defined antisocial personality disorder concept. Others have argued at a more basic level that DSM Axis II criteria do not meet scientific standards. Clark (1992) suggested that the Axis II personality criteria were not optimally grouped into "disorders" and do not accurately reflect trait dimensions. These individuals, somewhat optimistically, call for more research to clarify the issues.

These issues highlight some of the difficulties with alleged benefits of an "atheoretical" approach proclaimed by the architects of DSM-III and its successors. The development of DSM-III, really the culminating event of the so-called "neo-Kraepelinian" revolution in psychiatry (see Blashfield, 1984), justifiably sought a diagnostic system that would provide explicit, usually behavioral, criteria that could be reliably assessed. Such a methodological approach to the definition and operationalization of constructs was long known in psychology (see Cronbach & Meehl, 1955), and its utility was established. Therefore, many psychiatric and clinical psychology researchers welcomed the overhaul of the diagnostic system with open arms. Unfortunately, however, it is our sense that the rush for diagnostic reliability and the value placed upon reliability (something all could agree upon) became conflated with or necessarily implied the need for an "atheoretical" approach to diagnosis. The reasons for adopting an atheoretical approach in the contemporary DSM systems were surely complex and were likely a necessity in order to have the diagnostic systems adopted despite parochial interests of the various schools of psychotherapy and clinical practice. In other words, such an approach was necessary given that the product (i.e., DSM) was a quasi-political one, albeit one with important scientific impact. Our point should be obvious; we firmly endorse a methodological approach to diagnosis that is rigorous and displays adequate reliability and validity, but such an approach need not necessarily be "atheoretical." Therefore, in sharp relief, we present in this volume a variety of theories or models of personality pathology, precisely because theories will not only guide empirical measurement of personality pathology but also provide the context in which empirical results can be examined and understood.

ISSUES OF CONCERN FOR SCIENTIFIC THEORIES OF PERSONALITY DISORDER

As we noted above, the advent of Axis II in the multiaxial system introduced by DSM-III and the explicit definition of personality disorders have stimulated scientific and clinical interest in personality pathology. The effect of DSM-III on both research and practice has been unambiguous and rather dramatic, primarily leading to an increase in the rate at which Axis II diagnoses have been made in clinical settings (e.g., Loranger, 1990) but also a marked increase in the number of research studies directed at personality pathology. A review of articles in the prominent scientific psychopathology journals (e.g., *Archives of General Psychiatry, Journal of Abnormal Psychology*) since 1980 will reveal a noteworthy increase in the number of research reports on Axis-II-related topics. This era of scientific growth has been rapid enough, in fact, to warrant development and publication of the specialty journal *Journal of Personality Disorders* as well as the formation of the International Society for the Study of Personality Disorders. By almost any objective index, the rate of scholarly inquiry into personality pathology has seen dramatic growth, and the decades to come are almost certain to see sustained interest in the personality disorders.

The contributors to this volume have articulated their respective views on the nature and organization of personality pathology. In contrast to the "atheoretical" position of DSM-III-R, each of our contributors has taken a stand with respect to the fundamental nature of personality disorder, transcending an approach (i.e., DSM-III-R) that explicitly describes, but, unfortunately, eschews explanation. Consistent with the contents of this volume, our hope is that future scientific work in personality disorders will become increasingly theory-guided. The benefit of such a development in the scientific approach to personality pathology lies in the power achieved through formulating testable and falsifiable models that are not merely descriptive, but rather emphasize etiology, mechanism, and lifespan developmental sequelae of personality pathology. Additional benefits of theory-guided and empirically based models of personality pathology would be the further development and refinement of rational treatments for personality disorders that are more closely tailored to the specific deficits and dysfunctional attributes presented by individual personality pathologies, aims embodied in the clinical approach known as "differential therapeutics" or "systematic treatment selection" (Frances, Clarkin, & Perry, 1984; Beutler & Clarkin, 1990). Finally, with increased knowledge of etiology and mechanism, one could ultimately consider issues related to the prevention of personality disorders, though clearly a Herculean task that, at present, challenges the imagination. The importance of theory-guided approaches to personality pathology is only amplified when one considers the pervasiveness of personality disorders in general clinical practice, clinic populations, and the population at large. Although high-quality, epidemiologically derived estimates of the prevalence of Axis II disorders are not yet available (see "Study Populations and the Epidemiology of Personality Disorders," below), one need only consult DSM-IV (American Psychiatric Association, 1994) for educated prevalence "guesses," for example: borderline, histrionic, avoidant, dependent, compulsive, and narcissistic personality disorders are described as "apparently common," schizotypal personality disorder is thought to have a 3% general population prevalence, and antisocial affects 3% and 1% of male and female individuals respectively; data for schizoid, paranoid, and passive–aggressive personality disorders are lacking. It is not uncommon, however, to hear informed personality disorder researchers and experienced clinicians conjecture a general population prevalence for personality pathology between 10–15%, a range consistent with the most recent effort to determine a lifetime prevalence (Weissman, 1993). A recently completed two-stage case identification study using both a screening procedure and follow-up interviews conducted by skilled clinicians confirms a prevalence figure of approximately 10% (Lenzenweger, Loranger, Korfine, & Neff, 1995). Clearly, personality pathology is ubiquitous, and we are, therefore, challenged to understand the "hows" and "whys" of personality disorder development as well as to discern the most efficient and valid classification approach for such disorders.

We are committed to and advocate a scientific approach to the study of psychopathology, and the study of personality disorders is no exception. In this framework, the necessity of reliable assessments, measures, and procedures that possess suitable validity is axiomatic. However, despite good instrumentation, we anticipate that future personality disorder theories and research will be characterized by "false starts," forays down "blind alleys," and the customary slow progress of "normal science" punctuated by periodic substantive advances and moments of genuine clarity. This section of our introductory chapter is intended to highlight issues that any scientific theory of personality disorder will need to consider. We intend to raise questions rather than provide answers. As most research in personality disorders in the 1990s is probably best considered as occurring within the "context of discovery" (Reichenbach, 1938), it seems prudent to us to draw attention to a variety of substantive and methodological issues that should guide research in this rapidly developing area in psychopathology research. Personality disorders research is particularly interesting as it needs to draw upon the lessons we have learned, methodological and otherwise, from the study of other forms of severe psychopathology (e.g., schizophrenia, affective illness). However, it is ripe with challenges that are relatively unique to this domain of pathology. For example, where are the boundaries between "normal" personality and personality disorder? Can one define a "case" of personality disorder in the absence of marked impairment or distress? Furthermore, one could argue that some of the specific research challenges that personality disorder psychopathology affords may not be readily illuminated by the clues we have gleaned from other areas of study, and reliance upon previous insights may be less useful than having the wrong map for a territory. In short, the study of personality pathology will rely on the efforts and insights of many psychopathologists—including those contributing to this volume—to chart these new territories.

In citing several methodologic and/or substantive issues below, it is not our intention to suggest previous personality disorder research that has addressed these issues, directly or in part, has been somehow lax (though some clearly has been!). We are mindful that personality disorder research has only just "taken off" in the last 10 to 15 years (principally during the 1980s); since it is truly in its infancy, we therefore seek to encourage more extensive and ambitious work in this area. We suggest that we have come far enough along at this point in personality disorder research to highlight themes that remain troubling and/or challenging. Finally, we would like to stress the facts that the literature we cite below is necessarily highly selected because of space constraints, and our review is not intended to be exhaustive. Our examples, as one might anticipate, will hail primarily from recent research in personality disorders and will, therefore, be heavily influenced by the prevailing DSM-III (and DSM-III-R) nomenclature. Although many of the issues we shall raise will relate to DSM-III-R-defined personality pathology, we suggest our points are not intimately linked to that taxonomy. We view the following issues, not ordered in terms of importance, as largely unresolved and in need of further work as well as worthy of considerable attention by any comprehensive theory of personality disorder, including those contained in this volume.

Normal Personality and Personality Disorder: Questions of Continuity and Structure?

With the advent of specific diagnostic criteria and a polythetic approach to classification, Axis II of DSM-III represented an opportunity for rich theoretical discussion of and empirical research on the relationships between personality disorders as conceptualized by psychopathologists and normal personality as studied by academic personality psychologists. Theoretical discussion has focused on three key conceptual issues, namely, (1) the dimensional versus categorical nature of personality disorders (Widiger & Frances, 1985), (2) the distinction between normal and pathological personality features (e.g., social isolation as possibly representing low sociability vs. suicidal attempts as unrepresented on any "normal" dimension of personality; see Wiggins, 1982), and (3) the nature of the basic processes and structure underlying both personality disorders as well as normal personality (see Cloninger, 1987; Cloninger, Svrakic, & Przybeck, 1993; Lenzenweger & Depue, 1995; Depue, Chapter 6, this volume; Rutter, 1987). Although these issues are clearly of interest to psychopathologists and personality theorists alike, at this time, little substantive empirical research has been systematically directed at evaluating the nature of the relationships between DSM-III-R personality disorder features and contemporary conceptualizations of normal personality. To date, just three published studies have examined the associations between well established normative personality dimensions (i.e., the "Big Five" factors of Neuroticism, Extraversion, Openness, Agreeableness, Conscientiousness) and DSM-III-R-defined personality disorders (Wiggins & Pincus, 1989; Costa & McCrae, 1990; Trull, 1992). In short, the "normal" personality correlates, if any, of specific personality disorders remain but tentatively specified and, most importantly, it is unclear to what extent personality disorder symptoms are *continuous*, albeit exaggerated, extensions of normal traits. Furthermore, research to date has not effectively addressed the comparability or goodness of fit between the overall DSM-III-R/DSM-IV (American Psychiatric Association, 1994) personality disorder taxonomy and the empirically based dimensional structures observed in contemporary personality research such as the interpersonal circumplex (Leary, 1957; Wiggins, 1982) and established multidimensional/factorial models (e.g., the "Big Five" model, see Digman, 1990, or John, 1990, for excellent reviews and Block, 1995, for strident criticism; the "three superfactor" model of Tellegen, 1985; the three factor temperament model, Buss & Plomin, 1984). It is not clear how comparably personality pathology is organized at the latent level vis-à-vis normal personality. Stated differently, do three, four, or five major dimensions also *continuously* underlie personality disorders? Although normal personality research now suggests that somewhere between three and five factors adequately capture the variation in the primary descriptors of personality, the same cannot be said readily for personality pathology. Moreover, the correspondence between the primary factors of personality and personality disorder remains to be explored.

In the search for the personality correlates of personality disorder, the question of the meaning of discovered associations looms large. Many future studies will focus on the relationship between normal personality and personality disorder. It is likely that most of these studies will *not* directly address the issue of whether or not personality disorder symptoms are continuously versus discontinuously distributed in the population if they rely primarily on demonstrating correlations among these variables (i.e., are personality disorder symptoms exaggerations of normal traits?). An implicit assumption of the work seeking associations between normative and personality pathology measures has been (see Wiggins & Pincus, 1989; Costa & McCrae, 1990; Trull, 1992) that an association between such variables suggests a *continuity* between the phenomena. This implicit assumption is fraught with substantive and statistical pitfalls. It could quite conceivably be that in some instances no genuine (i.e., real, natural) connection between a dimension of personality and a personality disorder variable exists even though a statistically significant correlation may exist between them. To begin to address this issue, we would need to assess an exceptionally large, randomly ascertained general population sample of individuals for personality disorder symptoms. The distributions of these symptoms should be examined for the existence of qualitative discontinuities as evidenced, possibly, by "bimodality" (see Grayson, 1987, for a provocative review of this concept) *and* through application of complex statistical procedures such as an admixture analysis (e.g., Lenzenweger & Moldin, 1990) or taxometrics (Meehl, 1992, 1995; see Korfine & Lenzenweger, 1995; Lenzenweger & Korfine, 1992). Comparable work will need to be done on normative "dimensions" of personality as well before we can proceed to inferences concerning the continuous relationship between personality and personality disorder.

A question concerning the very existence of "dimensional" continuities and "categorical" (or "typological") discontinuities in either the personality or personality disorder realms remains controversial (see Gangestad & Snyder, 1985; Meehl, 1992). In short, regardless of the application of appropriate statistical procedures to such problems (techniques only recently refined sufficiently for reliable work), there remain quasi-ideological preferences for either dimensional or categorical conceptualizations of personality-related phenomena. The "dimensional versus categorical" issue has been discussed extensively in relation to personality pathology through the 1980s, with some psychologists advocating a dimensional approach (Widiger, 1992), whereas the psychiatric community remains essentially wed to a categorical framework (American Psychiatric Association, 1991). The reasons for such preferences are not always immediately discernible, though psychiatry has long preferred a typological approach to psychopathology (consistent with traditional medicine), and this approach is therefore familiar, facilitates communication, and is consistent with clinical decision making (American Psychiatric Association, 1991; Widiger, 1992). Normal personality research has long preferred a dimensional or continuum view of personality and of other behavioral phenomena (see Gangestad & Snyder, 1985; Meehl, 1992, 1995), due perhaps in part to reliance on parametric statistics and a focus on the study of normative aspects of psychological functioning. Interestingly as a "dimensional" approach to personality pathology has become increasingly of interest to psychiatry (see American Psychiatric Association, 1991), psychological research has seen a resurgence of interest in the detection of discontinuities, "types," or "taxa" in a variety of psychological and psychopathological realms (see Meehl, 1992, 1995; Lenzenweger & Korfine, 1992; Trull, Widiger, & Guthrie, 1990). For example, taxometric data generated using the maximum covariation analysis (MAXCOV) technique developed by Meehl suggest that schizotypy (Lenzenweger & Korfine, 1992; Korfine & Lenzenweger, 1995), borderline personality disorder (Trull et al., 1990), and psychopathy (Harris, Rice, & Quinsey, 1994) are all taxonic at the latent level.[1]

Other than the need for an appropriate methodological approach in the determination of continuity versus discontinuity between personality and personality disorder constructs, theoretical conjectures concerning the relationships between personality disorders (and personality disorder symptoms) and normal personality must take into account the divergent behavioral, affective, attitudinal, and cognitive domains covered by these two broad areas of scientific inquiry. Are there normative counterparts of accepted personality disorder symptoms? Clearly, some personality disorder symptoms will not be expected to have normative personality counterparts (e.g., suicidal behaviors, self-mutilation). The normative construct sociability, on the other hand, clearly ranges from "high" to "low," and, perhaps, a schizoid personality-disordered individual shares much in common with a person described as displaying low sociability. All things considered, it is somewhat unrealistic to conceive of precise one-to-one correspondences between personality disorder symptoms and normative personality traits (Cloninger, 1987; Costa & McCrae, 1986; Rutter, 1987; Widiger & Frances, 1985). We readily predict that noteworthy correspondences will be observed between several of the major dimensions underlying normal personality (or temperament) and personality disorder symptomatology. The meaning and interpretation of such correspondences should prove a challenge to personality disorder theorists. For example, recent data bearing on the interrelationships among biological sex, psychological gender, and Axis II disorders are considerably more complex than initially anticipated (see Korfine, Lenzenweger, & Hazan, 1994).

Finally, although DSM-III-R has presented us with a "structure" for organizing personality pathology, namely the disorders of Axis II, any meaningful consideration of the relationship(s) between personality pathology and normal personality must be cognizant of the possibility that the Axis II arrangement may have little genuine correspondence to the true (or, natural) latent organization of personality disorder symptomatology. By this we mean, in short, DSM-III-R/DSM-IV present us with 11 disorders grouped into three so-called clusters, the odd–eccentric, the impulsive–erratic, and the anxious–avoidant clusters. However there are no published data derived from a large sample ($n > 1,300$, assuming 10 subjects per Axis II diagnostic criterion) of carefully clinically assessed cases in which analyses, conducted at the level of individual items (i.e., criterion level), confirm the DSM-III-R/DSM-IV clustering structure or even the disorder structures themselves. Some factor analytic studies have obtained three factor solutions, corresponding broadly to the three "clusters" of the DSM-III-R/DSM-IV Axis II taxonomy. However, these studies analyzed data at the level of disorders, and they overlooked the fact that the analyzed data had been structured a priori by being organized into 11 predefined disorders.

Given the relatively high degree of overlap that can be found among the currently defined Axis II personality disorders, both in the form of correlations among symptom dimensions and/or rates of co-occurrence of categorical diagnoses (Korfine & Lenzenweger, 1991; Widiger et al., 1991), it seems quite reasonable to hypothesize that item-level multivariate analyses of the domain of symptoms found on Axis II will reveal but a handful of meaningful (i.e., interpretable) factors. While the preliminary work on this problem would by definition need to be more exploratory in nature, a confirmatory approach could be adopted for assessing the fit between an emergent structure or model and new sets of data. An illustration of such an approach can be found in the schizophrenia literature wherein the latent structure of positive

and negative symptoms was resolved through application of confirmatory factor analysis and the systematic comparison of multiple competing models of latent structure (Lenzenweger, Dworkin, &
Wethington, 1989; see also Lenzenweger & Dworkin, in press). Efforts
to discern the latent structure of personality disorder symptomatology,
whether specified by DSM-III-R or an alternative model such as one
of those in the present volume, must bear in mind the effect the use
of cases selected solely from clinical settings will have on obtained
results. In short, those individuals who come to hospitals and clinics
for treatment tend to be more severely affected in general, and this
fact alone will likely increase the degree of overlap (or correlation) seen
across forms of personality pathology. Moreover, the more ill a sample is, the less likely will be subthreshold cases, which are important
to "fill in" the range of personality pathology as it occurs naturally.
Thus the impact of sampling on efforts to illuminate the latent structure of personality pathology must be considered.

The State–Trait Issue in Relation to the Definition and Diagnosis of Personality Disorders

Implied in the DSM-III-R definition of personality disorder is the assumption that state factors such as anxiety and depression should not
substantively affect the assessment of personality pathology. DSM-III-R
clearly acknowledges that personality disorder symptoms may be
manifested during periods of acute illness (e.g., major depression),
however it is equally clear that personality disorder symptomatology
should be typical of a person's long-term functioning and not be limited
only to periods of acute illness (American Psychiatric Association, 1987,
p. 335). Although some data do suggest that certain normative personality features, assessed via self-report instruments, (not necessarily personality disorder symptoms) among clinically depressed patients do
vary over time as a function of changing levels of depression (Hirschfeld et al., 1983), at present neither the relationship between personality disorder symptoms and state disturbance within the context of
the cross-sectional diagnostic process (Frances, 1980) nor the relationship between longitudinal symptom stability and state variability is
resolved unambiguously for DSM-III-R personality disorders.

A recent study that employed structured interviews administered
by experienced clinicians (Loranger et al., 1991) found that changes
in clinical state (i.e., anxiety, depression) did *not* correspond significantly with changes in the number of DSM-III-R personality disorder
criteria met at two points in time. This finding has subsequently been
replicated by Loranger and Lenzenweger (1995) (see Zimmerman,

1994). Moreover, Trull and Goodwin (1993) recently reported that changes in mental state were not associated with either self-reported or interview-assessed personality pathology, although the levels of depression and anxiety characterizing the patients in the study were unusually low (perhaps not clinically significant in intensity). Current normal personality research acknowledges the importance of determining the influence of state factors on trait assessment (Tellegen, 1985), and normative trait-oriented, lifespan research now seeks to include state factors as important causal factors in longitudinal developmental models and research (Nesselroade, 1988). Therefore, a major focus of future research in personality pathology should be further clarification of the effect of anxiety and depression on both cross-sectional personality disorder symptom(s) and personality trait assessment as well as the effect of state factors on the longitudinal stability of personality disorder symptoms and traits. Any major theory of personality disorder will need to incorporate and address the role of state disturbances in the development and manifestation of personality pathology.

On a broadly related theme, the relatively robust association between personality pathology and affective disturbance raises an important issue specifically concerning less severe affective pathology that is frequently accompanied by personality pathology (Loranger et al., 1991; Klein, Riso, Anderson, 1993). For example, focusing on but one possible issue, we suggest that future research on personality-disordered populations as well as theories of personality disorder will need to address more directly the precise relationship between dysthymia and personality disorder. Klein et al. (1993, p. 234), in a careful examination of the dysthymia construct, outlines *four* plausible, though competing, conceptualizations of dysthymia in relation to personality disorder:

1. Dysthymia is a "characterological depression," essentially an attenuated form of major affective disorder, and this depression has an adverse impact on normative developmental processes, giving rise to the frequently co-occurring features of borderline, dependent, avoidant, and other personality disorder features.
2. Dysthymia is an "extreme" form of normally occurring depressive personality traits, a view deriving largely from psychodynamic theorists.
3. Dysthymia is the result or consequence of life stressors, notably those elicited by personality pathology.
4. Dysthymia is a "character spectrum disorder" in which the low-grade dysphoria of the illness is a complication of a primary personality disorder trait.

Simply stated, any theory of personality disorder must not only take into account the role of dysphoric emotional states in the assessment and definition of personality pathology, but also must make explicit its assumptions about the relationships hypothesized to exist between personality pathology, affect/emotion, and affective disorder.

Study Populations and the Epidemiology of Personality Disorders

An essential issue of concern in both future personality disorder research and theory is the representativeness of findings from studies and substantive conceptualizations based on hospitalized and/or clinic patient populations (vis-à-vis the general population at large) for furthering our understanding of the nature, course, and development of personality disorders (see Drake, Adler, & Vaillant, 1988; Kohlberg et al., 1972). There can be little doubt that additional studies using inpatient and/or outpatient samples represent a necessity in future personality disorder research. We suggest it is critical to recognize that many personality-disordered individuals exist in the community at large, and these people may never present themselves for psychiatric treatment (Dohrenwend & Dohrenwend, 1982) even though they may be quite impaired (Drake & Vaillant, 1985; Drake et al., 1988). This may be especially true for certain personality disorder diagnoses. For example, two studies that used clinically experienced raters found very low rates of schizoid and paranoid personality disorder in patient samples (Loranger, 1990; Pfohl et al., 1986), although population prevalence estimates for such pathology suggest many more people are affected by these conditions than those who seek treatment. Furthermore, given the polythetic nature of DSM-III-R/DSM-IV, personality-disordered individuals who are hospitalized may be defined by substantively different configurations of symptoms than those who are not hospitalized. For example, hospitalized borderline personality disorder patients might display more life-threatening and self-mutilating phenomenology than individuals who are also diagnosed borderline but who have not been hospitalized, although both would be validly diagnosed (the reader will recall that there are 93 "ways" to be diagnosed with borderline personality disorder according to DSM-III-R; see Clarkin, Widiger, Frauces, Hurt, & Gilmore, 1983). Moreover, as was established long ago in epidemiology, those individuals who present for hospital care for one condition are frequently afflicted with other conditions as well as driven by other factors to seek care. Consequently, generalizations based on the study of patient populations must always be made cautiously (i.e., "Berkson's bias"; Berkson, 1946). We argue that future studies of personality disorders that employ subjects drawn from nonclinical sources will likely represent useful adjuncts to the more traditional study of hospitalized patients and may lead to insights that reflect noteworthy differences between personality pathology that is observed in clinical versus nonclinical settings.

As noted above, there exist no comprehensive and high-quality data that speak to prevalence rates for personality pathology. An Epidemiologic Catchment Area (ECA) study equivalent has yet to be conducted for personality disorders other than antisocial personality disorder (Robins et al., 1984). A current estimate for the overall life-time rate for any Axis II disorder is in the range of 10–13% (Weissman, 1993; see Maier, Lichtermann, Klingler, Heun, & Hallmayer, 1992), however the data upon which this estimate is based are quite limited. The technology for cost-effective and efficient personality disorder di-agnosis on a relatively large scale using a general population approach does not appear to exist currently (Loranger, 1992). Whereas reliable structured interviews for Axis II personality pathology exist (Loranger, 1988, 1991a; Perry, 1992), these instruments typically require adminis-tration by clinically experienced diagnosticians and are known to take several hours to complete. These considerations make the logistic re-quirements of epidemiological study using currently available methods rather daunting. The possibility of using self-report methods to gener-ate epidemiological estimates of personality pathology is intriguing, however the correspondence between such currently published inven-tory measures of personality disorder and clinical diagnoses tends to be rather uninspiring (Loranger, 1992; Perry, 1992). If reasonably effi-cient self-report personality disorder screening measures could be de-veloped (i.e., ones that generate few false negatives even at the expense of false positives), then such measures could be used for an initial screening of a population for possible personality disorders (comparable to the psychometric high-risk strategy [see Chapman & Chapman, 1985; Lenzenweger, 1993]), and identified cases could then be evaluated us-ing structured clinical interviews, the two-phase procedure for case identification (e.g., Lenzenweger et al., 1995).

Longitudinal Course/Lifespan Perspectives on the Natural History of Personality Disorders

One of the cardinal assumptions concerning the nature of personality disorders, and perhaps most important from a theoretical perspective, is that they represent *enduring* conditions that are trait-like and, there-fore, relatively stable over time (American Psychiatric Association, 1980, 1987). In fact, DSM-III-R states, ''The manifestations of Personality Disorders are often recognizable by adolescence or earlier and continue throughout most of adult life, though they often become less obvious in middle or old age" (American Psychiatric Association, 1987, p. 335). However, with the possible exception of antisocial personality disorder (Glueck & Glueck, 1968; Robins, 1966, 1978), very little is known about the long-term longitudinal course, development, or natural history of personality disorders (Drake & Vaillant, 1988; Drake et al., 1988). Although several studies have supported the temporal stability of personality disorder features and diagnoses over relatively short time spans (e.g., 1 year or less) (Perry, 1993), evidence concerning long-term or lifespan stability of operationally defined personality disorders is conspicuously lacking in the empirical research literature (Drake & Vaillant, 1988; Drake et al., 1988). In fact, it is relatively safe to say that there currently exist *no* published data from a large-scale, prospective, multiwave longitudinal study of the full range of DSM-III-R personality disorders (see Perry, 1993 for a review of published test–retest studies). One of us (M. F. L.) is currently directing such a study at Cornell University in Ithaca, NY.

At this time, longitudinal studies support the general stability of *normal* personality traits and features in a variety of age groups, including college students and young adults (Block, 1971; Costa & McCrae, 1986, 1988; Finn, 1986; Haan & Day, 1974; Helson & Moane, 1987; McCrae & Costa, 1984; Mortimer, Finch, & Kumka, 1982; Nesselroade & Baltes, 1974; Vaillant, 1977). Given the body of evidence supporting the stability of normal personality, it is not unreasonable to expect that at least some personality disorder features will display significant long-term temporal stability, on the assumption they are reflective of normal personality variation in some manner. Particularly, for example, features such as schizoid social withdrawal, compulsive rigidity, and the "extraverted" or outwardly directed interpersonal style of the psychopath. However, lacking empirical evidence from longitudinal studies, it is difficult to determine to what extent personality disorders, at least individual features, are stable over time.

Long-term longitudinal work remains sorely needed in this area, and the preferable way to conduct such research will be to use "multiwave" panel design studies (Baltes, Reese, & Nesselroade, 1977; Kessler & Greenberg, 1981; Nesselroade, Stigler, & Baltes, 1980) with multiple indicators for all of the disorders (constructs) of interest. What this implies in practical terms are studies in which a large number of cases are examined at least three, and preferably more, times for personality pathology across meaningfully lengthy time intervals, with all cases being examined using the same measures (procedures) at each assessment point. The scientific utility of a multiwave design lies in the fact that it provides an opportunity for the most informative statistical analysis of empirical relationships among constructs over time (Baltes & Nesselroade, 1973; Bentler, 1980, 1984; Collins & Horn, 1991; Joreskog, 1979; Nesselroade & Baltes, 1979, 1984; Rogosa, 1979, 1988), a fact that is well established in the lifespan developmental research realm. Although there are a variety of studies that have used the basic test–retest study design in the examination of personality disorder stability and change over time (see Perry, 1993 for review), it is essential to note that as Rogosa, Brandt, and Zimowski (1982), the lifespan research methodologists, remark pointedly, ''Two waves of data are better than one, but maybe not much better'' (p. 744). Because of regression toward the mean effects (Nesselroade et al., 1980) and other difficulties (e.g., inability to estimate individual growth curves; inadequacy for study of individual differences in change; Rogosa, 1988) fundamentally inherent in simple test–retest design studies, we advocate strongly that all future prospective longitudinal studies of personality disorders employ multiwave designs, preferably multiple measures of each disorder (or construct) under consideration. Only through the multiwave study of personality pathology will we be able to illuminate accurately the temporal stability (or lack thereof) of personality disorders.

The longitudinal stability of personality disorders should clearly be a central focus in future personality disorder studies, and each of the models discussed later in this volume should be considered carefully with respect to its predictions concerning temporal stability (and change) for personality pathology. The reader is urged to bear in mind that stability is not necessarily as easy to investigate as one might initially think because changes over time in personality pathology could be the result of aging, treatment, and/or retest effects, although retest effects appear less relevant to personality assessments (Costa & McCrae, 1988). Longitudinal stability (and, by definition, change) of personality disorder features, can be evaluated from at least four different perspectives (following Kagan, 1980; Mortimer et al., 1982; Collins & Horn, 1991), namely structural invariance, rank-order stability, level stability, and ipsative (or intraindividual) stability. Structural invariance, or the maintenance of a temporally consistent factor structure and configuration of factor loadings, can be assessed using both confirmatory factor analysis and causal modeling techniques (Bentler, 1984; Joreskog, 1979; Nesselroade & Baltes, 1984; Rogosa, 1979). These statistical techniques are ideally suited for use in longitudinal research as they allow the investigator to use all available panel data simultaneously (Kessler & Greenberg, 1981; Rogosa, 1979), and they allow for direct comparison of alternative structural models of stability (Bentler,

1984; Nesselroade & Baltes, 1984). Rank-order, or "normative stability," concerns the extent to which individuals maintain their relative position within a group ranking on a variable of interest from time 1 to time 2. "Level stability" concerns the extent to which group means remain invariant over time on a variable (or disorder) of interest. Finally "ipsative stability" concerns *intra*individual consistency in the organization of personality disorder features or personality traits over time (see Mortimer et al., 1982).

In advocating the careful study of the longitudinal stability of personality disorders, we do not intend to suggest that such inquiry represents an end in itself, one that is but merely descriptive and statistical. But rather it should be viewed as a necessary first step in the ongoing exploration of the lifespan developmental course of personality pathology. Once established, we foresee studies moving away from simple demonstrations of stability (or lack thereof) but toward a lifespan view with an emphasis on discerning those biobehavioral and psychosocial processes and mechanisms that underlie the etiology and development of personality pathology (i.e., moving from description toward an explanatory framework).

Genetic and Biological Underpinnings of Personality Pathology

The role of genetic influences in the development and stability of normal personality as well as individual differences in personality is now well established and beyond dispute (Plomin, Chipuer, & Loehlin, 1990; McGue, Bacon, & Lykken, 1993), contrarian views being most likely expressed by those with sociopolitical agendas rather than rigorous scientific interests. Though the heritability estimates for features or dimensions of personality tend to be lower than those observed for intelligence or other cognitive abilities, it can be safely said that genetic factors play an influential role in determining personality— they have the status of fact at this point (see Plomin et al., 1990). The situation for personality disorders, however, is considerably less clear with respect to the role of genetic factors in the etiology of personality pathology. This is *not* to say that genetic factors do not play a role in determining these disorders but, rather, that the studies bearing on the determination of both familiality and heritability of personality disorders are only just beginning to appear, twin and adoption studies remain a rarity, and familial aggregation work is accumulating slowly. To date, the greatest amount of genetically relevant data can be found for schizotypal personality disorder, which by most accounts appears related genetically to schizophrenia, as well as borderline, antisocial, and obsessive–compulsive personality disorders. However, the genetic picture for even these disorders is unclear due in large part to an absence of data for the disorders themselves or putatively correlated dimensions (e.g., sociability in schizoid personality disorder) (Nigg & Goldsmith, 1994). Finally, quite apart from research on genetic factors, it is necessary to point out that the psychobiological underpinnings of personality pathology in terms of prominent central nervous system neurotransmitters and meaningful neurobehavioral circuitry remain in their infancy (see Cloninger et al., 1993; Coccaro, 1993; Coccaro et al., 1989; Depue, Chapter 6, this volume; Lenzenweger & Depue, 1995; Siever, Kalus, & Keefe, 1993).

The Axis I and Axis II Interface: Comorbidity, Causality, or Confusion?

All models of personality disorder are, by necessity, required to deal with the relationship between personality pathology and other major forms of psychopathology, such as affective illness, anxiety disorders, and even schizophrenia. Both clinical practice and available research data suggest strongly that an individual can suffer from both a major Axis I condition as well as a personality disorder simultaneously; a clinical reality typically discussed under the rubric of "comorbidity" (Widiger & Shea, 1991). The comorbidity issue is laden with a number of complex questions that speak not only to description, diagnosis, and classification, but also to etiology. For example, at the level of diagnosis, is it the case that comorbidity arises out of the fact that our current multiaxial system encourages multiple diagnoses (is it an artifact of the system?), or is it the case that people can actually suffer from two or more disorders simultaneously? Clearly, if one can have both pneumonia and heart disease simultaneously, can one have both depression and schizotypal personality disorder at the same time? Can one not have a personality disorder in the face of a psychotic illness—if so, what limitations or qualifications must attend the diagnosis of a personality disorder in such circumstances?

Future research will need to focus on the careful dissection of putatively highly comorbid conditions such as major depression and borderline personality disorder (e.g., Loranger, 1991b) along a variety of meaningful dimensions such as phenomenology, familiality, medication response, psychobiology, and pathogenesis (see Gunderson & Phillips, 1991, for an excellent demonstration). Such careful dissection of comorbid conditions will likely enhance our understanding not only of the boundaries existing between personality pathology and other major syndromes but also our notions regarding the development and etiology of personality disorders. What possible roles could a major Axis I disorder play in relation to personality pathology? For example, could the presence of a major psychiatric syndrome be shown to "causally" facilitate the development of a personality disorder or merely increase the statistical risk for the development of a personality disorder? Can an Axis I syndrome represent the more severe version of a broad class of psychopathology of which the related personality disorder is but a spectrum variant (cf. schizophrenia and schizotypal personality disorder)? Could it also not be that there is no etiologically relevant connection whatsoever between a major syndrome and a comorbid personality disorder?

For research into the comorbidity issue(s) to be maximally beneficial to the field, two fundamental methodological issues should be kept in mind. First, comorbidity work is badly in need of large n studies. If the natural association between conditions (e.g., borderline personality disorder and depression) is to emerge from data, then the most stable estimate of this association will come from data drawn from large samples. Second, future comorbidity research should be done on either a consecutive admissions basis at a clinical setting or in the general population from an epidemiological perspective (see National Comorbidity Survey by Kessler et al., 1994). Future reports on the comorbid diagnoses of those patients who happen to be in one's personality disorder protocol are not likely to be informative as any inherent sampling bias will misrepresent the natural rate of comorbidity.

Validity of Personality Pathology

Last, but by no means least, is the issue of validity in relation to personality disorder constructs. Despite the 16 years since publication of DSM-III, the validity of specific DSM-III-R personality disorder diagnoses remains a relatively open issue in psychopathology research; however the base of validity information is growing for most disorders, particularly schizotypal, borderline, and antisocial personality disorders. We take this opportunity to remind our reader that although reliable ratings of personality disorder symptoms are now possible, this does not necessarily ensure that the validity of the diagnoses has been established (Carey & Gottesman, 1978). This statement holds true for the DSM-III-R taxonomy as well as all of those models described in the present volume. Furthermore, no clear and compelling criteria of validity (Cronbach & Meehl, 1955) currently exist against which personality disorder diagnoses can be compared to assess their validity— not unlike other areas of psychopathology, there is no "gold standard" for validity in the personality disorder realm. Although Spitzer (1983) has proposed that the validity of personality disorder diagnoses might ultimately best be established by longitudinal studies of personality disorders that employ well-known expert raters as well as all available data useful for psychiatric diagnosis (the so-called LEAD standard—longitudinal data, expert raters, and all available diagnostic data), such a definitive study conducted on a large scale has yet to be undertaken because of the logistical difficulties and formidable expense most likely involved in such a project (see Pilkonis, Heape, Ruddy, & Serrao, 1991; see also Zimmerman, 1994).

LANDMARKS, CRITICAL JUNCTURES, AND FRONTIERS: A GUIDE TO EXPLORING THE MAJOR THEORIES OF PERSONALITY DISORDER

In closing this introductory chapter, we look back and see that we have raised a number of specific issues that can be counted among the most challenging and important in the area of personality disorders research. For this area of psychopathology research to move forward, greater clarity must be sought along each of the dimensions noted above. Our contributors, one and all, speak to various aspects of the issues raised above, and they can be fit into broader theoretical and scientific contexts as well. At the same time, we encourage you, our reader, to find how the theoreticians and researchers contributing to this volume deal with the specific substantive issues noted above. We should also like to encourage you to examine the following chapters using a common set of broader guidelines. By evaluating each of the following chapters along the general dimensions specified below, we believe consistencies and inconsistencies across the models as well as possibilities for new theory, research, and treatment will emerge. Consider the following dimensions with respect to each of the following theoretical models of personality disorder:

What Are the Substantive Foundations of the Model?

Can the roots of the model be traced to major historical or research traditions in psychology and/or psychiatry (e.g., psychoanalysis, behaviorism)? Does the author identify the level from which the data are derived that constitute the basis for classification, measurement, and treatment (e.g., intrapsychic, interpersonal, cognitive)? What is the primary focus of the model (e.g., etiologically oriented, therapeutically oriented)?

What Is the Formal Structure of the Model?

Have the core assumptions of the model been formally stated, and are the major explanatory principles clearly articulated? While models in psychopathology, unlike comprehensive theories, can be somewhat incomplete in their effort to explain a form of psychopathology (see Matthysse, 1993), has the model nonetheless been formulated in a manner that allows for its testability and falsifiability (and, therefore, possible refutation) (see Meehl, 1978, 1993)?

What Taxonomy Derives from the Model?

What is the nature of the taxonomy that derives from the model? For example, does the model admit of a structure that is hierarchic, based on a circumplex, or some alternative form of a multiaxial approach? Is the classification approach based on a prototypal, categorical, or dimensional methodology? Is variation personality pathology discussed in terms of degree (quantitative) or kind (qualitative)? How independent are the personality disorder syndromes in terms of etiological origins, and does this independence affect the taxonomy in any fashion? How does the model relate to DSM-III-R and the more recent DSM-IV?

Etiological and Developmental Considerations?

Does the model transcend a purely descriptive stance and speak to issues of "mechanisms" and "processes" that determine the development of a personality disorder? In short, does the model attempt to answer the question "how" with respect to the emergence of personality pathology? What are the principal components of the processes and mechanisms that are theorized to be etiologically relevant (e.g., genetic influences, neurobehavioral factors, temperamental dispositions; cognitive deficits; learned characteristics; other sources of disorder such as familial conflict and trauma or abuse)?

In the theories presented in this volume, one trend is quite clear—all of our contributors have clearly eschewed a merely descriptive approach in favor of an explanatory effort with clearcut implications for etiology. Furthermore, all of our contributors have proposed theoretical models that presume interaction across multiple levels of the individual, emphasizing not only behavioral and personality characteristics and factors but also neurobiological and environmental components as well. For example, although Otto Kernberg (Chapter 3) sees character pathology largely in terms of a developmental pathology of aggression, his theory incorporates temperament, affect, and trauma components in interaction. Richard Depue (Chapter 6) presents a fundamental model of personality as defined by interacting dimensions known to be rooted in neurobiological functions, and according to his model personality, pathology can also be viewed as the interactive result of these dimensions. For Theodore Millon and Roger Davis (Chapter 5), personality pathology emerges from a complex interaction of three fundamental polarities: self versus other, pleasure versus pain, and activity versus passivity. James Pretzer and Aaron Beck (Chapter 2) see personality pathology largely emerging from and being maintained by systematic biases in information processing and memory of events eliciting pathological cognitive, emotional, and behavioral responses.

How Are Assessment and Diagnosis Accounted for in the Model?

Does the model have an associated assessment and diagnostic approach? If so, what are the sources of the empirical data that are used for diagnosis according to the model? Does the assessment approach rely on therapeutic contexts, self-report inventories, or structured interviews? Has the author presented adequate information concerning the reliability and validity of the assessment and diagnostic procedures associated with the model?

Millon and Davis (Chapter 5) and Benjamin (Chapter 4), and, to a lesser extent, Pretzer and Beck (Chapter 2) have exerted a great deal of effort in operationalizing their personality pathology constructs in the form of assessment instruments covering the taxonomy of the personality disorders. Millon and Davis are guided by the DSM taxonomy to a great extent, whereas Benjamin has shown the consistency of her interpersonal approach with the DSM system.

Does the Model Articulate Therapeutic Procedures or, at Least, Highlight Implications for Treatment?

According to the model, how does one go about treating personality pathology and what are the treatment goals (e.g., symptom relief vs. reconstructive work)? In what tradition is the therapeutic work carried out (e.g., insight-oriented vs. cognitive vs. biological therapy)? Are the principles of change/improvement clearly articulated by the model? What are the limits of the therapeutic approach (i.e., Are there personality disorders for which the therapy would not be appropriate)?

While Benjamin (Chapter 4), Kernberg (Chapter 3), and Pretzer and Beck (Chapter 2) all relate their personality pathology constructs and theories to interventions, it is Kernberg and Beck who have articulated treatment manuals for these disorders.

Prospects for the Future:
Integration of Mind, Brain, and Behavior

To our minds, the tasks of future theorizing and empirical research in personality disorders will involve the effective integration of mind, brain, and behavior. Any comprehensive model of complex human behavior, particularly forms of psychopathology, will require a clear and genuine integration of ideas and research findings that cut across the levels of analysis linking mind, brain, and behavior. One thing is quite clear to us, as well as to the contributors of this volume, monolithic theories existing at but one level of analysis are sure to fail in their explanation of complex human behavior. For example, for years normative developmental psychologists have viewed personality and emotional development almost exclusively in terms of psychosocial influences, much to the exclusion of genetic and biological factors. Indeed, David Rowe (1994), the noted developmental behavioral geneticist, has termed this view of personality and psychological development "socialization science," and he has offered a pungent criticism of such a monolithic model, demonstrating effectively the relative importance of genetic factors vis-à-vis psychosocial influences for personality development. We maintain a similar position with respect to personality disorders—for example, personality disorders are not likely to be understood or explained solely in terms of psychosocial influences. A genuine integration of genetic factors, neurotransmitter models, and other neurobiological processes with psychosocial, cognitive, and environmental factors will be required to advance our knowledge of the personality disorders. The best models in some ultimate sense will be those that integrate across these levels (e.g., Meehl, 1990; see also Meehl, 1972). The importance of genetic factors in both normative and pathological development is indisputable (Rowe, 1994; Rutter, 1991), and the essential role of neurobiological factors in temperament (e.g., Kagan, 1994), emotion (Ekman & Davidson, 1994), personality development (e.g., Depue & Collins, in press), and the emergence of psychopathology (e.g., Breslin & Weinberger, 1990; Coccarro & Murphy, 1990; Grace, 1991) is axiomatic, some would even say confirmed. The meaningful integration of brain, emotion, behavior, and environmental influences currently represents exceptionally active research in various areas of psychological science, especially cognition and personality. Our belief is that personality disorders research will necessarily have to strive for similar integrative work for genuine advances to occur. Our contributors are clearly leading the way in this connection. For example: Depue (Chapter 6) seeks to integrate personality, behavior, and neurobiology in his model; Kernberg (Chapter 3) proposes complex interactions among temperament, trauma, and early experience; and Pretzer and Beck (Chapter 2) suggest biased cognition must be understood within a matrix that incorporates affect and emotion as well as interpersonal factors. Indeed, interesting differences have emerged among our theorists. For example, Kernberg (Chapter 3) argues that neurobiological factors, operating through temperament, have more of a *mediating* role in the determination of personality pathology, whereas Depue (Chapter 6) casts neurobiological processes, especially the role of serotonin, in a *modulating* framework. This is precisely the type of debate and discussion that will not only provide useful heuristics for future research directed at integrating mind, brain, and behavior, but it will ultimately allow us to better understand and care for our patients.

At this point we end our introduction and orientation and invite you the reader to sample from what we believe are the leading theories of personality disorder. We encourage you to view each of these chapters individually as an independent position statement by its author(s), but also collectively as the building blocks for what may ideally become a more comprehensive theory of personality pathology.

ACKNOWLEDGMENTS

We thank Armand W. Loranger and Lauren Korfine for useful discussions concerning critical substantive issues in personality disorders research. Development and preparation of this chapter was supported in part by Grant MH-45448 from the National Institute of Mental Health to Mark F. Lenzenweger. Completion of this chapter was also facilitated by generous sabbatical support provided to Mark F. Lenzenweger by Harvard University and the Laboratory of Psychology, McLean Hospital through Professor Philip S. Holzman.

NOTE

1. The MAXCOV data reported in Trull et al. (1990) for borderline personality disorder reveal the characteristic right-end peak suggestive of a low-base-rate latent taxon (see Meehl, 1992, 1995, or Korfine & Lenzenweger, 1995, for conceptual and mathematical rationale).

REFERENCES

Allport, G. W. (1937). *Personality: A psychological interpretation.* New York: Henry Holt.

American Psychiatric Association. (1952). *Diagnostic and statistical manual of mental disorders.* Washington, DC: Author.

American Psychiatric Association. (1968). *Diagnostic and statistical manual of mental disorders* (2nd ed.). Washington, DC: Author.

American Psychiatric Association. (1980). *Diagnostic and statistical manual of mental disorders* (3rd ed.). Washington, DC: Author.

American Psychiatric Association. (1987). *Diagnostic and statistical manual of mental disorders* (3rd ed., rev.). Washington, DC: Author.

American Psychiatric Association. (1991). *DSM-IV options book: Work in progress.* Washington, DC: Author.

American Psychiatric Association. (1994). *Diagnostic and statistical manual of mental disorders* (4th ed.). Washington, DC: Author.

Baltes, P., & Nesselroade, J. (1973). The developmental analysis of individual differences on multiple measures. In J. Nesselroade & H. Reese (Eds.), *Life-span developmental psychology: Methodological issues* (pp. 219–251). New York: Academic Press.

Baltes, P., Reese, H., & Nesselroade, J. (1977). *Life-span developmental psychology: Introduction to research methods.* Monterey, CA: Brooks/Cole.

Bentler, P. (1980). Multivariate analysis with latent variables: Causal modeling. *Annual Review of Psychology, 31,* 419–456.

Bentler, P. (1984). Structural equation models in longitudinal research. In S. Mednick, M. Harway, & K. M. Finello (Eds.), *Handbook of longitudinal research* (pp. 88–105). New York: Praeger.

Berkson, J. (1946). Limitations of the application of fourfold table analysis to hospital data. *Biometrics, 2,* 339–343.

Beutler, L., & Clarkin, J. F. (1990). *Systematic treatment selection: Toward targeted therapeutic interventions.* New York: Brunner/Mazel.

Blashfield, R. K. (1984). *The classification of psychopathology: Neo-Kraepelinian and quantitative approaches.* New York: Plenum Press.

Block, J. (1971). *Lives through time.* Berkeley, CA: Bancroft Books.

Block, J. (1995). A contrarian view of the five-factor approach to personality description. *Psychological Bulletin, 117,* 187–215.

Breslin, N. A., & Weinberger, D. R. (1990). Schizophrenia and the normal functional development of the prefrontal cortex. *Development and Psychopathology, 2,* 409–424.

Buss, A., & Plomin, R. (1984). *Temperament: Early developing personality traits.* Hillsdale, NJ: Erlbaum.

Carey, G., & Gottesman, I. (1978). Reliability and validity in binary ratings: Areas of common misunderstanding in diagnosis and symptom ratings. *Archives of General Psychiatry, 35,* 1454–1459.

Chapman, L., & Chapman, J. (1985). Psychosis proneness. In M. Alpert (Ed.), *Controversies in schizophrenia: Changes and constancies* (pp. 157–172). New York: Guilford Press.

Clark, L. A. (1992). Resolving taxonomic issues in personality disorders: The value of large-scale analyses of symptom data. *Journal of Personality Disorders, 6,* 360–376.

Clark, L. A. (1993). *Manual for the schedule for nonadaptive and adaptive personality (SNAP).* Minneapolis, MN: University of Minnesota Press.

Clarkin, J., Widiger, T., Frances, A., Hurt, S., & Gilmore, M. (1983). Prototypic typology and borderline personality disorder. *Journal of Abnormal Psychology, 92,* 263–275.

Cloninger, C. R. (1987). A systematic method for clinical description and classification of personality variants: A proposal. *Archives of General Psychiatry, 44,* 573–588.

Cloninger, C., Svrakic, D., & Przybeck, T. (1993). A psychobiological model of temperament and character. *Archives of General Psychiatry, 50,* 975–990.

Coccaro, E. (1993). Psychopharmacologic studies in patients with personality disorders: Review and perspective. *Journal of Personality Disorders, 7* (Suppl. Spring), 181–192.

Coccaro, E. F., & Murphy, D. L. (Eds.). (1990). *Serotonin in major psychiatric disorders.* Washington, DC: American Psychiatric Press.

Coccaro, E., Siever, L., Klar, H., Maurer, G., Cochrane, K., Cooper, T., Mohs, R., & Davis, K. (1989). Serotonergic studies in patients with affective and borderline personality disorders: Correlates with suicidal and impulsive aggressive behavior. *Archives of General Psychiatry, 46,* 587–599.

Collins, L., & Horn, J. (Eds.). (1991). *Best methods for the analysis of change: Recent advances, unanswered questions, future directions.* Washington, DC: American Psychological Association.

Costa, P., & McCrae, R. (1986). Personality stability and its implications for clinical psychology. *Clinical Psychology Review, 6,* 407–423.

Costa, P., & McCrae, R. (1988). Personality in adulthood: A six-year longitudinal study of self-reports and spouse ratings on the NEO personality inventory. *Journal of Personality and Social Psychology, 54,* 853–863.

Costa, P., & McCrae, R. (1990). Personality disorders and the five-factor model of personality. *Journal of Personality Disorders, 4,* 362–371.

Cronbach, L., & Meehl, P. (1955). Construct validity in psychological tests. *Psychological Bulletin, 52,* 281–302.

Depue, R. A., & Collins, P. (in press). *Neurobehavioral systems, personality, and psychopathology.* New York: Springer-Verlag.

Digman, J. (1990). Personality structure: Emergence of the five-factor model. *Annual Review of Psychology, 41,* 417–440.

Dohrenwend, B., & Dohrenwend, B. (1982). Perspectives on the past and future of psychiatric epidemiology. *American Journal of Public Health, 72,* 1271–1279.

Drake, R., Adler, D. A., & Vaillant, G. E. (1988). Antecedents of personality disorders in a community sample of men. *Journal of Personality Disorders, 2,* 60–68.

Drake, R., & Vaillant, G. (1985). A validity study of Axis II. *American Journal of Psychiatry, 142,* 553–558.

Drake, R., & Vaillant, G. (1988). Introduction: Longitudinal views of personality disorder. *Journal of Personality Disorders, 2,* 44–48.

Ekman, P., & Davidson, R. J. (1994). *The nature of emotion: Fundamental questions.* New York: Oxford University Press.

Finn, S. (1986). Stability of personality self-ratings over 30 years: Evidence for an age/cohort interaction. *Journal of Personality and Social Psychology, 50,* 813–818.

Frances, A. (1980). The DSM-III personality disorders section: A commentary. *American Journal of Psychiatry, 137,* 1050–1054.

Frances, A., Clarkin, J. F., & Perry, S. (1984). *Differential therapeutics: A guide to the art and science of treatment planning in psychiatry.* New York: Brunner/Mazel.

Freud, S. (1908). Character and eroticism. *Standard Edition, 9,* 169–175.

Gangestad, S., & Snyder, M. (1985). "To carve nature at its joints": On the existence of discrete classes in personality. *Psychological Review, 92,* 317–349.

Glueck, S., & Glueck, E. (1968). *Delinquents and non-delinquents in perspective.* Cambridge, MA: Harvard University Press.

Grace, A. A. (1991). Phasic versus tonic dopamine release and the modulation of dopamine system responsivity: A hypothesis for the etiology of schizophrenia. *Neuroscience, 41,* 1–24.

Grayson, D. (1987). Can categorical and dimensional views of psychiatric illness be distinguished? *British Journal of Psychiatry, 151,* 355–361.

Gunderson, J., & Phillips, K. (1991). A current view of the interface between borderline personality disorder and depression. *American Journal of Psychiatry, 148,* 967–975.

Haan, N., & Day, D. (1974). A longitudinal study of change and sameness in personality development: Adolescence to early adulthood. *International Journal of Aging and Human Development, 5,* 11–39.

Harris, G. T., Rice, M. E., & Quinsey, V. L. (1994). Psychopathy as a taxon: Evidence that psychopaths are a discrete class. *Journal of Consulting and Clinical Psychology, 62,* 387–397.

Hathaway, S. R., & McKinley, J. C. (1983). *The Minnesota Multiphasic Personality Inventory manual.* New York: Psychological Corporation, 1943.

Helson, R., & Moane, G. (1987). Personality change in women from college to midlife. *Journal of Personality and Social Psychology, 53,* 176–186.

Hirschfeld, R. M. A., Klerman, G. L., Clayton, P. J., Keller, M. B., MacDonald-Scott, P., & Larkin, B. H. (1983). Assessing personality: Effects of the depressive state on trait measurement. *American Journal of Psychiatry, 140,* 695–699.

Jacob, F. (1982). *The logic of life: A history of heredity.* New York: Pantheon Books.

John, O. (1990). The "big five" factor taxonomy: Dimensions of personality in the natural language and in questionnaires. In L. Pervin (Ed.), *Handbook of personality: Theory and research* (pp. 66–100). New York: Guilford Press.

Joreskog, K. G. (1979). Statistical estimation of structural equations in longitudinal-developmental investigations. In J. Nesselroade & P. Baltes (Eds.), *Longitudinal research in the study of behavior and development.* New York: Academic Press.

Kagan, J. (1980). Perspectives on continuity. In O. Brim & J. Kagan (Eds.),

Constancy and change in human development (pp. 26–74). Cambridge, MA: Harvard University Press.

Kagan, J. (1994). *Galen's prophecy: Temperament in human nature.* New York: Basic Books.

Kessler, R., & Greenberg, D. (1981). *Linear panel analysis: Models of quantitative change.* New York: Academic Press.

Kessler, R., McGonagle, K., Zhao, S., Nelson, C., Hughes, M. Eshleman, S., Wittchen, H.-U., & Kendler, K. (1994). Lifetime and 12-month prevalence of DSM-III-R psychiatric disorders in the United States: Results from the National Comorbidity Survey. *Archives of General Psychiatry, 51,* 8–19.

Klein, D., Riso, L., & Anderson, R. (1993). DSM-III-R dysthymia: Antecedents and underlying assumptions. In L. Chapman, J. Chapman, & D. Fowles (Eds.), *Progress in experimental personality and psychopathology research* (Vol. 16, pp. 222–253). New York: Springer.

Kohlberg, L., LaCrosse, J., & Ricks, D. (1972). The predictability of adult mental health from childhood behavior. In B. Wolman (Ed.), *Manual of child psychopathology.* New York: McGraw-Hill.

Korfine, L., & Lenzenweger M. F. (1991, December). *The classification of DSM-III-R Axis II personality disorders: A meta-analysis.* Paper presented at the sixth annual meeting of the Society for Research in Psychopathology, Harvard University, Cambridge, MA.

Korfine, L., & Lenzenweger, M. F. (1995). The taxonicity of schizotypy: A replication. *Journal of Abnormal Psychology, 104,* 26–31.

Korfine, L., Lenzenweger, M. F., & Hazan, C. (1994). *Sex, gender, and personality disorders.* Manuscript submitted for publication.

Kraepelin, E. (1907). *Clinical psychiatry* (A. R. Diefendorf, Trans.). New York: Macmillan.

Leary, T. (1957). *Interpersonal diagnosis of personality.* New York: Ronald.

Lenzenweger, M. F. (1993). Explorations in schizotypy and the psychometric high-risk paradigm. In L. Chapman, J. Chapman, & D. Fowles (Eds.), *Progress in experimental personality and psychopathology research* (Vol. 16, pp. 66–116). New York: Springer.

Lenzenweger, M. F., & Depue, R. A. (1995). *Mind, brain, and behavior: Toward an integrated model of personality, personality disorder, and neurobiology.* Manuscript in preparation.

Lenzenweger, M. F., & Dworkin, R. H. (in press). The dimensions of schizophrenia phenomenology? Not one or two, at least three, perhaps four. *British Journal of Psychiatry.*

Lenzenweger, M. F., Dworkin, R., & Wethington, E. (1989). Models of positive and negative symptoms in schizophrenia: An empirical evaluation of latent structures. *Journal of Abnormal Psychology, 98,* 62–70.

Lenzenweger, M. F., & Korfine, L. (1992). Confirming the latent structure and base rate of schizotypy: A taxometric approach. *Journal of Abnormal Psychology, 101,* 576–571.

Lenzenweger, M. F., Loranger, A. W., Korfine, L., & Neff, C. (1995). *Detecting DSM-III-R personality disorders in a nonclinical population: Application of a two-stage procedure for case identification.* Manuscript submitted for publication.

Lenzenweger, M. F., & Moldin, S. (1990). Discerning the latent structure of hypothetical psychosis proneness through admixture analysis. *Psychiatry Research, 33*, 243–257.

Loranger, A. (1988). *The Personality Disorder Examination (PDE) manual.* Yonkers, NY: DV Communications.

Loranger, A. (1990). The impact of DSM-III on diagnostic practice in a university hospital: A comparison of DSM-II and DSM-III in 10,914 patients. *Archives of General Psychiatry, 47*, 672–675.

Loranger, A. (1991a). Diagnosis of personality disorders: General considerations. In R. Michels, A. Cooper, S. Guze, L. Judd, G. Klerman, A. Solnit, & A. Stunkard (Eds.), *Psychiatry* (Rev. ed., Vol. 1, pp. 1–14). New York: Lippincott.

Loranger, A. (1991b, May). *Comorbidity of borderline personality disorder.* Paper presented at the 144th annual meeting of the American Psychiatric Association, New Orleans, LA.

Loranger, A. (1992). Are current self-report and interview measures adequate for epidemiological studies of personality disorders? *Journal of Personality Disorders, 6*, 313–325.

Loranger, A., & Lenzenweger, M. (1995). *Trait–state artifacts and the diagnosis of personality disorders: A replication.* Manuscript in preparation.

Loranger, A., Lenzenweger, M., Gartner, A., Susman, V., Herzig, J., Zammit, G., Gartner, J., Abrams, R., & Young, R. (1991). Trait–state artifacts and the diagnosis of personality disorders. *Archives of General Psychiatry, 48*, 720–728.

Maier, W., Lichtermann, D., Klingler, T., Heun, R., & Hallmayer, J. (1992). Prevalences of personality disorders (DSM-III-R) in the community. *Journal of Personality Disorders, 6*, 187–192.

Matthysse, S. (1993). Genetics and the problem of causality in abnormal psychology. In P. Sutker & H. Adams (Eds.), *Comprehensive handbook of psychopathology* (pp. 178–186). New York: Springer-Verlag.

McCrae, R., & Costa, P. (1984). *Emerging lives, enduring dispositions: Personality in adulthood.* Boston: Little, Brown.

McGue, M., Bacon, S., & Lykken, D. (1993). Personality stability and change in early adulthood: A behavioral genetic analysis. *Developmental Psychology, 29*, 96–109.

Meehl, P. E. (1972). Specific genetic etiology, psychodynamics, and therapeutic nihilism. *International Journal of Mental Health, 1*, 10–27.

Meehl, P. E. (1978). Theoretical risks and tabular asterisks: Sir Karl, Sir Ronald, and the slow progress of soft psychology. *Journal of Consulting and Clinical Psychology, 46*, 806–834.

Meehl, P. E. (1990). Toward an integrated theory of schizotaxia, schizotypy, and schizophrenia. *Journal of Personality Disorders, 4*, 1–99.

Meehl, P. E. (1992). Factors and taxa, traits and types, differences of degree and differences in kind. *Journal of Personality, 60*, 117–174.

Meehl, P. E. (1993). Philosophy of science: Help or hindrance? *Psychological Reports, 72*, 707–733.

Meehl, P. E. (1995). Bootstraps taxometrics: Solving the classification problem in psychopathology. *American Psychologist, 50*, 266–275.

Millon, T. (1982). *Disorders of personality.* New York: Wiley.

Mortimer, J., Finch, M., & Kumka, D. (1982). Persistence and change in development: The multidimensional self-concept. In P. Baltes & O. Brim (Eds.), *Life-span development and behavior* (Vol. 4, pp. 263–313). New York: Academic Press.

Murray, H. A. (1938). *Explorations in personality.* New York: Wiley.

Nesselroade, J. (1988). Some implications of the trait–state distinction for the study of development over the life-span: The case of personality. In P. Baltes, D. L. Featherman, & R. M. Lerner (Eds.), *Life-span development and behavior* (Vol. 8, pp. 163–189). Hillsdale, NJ: Erlbaum.

Nesselroade, J., & Baltes, P. (1974). Adolescent personality development and historical change: 1970–1972. *Monographs of the Society for Research in Child Development, 39*(1, Whole No. 154).

Nesselroade, J., & Baltes, P. (1979). *Longitudinal research in the study of behavior and development.* New York: Academic Press.

Nesselroade, J., & Baltes, P. (1984). From traditional factor analysis to structural causal modeling in developmental research. In V. Sarris & A. Parducci (Eds.), *Perspectives in psychological experimentation: Toward the year 2000* (pp. 267–287). Hillsdale, NJ: Erlbaum.

Nesselroade, J., Stigler, S., & Baltes, P. (1980). Regression toward the mean and the study of change. *Psychological Bulletin, 88*, 622–637.

Nigg, J., & Goldsmith, H. (1994). Genetics of personality disorders: Perspectives from psychology and psychopathology research. *Psychological Bulletin, 115*, 346–380.

Perry, J. (1992). Problems and considerations in the valid assessment of personality disorders. *American Journal of Psychiatry, 149*, 1645–1653.

Perry, J. (1993). Longitudinal studies of personality disorders. *Journal of Personality Disorders, 7*(Suppl. Spring), 63–85.

Pervin, L. A. (1990). A brief history of modern personality theory. In L. A. Pervin (Ed.), *Handbook of personality: Theory and research* (pp. 3–18). New York: Guilford Press.

Pfohl, B., Coryell, W., Zimmerman, M., & Stangl, D. (1986). DSM-III personality disorders: Diagnostic overlap and internal consistency of individual DSM-III criteria. *Comprehensive Psychiatry, 27*, 21–34.

Pilkonis, P., Heape, C., Ruddy, J., & Serrao, P. (1991). Validity in the diagnosis of personality disorders: The use of the LEAD standard. *Psychological Assessment: A Journal of Consulting and Clinical Psychology, 3*, 46–54.

Plomin, R., Chipuer, H., & Loehlin, J. (1990). Behavioral genetics and personality. In L. Pervin (Ed.), *Handbook of personality: Theory and research* (pp. 225–243). New York: Guilford Press.

Rapaport, D., Gill, M. M., & Schafer, R. (1968). *Diagnostic psychological testing* (Rev. ed.; R. R. Holt, Ed.). New York: International Universities Press.

Reichenbach, H. (1938). *Experience and prediction.* Chicago: University of Chicago Press.

Robins, L. (1966). *Deviant children grown up.* Baltimore: Williams & Wilkins.

Robins, L. (1978). Sturdy childhood predictors of adult anti-social behavior: Replications from longitudinal studies. *Psychological Medicine, 8*, 611–622.

Robins, L., Helzer, J., Weissman, M., Orvaschel, H., Gruenberg, E., Burke,

J., & Regier, D. (1984). Lifetime prevalence of specific psychiatric disorders in three sites. *Archives of General Psychiatry, 41,* 949–958.

Rogosa, D. (1979). Causal models in longitudinal research: Rationale, formulation, and interpretation. In J. Nesselroade & P. Baltes (Eds.), *Longitudinal research in the study of behavior and development* (pp. 263–302). New York: Academic Press.

Rogosa, D. (1988). Myths about longitudinal research. In K. Shaie, R. Campbell, W. Meredith, & S. Rawlings (Eds.), *Methodological issues in aging research* (pp. 171–209). New York: Springer.

Rogosa, D., Brandt, D., & Zimowski, M. (1982). A growth curve approach to the measurement of change. *Psychological Bulletin, 90,* 726–748.

Rowe, D. C. (1994). *The limits of family influence: Genes, experience, and behavior.* New York: Guilford Press.

Rutter, M. (1987). Temperament, personality, and personality disorder. *British Journal of Psychiatry, 150,* 443–458.

Rutter, M. (1991). Nature, nurture, and psychopathology: A new look at an old topic. *Development and Psychopathology, 3,* 125–136.

Schroeder, M. L., Wormworth, J. A., & Livesley, W. J. (1994). Dimensions of personality disorder and the five-factor model of personality. In P. T. Costa & T. A. Widiger (Eds.), *Personality disorders and the five-factor model of personality* (pp. 117–130). Washington, DC: American Psychological Association.

Siever, L., Kalus, O., & Keefe, R. (1993). The boundaries of schizophrenia. *Psychiatric Clinics of North America, 16,* 217–244.

Spitzer, R. (1983). Psychiatric diagnosis: Are clinicians still necessary? *Comprehensive Psychiatry, 24,* 399–411.

Spitzer, R., Williams, J., & Gibbon, M. (1987). *Structured Clinical Interview for DSM-III-R Personality Disorders (SCID-II).* New York: New York State Psychiatric Institute.

Tellegen, A. (1985). Structure of mood and personality and their relevance for assessing anxiety, with an emphasis on self-report. In A. Tuma & J. Maser (Eds.), *Anxiety and the anxiety disorders* (pp. 681–706). Hillsdale, NJ: Erlbaum.

Trull, T. (1992). DSM-III-R personality disorders and the five-factor model of personality: An empirical comparison. *Journal of Abnormal Psychology, 101,* 553–560.

Trull, T., & Goodwin, A. (1993). Relationship between mood changes and the report of personality disorder symptoms. *Journal of Personality Assessment, 61,* 99–111.

Trull, T., Widiger, T., & Guthrie, P. (1990). Categorical versus dimensional status of borderline personality disorder. *Journal of Abnormal Psychology, 99,* 40–48.

Vaillant, G. (1977). *Adaptation to life.* Boston: Little, Brown.

Vaillant, G. E., & Perry, J. C. (1985). Personality disorders. In H. I. Kaplan & B. J. Sadock (Eds.), *Comprehensive textbook of psychiatry/IV* (4th ed., Vol. 1, pp. 958–986). Baltimore: Williams & Wilkins.

Weissman, M. (1993). The epidemiology of personality disorders: A 1990 update. *Journal of Personality Disorders, 7*(Suppl. Spring), 44–62.

Widiger, T. (1992). Categorical versus dimensional classification. *Journal of Personality Disorders, 6,* 287–300.

Widiger, T., & Frances, A. (1985). The DSM-III personality disorders: Perspectives from psychology. *Archives of General Psychiatry, 42,* 615–623.

Widiger, T., Frances, A., Harris, M., Jacobsberg, L., Fyer, M., & Manning, D. (1991). Comorbidity among Axis II disorders. In J. Oldham (Ed.), *Personality disorders: New perspectives on diagnostic validity* (pp. 163–194). Washington, DC: American Psychiatric Press.

Widiger, T., & Shea, T. (1991). Differentiation of Axis I and Axis II disorders. *Journal of Abnormal Psychology, 100,* 399–406.

Widiger, T. A., Trull, T. J., Clarkin, J. F., Sanderson, C., & Costa, P. T. (1994). A description of the DSM-III-R and DSM-IV personality disorders with the five-factor model of personality. In P. T. Costa & T. A. Widiger (Eds.), *Personality disorders and the five-factor model of personality* (pp. 41–58). Washington, DC: American Psychological Association.

Wiggins, J. (1982). Circumplex models of interpersonal behavior in clinical psychology. In P. Kendall & J. Butcher (Eds.), *Handbook of research methods in clinical psychology* (pp. 183–221). New York: Wiley.

Wiggins. J., & Pincus, A. (1989). Conceptions of personality disorders and dimensions of personality. *Psychological Assessment: A Journal of Consulting and Clinical Psychology, 1,* 305–316.

Zimmerman, M. (1994). Diagnosing personality disorders: A review of issues and research methods. *Archives of General Psychiatry, 51,* 225–245.

2

A Cognitive Theory
of Personality Disorders

JAMES L. PRETZER
AARON T. BECK

Clients with personality disorders are among the most complex and demanding clients whom therapists face. Personality disorders are encountered frequently in many clinical settings and often co-occur with Axis I disorders (e.g., Black, Yates, Noyes, Pfohl, & Kelley, 1989; Freidman, Shear, & Frances, 1987; Overholser, 1991; Turner, Bidel, Borden, Stanley, & Jacob, 1991). When this is the case, the presence of an Axis II disorder can have a significant effect on the clinical presentation, development, and course of the Axis I disorder. It has even been suggested that clients with personality disorders may account for a substantial proportion of those individuals for whom psychotherapy proves ineffective or deleterious (Mays & Franks, 1985). Clearly, the development of effective approaches to understanding and treating individuals with personality disorders is of great importance. In recent years, major advances have been made in applying the principles of cognitive therapy[1] with this difficult population.

Cognitive therapy is an active, problem-focused approach to psychotherapy based on contemporary understandings of the role of thought, feeling, and action in psychopathology. This approach may have particular potential for overcoming some of the problems encountered in attempting to understand and treat individuals with personality disorders. First, persons with personality disorders are often difficult to conceptualize clearly. Cognitive therapy provides a conceptual framework that is straightforward and easy to grasp and that can make therapy with complex clients less confusing and frustrating. Second, individuals with personality disorders often present a wide range of symptoms that demand immediate attention. Cognitive therapy provides a coherent framework within which a wide range of interventions can be used flexibly and strategically. These interventions include specialized cognitive-behavioral techniques that provide powerful tools both for alleviating current distress and for accomplishing the lasting changes needed to head off future difficulties. Finally, many approaches to psychotherapy have only a limited empirical base. Cognitive therapy is supported by a large body of empirical research on both the validity of the theory and the effectiveness of the treatment. While research into cognitive therapy with personality disorders is in its initial stages, there are preliminary indications that it will prove to be an effective treatment for these complex disorders.

However, despite these arguments in favor of cognitive therapy as an approach to understanding and treating personality disorders, there is increasing evidence that cognitive-behavioral treatment frequently proves ineffective or counterproductive for individuals with Axis II diagnoses if the treatment approach is not modified to account for the presence of a personality disorder (Fleming & Pretzer, 1990; Pretzer & Fleming, 1990). For example, Turner (1987) found that social phobics without concurrent Axis II diagnoses improved markedly during a 15-week, time-limited cognitive-behavioral treatment for social phobia, whereas patients who had concomitant Axis II diagnoses failed to respond to this treatment regimen. Similarly, Persons, Burns, and Perloff (1988) found that premature termination of "standard" cognitive therapy and the consequent ineffectiveness of therapy were more likely when depressed patients had concurrent personality disorders.

Personality disorders are among the most difficult and least understood problems faced by therapists regardless of the therapist's orientation. The treatment of clients with these disorders can be just as complex and frustrating for cognitive therapists as it is for other therapists. For example:

> Gary, a young radiologist, contacted a therapist (J. L. P.) seeking treatment for persistent anxiety which aggravated a long-standing problem with irritable bowel syndrome. Initially, the case seemed fairly straightforward, and initial interventions directed toward helping him to learn more effective ways of coping with stress and to learn to control his excessive worries proved effective. However, after six sessions of apparently successful treatment, Gary reported that the relaxation techniques that had been quite effective had

now "quit working," and he seemed increasingly unwilling to relax his vigilance and worry. As treatment progressed, his therapist discovered that he had a persistent view of others as hostile and malicious, that he had recurrent encounters with his family of origin and with co-workers that seemed to confirm this negative view of others, and that he was enmeshed in a complex dysfunctional relationship with his alcoholic girlfriend. It turned out that in addition to the generalized anxiety disorder that had initially brought him to treatment, Gary met DSM-III-R criteria for dysthymic disorder and paranoid personality disorder as well.

"Standard" interventions were proving ineffective with Gary, as they do with many individuals with personality disorders. Would it be necessary to abandon cognitive therapy and switch to some other type of therapy? Were major revisions of cognitive therapy called for? Or would it simply be a matter of taking Gary's personality disorder into account in planning therapeutic interventions?

For cognitive therapy to live up to its promise as an approach to understanding and treating personality disorders, it is necessary to tailor the approach to the characteristics of individuals with personality disorders rather than simply using "standard" cognitive therapy without modification. Actually, it is not surprising that Gary's treatment reached an impasse, since the interventions that were proving ineffective were based on a very incomplete conceptualization of Gary's problems. His paranoia had not been apparent before this impasse in treatment arose, and the treatment plan the therapist had in mind did not take it into account at all. In order to intervene effectively, Gary's therapist needed to develop a treatment plan based on a clear conceptualization that encompassed both Gary's problems with anxiety and his personality disorder. However, this presents a problem. . . . How is one to understand personality disorders in cognitive-behavioral terms?

PHILOSOPHICAL FOUNDATIONS
OF COGNITIVE THERAPY

Cognitive therapy's basic philosophical orientation is phenomenological. It assumes that the individual's perception and interpretation of situations shape the emotional and behavioral responses to the situation. This is hardly a radical view. Thinkers from Buddha and the ancient Stoic philosophers up to the present have emphasized the idea that humans react to their interpretation of events, not to the actual events themselves and have argued that misperceptions and misinterpretations of events result in much unnecessary distress.

Cognitive therapy is based on the proposition that much psychopathology is the result of systematic errors, biases, and distortions in perceiving and interpreting events. These cognitive factors are seen as resulting in dysfunctional responses to events, which, in turn, may have consequences that serve to perpetuate the dysfunctional cognitions. Theoretically, the focus is strongly on the interaction between the individual and his/her environment rather than emphasizing either individual or situational factors in isolation (for a detailed example see Pretzer, Beck, & Newman, 1990). Individuals' interpretations of events are seen as playing a central role in many forms of psychopathology, and these interpretations are seen as being the product of the interaction between the characteristics of the individual and the nature of the events the individual encounters. However, in discussing treatment, much more emphasis is placed on individual factors (such as dysfunctional beliefs) than on situational factors (such as negative life events) because therapist and client are more able to modify individual factors than situational ones.

Some phenomenological approaches are highly subjective in orientation and assume that objective reality is unknowable. Cognitive therapy, however, has a strongly empirical orientation. Given our assumption that individuals' perceptions are subject to errors, biases, and distortions that can lead to misperceptions, misunderstandings, and dysfunctional responses, we also assume that we need to be aware of the potential for errors, biases, and distortions in our own thinking as therapists. Thus we need to make efforts both to minimize biases and distortions in our observations and to test the validity of our conclusions rather than to assume that clinical observation and logical analysis will lead us to "the truth." Cognitive therapy has a strong tradition of empirical research but our empirical orientation goes far beyond conducting outcome research, testing hypotheses based on cognitive models of specific forms of psychopathology, or making use of the available empirical research in developing cognitive conceptualizations of various disorders. The idea of "collaborative empiricism" is central to the practice of cognitive therapy. In the course of therapy, the cognitive therapist works with his or her client to collect detailed information regarding the specific thoughts, feelings, and actions that occur in problem situations. These observations are used as a basis for developing an individualized understanding of the client, which provides a basis for strategic intervention. Collaborative empiricism continues to play an important role as the focus of therapy shifts from assessment to intervention. Many of the specific techniques used to modify dysfunctional thoughts, beliefs, and strategies emphasize using first-hand observation and "behavioral experiments" to test the validity of dysfunctional automatic thoughts or dysfunctional beliefs and to develop more adaptive alternatives. Rather than relying on the therapist's expertise, theoretical deductions, or logic, cognitive therapy assumes that empirical observation is the most reliable means for developing valid conceptualizations and effective interventions.

This emphasis on an empirical approach does not mean that we emphasize objective reality over subjective experience but that we try to develop accurate understandings of both. Cognitive theory asserts that it is the subjective experience of events that shapes the individual's emotional and behavioral responses, but it also asserts that the individual's emotional and behavioral responses are likely to prove to be dysfunctional when there is a substantial discrepancy between subjective experience and objective reality. In order for the cognitive therapist to intervene effectively, he or she must endeavor both to understand the individual's subjective experience and to perceive objective reality accurately. In attempting to do this, it is often necessary to rely on client self-reports because some of the factors that are of interest to cognitive therapists, such as automatic thoughts and dysfunctional beliefs, are not directly observable and because it is often impractical for the therapist to do extensive in vivo observation. We recognize that self-reports may be an imperfect source of data, since they are open to a wide range of potential biases and distortions. However, they are often the most practical source of information regarding the client's day-to-day experiences.[2]

In considering the role of cognition in psychopathology, cognitive therapy uses the term "cognition" broadly to refer to much more than verbal thought of which the individual is self-consciously aware. "Cognition" is treated as synonymous with information processing and no a priori assumption is made that all important aspects of cognition are verbally mediated, are easily accessible to the individual's awareness, or are subject to the individual's volitional control. In fact, much cognition occurs outside of awareness simply because the individual is not paying attention to it or because the processes involved are automatic and occur without a need for awareness or volitional control. Cognition is not necessarily verbally mediated. It can also be mediated by mental imagery or can involve more abstract modes of information processing. Obviously, when discussing cognition, it is necessary to translate nonverbal cognitions, such as mental images, into words in order to facilitate communication. In discussing cognition and other aspects of individual functioning, cognitive investigators have tried to avoid the tendency to generate specialized technical terms and instead have relied heavily on "natural language" along with terms borrowed from cognitive psychology. The advantages of using a straightforward, easily understood vocabulary greatly outweigh the supposed advantages of a more precise technical vocabulary.

Above all, cognitive therapy is a practical approach that has emphasized effective treatment rather than abstract theory. We emphasize basing interventions on an individualized conceptualization of the client's problems not because of any inherent commitment to theory but because strategic interventions based on a clear conceptualization are more efficient and more effective. Similarly, cognitive therapy's emphasis on the "here-and-now" is a matter of practicality rather than philosophy. We find that time spent investigating the factors that perpetuate the psychopathology in the present is usually more productive than time spent investigating the individual's past. This does not mean that cognitive therapists ignore the individual's past. In fact it can be quite valuable for therapist and client to recreate past traumatic events at times. Cognitive therapists, however, attempt to focus on the past only to the extent that this contributes to understanding and/or modifying the factors that perpetuate the disorder in the present.

To return to the question of how to develop a cognitive conceptualization of a person such as Gary, the young radiologist discussed above, cognitive therapy's orientation is directed toward attempting to develop an accurate understanding of both Gary's subjective experience of events and the objective reality he faces. In order to minimize the problems that can arise from the therapist's own misperceptions and misunderstandings, an attempt will be made to make use of knowledge acquired through empirical research and direct observation insofar as possible; however, because of practical constraints, it will be necessary to rely heavily on Gary's reports both of the situations he encounters and of his cognitive, emotional, and behavioral responses to them. The focus in therapy will be primarily on the here-and-now, on the interaction between Gary and the situations in which he finds himself, and on identifying the factors or processes that perpetuate Gary's problems. It is anticipated that when Gary's perception of a situation differs substantially from the reality of the situation, his responses are likely to prove dysfunctional. However, this general philosophical orientation does not provide a detailed enough conceptual framework to permit us to develop a clear understanding of Gary's problems or to develop a promising approach to intervention. A more detailed theoretical framework is needed.

THEORETICAL FOUNDATIONS OF COGNITIVE THERAPY

Precursors

The evolution of cognitive therapy has been influenced by a wide range of theorists and clinicians, and it can be argued that cognitive therapy is a highly integrative approach (Alford & Norcross, 1991; Beck, 1991). The three primary theoretical influences have been the phenomenological approach to psychology, psychodynamic depth psychology, and cognitive psychology. The clinical practice of cognitive therapy has been strongly influenced by client-centered therapy and by contemporary behavioral and cognitive-behavioral approaches to therapy. Among the influences that Beck (Beck, 1985; Beck & Weishaar, 1989) considers to have been most important are: phenomenological perspectives dating back to the Greek Stoic philosophers and presented more recently by Alfred Adler, Otto Rank, and Karen Horney; the structural theory and depth psychology of Immanuel Kant and Sigmund Freud; the cognitive perspectives of George Kelley, Magda Arnold, and Richard Lazarus; the emphasis on a specific, here-and-now approach to problems taken by Austen Riggs and Albert Ellis; Carl Rogers's client centered therapy; the idea of preconscious cognition from writers such as Leon Saul; and the work of cognitive-behavioral investigators including Albert Bandura, Marvin Goldfried, Michael Mahoney, Donald Meichenbaum, and G. Terence Wilson.

The Development of Cognitive Therapy

Aaron Beck's initial training and therapeutic orientation were psychodynamic. He accepted the psychodynamic view of the day that depression, anxiety disorders, and other disorders were only the surface manifestation of an underlying personality defect or disorder. Cognitive therapy developed out of his attempts to substantiate Freud's theory that the core of depression was "anger turned on the self." Beck initially set out to examine the thoughts and dreams of depressed individuals expecting to discover indications of hostility turned inward and thus to provide empirical support for psychoanalytic theory. However, he consistently noted themes of defeat, deprivation, and despair rather than the hostility turned inward that Freud postulated. Further empirical research and clinical observation led him to the realization that an understanding of the content of depressed individuals' appraisals of the situations and events that they encountered did much to explain their mood and behavior and revealed a consistent negative bias in information processing. Beck initially developed a cognitive model of emotional disorders to explain the biases and distortions in information processing that he observed in depressed individuals.

This cognitive understanding of psychopathology led naturally to attempts to modify the cognitive processes that appeared to play a major role in psychopathology. It was soon discovered that when the therapist engaged in an active dialogue with depressed clients and focused on the clients' thoughts and beliefs, it was possible to help them to consciously correct the biases and distortions in their information processing and consequently to alleviate their depression. Albert Ellis's (1962) initial work on rational–emotive therapy was concurrent with Beck's research and shared a focus on the client's thoughts and beliefs and an active, problem-focused approach to therapy. Despite important conceptual and stylistic differences, the two approaches have developed concurrently and have influenced each other in many ways.

The "cognitive revolution" in behavior therapy occurred at the same time as cognitive therapy was evolving and had important influences on both the theory and the clinical practice of cognitive therapy. Bandura's social learning theory (Bandura, 1977) contributed an emphasis on the interaction between the individual and the environment, modeling, vicarious learning, and concepts of expectancy of reinforcement and self- and outcome efficacies. Similarly, Mahoney's (1974, 1977) emphasis on the cognitive mediation of human learning was an important theoretical influence. Behavior therapy also had important influences on cognitive therapy's developing approach to clinical intervention with its emphasis on detailed, objective clinical observation, its problem-focused approach to intervention, its emphasis on empirical evaluation of interventions, and its wide range of specific intervention techniques.

The investigators who have collaborated with Beck in the development of cognitive therapy have come from a variety of backgrounds but have not clung to their preconceptions or theoretical assumptions. The emphasis within cognitive therapy has been on taking theoretical concepts, whatever their origin, as hypotheses to be tested empirically and clinically with the goal of developing a coherent, empirically validated understanding of psychopathology and an effective approach to psychotherapeutic intervention. The result has been a truly integrative approach (Alford & Norcross, 1991; Beck, 1991) that emphasizes the importance of understanding individuals' subjective experience, of accurately observing the objective situation and the individual's response to it, and of addressing the discrepancies between subjective experience and objective reality. While the individual's cognitive processes have been an important focus of cognitive therapy, affect and interpersonal behavior have always played an important role as well, and they have received increasing attention in recent years.

COGNITION AND PSYCHOPATHOLOGY

Core Assumptions

The cognitive view of psychopathology is essentially an information-processing model. It assumes that in order to function in the wide range of life situations that they encounter, humans are constantly perceiving, recalling, interpreting, and storing data from the environment and that these continuous, automatic processes elicit the individual's cognitive, emotional, and behavioral responses to events. It also assumes that biases, distortions, or defects in perception and interpretation of experiences can result in maladaptive responses and that persistent, systematic errors in information processing play an important role in many forms of psychopathology. Thus an individual who accurately perceives a particular situation as benign is likely to respond adaptively. In contrast, an individual who erroneously perceives a single benign situation as dangerous will experience a "false alarm" and will respond as though the situation is dangerous. This reaction, by itself, is not likely to result in a significant problem; however, the individual who *consistently misperceives benign situations as dangerous* is likely to manifest problematic levels of anxiety and avoidance behavior.

This view might seem to presume that individuals normally respond to events in a logical, rational, computer-like manner and that psychopathology is the result of irrational or illogical responses, but this is not our assumption at all. We argue that much information processing occurs automatically and outside of awareness and that, furthermore, the processes involved are not necessarily logical, rational, or veridical. The processes through which humans interact with their environment evolved to serve the basic requirements of the organism in an environment that was substantially different from the environments in which humans find themselves today. Some biases in information processing may have had important advantages for the organism. For example, an optimistic bias in mate selection may have promoted bonding and reproductive success, whereas a tendency to exaggerate the degree of danger presented by risk situations may have maximized the likelihood of avoiding real danger and have promoted survival (Beck, 1992). On the one hand, humans may have biases in information processing that prove to be more adaptive than purely objective information processing would be. On the other hand, as human social change has outstripped physiological evolution, we may well have also retained some biases in information processing that now tend to be maladaptive.

The cognitive view of human functioning (Figure 2.1) emphasizes three aspects of cognition. First, an individual's "automatic thoughts," his/her immediate, spontaneous appraisal of the situation, are seen as playing a central role in eliciting and shaping an individual's emotional and behavioral response to a situation. For example, when Gary (the young radiologist described above) and his therapist examined one of the situations in which the progressive relaxation exercises "didn't work," Gary reported remembering[3] that his immediate reaction as a colleague approached was "He'll catch up with me and see what I'm doing. I don't want him stealing my idea." Given that he perceived the situation as one in which he needed to be vigilant in order

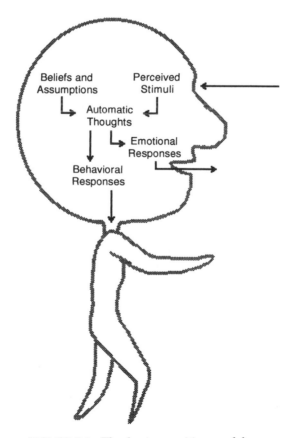

FIGURE 2.1. The basic cognitive model.

to prevent a rival at work from "stealing" his ideas, it isn't surprising that he was unable to relax. Unfortunately for Gary, he was prone to conclude that he had to be vigilant and on guard in a wide range of situations where vigilance was actually unnecessary and where the resulting tension and anxiety were seriously maladaptive.

How could an intelligent, perceptive person like Gary consistently misperceive mundane situations? Certainly one possibility is that the type of evolutionarily based biases in information processing discussed above could contribute to a tendency to misperceive certain types of situations. However, our view is that many misperceptions and misinterpretations result from the effects of schemas, cognitive structures containing the individual's basic beliefs and assumptions, which shape the individuals' perceptions of events and their responses to them. Humans do not "start from scratch" in perceiving and interpreting each event or situation they encounter. For example, when an individual encounters a large quadruped covered with shaggy hair, that person can easily classify it as a dog and interpret its wagging tail as indicative of benign intentions even if he/she has not previously encountered a Briard (a French breed of sheep dog) and has never seen a dog that looks quite like this one. This is because the individual has retained a set of related concepts regarding the characteristics that characterize dogs, important aspects of canine behavior, and human-canine interaction. These concepts are automatically used in interpreting a relevant stimulus. This set of related concepts, termed a "schema," is based on the individual's previous experience with dogs, his or her observations of other persons' experience with dogs, verbal and nonverbal communications from others regarding dogs, and so forth.

A given individual will have an assortment of schemas that are relevant to hairy quadrupeds, but these are not simply applied randomly in perceiving our Briard. The context automatically influences the selection of schemas so that those that seem most likely to be relevant to the situation are tried first, and a series of schemas are tried until a "good fit" is achieved. Thus, if the Briard is encountered at a dog show, the individual's "dog schema" is likely to be applied first, and the Briard is likely to be perceived correctly at once. If the Briard is encountered in a cage at the zoo, more exotic schemas are likely to be applied first and it is likely to take longer for the individual to correctly perceive it as a dog. If the Briard is encountered among a collection of rare breeds of sheep and goats, its size, shaggy coat, and so forth, may well result in its being misperceived as an unusual type of goat until it emits some behavior, such as barking, that is incompatible with the individual's "goat schema." As soon as the animal is correctly identified as an unfamiliar breed of dog, the individual automatically uses an assortment of generalizations about canine behavior to interpret the dog's current behavior and to anticipate what the dog is likely to do in the future.

Normally, schemas greatly facilitate our responses to the situations we encounter. Life would be impossibly cumbersome if we had to start de novo in interpreting each organism and object that we encountered. However, schemas can also play an important role in maladaptive responses to stimuli. For example, an individual with a dog phobia is likely to have a schema regarding dogs that differs from the average individual's "dog schema" by emphasizing potentially dangerous aspects of dogs and canine behavior. As a result, the dog phobic correctly identifies the Briard as a dog but is likely automatically to classify it as dangerous and to respond with a range of physiological reactions, a subjective surge of anxiety, and an abrupt departure.

Gary, had operated on a long-standing conviction that other persons were malicious, deceptive, and hostile and would take advantage of him or attack him if given a chance (see Figure 2.2). These assumptions had important effects on the way in which Gary interpreted experiences. First, since he anticipated that others would be malicious and deceptive, he was alert for signs of deceit, deception, and malicious intentions. This selective attention resulted in his being quick to recognize those occasions when others were being dishonest or untrustworthy. In addition, many interpersonal interactions are ambiguous enough to be open to a variety of interpretations. Given his hypervigilance, Gary was quick to respond to ambiguous situations

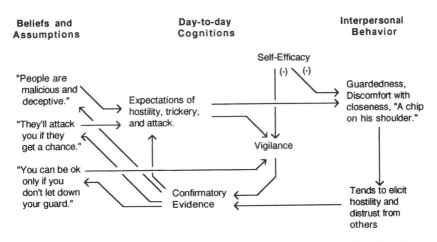

FIGURE 2.2. Cognitive conceptualization of paranoid personality disorder.

on the assumption that others had malicious intentions without pausing to consider other possibilities. Thus, his world view resulted in his being vigilant for signs of maliciousness and deception in a way that tended to result in his perceiving many of his experiences in a way that was congruent with his world view. Furthermore, when he did have an experience of someone's proving trustworthy or benevolent, his assumption that others are deceptive led to his concluding that the other person was trying to "set him up" rather than his concluding that the person was genuinely being trustworthy. In short, Gary's vigilance for experiences that appeared to confirm his preconceptions and his tendency to discount experiences that appeared to be inconsistent with his world view tended to confirm and perpetuate his assumptions about others.

In addition to their beliefs and assumptions about "the way things are," individuals also hold beliefs and assumptions about what one should do about this that can be termed "interpersonal strategies." For example, in addition to his assuming that others were malicious and deceptive, Gary believed that the way to be safe was to be vigilant, on guard, and to be quick to react to any offense. This reaction had a major impact on his interpersonal relationships. He tended to be quite guarded and defensive in interpersonal interactions, to avoid closeness, and to react quickly and strongly to any perceived mistreatment. He also assumed that assertion would prove ineffective or counterproductive, so instead of speaking up for himself when he felt mistreated, he often overreacted dramatically.

A third aspect of cognition that can contribute to persistent misperceptions of situations are systematic errors in reasoning, termed "cognitive distortions." Humans are prone to a variety of errors in logic that can contribute to misinterpretations of events and that can amplify the impact of schemas (see Table 2.1). Gary viewed trustworthiness in a dichotomous manner (see "dichotomous thinking" in Table 2.1). As he saw it, one is either trustworthy or untrustworthy, with no gradation in between. As he approached interpersonal interactions, he was vigilant for signs of deceit, deception, or malicious intentions, and once he observed any indication that the individual was not perfectly trustworthy, Gary automatically classified the other person as untrustworthy. Because of Gary's dichotomous view, intermediate categories such as "not very trustworthy" or "usually reliable" were not considered. Individuals were seen as trustworthy only if they had proven to be completely trustworthy and were considered to be untrustworthy as soon as a single apparent lapse in trustworthiness was observed. This, of course, contributed to Gary's view that people in general were untrustworthy, since very few of the people he knew managed to prove perfectly trustworthy for long.

TABLE 2.1. Common Cognitive Distortions

Dichotomous thinking: Viewing experiences in terms of two mutually exclusive categories with no "shades of gray" in between. For example, believing that one is *either* a success *or* a failure and that anything short of a perfect performance is a total failure.

Overgeneralization: Perceiving a particular event as being characteristic of life in general rather than as being one event among many. For example, concluding that an inconsiderate response from one's spouse shows that she doesn't care despite her having showed consideration on other occasions.

Selective abstraction: Focusing on one aspect of a complex situation to the exclusion of other relevant aspects of the situation. For example, focusing on the one negative comment in a performance evaluation received at work and overlooking the positive comments contained in the evaluation.

Disqualifying the positive: Discounting positive experiences that would conflict with the individual's negative views. For example, rejecting positive feedback from friends and colleagues on the grounds that "They're only saying that to be nice" rather than considering whether the feedback could be valid.

Mind reading: Assuming that one knows what others are thinking or how others are reacting despite having little or no evidence. For example, thinking "I just know he thought I was an idiot!" despite the other person's having given no apparent indications of his reactions.

Fortune telling: Reacting as though expectations about future events are established facts rather than recognizing them as fears, hopes, or predictions. For example, thinking "He's leaving me, I just know it!" and acting as though this is definitely true.

Catastrophizing: Treating actual or anticipated negative events as intolerable catastrophes rather than seeing them in perspective. For example, thinking "Oh my God, what if I faint!" without considering that while fainting may be unpleasant or embarrassing, it is not terribly dangerous.

Maximization/minimization: Treating some aspects of the situation, personal characteristics, or experiences as trivial and others as very important independent of their actual significance. For example, thinking "Sure, I'm good at my job, but so what? My parents don't respect me."

Emotional reasoning: Assuming that one's emotional reactions necessarily reflect the true situation. For example, concluding that because one feels hopeless, the situation must really be hopeless.

"Should" statements: The use of "should" and "have to" statements that are not actually true to provide motivation or control over one's behavior. For example, thinking "I shouldn't feel aggravated. She's my mother; I have to listen to her."

Labeling: Attaching a global label to oneself rather than referring to specific events or actions. For example, thinking "I'm a failure!" rather than "Boy, I blew that one!"

Personalization: Assuming that one is the cause of a particular external event when, in fact, other factors are responsible. For example, thinking "She wasn't very friendly today, she must be mad at me" without considering that factors other than one's own behavior may be affecting the other individual's mood.

Ideally an individual perceives situations accurately, interprets them correctly, and consequently manifests cognitive, emotional, and behavioral responses that are appropriate to the situation and that prove to be adaptive. According to the cognitive model, on those occasions when the individual's perception of the situation is biased or on which the perceived situation is interpreted incorrectly, the cognitive, emotional, and/or behavioral responses will be inappropriate to the situation or maladaptive to some extent. However, in most situations, the individual's perception and interpretation of subsequent events should provide feedback that reveals the extent to which the responses were inaccurate or maladaptive. Once this feedback is perceived and interpreted, it not only corrects the specific misperceptions and misinterpretations that occurred but also is stored in memory to aid in accurately perceiving and interpreting future events.

Thus, the cognitive view is that, given the complexity of daily life and the ambiguity of many interpersonal interactions, occasional misperceptions and misinterpretations of events are inevitable. However, isolated misperceptions and misinterpretations give rise to isolated maladaptive responses that are easily corrected by subsequent experiences. In order for seriously maladaptive responses to develop, a systematic bias in perception, recall, or interpretation would be required. This would result in more persistent maladaptive responses than would result from "normal" misperceptions and misinterpretations. If it also distorted the feedback process either by strongly biasing the interpretation of events or by influencing the responses of others, it could result in very persistent maladaptive responses.

Since the individual's schemas, beliefs, and assumptions have a major impact on the perception, recall, and interpretation of events, they are one possible source of such a systematic bias. However, they are not the only possible source of a systematic bias in the perception, recall, and interpretation of events. Despite cognitive therapy's name, the model in not exclusively cognitive. Rather, the cognitive model focuses on the interplay between cognition, affect, and behavior in psychopathology (see Figure 2.3). The effect of Gary's beliefs and assumptions on his perception of events and on his interpersonal behavior was discussed above, but the cycle does not end with the effects of cognition on behavior. A person's interpersonal behavior influences the responses of others, and their responses can, in turn, result in experiences that can influence the first individual's beliefs and assumptions. For example, Gary's guardedness, defensiveness, and his reluctance to be assertive did not endear him to others. Instead, his interpersonal behavior seemed to provoke hostility and bad treatment from others, and these responses from others provided additional experiences that seemed to confirm his negative world view.

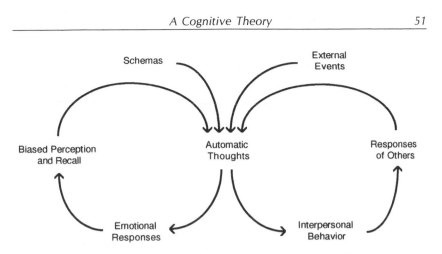

FIGURE 2.3. The role of cognition in psychopathology.

Also, while the cognitive model assumes that the individual's interpretation of events shapes his/her emotional response to the situation, we also argue that the individual's emotional state has important effects on cognition. A large body of research has demonstrated that affect tends to influence both cognition and behavior in mood-congruent ways (Isen, 1984). A number of studies have demonstrated that even a mild, experimentally induced depressed mood biases perception and recall in a depression-congruent way (see Watkins, Mathews, Williamson, & Fuller, 1992, for a recent discussion). This means that a depressed mood increases the likelihood that the individual will focus on negative aspects of the situation and preferentially recall negative experiences that occurred in the past. Although this phenomenon has not been investigated extensively for most other moods, it appears that many moods tend to bias perception and recall in a mood-congruent way. Thus, as an individual's level of anxiety increases, attentional processes appear to be biased in favor of signs of threat (Watkins et al., 1992). This phenomenon lays the foundation for a potentially self-perpetuating cycle where the individual's automatic thoughts elicit a particular mood, the mood biases perception and recall in a mood-congruent way, this increases the likelihood of additional mood-eliciting automatic thoughts, which elicit more of the mood in question, which further biases perception and recall, and so on, until something happens to disrupt the cycle.

For example, Gary's assumptions led him to interpret mundane interpersonal interactions as presenting a risk of malicious treatment and to interpret unremarkable interpersonal interactions as thinly disguised abuse. As a result, he experienced recurrent feelings of anxiety and resentment. On those occasions when he happened to be feeling relatively calm and peaceful, Gary showed only mild vigilance for interpersonal threats and only mild hypersensitivity to mistreatment. However, as soon as some event or spontaneous thought elicited feelings of anxiety and resentment, his vigilance for interpersonal danger and his sensitivity to mistreatment immediately increased substantially. This increased the likelihood of his interpreting subsequent events in a way that would elicit additional anxiety and resentment, and thus his moods tended to "snowball" quite quickly. Once Gary's anxiety and resentment built to clinical levels, they tended to be persistent.

Affect can play an important role in an individual's functioning in another way as well. As Taylor and Rachman (1991, 1992) have noted, individuals may fear certain emotions and may strive to avoid the emotion itself, may seek to escape from experiencing the emotion as quickly as possible, or may attempt to avoid thoughts, memories, or situations that they expect to elicit the emotion. Gary was unwilling to tolerate a number of emotions that he perceived as "weak" including feelings of sadness, loneliness, and vulnerability. Consequently he avoided situations he perceived as likely to elicit these feelings, was quick to intentionally focus his attention on perceived mistreatment by others in order to feel angry rather than sad, and refused to acknowledge or express these "weak" feelings. This further complicated commonplace interpersonal situations such as coping with periods of estrangement from his girlfriend.

It is important to notice that the cognitive model does *not* assert that cognition causes psychopathology. We view cognition as an important part of the cycle through which humans perceive and respond to events and thus as having an important role in pathological responses to events. However, we view it as a part of a cycle and as a promising point for intervention, not as the cause.

Cognitive Therapy and the Personality Disorders

Beck's initial training was predominantly psychoanalytic, and he believed, in line with the psychodynamic view of the day, that depression, phobias, and other problems that we would now classify as Axis I disorders were only the surface manifestation of underlying personality problems. This view held that since the hypothesized personality problems were the "cause" of depression, anxiety, and so forth, if the personality problems were cured, the neurosis would be cured as well. However, when Beck's early research into the psychoanalytic theory of depression produced results not compatible with the psychoanalytic views of that day, he began to reevaluate these assumptions. As cognitive therapy of depression evolved, Beck's thinking was influenced by the behavior therapy movement, and he accepted the view that the behavioral (and cognitive and emotional) manifestations of depression *were* the problem and that there was no deeper underlying cause that had to be treated. This formulation fit well with clinical experience and empirical research into cognitive therapy of depression available at that time. For example, when patients recovered from depression, their problematic "personality" characteristics such as overdependency, demandingness, and negativism often were no longer apparent. Apparently, curing the "symptoms" made the supposed personality defects go away.

At the same time that cognitive therapy was evolving, behavior therapy first incorporated cognitive perspectives and then began to consider personality disorders. Behaviorists have had a long tradition of rejecting the idea that personality traits could be important determinants of behavior and of emphasizing the situational determinants of behavior. Behavior therapy's rejection of the concept of personality was based in part on the assumption that only variables that can be observed directly can be studied scientifically and in part on a large body of research that appeared to demonstrate that personality variables accounted for little of the variance in human behavior, while situational variables accounted for a much larger portion of the variance. Since the term "personality disorder" was regarded as implying that individuals with Axis II diagnoses suffered from a disordered personality, behaviorists' initial reaction was to reject the concept of personality disorder. However, as it became clear that individuals diagnosed as having personality disorders were relatively common in clinical practice and were as difficult for behaviorists to treat as they were for other clinicians, behaviorists began to reconsider these individuals.

Over the interval during which most behaviorally oriented authors had ignored personality disorders, much had changed. First, behaviorists had accepted the idea of considering cognition and emotion as important aspects of human behavior even though they are not directly observable. Second, more sophisticated research into personality had shown that personality variables can account for a substantial amount of variance in behavior under at least some conditions (Epstein, 1979). Finally, DSM-III redefined personality disorders as "enduring patterns of perceiving, relating to, and thinking about the environment and oneself" which "are exhibited in a wide range of important social and personal contexts" and which "are inflexible and maladaptive and cause either significant functional impairment or subjective distress" (American Psychiatric Association, 1987, p. 335). Some behaviorists began to realize that, given this definition of "personality disorder," one need not presume that such patterns of cognition and behavior are the product of a disordered personality (Turner & Hersen, 1981).

During the past decade or so, behaviorists have seriously considered the topic of personality disorders, and behavioral perspectives on the personality disorders have rapidly evolved from simply seeing personality disorders as a collection of isolated symptoms that could each be treated separately (Stephens & Parks, 1981), to viewing them as disorders of interpersonal behavior (Turner & Hersen, 1981), then to seeing them as the product of dysfunctional schemas (Beck, 1964, 1967; Young, 1987), and most recently to conceptualizing personality disorders in terms of self-perpetuating cognitive-interpersonal cycles (see Fleming & Pretzer, 1990, and Pretzer & Fleming, 1990, for recent overviews of contemporary behavioral and cognitive-behavioral approaches to conceptualizing and treating personality disorders).

Cognitive therapy itself evolved primarily within the rapidly changing behavioral camp along with a range of other cognitive-behavioral approaches. It was developed initially as a short-term treatment for depression, and, after an extensive focus on understanding and treating depression, it was applied to a wider range of psychopathology. It was not until the early 1980's that the first systematic efforts to apply the cognitive approach with personality disorders began (Fleming, 1983; Pretzer, 1983; Simon, 1983; Young, 1983).

In the decade since then, a clinically based approach has been used by cognitive investigators in developing detailed conceptualizations and treatment strategies for each of the personality disorders (Beck, Freeman, & Associates, 1990; Fleming, 1983; 1985; 1988; Freeman et al., 1990; Pretzer, 1983, 1985, 1988; Simon, 1983, 1985). These authors began with a detailed evaluation of specific clients, developed individualized conceptualization of the client's problems, and generated treatment plans based on the conceptualizations. The conceptualizations were then tested through clinical observation and through noting the results of therapeutic interventions. This approach has led to the development of generalized conceptualizations and treatment strategies for each of the major personality disorders based on the commonalities observed among individuals manifesting the same disorder.

Cognitive therapy's general view of psychopathology applies directly to conceptualizing personality disorders. Returning to the case of ''Gary,'' it is important to note that Gary's beliefs and assumptions, his interpretation of events, his affect, his interpersonal behavior, and the reactions he evoked from others interacted in ways that were strongly self-perpetuating. First, his vigilance for signs of untrustworthiness and maliciousness in others resulted in observations that seemed to confirm his preconceptions about others. Second, his guardedness and defensiveness tended to elicit bad treatment from many of his acquaintances and co-workers, which again seemed to confirm his preconceptions. Finally, since his experience seemed to demonstrate that his vigilance and guardedness were necessary, he was unwilling either to relax his vigilance or to risk interacting with others less defensively.

This type of self-perpetuating cognitive-interpersonal cycle can be quite persistent and resistant to change. Once such a pattern is established, the individual's schemas tend to bias his or her perception of events in such a way that experiences that otherwise would contradict his/her assumptions are overlooked, discounted, or misinterpreted while, at the same time, his/her interpretation of events and his/her interpersonal behavior result in experiences which seem to confirm his/her dysfunctional schemas. We would argue that the cognitive and interpersonal processes that occur in individuals who qualify for Axis II diagnoses are the same as occur in any other nonpsychotic, neurologically intact individual except that, in individuals with Axis II diagnoses, strongly self-perpetuating, dysfunctional cognitive-interpersonal cycles have evolved. The cognitive view of "personality disorder" is that this is simply the term that is used to refer to individuals with *pervasive, self-perpetuating cognitive-interpersonal cycles* that are dysfunctional enough to come to the attention of mental health professionals.

It is important to note that the conceptualization summarized in Figure 2.2 is specific to Gary and that the details of the cognitive conceptualization of an individual with a personality disorder would be similar to this only for other individuals with paranoid personality disorder. For other personality disorders, there would be major differences in the particular schemas, beliefs, and assumptions that would be emphasized, in the interplay between cognitions and interpersonal behavior that would be anticipated, and in the types of interventions that would be proposed. For comparison, a recent cognitive conceptualization of borderline personality disorder is shown in Figure 2.4. It is immediately obvious that there are major differences between this model and the model of paranoid personality disorder shown in Figure 2.2. While individuals with borderline personality disorder are seen as sharing the paranoid's view of the world as a dangerous place where one is open to attack from others, they are not seen as sharing the paranoids' belief that one can stay safe by relying on one's own capabilities. Instead they are seen as believing that they are relatively weak and vulnerable and also as holding a conviction that they are flawed in some way that inherently will lead to rejection. These differences in basic assumptions lead to very different patterns of interpersonal interaction, elicit different responses from others, and establish a

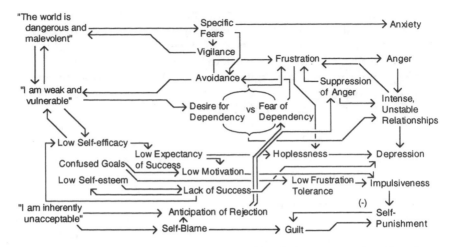

FIGURE 2.4. Cognitive conceptualization of borderline personality disorder.

cognitive-interpersonal cycle that is strongly self-perpetuating but quite different from that manifested in paranoid personality disorder. A discussion of the cognitive conceptualization of each of the personality disorders is beyond the scope of this chapter. Interested readers can find detailed discussions of cognitive conceptualizations of each of DSM-III-R personality disorders in *Cognitive Therapy of Personality Disorders* (Beck et al., 1990) or *Clinical Applications of Cognitive Therapy* (Freeman et al., 1990).

Some cognitively oriented authors have argued that in order to adequately account for the characteristics of individuals with personality disorders, cognitive therapy needs significant revision and have proposed their own modifications of cognitive therapy (Liotti, 1992; Lockwood, 1992; Lockwood & Young, 1992; Rothstein & Vallis, 1991; Safran & McMain, 1992; Young, 1990; Young & Lindemann, 1992). These approaches, variously termed "structural," "constructivist," or "postrationalist" by their advocates, propose adding new concepts or concepts borrowed from other theoretical systems to existing cognitive-behavioral approaches. For example, Young (1987, 1990; Young & Lindemann, 1992; Young & Swift, 1988) has advocated adding a "fourth level of cognition" which he terms "early maladaptive schemas" (EMS), Lockwood (1992) advocates integrating concepts from object relations theory into cognitive therapy, and Liotti (1992) emphasizes the role of egocentrism in the personality disorders.

These various modifications of theory and therapeutic approach have not been greeted with universal enthusiasm. For example,

Padesky (1986, 1988) has argued that there is no need to hypothesize that EMS are qualitatively different from other schemas in order to account for the persistence of dysfunctional cognitive and interpersonal patterns observed in clients with personality disorders. She points out that the tendency of schemas, beliefs, and behavior patterns to persist even after they have become seriously dysfunctional can easily be understood in terms of the effect they have on the perception and processing of new experiences.

It is interesting to note that many of the authors who argue that cognitive therapy needs substantial revision in order to deal adequately with personality disorders make no reference to the extensive work that has been done on conceptualizing and treating personality disorders within the existing cognitive framework (i.e., Beck et al., 1990; Fleming, 1983, 1985, 1988; Freeman et al., 1990; Padesky 1986, 1988; Pretzer, 1983, 1985, 1988; Simon, 1983, 1985). Many of the points the constructivists emphasize, such as the strongly self-perpetuating nature of personality disorders, the role of family relationships in the etiology of personality disorders, and the importance of the therapist–client relationship in treating these disorders, have been emphasized for some time by the authors who are working within the existing cognitive model. Since those who advocate revising cognitive therapy have yet to present detailed conceptualizations of specific personality disorders or to propose treatment strategies that are tailored to the characteristics of specific personality disorders, it is too early to determine whether their proposals contain important new contributions or not.

Propositional Testability

The cognitive theory of personality disorders is empirically testable, at least in principle, in that it generates specific, testable propositions. However, this does not mean that it is testable in its current form. In order for cognitive conceptualizations of the personality disorders to be truly testable, the general principles embodied in cognitive conceptualizations of the personality disorders will need to be elaborated into unambiguous propositions, more valid methods for quantifying cognitive and interpersonal variables will need to be developed, and experimental designs that overcome the practical problems encountered in attempting to assemble a large sample of subjects with a given personality disorder will need to be developed. There is potential for achieving each of these objectives, and possible methods for doing so are discussed later in this chapter, but much remains to be done in order to make the cognitive model of personality disorders truly testable.

TOWARD A COGNITIVE TAXONOMY
OF PERSONALITY DISORDERS

Because cognitive therapy's initial emphasis in conceptualizing personality disorders was on clinical practice, the focus has been on developing functional analyses of the various personality disorders to serve as a basis for strategic intervention. Work on developing comprehensive models of personality disorders or on analyzing the similarities and differences among the various personality disorders is of a more recent vintage (e.g., Beck et al., 1990, Chap. 3). The DSM-III-R classification system has been used in cognitive discussions of personality disorders for purely practical reasons, and cognitive authors generally have not focused on the question of whether there are better ways to classify personality disorders. While there has been no explicit discussion of the merits of the various approaches to classifying personality disorders (categorical vs. dimensional vs. prototypal), a prototypal view is implicit in much that has been written about cognitive therapy with personality disorders. The typical approach used by cognitive authors has been to present conceptualizations and treatment recommendations based on experience with individuals who seem typical of persons with a particular personality disorder. The assumption has been that when an individual presents features of a second personality disorder or meets criteria for two personality disorder diagnoses, the clinician will need to interpolate between the two conceptualizations and treatment approaches.

While the basic idea that personality disorders are manifestations of self-perpetuating cognitive/interpersonal cycles as discussed above applies to all of the personality disorders, cognitive therapy's functional approach to conceptualizing personality disorders has resulted in the development of distinct conceptualizations for each of the personality disorders. For example, current cognitive views suggest that whereas individuals who view the world as a hostile demanding place where one can be safe only by being alert, vigilant, and defensive are seen as being likely to manifest paranoid personality disorder (Beck et al., 1990, Chap. 6; Freeman et al., 1990, Chap. 7; Pretzer, 1988), individuals who see the world as being a dangerous place but who do not believe that they have the skills and capabilities needed to fend for themselves must find another solution. One obvious alternative is for them to endeavor to find someone strong and capable who can take care of them. Individuals who believe that "the way to be taken care of is to make your helplessness and neediness obvious to others and to passively subordinate your wants and preferences to those who are willing to take care of you" are likely to develop dependent personality disorder (Beck et al., 1990, Chap. 13; Fleming, 1985; Freeman et al., 1990, Chap. 12). Individuals who share the same view of the demands of daily life and of their capabilities for coping successfully on their own but who believe that the way to be taken care of is to actively work to attract and hold the other person's attention through being dramatic, seductive, and so forth are seen as being likely to manifest very different interpersonal behavior, elicit very different responses from others, and develop histrionic personality disorder (Beck et al., 1990, Chap. 10; Fleming, 1983, 1988; Freeman et al., 1990, Chap. 9).

We would argue that there are commonalities and differences in the underlying assumptions and interpersonal strategies held by individuals that result in systematic differences in momentary cognitions, in interpersonal behavior, and in the responses elicited from others, which in turn play important roles in the development of personality disorders. This view suggests that it should be possible to develop a cognitive typology of personality disorders based on the similarities and differences among the underlying assumptions and interpersonal strategies characteristic of different personality disorders. Such a typology might well highlight important commonalities in etiological influences or aid in the selection of appropriate approaches to intervention. A number of authors have begun to work toward such a typology by attempting to list and categorize the cognitive and behavioral characteristics of the various personality disorders (Beck et al., 1990, Chap. 3 and Appendix A; Pretzer, 1992; Young, 1990). The most advanced work in this direction is Beck's recent summarization of the cognitive characteristics of nine of the personality disorders that is seen in Table 2.2. However, more work remains to be done in order to develop a comprehensive cognitive typology of the personality disorders.

THE DEVELOPMENTAL ORIGINS
OF PERSONALITY DISORDERS

Inherited Predispositions

A number of heritable characteristics are relevant to understanding the development of personality disorders. First, it can be argued that, over the course of evolution, natural selection molded durable predispositions into humans that served the basic evolutionary goals of survival and reproduction. As our social milieu has changed from small groups subsisting in the wild to an advanced technological society, evolution may not have kept pace with social change, and thus there may well

TABLE 2.2. Profile of Characteristics of Personality Disorders

Personality disorder	View of self	View of others	Main beliefs	Main strategy
Avoidant	Vulnerable to depreciation, rejection Socially inept Incompetent	Critical Demeaning Superior	It's terrible to be rejected, put down If people know the real me they will reject me Can't tolerate unpleasant feelings	Avoid evaluative situations Avoid unpleasant feelings or thoughts
Dependent	Weak Needs Helpless Incompetent	(Idealized) Nurturant Supportive Competent	Need people to survive, be happy Need for steady flow of support, encouragement	Cultivate dependent relationships
Passive-aggressive	Self-sufficient Vulnerable to control, interference	Intrusive Demanding Interfering Controling Dominating	Others interfere with my freedom of action Control by others is intolerable Have to do things my own way	Passive resistance Surface submissiveness Evade, circumvent rules
Obsessive-compulsive	Responsible Accountable Fastidious Competent	Irresponsible Casual Incompetent Self-indulgent	I know what's best Details are crucial People *should* do better, try harder	Apply rules Perfectionisms Evaluates, control "Shoulds," criticize, punish
Paranoid	Righteous Innocent, noble Vulnerable	Interfering Malicious Discriminatory Abusive motives	Motives are suspect Be on guard Don't trust	Wary Look for hidden motives Accuse Counterattack
Antisocial	A loner Autonomous Strong	Vulnerable Exploitative	Entitled to *break* rules Others are patsies, wimps Others are exploitative	Attack, rob Deceive, manipulate
Narcissistic	Special, unique Deserve special rules; superior Above the rules	Inferior Admirers	Because I'm special, I *deserve* special rules I'm above the rules I'm better than others	Use others Transcend rules Manipulative Competitive
Histrionic	Glamorous Impressive	Seducible Receptive Admirers	People are there to serve or admire me They have no right to deny me my just deserts I can go by my feeling	Use dramatics, charm; temper tantrums, crying, suicide Gestures
Schizoid	Self-sufficient Loner	Intrusive	Others are unrewarding Relationships are messy, undesirable	Stay away

be areas of "poor fit" between our inherited predispositions and the demands of modern society that tend to cause problems for humans in general. If individuals differ in the strength or nature of these inherited predispositions, this could predispose certain individuals toward the development of particular problems. Beck (1992) has hypothesized that inherited predispositions toward certain "primeval strategies" (see Table 2.3) may contribute to the development of certain personality traits.

Several cognitive-behavioral authors have hypothesized that inborn defects or deficits play an important role in the development of personality disorders. For example, Linehan (1987a, 1987b, 1987c) has hypothesized that individuals with borderline personality disorder have an inherent defect in the regulation of emotion. She argues that this inborn defect interacts with a learning history that did not support the adaptive expression of emotion to result in intense, poorly controlled emotional responses. Similarly, Turner (1986) argues that borderlines have a biological predisposition toward low-stress tolerance that interacts with maladaptive schemas to distort information processing. However, recent cognitive conceptualizations of borderline personality disorder (Beck et al., 1990, Chap. 9; Freeman et al., 1990, Chap. 8; Pretzer, 1983) have argued that these phenomena can be understood in terms of the effects of dysfunctional beliefs, cognitive distortions, and learning history without any need to postulate any inborn differences between individuals who develop borderline personality disorder and those who do not (see Figure 2.4). Certainly, if inborn defects in information processing, regulation of affect, or in interpersonal behavior occur with sufficient frequency, this would be relevant for understanding the development of personality disorders. However, it is

TABLE 2.3. Primeval Strategies and Their Representation in Personality Disorders

"Strategy"	Personality disorder
Predatory	Antisocial
Help-eliciting	Dependent
Competitive	Narcissistic
Exhibitionistic	Histrionic
Autonomous	Schizoid
Defensive	Paranoid
Withdrawal	Avoidant
Ritualistic	Compulsive

not yet clear if such defects actually play a significant role in the development of personality disorders or not.

A potentially heritable aspect of individual development relevant to understanding the development of personality disorders is the infant's temperament. If one infant inherits a tendency to be extroverted and confident while another inherits a tendency to be shy and retiring, we would expect the shy, retiring infant to be more likely to eventually develop avoidant personality disorder. However, the development of schemas as well as the development of interpersonal strategies are both strongly influenced by life experience. An inherently shy and retiring child who experiences day-to-day life as calm and secure might gradually risk being a bit more adventuresome. If his/her initial attempts at being somewhat bolder seem to work out well, he/she might conclude that risk-taking is a good idea and gradually become less shy and retiring or might develop adaptive ways of coping with his/her shyness. However, a child who experiences daily life as frightening might avoid risk-taking as much as possible and therefore not have the experiences which would lead him/her to conclude that risk taking is a good idea. Similarly, a child who experiments with being a bit more adventuresome and perceives his or her boldness to have bad consequences is not likely to persist with risk taking. Either of these children might well persist in being shy and retiring, fall behind his/her peers in developing social skills, and become more and more socially isolated.

However, the role of these possible inherited predispositions toward certain personality disorders is not a simple, straightforward one. First, the interaction among the child's predispositions, his/her family environment, and significant life events would shape development rather than inherited predispositions alone shaping development. Second, it is important to note that it is not objective events but the child's *perception* of events that influences the development of schemas and interpersonal strategies. Since cognitive development occurs in a series of stages over the course of childhood and adolescence, children are at a substantial disadvantage in attempting to understand the complexities of daily life. Misunderstandings and misinterpretations can easily occur because of the child's limited life experience and limitations imposed by the stage of cognitive development that he or she has attained.

Learned Characteristics

The many processes involved in social learning are also likely to play major roles in the development of personality disorders. Parents and significant others influence the developing child through verbal communication and explicit teaching, through their modeling of behaviors, through the contingencies they impose on the child, and through the cultural influences they transmit. A shy, retiring child might be explicitly or implicitly taught by his/her parents that one should avoid uncomfortable situations or might be taught that one should face one's fears. This would have obvious influences on the child's development. However, the parents might well give conflicting messages because the two parents disagree with each other, because one or both of the parents may be ambivalent about the wisdom of facing one's fears, or because the parents' words are not consistent with their actions. As the child implicitly experiments with ways of understanding and responding to a particular type of recurrent situation and finds an approach that seems to work, the child may well "specialize" in a particular approach because it is strongly reinforced by the responses of others, because the situation seems risky enough to discourage further experimentation, or simply because it is the best approach the child has been able to discover.

The Developmental Impact of Traumatic Experiences

The long-term effects of traumatic events have been emphasized in many traditional perspectives on personality development. According to cognitive theory, the underlying assumptions and interpersonal strategies that are emphasized in the cognitive model of personality disorders are based on the individual's previous experience, and this certainly would include any traumatic events that have occurred. The extreme experiences that some children encounter (see Bowlby, 1985, for striking examples) certainly can have important and lasting impacts on an individual's development. It may be possible for a single, dramatic experience to have lasting effects, but we would expect experiences that are recurrent, that are part of a consistent pattern of events, or that strengthen existing preconceptions to be particularly likely to have lasting effects.

An individual's early experiences play an important role in the development of personality disorders and other psychopathology for several reasons. After all, childhood experiences occur during the period where initial schemas are being established, the child is exposed to the family environment daily over a period of years, parents are emotionally important to the growing child, and parents have control over powerful reinforcers and punishers. Childhood experiences are particularly important because once a child's initial schemas and interpersonal strategies are established, they shape the perception and interpretation of subsequent experiences in a way that tends to produce a "confirmatory bias" or "feed-forward mechanism" (Mahoney, 1974, 1977). Individuals tend to selectively attend to experiences that are consistent with their preconceptions and to be biased toward interpreting their experiences as confirming these preconceptions in such a way that once schemas are established, they tend to function as self-fulfilling prophecies. Therefore these cognitive structures tend to persist once they are established.

To return to our case example, Gary believed that people in general were malicious and deceptive, that they would attack him if they got a chance, and that the way to be safe was to be vigilant, on guard, and ready to defend himself. How did he come to hold these views? According to Gary's descriptions, he grew up in a family where a suspicious, vigilant approach to the outside world was explicitly taught by his parents both through their words and their example. In addition, family members had been physically and verbally abusive of him and each other throughout his childhood and had frequently taken advantage of him from childhood through the present. In short, he reported growing up in a family environment where his world view and interpersonal strategies were explicitly taught and were strongly reinforced by repeated experiences. Of course, we cannot be certain regarding the accuracy of Gary's perception and recall of interactions in his family of origin. However, it was his subjective experience rather than objective reality which, over time, gave rise to generalized beliefs about his world and his role in it. To a certain extent, the objective reality is unimportant, since it is the individual's interpretation of experience that gives rise to both immediate responses and more persistent memories, beliefs, and assumptions.

The question of the extent to which there are inherent differences between individuals with personality disorders and individuals who do not have personality disorders is likely to remain a matter of theoretical debate until there are long-term longitudinal studies that examine the extent to which differences observed in infancy predict the subsequent development of personality disorders. When differences between individuals with a given personality disorder and "normal" individuals are identified in cross-sectional research, it can be difficult to determine to what extent an observed difference between groups is an inherent difference that contributed to the development of the disorder, to what extent the difference reflects characteristics that were acquired in the course of development, and to what extent the difference is a product of the individual's disorder. However, this question is of limited relevance for clinical practice. It is much more important clinically to identify methods for accomplishing therapeutic changes than to identify inherent differences.

ASSESSMENT INSTRUMENTATION

Since many of the concepts central to the cognitive view of psychopathology in general and personality disorders in particular are not directly observable, the development of effective assessment procedures has been an on-going concern of cognitive therapists. While much progress has been made since the days when behaviorists rejected cognition as being inaccessible to scientific investigation, cognitive therapy's emphasis on variables that cannot be directly observed presents practical problems both in clinical practice and in empirical research. The task of identifying individuals' thoughts, feelings, assumptions, interpersonal strategies, and overt behavior is not a simple one. After all, individuals are often oblivious to many of their thoughts, feelings, assumptions, strategies, and even actions. When an individual seems to be able to report this information, we are faced by the problem of deciding to what extent his/her self-reports are inaccurate, biased, or censored.

Many techniques have been developed for assessing cognition (Merluzzi, Glass, & Genest, 1981), emotion (Isen, 1984), and behavior (Cone & Hawkins, 1977). Unfortunately, a great number of these techniques are impractical for regular clinical use because of the time, effort, and expense involved. In practice, cognitive therapists rely heavily on clinical interview, in vivo observation and interview, client self-monitoring, and self-report questionnaires. While these methods are not technologically sophisticated, they prove practical and effective in clinical practice (see Freeman et al., 1990, Chap. 2, for a more detailed discussion of clinical assessment in cognitive therapy).

The obvious problems with relying on self-report have received considerable discussion and empirical investigation over the years. It seems clear that the method used in eliciting descriptions of internal processes exercises a strong influence on the validity of the descriptions, and that properly obtained reports can be quite useful (Ericsson & Simon, 1980). It is necessary for cognitive therapists to rely on individuals' self-reports as an important source of data despite these problems because we have no other way of assessing the content of thoughts, schemas, assumptions, and behavioral strategies independent of self-report. Freeman et al. (1990, Chap. 2) have summarized a set of guidelines intended to increase the validity of individuals' self-reports (see Table 2.4) and have discussed evaluating the validity of self-reports obtained in clinical practice.

In considering cognitive assessment procedures, it is important to maintain a clear distinction between clinical assessment and assessment procedures to be used in empirical research because these two purposes call for very different approaches to assessment. It can be argued that, in clinical practice, the ultimate test of the value of self-reports is their utility in guiding clinical interventions (Kendall & Hollon, 1981). Clinical assessment can be a self-correcting process if therapist and client work together to collect needed information, implement therapeutic interventions based on the resulting conceptualizations, and then use the results of their interventions as a source of corrective feedback. Successful interventions both accomplish desired changes and provide evidence of the clinical utility of the conceptualizations on which the interventions were based. Unsuccessful or partially successful interventions highlight areas in which the current conceptualizations are not adequate. Observations regarding the actual effects of the unsuccessful interventions and the factors that influenced this outcome can serve as a basis for a revised conceptualization that can again be tested in practice. When clinical assessment is integrated with intervention in this way, this self-correcting process can make the most of rich data, even if the reliability and validity of a particular observation or self-report are uncertain.

Empirical research, in contrast, generally calls for standardized assessment procedures that produce numerical scores having respectable levels of reliability and validity. A variety of methods ranging from self-report questionnaires to structured self-monitoring to performance on experimental tasks have been used in cognitive-behavioral research with varying degrees of success. Many investigators have relied on minimally validated self-report questionnaires because they are easy to develop and inexpensive to use. While the use of a neatly printed, computer-scored questionnaire gives the appearance that one is proceeding very scientifically, the use of such measures presumes that subjects have sufficient self-knowledge to report the cognitions in question accurately and presumes that the subjects are willing and able to provide unbiased, uncensored reports of their cognitions. Although this unsophisticated approach to assessing cognitive variables has produced some useful findings, there is a need for more rigorous approaches to assessment in cognitive-behavioral research (for recent overviews of cognitive assessment procedures, see Freeman et al., 1990, Chap. 3, and Parks & Hollon, 1988).

TABLE 2.4. Guidelines for Increasing the Validity of Self-Reports

1. *Motivate the client to be open and forthright.* Make sure that it is clear that providing full, honest, detailed reports is in the client's interest by (a) providing a clear rationale for seeking the information, (b) demonstrating the relevance of the information being requested to the client's goals, and (c) demonstrating the value of clear, specific information by explicitly making use of the information.

2. *Minimize the delay between event and report.* This will result in more detailed information and will reduce the amount of distortion resulting from imperfect recall. For events occurring outside of the therapist's office, use an in vivo interview or self-monitoring techniques when possible.

3. *Provide retrieval cues.* Review the setting and the events leading up to the event of interest either verbally or by using imagery to improve recall.

4. *Avoid possible biases.* Begin with open-ended questions that ask the client to describe his or her experience without suggesting possible answers or requiring inference. Focus on "What happened?" not on "Why?" or "What did it mean?" Do not ask clients to infer experiences they cannot remember. Wait until after the entire experience has been described to test your hypotheses or ask for specific details.

5. *Encourage and reinforce attention to thoughts and feelings.* Clients who initially have difficulty monitoring their own cognitive processes are more likely to gradually develop increased skill if they are reinforced for accomplishments than if they are criticized for failures. Some clients may need explicit training in differentiating between thoughts and emotions, in attending to cognitions, or in reporting observations rather than inferences.

6. *Encourage and reinforce acknowledgement of limitations in recall.* If the therapist accepts only long, detailed reports, this increases the risk of the client's inventing data in order to satisfy the therapist. It is important for the therapist to appreciate the information the client can provide and to encourage the client to acknowledge his or her limits in recalling details, because incomplete but accurate information is much more useful than detailed reports fabricated in order to please the therapist.

7. *Watch for indications of invalidity.* Be alert for inconsistency within the client's report, inconsistency between the verbal report and nonverbal cues, and inconsistency between the report and data obtained previously. If apparent inconsistencies are observed, explore them collaboratively with the client without being accusatory or judgmental.

8. *Watch for factors that may interfere.* Be alert for indications of beliefs, assumptions, expectancies, and misunderstandings which may interfere with the client's providing accurate self-reports. Common problems include (a) the fear that the therapist will be unable to accept the truth and will become angry, shocked, disgusted, or rejecting if the client reports his or her experiences accurately, (b) the belief that the client must do a perfect job of observing and reporting the experiences and that he or she is a failure if the reports are not perfect from the beginning, (c) the fear that the information revealed in therapy may be used against the client or may give the therapist power over him or her, (d) the belief that it is dangerous to examine experiences involving strong or "crazy" feelings closely for fear that the feelings will be intolerable or will "get out of control."

COGNITIVE THERAPY OF PERSONALITY DISORDERS

Goals of Treatment

In cognitive therapy the goals of treatment are agreed upon collaboratively between therapist and client and therefore vary from client to
client. The goals typically involve achieving alleviation of the client's
distress as efficiently as is feasible and also achieving whatever changes
are necessary for the improvement to persist over time and for the client
to lead a happy, productive life. When an individual seeks treatment
for a specific, focused problem, cognitive therapy may involve very
focused interventions that have little impact on the rest of the client's
life. However, it is generally true that the greater the extent to which
the client's problems have broad effects throughout the client's life,
the broader the changes needed to alleviate the client's distress. Since
personality disorders, by definition, have pervasive effects throughout the individual's life, cognitive therapy with personality disorders
often involves a set of interventions intended to have broad effects
throughout the client's life. This does not mean that "personality re-
structuring" is the goal of cognitive therapy. The primary goals of therapy are generally to alleviate the client's distress, to improve the client's
day-to-day functioning, and to accomplish the lasting changes needed for these improvements to persist. Broad personality changes may
well be a necessary means toward these ends, but they are not inevitable goals of cognitive therapy. In particular, the practical constraints
imposed by limits on health insurance coverage, agency policies, and
client motivation mean that the goals of treatment in a given case may
be much more limited than this ideal. Cognitive therapy can be used
effectively in a very focused, time-limited way to accomplish limited
goals or in an open-ended way when the goals are defined much more
broadly.

Principles of Cognitive Therapy

The cognitive model of psychopathology emphasizes the effects of dysfunctional automatic thoughts, dysfunctional schemas, beliefs and assumptions, and dysfunctional interpersonal behavior. Therefore, each
of these are important targets for intervention in cognitive therapy.
The initial goal of cognitive therapy is to break the cycle or cycles that
perpetuate and amplify the client's problems (see Figure 2.3). This
could potentially be done by modifying the client's automatic thoughts,
by improving the client's mood, by working to counteract the biasing
impact of mood on recall and perception, and/or by changing the

client's behavior. In theory, these interventions could break the cycle or cycles that perpetuate the problems and thus could alleviate the client's immediate distress. However, if the therapist only does this, the client would be at risk for a relapse whenever he/she experienced events similar to the ones that precipitated the current problems. In order to achieve lasting results, it would also be important to modify the schemas, beliefs, and assumptions that predispose the client to his/her problems and to help the client plan effective ways to handle situations that might precipitate a relapse.

Our view is that many dysfunctional cognitions persist because:

1. Many individuals are unaware of the role their thoughts play in their problems.
2. The dysfunctional cognitions often seem so plausible that individuals fail to examine them critically.
3. Selective perception and cognitive biases often result in the individual's ignoring or discounting experiences that would otherwise conflict with the dysfunctional cognitions.
4. Cognitive distortions often lead to erroneous conclusions.
5. The individual's dysfunctional interpersonal behavior often can produce experiences that seem to confirm dysfunctional cognitions.
6. Individuals who are reluctant to tolerate aversive affect may consciously or nonconsciously avoid memories, perceptions, and/or conclusions that would elicit strong emotional responses.

This view suggests that cognitive interventions should be directed toward identifying the specific dysfunctional beliefs that play a role in the individual's problems and examining them critically while correcting for the effects of selective perception, biased cognition, and cognitive distortions and helping the individual to face and tolerate aversive affect. Logical or intellectual analysis of dysfunctional cognitions is usually not sufficient to accomplish substantive change. Individuals often find that within-session interventions can be intellectually convincing but that to be convinced "on the gut level," and to have the change in cognitions be manifested in their behavior, it is usually necessary to test the new cognitions in real-life situations. These "behavioral experiments" (see Beck, Rush, Shaw, & Emery, 1979, p. 56, or Freeman et al., 1990, pp. 76–77) are often much more convincing than any amount of intellectual insight. When dysfunctional cognitions are strongly supported by interpersonal experience, it may be necessary to accomplish changes in interpersonal behavior and/or in the individual's environment in order to challenge the cognitions effectively. It is our view that many dysfunctional behaviors persist because (1) they are a product of persistent dysfunctional beliefs; (2) expectations regarding the consequences of possible actions encourage behaviors that actually prove to be dysfunctional and/or discourage behaviors that would prove adaptive; (3) the individual lacks the skills needed to engage in potentially adaptive behavior; or (4) the environment reinforces dysfunctional behavior and/or punishes adaptive behavior. This view suggests that to change dysfunctional behavior it may be necessary to modify long-standing cognitions, to examine the individual's expectations regarding the consequences of his/her actions, to modify the individual's environment, or to help the individual master the cognitive or behavioral skills needed to successfully engage in more adaptive behavior.

It is interesting to note that when dysfunctional behavior is strongly maintained by dysfunctional cognitions, it may be necessary to modify the cognitions first, and that when dysfunctional cognitions are strongly maintained by the effects of dysfunctional behavior, it may be necessary to modify the dysfunctional behavior first. This suggests that if it is true that personality disorders are characterized by self-perpetuating cognitive-interpersonal cycles where dysfunctional cognitions strongly maintain dysfunctional behavior and dysfunctional behavior strongly maintains dysfunctional cognition, it may be difficult to find ways to intervene effectively. We argue that when a self-perpetuating cognitive-interpersonal cycle exists it may not be possible to effectively modify either cognitions or behavior in isolation and that a strategic intervention approach based on a clear conceptualization is likely to be necessary.

The Process of Cognitive Therapy

Obviously there are a wide variety of approaches that could be used to achieve the changes in cognition and behavior we see as being necessary to produce lasting improvement. The approach used in cognitive therapy has been described as "collaborative empiricism" (Beck et al., 1979, Chap. 3). The therapist endeavors to work *with* the client to help him/her to recognize the factors that contribute to problems, to test the validity of the thoughts, beliefs, and assumptions that prove important, and to make the necessary changes in cognition and behavior. While it is clear that very different therapeutic approaches ranging from philosophical debate to operant conditioning can be effective with at least some clients, collaborative empiricism has substantial advantages. By actively collaborating with the client, the therapist minimizes the resistance and oppositionality that are often elicited by taking an authoritarian role, yet the therapist is still in a position to structure each session as well as the overall course of therapy so as to be as efficient and effective as possible (Beck et al., 1979, Chap. 4).

One part of this collaborative approach is an emphasis on a process of "guided discovery." If the therapist guides the client by asking questions, making observations, and asking the client to monitor relevant aspects of the situation, the therapist can help the client develop an understanding of his or her problems, explore possible solutions, develop plans for dealing with the problems, and implement the plans quite effectively. Guided discovery has an advantage over approaches in which the therapist unilaterally develops an understanding of the problems and proposes solutions in that it maximizes client involvement in therapy sessions and minimizes the possibility of the client's feeling that the therapist's ideas are being imposed on the client. In addition, since the client is actively involved in the process of developing an understanding of the problems and coming up with a solution, the client also has an opportunity to learn an effective approach to dealing with problems and should be better able to deal with future problems when they arise.

Conceptualization of the Case

In cognitive therapy, a strategic approach to intervention is emphasized (Persons, 1991). Our view is that therapy is most effective and most efficient when the therapist thinks strategically about intervention and uses a clear conceptualization of the client's problems as a basis for selecting the most productive targets for intervention and the most appropriate intervention techniques. When the therapist intervenes without pausing to develop a conceptualization of the client's problems and without using that conceptualization to select the most appropriate interventions, much time and effort can be expended on interventions that prove ineffective or minimally relevant. This strategic approach is quite unlike therapies in which the therapist uses a standard therapeutic approach with all clients in the hope that by being "therapeutic in general" he/she will eventually address the most important issues. It is also quite different from technique-oriented approaches where intervention A is automatically used with problem A and intervention B is automatically used with problem B.

In order to take a strategic approach to therapy, the therapist must develop an understanding of the client and that client's problems. Therefore, the first step in cognitive therapy is an initial assessment that provides a foundation for intervention (Beck et al., 1979, Chap. 5). By beginning with a systematic evaluation, the therapist can develop an initial conceptualization quickly rather than waiting for an understanding of the client to develop gradually over the first few months of therapy; thus the therapist can be in a position to intervene effectively early in therapy. A clear conceptualization provides a basis for an individualized treatment plan that allows the therapist to be selective and efficient in employing the wide range of interventions and therapeutic techniques that are available.

The Therapeutic Relationship

In cognitive therapy, the initial therapy sessions are also important because they provide an opportunity for the therapist to establish a solid foundation for therapy before plunging into intervention (Beck et al., 1979, Chap. 3; Beck et al., 1990, pp. 64–79). The effectiveness of any psychotherapy depends on a relationship of confidence, openness, caring, and trust established between client and therapist. The cognitive therapist takes an active, directive role in treatment and thus can work actively to develop the therapeutic relationship rather than waiting for it to develop gradually over time. With many clients, this is more easily said than done. The complexities and difficulties encountered in the therapeutic relationship are particularly important in the treatment of clients with personality disorders.

In order to collaborate effectively, therapist and client must agree on what they are trying to accomplish. Therefore, following the initial evaluation, the therapist works with the client to specify goals for therapy and to prioritize them. These goals include the problems that the client wishes to overcome and the positive changes he/she wants to work toward; they should be operationalized clearly and specifically enough so that both therapist and client can tell if progress is being made. In considering the sequence in which to work on the goals, a number of factors are considered including the client's preferences regarding which issues to work on first, the therapist's conceptualization, which problems seem most likely to respond to early interventions, and any practical considerations that are relevant.

There is considerable advantage in working initially toward a goal that appears manageable even if it is not the goal that is most important to the client. If it proves possible to make demonstrable progress toward a valued goal, the client will be encouraged, and this will increase his/her motivation for therapy. The process of jointly agreeing on goals and priorities maximizes the likelihood that therapy will accomplish what the client is seeking. At the same time, it establishes the precedent of the therapist's soliciting and respecting the client's input while being open regarding the therapist's own views. Thus, it lays the foundation for therapist and client to work together collaboratively, and it makes clear to the client that his/her concerns are understood and respected. The time and effort spent on establishing mutually agreed upon goals and priorities are more than compensated for by the resulting increase in client involvement, decrease in resistance, and decrease in time and effort wasted on peripheral topics.

Another issue that is important in a collaborative approach to therapy is to introduce the client to the therapist's understanding of the problems and to his/her approach to therapy. While this could be done as a "minilecture" about psychopathology and psychotherapy, it is generally easier and more effective to use a guided-discovery approach and to base the explanation on the thoughts and feelings the client reports experiencing on particular occasions when his/her problems were occurring (see Freeman et al., 1990, pp. 94–95).

Intervention Techniques

Cognitive therapy is a "technically eclectic" approach in that a wide range of intervention techniques can be used flexibly within a coherent conceptual framework. As therapist and client endeavor to work together toward their shared goals, the therapist is free to select from the full range of intervention techniques. One of the primary interventions used in cognitive therapy is helping the client to identify the specific automatic thoughts that occur in problem situations, to recognize the effects these thoughts have on the client's emotions and behavior, and to respond effectively to those thoughts that prove problematic (Beck et al., 1979, Chap. 8; Beck et al., 1990, pp. 80–90; Freeman et al., 1990, pp. 49–68). Negative, self-deprecating, or other problematic thoughts typically are a habitual part of the client's life and come "fast and furious" without the client necessarily being aware of their presence or their relationship to his/her distress. By using interview and self-monitoring techniques, the client can learn to recognize dysfunctional thinking, to understand its impact on moods and actions, and to develop increased control over it.

Behavioral interventions are also used frequently in cognitive therapy to alleviate depressed mood, to improve coping skills, to replace dysfunctional interpersonal behavior with more adaptive responses, and to challenge dysfunctional cognitions. However, cognitive therapy is not limited to cognitive and behavioral interventions even though these are the most commonly used interventions. The full range of therapeutic techniques can be used as long as they are appropriate to the goals being pursued at the moment, are compatible with the current conceptualization of the client's problems, and are used collaboratively.

"Homework assignments" are used extensively throughout cognitive therapy (Beck et al., 1979, Chap. 13). Clients who actively engage in some of the work of therapy between sessions accomplish more than those who passively wait for their weekly hour with the therapist (Persons et al., 1988). In addition, clients are in a position to collect data and test the effects of cognitive and behavioral changes in daily life in ways that would be difficult to duplicate within the therapy session. Noncompliance often occurs when homework assignments are used. However, rather than being a problem, noncompliance is often quite useful in identifying problems in the therapist–client relationship and in identifying the factors that block the client from making the desired changes (Beck et al., 1990, pp. 66–77).

The Termination of Therapy

The cognitive model of psychopathology asserts that, in addition to modifying dysfunctional automatic thoughts, it is important to also address the client's underlying assumptions, and a variety of techniques for doing this have been developed (Beck et al., 1979, Chap. 12). Otherwise it is possible to resolve the client's current problems but still leave the client prone to relapse. In theory, effectively modifying the client's basic assumptions and any dysfunctional interaction patterns should leave him/her no more prone to future problems than anyone else. However, it is often hard for a therapist to gauge whether interventions have been completely effective. Therefore, cognitive therapy ends by explicitly working to prepare the client to deal with future setbacks (Beck et al., 1979, Chap. 15). This work, based on Marlatt and Gordon's (1985) research on relapse prevention, consists of helping the client to become aware of high-risk situations, to identify early warning signs of impending relapse, and to develop explicit plans for handling high-risk situations and heading off potential relapse.

Preferably, when the client has attained his/her goals for therapy, work on relapse prevention has been completed, and the client's progress has been maintained long enough for him/her to have a reasonable amount of confidence that he/she will be able to cope with problems as they arise, the decision to terminate is made. In the typical case, the therapist and client agree to "taper off" by shifting from weekly sessions to biweekly and, possibly, monthly sessions when the time for termination is near. This not only makes the ending of therapy less abrupt but also provides therapist and client with an opportunity to discover how well the client handles problems without the therapist's help and to discover whether any additional issues need to be addressed. The client is also offered the opportunity to return for "booster sessions" if problems arise, in the hopes that early intervention with future problems may forestall major difficulties.

Application of Cognitive Therapy to Treatment of Personality Disorders

The basic cognitive therapy approach to treating individuals with personality disorders is the same as cognitive therapy with other clients. However, a number of important modifications are needed to accommodate to the characteristics of individuals with personality disorders and to avoid problems frequently encountered in treating individuals with personality disorders. Pretzer and Fleming have proposed a number of general guidelines for cognitive therapy with clients who have personality disorders (Beck et al., 1990, pp. 351–358; Fleming & Pretzer, 1990; Pretzer & Fleming, 1990):

1. *Interventions are most effective when based on an individualized conceptualization of the client's problems.* Clients with personality disorders are complex, and the therapist is often faced with choosing among many possible targets for intervention and a variety of possible intervention techniques. Not only does this present a situation in which intervention can easily become confused and disorganized if the therapist does not have a clear treatment plan, but the interventions that seem appropriate after a superficial examination of the client can easily prove ineffective or counterproductive. The practice of developing a clear conceptualization of the client's problems on the basis of a detailed evaluation and then revising this conceptualization on the basis of clinical observation and the results of clinical interventions aids in the development of an effective treatment plan and minimizes the risk of the therapist being confused by the sheer complexity of the client's problems.

2. *It is important for therapist and client to work collaboratively toward clearly identified, shared goals.* With clients as complex as those with personality disorders, clear, consistent goals for therapy are necessary to avoid skipping from problem to problem without making any lasting progress. However, it is important for these goals to be mutually agreed upon in order to minimize the noncompliance and power struggles that often impede treatment of clients with personality disorders. It can be difficult to develop shared goals for treatment, since many of these clients present numerous vague complaints and, at the same time, may be unwilling to modify some of the behaviors that the therapist sees as particularly problematic. However, the time and effort spent developing mutually acceptable goals can be a good investment.

3. *It is important to focus more than the usual amount of attention on the therapist–client relationship.* While a good therapeutic relationship is as necessary for effective intervention in cognitive therapy as in any other approach to therapy, behavioral and cognitive-behavioral therapists are generally accustomed to being able to establish a fairly straightforward therapeutic relationship at the outset of therapy and then proceed without paying much attention to the interpersonal aspects of therapy. However, this is not usually the case when a therapist is working with clients who have personality disorders. The dysfunctional schemas, beliefs, and assumptions that bias clients' perceptions of others are likely to bias their perception of the therapist as well, and the dysfunctional interpersonal behaviors these clients manifest in relationships outside of therapy are likely to manifested in the therapist–client relationship as well. While the interpersonal difficulties that are manifested in the therapist–client relationship can disrupt therapy if they are not addressed effectively, they also provide the therapist with the opportunity to do in vivo observation and intervention (Freeman et al., 1990; Linehan, 1987c; Mays, 1985; Padesky, 1986) rather than having to rely on the client's report of interpersonal problems occurring between sessions.

One type of problem in the therapist–client relationship that is more common among individuals with personality disorders than other individuals in cognitive therapy is the phenomenon traditionally termed "transference" when the client manifests an extreme or persistent misperception of the therapist that is based on his/her previous experience in significant relationships rather than on the therapist's behavior. This can be understood in cognitive terms as the individual overgeneralizing beliefs and expectancies acquired in significant relationships. Individuals with personality disorders are typically vigilant for any sign that their fears may be realized, and they are prone to react quite intensely when the therapist's behavior appears to confirm their anticipations. When these strongly emotional reactions occur, it is important for the therapist to recognize what is happening, quickly develop an understanding of what the client is thinking, and directly but sensitively clear up the misconceptions before they disrupt therapy. While these reactions can be quite problematic, it is also true that they provide opportunities to identify beliefs, expectations, and interpersonal strategies that play an important role in the client's problems and that they provide an opportunity to respond to the client in ways that tend to disconfirm his/her dysfunctional beliefs and expectancies.

4. *Consider beginning with interventions that do not require extensive self-disclosure.* Many clients with personality disorders are quite uncomfortable with self-disclosure due to a lack of trust in the therapist, dis-

comfort with even mild levels of intimacy, fear of rejection, and so forth. While it is sometimes necessary to begin treatment with interventions that require extensive discussion of the client's thoughts and feelings, sometimes it can be useful to begin treatment by working on a problem that can be approached through behavioral interventions that do not require extensive self-disclosure. This allows time for the client to gradually become more comfortable with therapy and for the therapist to gradually address the client's discomfort with self-disclosure (Freeman et al., 1990, Chap. 8).

5. *Interventions that increase the client's sense of self-efficacy*[4] *often reduce the intensity of the client's symptomatology and facilitate other interventions.* The intensity of the emotional and behavioral responses manifested by individuals with personality disorders is often in part the result of the individual's doubting his/her ability to cope effectively with particular problem situations. This doubt regarding one's ability to cope effectively not only intensifies emotional responses to the situation but also predisposes the individual to drastic responses. If it is possible to increase the individual's confidence that he/she will be able to handle these problem situations if they arise, this often lowers the client's level of anxiety, moderates his/her symptomatology, enables him/her to react more deliberately, and makes it easier to implement other interventions. The individual's sense of self-efficacy, his/her confidence that he/she can deal effectively with specific situations when they arise, can be increased through interventions that correct any exaggerations of the demands of the situation or minimization of the individual's capabilities, through helping the individual to improve his/her coping skills, or through a combination of the two (Freeman et al., 1990, Chap. 7; Pretzer, et al., 1990).

6. *Do not rely primarily on verbal interventions.* The more severe a client's problems are, the more important it is to use behavioral interventions to accomplish cognitive as well as behavioral change (Freeman et al., 1990, Chap. 3). A gradual hierarchy of "behavioral experiments" not only provides an opportunity for desensitization to occur and for the client to master new skills, but they also can be quite effective in challenging unrealistic beliefs and expectations.

7. *Try to identify and address the client's fears before implementing changes.* Clients with personality disorders often have strong but unexpressed fears about the changes they seek or are asked to make in the course of therapy, and attempts to induce the client to simply go ahead without addressing these fears are often unsuccessful (Mays, 1985). If the therapist makes a practice of discussing the client's expectations and concerns before each change is attempted, this is likely to reduce the client's level of anxiety regarding therapy and improve compliance.

8. *Help the client deal adaptively with aversive emotions.* Clients with personality disorders often experience very intense aversive emotional reactions in specific situations. These intense reactions can be a significant problem in their own right, but in addition, the individual's attempts to avoid experiencing these emotions, his/her attempts to escape the emotions, and his/her cognitive and behavioral response to the emotions often play an important role in the client's problems in living. Often, the individual's unwillingness to tolerate aversive affect blocks him/her from handling the emotions adaptively and perpetuates fears about the consequences of experiencing the emotions. If the individual is willing to face the emotions long enough to handle them adaptively, he/she may well also need to acquire some of the cognitive and/or behavioral skills needed to handle the emotions effectively.

9. *Anticipate problems with compliance.* Many factors contribute to a high rate of noncompliance among clients with personality disorders. In addition to the complexities in the therapist–client relationship and the fears regarding change discussed above, the dysfunctional behaviors of individuals with personality disorders are strongly ingrained and often are reinforced by aspects of the client's environment. However, rather than simply being an impediment to progress, episodes of noncompliance can provide an opportunity for effective intervention. When noncompliance is predictable, addressing the issues beforehand may not only improve compliance with that particular assignment but may also prove helpful with other situations where similar issues arise. When noncompliance arises unexpectedly, it provides an opportunity to identify issues that are impeding progress in therapy so that they can be addressed.

10. *Do not presume that the client exists in a reasonable environment.* Some behaviors, such as assertion, are so generally adaptive that it is easy to assume that they are always a good idea. However, clients with personality disorders are often the product of seriously atypical families and live in atypical environments. When implementing changes, it is important to assess the likely responses of significant others in the client's environment rather than to presume that they will respond in a reasonable way.

11. *Attend to your own emotional reactions during the course of therapy.* Interactions with clients with personality disorders can elicit emotional reactions from the therapist ranging from empathic feelings of depression to strong anger, discouragement, fear, or sexual attraction. It is important for the therapist to be aware of these responses so that they do not unduly influence or disrupt the therapist's work with the client, and so that they can be used as a source of potentially useful data. Since emotional responses do not occur randomly, an unusually

strong emotional response is likely to be a reaction to some aspect of the client's behavior. Since a therapist may respond *emotionally* to a pattern in the client's behavior long before it has been recognized *intellectually*, accurate interpretation of one's own responses can speed recognition of these patterns. Careful thought is needed regarding whether to disclose these reactions to the client or not. On one hand, clients with personality disorders often react strongly to therapist self-disclosure and may find it very threatening. However, on the other hand, if the therapist does not disclose an emotional reaction that is apparent to the client from nonverbal cues or that the client anticipates on the basis of experiences in other relationships, this can easily lead to misunderstandings or distrust. Therapists may benefit from using cognitive techniques (such as the dysfunctional thought record; Beck et al., 1979) and/or from seeking consultation with an objective colleague when their own emotional reactions complicate therapy.

12. *Be realistic regarding the length of therapy, goals for therapy, and standards for therapist self-evaluation.* Many therapists using behavioral and cognitive-behavioral approaches to therapy are accustomed to accomplishing substantial results relatively quickly. One can easily become frustrated and angry with the "resistant" client when therapy proceeds slowly or become self-critical and discouraged when therapy goes badly. Behavioral and cognitive-behavioral interventions can accomplish substantial, apparently lasting changes in some clients with personality disorders, but more modest results are achieved in other cases, and little is accomplished in others (Fleming & Pretzer, 1990; Freeman et al., 1990; Turkat & Maisto, 1985). When therapy proceeds slowly, it is important neither to give up prematurely nor to perseverate with an unsuccessful treatment approach. When treatment is unsuccessful, it is important to remember that therapist competence is not the only factor influencing the outcome of therapy.

Just as in cognitive therapy with other problems, the basic strategy in cognitive therapy with personality disorders is to develop an initial conceptualization based on the initial evaluation and then to intervene strategically, focusing both on alleviating the individual's current distress and on accomplishing lasting changes. In the case of Gary, the conceptualization of his problems summarized in Figure 2.2 may seem to provide little chance for effective intervention. One goal of therapy would be to modify Gary's basic assumptions since these are the foundation of the disorder. However, how can one hope to challenge Gary's conviction that others are malicious and deceptive effectively while his vigilance and guardedness constantly produce experiences that seem to confirm his assumptions? If it were possible to

induce Gary to relax his vigilance and defensiveness, this would simplify the task of modifying his assumptions. But how can we hope to
do this as long as he is convinced that people have malicious intentions? Fortunately, the client's sense of self-efficacy plays an important role in the model as well and provides a promising point for
intervention.

The paranoid individual's intense vigilance and defensiveness is
a product of the belief that constant vigilance and defensiveness are
necessary in order to stay safe. If it is possible to increase the client's
sense of self-efficacy regarding problem situations to the point that
he/she is confident of being able to handle problems as they arise, then
the intense vigilance and defensiveness seem less necessary, and it may
be possible for the client to relax both to some extent. This can reduce
the intensity of the client's symptomatology substantially, make it much
easier to address the client's cognitions through conventional cognitive therapy techniques, and make it more possible to persuade the
client to try alternative ways of handling interpersonal conflicts. Therefore, the initial strategy in the cognitive treatment of paranoid personality disorder is to work to increase the client's sense of self-efficacy.
This is followed by attempts to modify other aspects of the client's automatic thoughts, interpersonal behavior, and basic assumptions.

Self-efficacy can be increased in two basic ways. Since it is essentially a subjective evaluation of the demands inherent in a situation
and the individual's ability to successfully meet those demands, an
unrealistically low sense of self-efficacy can result if individuals over-
estimate the demands of the situation or underestimate their ability
to handle the situation. When this is the case, cognitive interventions
that result in a more realistic evaluation of the situation can increase
self-efficacy. A low sense of self-efficacy can also result when individuals realistically conclude that they do not have the skills or capabilities
needed to handle the situation effectively. In that case, self-efficacy
can be increased through interventions that increase the client's coping skills. This can be a matter of helping the client master new coping skills, helping him/her muster the needed resources, helping
him/her plan how best to use the skills and resources he/she does have,
and so forth.

With Gary, his paranoid personality disorder was not recognized
until the seventh therapy session, and the stress-management interventions that began earlier in therapy had already raised his sense of
self-efficacy substantially. However, he still felt that vigilance was
necessary in many innocuous situations because he doubted his ability to cope if he was not constantly vigilant. This stemmed from his
persistently labeling himself as "incompetent" despite his skills and

accomplishments. When this issue was explored in therapy, it became clear that he had very strict idiosyncratic standards for competence and viewed competence dichotomously. He believed that one was either fully competent or totally incompetent. Since he manifested a dichotomous view of competence, the "continuum technique," a cognitive technique used specifically to counteract dichotomous thinking was used:

THERAPIST: It sounds like a lot of your tension and your spending so much time double-checking your work is because you see yourself as basically incompetent and think, "I've got to be careful or I'll really screw up."

GARY: Sure. But it's not just screwing up something little, someone's life could depend on what I do.

THERAPIST: Hmm. We've talked your competence in terms of how you were evaluated while you were in training and how well you've done since then without making much headway. It occurs to me that I'm not sure exactly what "competence" means for you. What does it take for somebody to really qualify as competent? For example, if a martian came down knowing nothing of humans and he wanted to know how to tell who was truly competent, what would you tell him to look for?

GARY: It's someone who does a good job at whatever he's doing.

THERAPIST: Does it matter what the person is doing? If someone does well at something easy, do they qualify as competent in your eyes?

GARY: No, to really be competent they can't be doing something easy.

THERAPIST: So it sounds like they've got to be doing something hard and getting good results to qualify as competent.

GARY: Yeah.

THERAPIST: Is that all there is to it? You've been doing something hard and doing well at it, but you don't feel competent.

GARY: But I'm tense all the time, and I worry about work.

THERAPIST: Are you saying that a truly competent person isn't tense and doesn't worry?

GARY: Yeah. They're confident. They relax while they're doing it, and they don't worry about it afterward.

THERAPIST: So a competent person is someone who takes on difficult tasks and does them well, is relaxed while he's doing them, and doesn't worry about it afterwards. Does that cover it or is there more to competence?

GARY: Well, he doesn't have to be perfect as long as he catches his mistakes and knows his limits.

THERAPIST: What I've gotten down so far [the therapist has been taking notes] is that a truly competent person is doing hard tasks well and getting good results, he's relaxed while he does this and doesn't worry about it afterward, he catches any mistakes he makes and corrects them, and he knows his limits. Does that capture what you have in mind when you use the word "competent"?

GARY: Yeah, I guess it does.

THERAPIST: From the way you've talked before, I've gotten the impression that you see competence as pretty black and white. Either you're competent or you aren't.

GARY: Of course. That's the way it is.

THERAPIST: What would be a good label for the people who aren't competent? Does incompetent capture it?

GARY: Yeah, that's fine.

THERAPIST: What would characterize incompetent people? What would you look for to spot them?

GARY: They screw everything up. They don't do things right. They don't even care whether it's right or how they look or feel. You can't expect results from them.

THERAPIST: Does that cover it?

GARY: Yeah, I think so.

THERAPIST: Well, let's look at how you measure up to these standards. One characteristic of an incompetent person is that he screws everything up. Do you screw everything up?

GARY: Well, no. Most things I do come out OK, but I'm real tense while I do them.

THERAPIST: And you said that an incompetent person doesn't care whether it comes out right or how they look to others; so your being tense and worrying doesn't fit with the idea that you're incompetent. If you don't qualify as incompetent, does that mean that you're completely competent?

GARY: I don't feel competent.

THERAPIST: And by these standards you aren't. You do well with a difficult job, and you've been successful at catching the mistakes you do make, but you aren't relaxed and you do worry. By these standards you don't qualify as completely incompetent or totally competent. How does that fit with the idea that a person's either competent or incompetent?

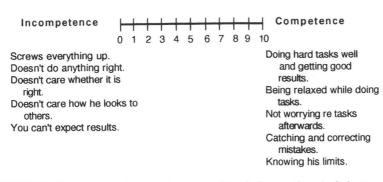

Incompetence |—+—+—+—+—+—+—+—+—+—+—| Competence
0 1 2 3 4 5 6 7 8 9 10

Screws everything up.
Doesn't do anything right.
Doesn't care whether it is
   right.
Doesn't care how he looks to
   others.
You can't expect results.

Doing hard tasks well
   and getting good
   results.
Being relaxed while doing
   tasks.
Not worrying re tasks
   afterwards.
Catching and correcting
   mistakes.
Knowing his limits.

FIGURE 2.5. Continuum of competence used to challenge Gary's dichotomous view of competence.

GARY: I guess maybe it's not just one or the other.

THERAPIST: While you were describing how you saw competence and incompetence I wrote the criteria here in my notes. Suppose we draw a scale from zero to ten here where zero is absolutely, completely incompetent and ten is completely competent, all the time [see Figure 2.5]. How would you rate your competence in grad school?

GARY: At first I was going to say three, but, as I think about it, I'd say a seven or eight except for my writing, and I've never worked at that until now.

THERAPIST: How would you rate your competence on the job?

GARY: I guess it would be an eight or nine in terms of results; but I'm not relaxed, that would be about a three. I do a good job of catching my mistakes as long as I'm not worrying too much, so that would be an eight, and I'd say a nine or ten on knowing my limits.

THERAPIST: How would you rate your skeet shooting?

GARY: That would be a six, but it doesn't matter; I just do it for fun.

THERAPIST: So I hear several important points. First, when you think it over, competence turns out not to be all or nothing. Someone who's not perfect isn't necessarily incompetent. Second, the characteristics you see as being signs of competence don't necessarily hang together real well. You rate an eight or nine in terms of the quality of your work but a three in being relaxed and not worrying. Finally, there are times, such as when you're at work, when being competent is very important to you and other times, like skeet shooting, when its not very important.

GARY: Yeah, I guess I don't have to be at my peak all the time.

THERAPIST: What do you think of this idea that if a person's competent they'll be relaxed, and if they're tense that means they're not
competent?

GARY: I don't know.

THERAPIST: It certainly seems that if a person's sure they can handle
the situation they're likely to be less tense about it. But I don't know
about the flip side, the idea that if you're tense, that proves you're
incompetent. When you're tense and worried, does that make it
easier for you to do well or harder for you to do well?

GARY: It makes it a lot harder for me to do well. I have trouble concentrating and keep forgetting things.

THERAPIST: So if someone does well despite being tense and worried,
they're overcoming an obstacle.

GARY: Yeah, they are.

THERAPIST: Some people would argue that doing well despite having
to overcome obstacles shows greater capabilities than doing well
when things are easy. What do you think of that idea?

GARY: It makes sense to me.

THERAPIST: Now, you've been doing a good job at work despite being real tense and worried. Up to this point you've been taking
your tenseness as proof that you're really incompetent and have
just been getting by because you're real careful. This other way
of looking at it would say that being able to do well despite being
anxious shows that you really are competent, not that you're incompetent. Which do you think is closer to the truth?

GARY: I guess maybe I'm pretty capable after all, but I still hate being so tense.

THERAPIST: Of course, and we'll keep working on that, but the key
point is that being tense doesn't necessarily mean you're incompetent. Now, another place where you feel tense and think you're
incompetent is in social situations. Let's see if you're as incompetent as you feel there. . . .

Once Gary accepted the idea that his ability to handle stressful situations well despite his stress and anxiety was actually a sign of his
capabilities rather than being a sign of incompetence, his sense of self-
efficacy increased substantially. Following this increase in self-efficacy,
he was substantially less defensive and was more willing to disclose
his thoughts and feelings in therapy. He also was more willing to look
critically at his beliefs and assumptions and to test new approaches

to problem situations. This made it possible to use standard cognitive techniques with greater effectiveness.

Another series of interventions that was particularly impactful with Gary was using the continuum technique to challenge his dichotomous view of trustworthiness, then introducing the idea that he could learn which persons were likely to prove trustworthy by noticing how well they followed through when trusted on trivial issues. As he reexamined the trustworthiness of the people he interacted with, he concluded that his family members were truly malicious and deceptive but that they were not typical of people in general. He was able to gradually test his negative view of others' intentions by trusting colleagues and acquaintances in small things and observing their performance. He was pleasantly surprised to discover that the world at large was much less malevolent than he had assumed, that it contained benevolent and indifferent people as well as malevolent ones, and that on those occasions when he was treated badly he could deal with the situation effectively.

Concurrently with these primarily cognitive interventions, it was important to work to modify Gary's dysfunctional interpersonal interactions so that he would be less likely to provoke hostile reactions from others that would support his paranoid views. This required focusing on specific problem situations as they arose and identifying and addressing the cognitions that blocked appropriate assertion. These included, "It won't do any good," "They'll just get mad," and "If they know what I want, they'll use that against me." It was also necessary to work to improve Gary's skills in assertion and clear communication through assertion training. When this resulted in improvements in his relationships with colleagues and in his relationship with his girlfriend, it was fairly easy to use guided discovery to help him recognize the ways in which his previous interaction style had inadvertently provoked hostility from others.

THERAPIST: So it sounds like speaking up for yourself directly has been working out pretty well. How do the other people seem to feel about it?

GARY: Pretty good I guess. Sue and I have been getting along fine, and things have been less tense at work.

THERAPIST: That's interesting. I remember that one of your concerns was that people might get mad if you spoke up for yourself. It sounds as though it might be helping things go better instead.

GARY: Well, I've had a few run-ins, but they've blown over pretty quickly.

THERAPIST: That's a change from the way things used to be right there. Before, if you had a run-in with somebody, it would bug you for a long time. Do you have any idea what's made the difference?

GARY: Not really. It just doesn't seem to stay on my mind as long.

THERAPIST: Could you fill me in on one of the run-ins you had this week? (*They discuss a disagreement with his boss in detail.*)

THERAPIST: It sounds like two things were different from the old way of handling this sort of situation. You stuck with the discussion rather than leaving angry, and you let him know what was bugging you. Do you think that had anything to do with it blowing over more quickly than usual?

GARY: It might.

THERAPIST: It works that way for a lot of people. If it turns out to work that way for you that would be another payoff to speaking up directly. If they go along with what you want there's no problem, and if they don't, at least it blows over more quickly. Do you remember how you used to feel after leaving a disagreement unresolved?

GARY: I'd think about it for days. I'd be tense and jumpy and little things would bug me a lot.

THERAPIST: How do you think it was for the people at work?

GARY: They'd be pretty tense and jumpy too. Nobody'd want to talk to each other for a while.

THERAPIST: That makes it sound like it would be easy for a little mistake or misunderstanding to set off another disagreement.

GARY: I think you're right.

THERAPIST: You know, it seems pretty reasonable for a person to assume that the way to have as little conflict and tension as possible is to avoid speaking up about things that bug him and to try not to let his aggravation show but it doesn't seem to work that way for you. So far it sounds like when you speak up about things that bug you, there are fewer conflicts, and the conflicts that happen blow over more quickly.

GARY: Yeah.

THERAPIST: Do you think that your attempts to keep from aggravating people may have actually made things more tense?

GARY: It sounds like it.

Toward the close of therapy, it was possible to improve Gary's understanding of others and his interpersonal skills further by working to help him better understand the perspectives of others and to empathize with them. This was done through asking questions that required Gary to anticipate the impact of his actions on others, to consider how he would feel if the roles were reversed, or to infer the thoughts and feelings of the other person from that person's actions and then to examine the correspondence between his conclusions and the available data. Initially Gary found these types of questions difficult to answer, but as he received feedback both from the therapist and from subsequent interactions with the individuals in question, his ability to grasp the other person's perspective increased steadily. Gary discovered that aggravating actions by others were not necessarily motivated by malicious intentions, that understanding the other person's point of view often made situations less aggravating, and that this increased his ability to deal effectively with interpersonal conflicts.

At the close of therapy, Gary was noticeably more relaxed and was only bothered by symptoms of stress and anxiety at times when it is common to experience mild symptoms, such as immediately before major examinations. He reported being much more comfortable with friends and colleagues, was socializing more actively, and seemed to feel no particular need to be vigilant. When he and his girlfriend began having difficulties, in part because of her discomfort with the increasing closeness in their relationship, he was able to suspend his initial feelings of rejection and his desire to retaliate long enough to consider her point of view. He then was able to take a major role in resolving their difficulties by communicating his understanding of her concerns ("I know that after all you've been through it's pretty scary when we start talking about marriage"), by acknowledging his own fears and doubts ("I get pretty nervous about this too"), and by expressing his commitment to their relationship ("I don't want this to tear us apart"). Thus this approach to intervention resulted both in substantial improvement in his presenting problems and in substantial changes in the way in which he related to others. He continued to maintain these improvements when he returned to therapy briefly several years later for help in dealing with his girlfriend's excessive drinking and conflicting feelings over a career change.

Differential Treatment for Personality Disorders

It is important to note that the intervention approach used with Gary is specific to paranoid personality disorder. Since cognitive therapy sees each personality disorder as embodying a distinct set of schemas, assumptions, and interpersonal strategies, there are important differences in the intervention approaches used with each. For example, Fleming presents a view of histrionic personality disorder (Beck et al.,

1990, Chap. 10; Fleming, 1983, 1988; Freeman et al., 1990, Chap. 9) which hypothesizes that a history of being rewarded from an early age for enacting certain roles rather than for competence or ability results in the individual learning to focus attention on the playing of roles and "performing" for others rather than on developing his or her own capabilities. As a consequence, the individual comes to assume "I am inadequate and unable to handle life on my own," and "It is necessary to be loved and approved of by everyone," and to have a very strong fear of rejection.

Fleming argues that histrionic individuals' learning histories result in their adopting interpersonal strategies that account for much of the histrionic's dysfunctional behavior. Since they have been rewarded for the enactment of certain roles rather than for careful observation and planning, they attempt to interact with others on the basis of stereotyped roles rather than systematically planning ways to please or impress their audience. When problems arise, the histrionic's fear of disapproval and rejection leads to indirect manipulation rather than assertive responses. However, since the approval of others is assumed to be a dire necessity, the histrionic is quick to become desperate if these methods seem to be failing and to resort to threats, coercion, and temper tantrums as desperation overcomes fear of rejection. This extreme approach to interpersonal relationships is often effective enough to maintain lasting, if tempestuous, relationships. The histrionic's preoccupation with relationships leads him or her to focus predominantly on interpersonal stimuli while his or her tendency to rely on role enactment and manipulation rather than analysis and planning in dealing with problems results in a characteristic thought style that is global, impressionistic, and vivid but is lacking in detail and focus. Global, impressionistic thoughts about interpersonal interactions lead to dramatic reactions that can be intense, labile, and difficult to control, leaving the person subject to explosive outbursts. The resulting difficulties in coping effectively with problem situations serve to further strengthen the histrionic's belief that he or she is inadequate to cope with life alone and needs to rely on the help of others.

Cognitive therapy with histrionic personality disorder is complicated by the fact that the histrionic patient comes to therapy with an approach to life that is diametrically opposed to the systematic, problem-solving approach typically used by cognitive-behavioral therapists. Fleming argues that with such different basic styles, both the therapist and the patient can find therapy quite difficult and frustrating; but she also argues that, if it is possible to bridge this difference in styles, the skills required simply to take part in therapy can constitute an important and useful part of the treatment. She proposes a treatment approach that involves extensive attention to manifestations of the client's histrionic interpersonal style within the therapy relationship, the gradual shaping of effective problem-solving skills, and the development of a more adaptive approach to interpersonal relationships and emphasizes the interplay between cognitive and interpersonal factors:

> Challenging their immediate thoughts may not be sufficient, however, since histrionic individuals so often use emotional outbursts to as a way to manipulate situations. Thus, if a woman with HPD has a tantrum because her husband came home late from work, her immediate thoughts may include, "How can he do this to me? He doesn't love me any more! I'll die if he leaves me!" As a result of her tantrum, however, she may well receive violent protestations of his undying love for her which satisfy her desire for reassurance. Thus, in addition to directly challenging her thoughts when she gets emotionally upset, she also needs to learn to ask herself, "What do I really want now?" and explore alternative options for achieving this.
>
> Once patients can learn to stop reacting and to determine what they want out of the situation (which, with histrionic patients, is often reassurance and attention), they can apply their problem-solving skills by exploring the various methods for achieving that goal and looking at the advantages and disadvantages of each. Thus, rather than automatically having a temper tantrum, they are confronted with a choice between having a temper tantrum and trying other alternatives. (Beck et al., 1990, p. 228)

Thus, despite a shared theoretical framework and therapeutic approach, cognitive therapy with histrionic personality disorder differs from cognitive therapy with paranoid personality disorder in many ways. Discussion of cognitive therapy's conceptualizations of each of the personality disorders and proposed approaches to intervention with each is beyond the scope of this chapter. The interested reader is referred to Beck et al. (1990) or Freeman et al. (1990) for detailed discussions of cognitive therapy with each of the personality disorders.

EMPIRICAL EVALUATION

In examining the empirical status of the cognitive approach to personality disorders there are two important areas to consider. One is empirical evidence regarding the validity of cognitive conceptualizations of personality disorders and the second is empirical evidence regarding the effectiveness of cognitive therapy as a treatment for individuals with personality disorders. While the ideal would be for a particular

approach to any area of psychopathology to provide both a valid conceptualization and an effective approach to treatment, the two do not
necessarily go hand in hand.

The Validity of Cognitive Conceptualizations of Personality Disorder

Cognitive conceptualizations of personality disorders are of recent vintage and, consequently, little research into the validity of these conceptualizations has been reported thus far. In fact, a computerized
literature search identified only two empirical studies that examined
the role of cognitive variables in personality disorders.

One of these studies (O'Leary et al., 1991) examined the role of
dysfunctional beliefs and assumptions in borderline personality disorder. These investigators administered the Dysfunctional Attitude
Scale (Weisman & Beck, 1978), a self-report measure of dysfunctional
attitudes emphasized in cognitive therapy of depression, to a sample
of 46 patients diagnosed as having borderline personality disorder and
27 normal controls. They found that the borderlines' scores were significantly higher than those of the normal controls and were among
the highest of any diagnostic group reported previously. Furthermore,
the borderlines' scores were not related to the presence or absence of
a concurrent major depression, to history of a previous major depression, or to clinical status.

The second study (Gasperini et al., 1989) investigated the relation-
ship(s) among mood disorders, personality disorders, automatic
thoughts, and coping strategies. These investigators administered the
Automatic Thoughts Questionnaire (ATQ; Hollon & Kendall, 1980) and
the Self-Control Schedule (SCS; Rosenbaum, 1980), among other measures, to a sample of depressed outpatients and a control group of medical inpatients who did not manifest any Axis I disorders. All subjects
were evaluated for Axis II diagnoses using the structured interview
for DSM-III personality disorders (Stangl, Pfohl, Zimmerman, Bowers, & Carenthal, 1985). The relationships among diagnostic status and
the measures used in this study were then explored through factor analyses. These analyses revealed that the first factor that emerged from
the factor analysis of ATQ and SCS items reflected the presence of a
"Cluster B" personality disorder (narcissistic, histrionic, borderline,
and antisocial), whereas the second factor reflected the presence of a
"Cluster C" personality disorder (compulsive, dependent, avoidant,
and passive–aggressive). "Cluster A" personality disorders (paranoid,
schizoid, and schizotypal) were unrelated to any of the factors that
emerged from the factor analysis; however, few subjects received

Cluster A diagnoses, and the lack of relationship could easily be due to this alone.

Both of these studies provide support for the general proposition that dysfunctional cognitions play a role in personality disorders. Unfortunately, they have only a very limited bearing on the theoretical model presented in this chapter. While the finding of O'Leary et al. (1991) that borderlines have highly elevated scores on a measure of dysfunctional beliefs is consistent with the idea that dysfunctional beliefs and assumptions play a role on personality disorders, the investigators only considered subjects' total scores on the DAS and did not examine the degree to which they endorsed the specific dysfunctional beliefs that have been hypothesized to play a role in borderline personality disorder. Thus, the study does not provide a direct test of the cognitive model of borderline personality disorder. Similarly, Gasperini et al. (1989) did not use measures that assessed any of the specific schemas or dysfunctional beliefs that have been emphasized in cognitive conceptualizations of personality disorders and did not test any hypotheses derived from cognitive theory. Their finding that the presence of a Cluster B or Cluster C personality disorder accounted for factors that consisted largely of ATQ items assessing the occurrence of specific automatic thoughts is consistent with the general proposition that automatic thoughts are related to personality disorders in some way. However, it falls far short of testing the cognitive model of personality disorders.

In short, the available evidence is consistent with the proposition that cognitive variables are related to personality disorders in some way; however, no empirical studies have yet been reported that test hypotheses based on cognitive conceptualizations of personality disorders. Until such research is conducted, it will not be clear whether the model we have presented suffers from serious conceptual deficiencies or not.

The Effectiveness of Cognitive Therapy with Personality Disorders

The effectiveness of cognitive therapy as a treatment for unipolar depression is well established, and there are at least preliminary indications that it holds promise as an approach to treating a range of other disorders (i.e., Simon & Fleming, 1985). However, most research into the effectiveness of cognitive therapy and related approaches as treatments for individuals with personality disorders is of recent vintage. Less than a decade ago, Kellner (1986) concluded that there were too few adequately controlled studies of behavioral or cognitive-behavioral treatment approaches with subjects clearly diagnosed as having personality disorders to provide an empirical basis for recommending specific interventions for clients with personality disorders. In recent years, the number and quality of empirical studies of cognitive-behavioral treatment of personality disorders have improved substantially, but the overall situation has not yet changed dramatically.

Several recent reviews of empirical studies of behavioral and cognitive-behavioral approaches to treating personality disorders have appeared (Beck et al., 1990, pp. 11–21; Fleming & Pretzer, 1990; Pretzer & Fleming, 1990). Table 2.5 provides an overview of the available evidence regarding the effectiveness of cognitive-behavioral interventions in the treatment of individuals diagnosed as having personality disorders. It is immediately apparent from this table that there have been many uncontrolled clinical reports that assert that cognitive-behavioral therapy can provide effective treatment for personality disorders. However, there are few controlled outcome studies to provide support for these assertions.

A number of studies have examined the effectiveness of cognitive-behavioral treatment for Axis I disorders with subjects who are also diagnosed as having personality disorders and have found that the presence of an Axis II diagnosis greatly decreases the likelihood of treatments being effective. For example, Turner (1987) found that socially phobic patients without personality disorders improved markedly after a 15-week group treatment for social phobia and maintained their gains at a 1-year follow-up. However, patients with personality disorder diagnoses in addition to social phobia showed little or no improvement both posttreatment and at the 1-year follow-up.

Mavissakalian and Hamman (1987) obtained similar results in a study of the treatment of agoraphobia. In their study, 75% of agoraphobic subjects rated as being low in personality disorder characteristics responded well to a time-limited behavioral and pharmacological treatment for agoraphobia, while only 25% of the subjects rated as being high in personality disorder characteristics responded to this treatment. However, it is interesting that Mavissakalian and Hamman (1987) also found that four of seven subjects who had met diagnostic criteria for a single personality disorder diagnosis before treatment no longer met criteria for a personality disorder diagnosis following treatment, while subjects diagnosed as having more than one personality disorder did not show a similar improvement. Apparently, while subjects with Axis II diagnoses generally responded poorly to treatment, some subjects with Axis II diagnoses not only showed improvement in symptoms of agoraphobia but also showed broader benefits from time-limited treatment.

TABLE 2.5. The Effectiveness of Cognitive-Behavioral Treatment with Personality Disorders

Personality disorder	Uncontrolled clinical reports	Single-case design	Effects of personality disorders on outcome	Controlled outcome
Antisocial	+	−	+	[a]
Avoidant	+	+	±	+
Borderline	±	−	+	±
Dependent	+	+	+	
Histrionic	+		−	
Narcissistic	+	+		
Obsessive–compulsive	+	−		
Paranoid	+	+		
Passive–aggressive	+		+	
Schizoid	+			
Schizotypal				

Note. + Cognitive-behavioral interventions found to be effective; − cognitive-behavioral interventions found not to be effective; ± mixed findings.
[a]Cognitive-behavioral interventions were effective with antisocial personality disorder subjects only when the individual was depressed at pretest.

The studies that have examined the effectiveness of cognitive-behavioral treatment for Axis I disorders with individuals who also have personality disorders consistently show that the presence of Axis II diagnoses substantially decreases the likelihood of successful treatment. However, these studies examined the effectiveness of treatment approaches that did not take the presence of personality disorders into account. The few controlled studies that have focused specifically on cognitive-behavioral treatment of individuals with personality disorders have produced more encouraging results.

In a study of the treatment of opiate addicts in a methadone maintenance program, Woody, McLellan, Luborsky, and O'Brien (1985) found that subjects who met DSM-III diagnostic criteria for both major depression and antisocial personality disorder responded well to both cognitive therapy and a supportive–expressive psychotherapy systematized by Luborsky (Luborsky, McLellan, Woody, O'Brien, & Auerbach, 1985). The subjects showed statistically significant improvement on 11 of 22 outcome variables used, including psychiatric symptoms, drug use, employment, and illegal activity. Subjects who met criteria for antisocial personality disorder but not major depression showed little response to treatment, improving on only 3 of 22 variables. This pattern of results was maintained at a 7-month follow-up. While subjects not diagnosed with antisocial personality disorder responded to treat ment better than the sociopaths did, sociopaths who were initially depressed did only slightly worse than the nonsociopaths, whereas the nondepressed sociopaths did much worse. The finding that two dissimilar treatment approaches were both effective might suggest that the improvement was due to nonspecific treatment effects. However, the finding that the degree to which therapists adhered to the relevant treatment manual was significantly correlated with degree of improvement (Luborsky et al., 1985) suggests that each treatment approach proved effective in its own right.

Studies of the treatment of avoidant personality disorder have also provided encouraging results. Both short-term social skills training and social skills training combined with cognitive interventions have been demonstrated to be effective in increasing the frequency of social interaction and decreasing social anxiety in subjects with avoidant personality disorder (Stravynski, Marks, & Yule, 1982). Stravynski et al. (1982) interpreted this finding as demonstrating the "lack of value" of cognitive interventions, but it should be noted that all treatments were provided by a single therapist (who was also principal investigator) and that only one of many possible cognitive interventions (disputation of irrational beliefs) was used. In a subsequent study, Greenberg and Stravynski (1985) reported that the avoidant client's fear of ridicule appears to contribute to premature termination in many cases and suggest that interventions that modify relevant aspects of the clients' cognitions might add substantially to the effectiveness of intervention.

Linehan and her colleagues (Linehan, Armstrong, Allmon, Suarez, & Miller, 1988; Linehan, Armstrong, Suarez, & Allmon, 1988) have conducted an outcome study of Linehan's cognitive-behavioral approach, which she terms "dialectical behavior therapy," with a sample of chronically parasuicidal borderline subjects. The patients in the dialectical behavior therapy condition had a significantly lower rate of premature termination of therapy and significantly less self-injurious behavior at the close of 1 year of treatment than a control group that received "treatment as usual" in the community. However, they did not show significant over-all improvement in depression or other symptomatology. Although these results are modest, it is important to note that this study was conducted with a sample of subjects who not only met diagnostic criteria for borderline personality disorder but who also were chronically parasuicidal, had histories of multiple psychiatric hospitalizations, and were unable to maintain employment as a result of their psychiatric symptoms. It is encouraging to find that 1 year of cognitive-behavioral treatment can produce any significant improvement in such a severely impaired population.

In clinical practice, most therapists do not apply a standardized treatment protocol with a homogeneous sample of individuals who share a common diagnosis. Instead, clinicians face a variety of clients and take an individualized approach to treatment. A recent study of the effectiveness of cognitive therapy under such "real world" conditions provides important support for the clinical use of cognitive therapy with clients who are diagnosed as having personality disorders. Persons et al. (1988) conducted an interesting empirical study of clients receiving cognitive therapy for depression in private practice settings. The subjects were 70 consecutive individuals seeking treatment from Dr. Burns or Dr. Persons in their own practices. Both therapists are established cognitive therapists who have taught and published extensively, and in this study, both therapists conducted cognitive therapy as they normally do. This meant that treatment was open-ended, it was individualized rather than standardized, and medication and inpatient treatment were used as needed.

The primary focus of the study was on identifying predictors of dropout and treatment outcome in cognitive therapy for depression. However, it is interesting for our purposes to note that 54.3% of the subjects met DSM-III criteria for a personality disorder diagnosis and that the investigators considered the presence of a personality disorder diagnosis as a potential predictor of both premature termination of therapy and therapy outcome. The investigators found that while patients with personality disorders were significantly more likely to drop out of therapy prematurely than patients without personality disorders, those patients with personality disorder diagnoses who persisted in therapy through the completion of treatment showed substantial improvement and did not differ significantly in degree of improvement from patients without personality disorders.

While the number of published studies is quite limited and some studies suffer from methodological problems, several general conclusions are suggested by the available research (see Beck at al., 1990, pp. 11–21, or Fleming & Pretzer, 1990, for comprehensive recent reviews). First, many authors report that standard cognitive-behavioral treatments for Axis I disorders often prove ineffective when used with individuals who have concurrent Axis II disorders and that this is true even if the treatments are quite effective with subjects who do not have Axis II disorders. Second, the available findings suggest that, for some individuals with an Axis I disorder and a concurrent Axis II disorder, behavioral or cognitive-behavioral treatment for the Axis I disorder not only can be effective as a treatment for the Axis I disorder but also can result in overall improvement in the Axis II disorder as well. Third, clinical reports assert that cognitive therapy can be an effective treatment approach for most of the personality disorders, but we do not yet have adequate empirical data to support this enthusiasm. Finally, we have little evidence to provide grounds for comparing cognitive therapy with alternative approaches to treating personality disorders.

The findings reported by Persons et al. (1988) are quite encouraging. They suggest that while the presence of a personality disorder increases the likelihood of cognitive therapy's proving ineffective (if the client discontinues therapy prematurely), if it is possible to induce the client to persist in treatment, cognitive therapy can prove quite useful. It should be noted that the subjects in the study of Persons et al. (1988) received treatment in the period before the recent advances in cognitive therapy with personality disorders were widely published. Hopefully, the effectiveness of cognitive therapy as a treatment for individuals with personality disorders has increased in recent years.

FUTURE DIRECTIONS

Clearly, cognitive therapy for personality disorders is still under development and is in need of continued theoretical refinement, clinical innovation, and empirical research. With some personality disorders, such as paranoid personality disorder, cognitive conceptualizations have been developed in considerable detail, and specific treatment approaches have been proposed. These disorders are ripe for empirical tests of the validity of the conceptualization, of the overall effectiveness of the proposed treatment approach, and of the effects of particular interventions. With other personality disorders, such as schizotypal personality disorder, both the conceptualization and the treatment approach are much less developed and would need further refinement in order to be suitable for empirical testing.

While research to test the effectiveness of cognitive therapy as a treatment for individuals with a number of personality disorders is under way, more than simple outcome studies are needed. Evidence of the effectiveness of a given treatment approach does not necessarily demonstrate the validity of the conceptualization on which the treatment is based or suggest ways in which the treatment approach can be improved. If the cognitive perspective on personality disorders is to advance, it will be important to test specific hypotheses derived from cognitive conceptualizations of each of the personality disorders. It is only through such hypothesis testing that it will be possible to identify the conceptual deficiencies of our current models and refine them into conceptualizations that facilitate more effective intervention.

Empirical tests of the actual effects of the particular intervention approaches have much potential for increasing the effectiveness of cognitive therapy with personality disorders. For example, it has been suggested that the use of the "continuum technique" to counteract dichotomous thinking in clients with borderline personality disorder can decrease the intensity of borderlines' remarkable mood swings and can facilitate other interventions (Beck et al., 1990, pp. 199–201; Freeman et al., 1990, p. 198). An empirical test of the degree to which this intervention actually produces the desired results and an investigation of conditions that may facilitate or block the technique's effects could be quite useful in refining treatment recommendations. Many other specific cognitive, behavioral, and interpersonal intervention techniques have been recommended in various discussions of cognitive therapy with personality disorders. An empirically based understanding of the effects of various interventions and the factors that influence their effectiveness would be quite useful to the therapist who is faced with the dilemma of choosing between many possible interventions or who must choose the most promising time to attempt a given intervention.

One area that needs theoretical attention and empirical investigation is the question of how to best conceptualize and treat individuals who are diagnosed as having mixed personality disorder or who satisfy diagnostic criteria for more than one personality disorder. This issue has received little explicit attention, and it is not at all clear if one can best conceptualize and treat an individual who meets DSM-III-R criteria for both paranoid personality disorder and histrionic personality disorder, for example, simply by combining the conceptualizations and treatment approaches that have been developed for each disorder separately. If it were possible to develop a comprehensive cognitive typology of the personality disorders, this could simplify the task of exploring the similarities and differences among the personality disorders and could make it easier to develop clear conceptualizations of individuals who merit more than one personality disorder diagnosis.

One impediment to empirical research on personality disorders is the difficulty of using traditional research designs that require one to assemble a large, homogeneous sample of subjects. The practical problems encountered in attempting to assemble a group of individuals with a given personality disorder and then to collect detailed data regarding their cognitions and behavior can be substantial. Turkat and his colleagues (see Turkat, 1990; Turkat & Maisto, 1985) have broken important new ground by presenting an innovative single-case experimental design that has proven useful in developing and testing cognitive-behavioral conceptualizations of clients with personality disorders. In their approach, a thorough clinical assessment is used as a basis for developing a detailed formulation of a particular individual's problems. Specific hypotheses based on this conceptualization are then generated and are tested using the most appropriate available measures. Positive results from this hypothesis testing are interpreted as validating the conceptualization, and negative results are used to identify portions of the conceptualization that are in need of revision. Finally, a treatment plan is developed on the basis of this case formulation, and as treatment is implemented, successful interventions are seen as validating the case formulation, while unsuccessful interventions are taken as indicating a need for reevaluation of the case formulation. This experimental method reduces many of the practical problems encountered in trying to assemble a homogeneous sample of individuals with the same personality disorder as well as the logistical problems encountered when attempting to conduct detailed data collection on a large sample of individuals who may well be in need of immediate treatment. At the same time, it avoids many of the biases that can creep into unstructured clinical exploration. Although this type of experimental design will not replace traditional nomothetic research, it can provide a practical method for developing and refining conceptualizations of specific personality disorders that can then be tested more conclusively using more traditional experimental designs.

A second impediment to research into the cognitive approach to personality disorders, as well as into other areas, is the tendency of cognitive-behavioral researchers to rely on simple self-report questionnaires as the primary means of assessing cognitive variables. As noted earlier, the use of self-report questionnaires presumes that respondents both are capable of accurately reporting the desired information and are willing to do so. These assumptions may be valid in a one-on-one psychotherapeutic relationship where the client can receive training in monitoring and reporting cognitions, where it is to the client's advantage to provide the therapist with the information needed for effective intervention, and where any inconsistencies within the clients' reports of their cognitions or discrepancies between reports of cognitions and reports of emotions and behavior can be explored. However, self-report measures of cognitions have often been used for research purposes without subjects receiving training in monitoring and reporting cognitions, with responses being based on recollection rather than self-monitoring, without an incentive for subjects to provide uncensored reports of their cognitions, and/or without any attention to inconsistencies within the reports or discrepancies between reports of cognitions and other data. Clearly, more attention to obtaining valid measures of cognitive variables could do much to advance cognitive-behavioral research in many areas.

The wider application of laboratory methods used in basic research into cognitive processes to research on clinically relevant topics has considerable potential for providing more valid and more objective measures of cognitive variables. For example, recent studies have successfully used the Stroop color-naming task to investigate selective processing of threat cues in panic disorder (McNally, Riemann, & Kim, 1990), to examine cognitive aspects of posttraumatic stress disorder (Cassiday, McNally, & Zeitlin, 1992), and to assess the self-schema in an individual diagnosed as having a multiple personality (Scott, 1992). Other examples of promising approaches are the use of measures of eye fixation (Matthews & Antes, 1992) and performance on dichotic listening tasks (Klinger, 1978) to investigate attentional biases and the use of thought-sampling procedures (Hurlburt, Leach, & Saltman, 1984) to obtain more accurate data regarding the content of an individual's thoughts. These sorts of methods for measuring cognition without relying exclusively on self-report questionnaires have much potential for advancing cognitive-behavioral research.

Given the prevalence of personality disorders and the consensus that treatment of clients with personality disorders is difficult and complex no matter what treatment approach is used, it is clearly important that these disorders be a continued focus of empirical research, theoretical innovation, and clinical experimentation. For the time being, treatment recommendations based on clinical observation and a limited empirical base are the best that cognitive therapy can offer to clinicians who must try to work with personality disorder clients today rather than waiting for empirically validated treatment protocols to be developed at some point in the future. Fortunately, the authors' experience has been that when cognitive-behavioral interventions are based on an individualized conceptualization of the client's problems and the interpersonal aspects of therapy receive sufficient attention, many clients with personality disorders can be treated quite effectively.

NOTES

1. A number of different cognitive and cognitive-behavioral approaches to therapy have been developed in recent years. While these various approaches have much in common, there are important conceptual and technical differences among them. In order to minimize confusion, the specific approach developed by Aaron T. Beck and his colleagues will be referred to as cognitive therapy, whereas the term "cognitive-behavioral" will be used to refer to the full range of cognitive and cognitive-behavioral approaches.

2. A variety of methods are available for increasing the validity and usefulness of self reports. For an overview, see Freeman, Pretzer, Fleming, and Simon (1990, Chap. 2).

3. It is important to note that individuals are not necessarily aware of automatic thoughts as they occur and that when they do become aware of the automatic thoughts, these thoughts typically are so plausible that the individual does not think of examining them critically.

4. The term "self-efficacy" refers to expectations regarding one's ability to deal effectively with a specific situation (Bandura, 1977). An individual's level of self-efficacy regarding a particular situation is believed to have an important effect both on the the individual's anxiety level and his/her coping behavior in that situation.

REFERENCES

Alford, B. A., & Norcross, J. C. (1991). Cognitive therapy as integrative therapy. *Journal of Psychotherapy Integration, 1,* 175–190.

American Psychiatric Association. (1987). *Diagnostic and statistical manual of mental disorders* (3rd ed., rev.). Washington, DC: Author.

Bandura, A. (1977). *Social learning theory.* Englewood Cliffs, NJ: Prentice-Hall.

Beck, A. T. (1964). Thinking and depression: 2. Theory and therapy. *Archives of General Psychiatry, 10,* 561–571.

Beck, A. T. (1967). *Depression: Clinical, experimental, and theoretical aspects.* New York: Harper & Row. (Reprinted 1972 as *Depression: Causes and treatment.* Philadelphia: University of Pennsylvania Press)

Beck, A. T. (1985). Cognitive therapy. In H. I. Kaplan & B. J. Sadock (Eds.), *Comprehensive textbook of psychiatry/IV* (Vol. 2). Baltimore: Williams & Wilkins.

Beck, A. T. (1991). Cognitive therapy as *the* integrative therapy: Comments on Alford and Norcross. *Journal of Psychotherapy Integration, 1,* 191–198.

Beck, A. T. (1992). Personality disorders (and their relationship to syndromal disorders). *Across-Species Comparisons and Psychiatry Newsletter, 5,* 3–13.

Beck, A. T., Freeman, A., & Associates. (1990). *Cognitive therapy of personality disorders.* New York: Guilford Press.

Beck, A. T., Rush, A. J., Shaw, B. F., & Emery, G. (1979). *Cognitive therapy of depression.* New York: Guilford Press.

Beck, A. T., & Weishaar, M. (1989). Cognitive therapy. In A. Freeman, K. M. Simon, L. E. Beutler, & H. Arkowitz (Eds.), *Comprehensive handbook of cognitive therapy.* New York: Plenum Press.

Black, D. W., Yates, W. R., Noyes, R., Pfohl, B., & Kelley, M. (1989). DSM-III personality disorder in obsessive compulsive study volunteers: A controlled study. *Journal of Personality Disorders, 3,* 58–62.

Bowlby, J. (1985). The role of childhood experience in cognitive disturbance. In M. J. Mahoney & A. Freeman (Eds.), *Cognition and psychotherapy.* New York: Plenum Press.

Cassiday, K. L., McNally, R. J., & Zeitlin, S. B. (1992). Cognitive processing of trauma cues in rape victims with post-traumatic stress disorder. *Cognitive Therapy and Research, 16,* 283–295.

Cone, J. D., & Hawkins, R. P. (1977). *Behavioral assessment: New directions in clinical psychology.* New York: Brunner/Mazel.

Ellis, A. (1962). *Reason and emotion in psychotherapy.* New York: Lyle Stuart.

Epstein, S. (1979). The stability of behavior: I. On predicting most of the people much of the time. *Journal of Personality and Social Psychology, 37,* 1097–1126.

Ericsson, K. A., & Simon, H. A. (1980). Verbal reports as data. *Psychological Review, 87,* 215–251.

Fleming, B. (1983, August). *Cognitive therapy with histrionic patients: Resolving a conflict in styles.* Paper presented at the meeting of the American Psychological Association, Anaheim, CA.

Fleming, B. (1985). *Dependent personality disorder: Managing the transition from dependence to autonomy.* Paper presented at the meeting of the Association for Advancement of Behavior Therapy, Houston, TX.

Fleming, B. (1988). CT with histrionic personality disorder: Resolving a conflict of styles. *International Cognitive Therapy Newsletter, 4,* 4, 8–9, 12.

Fleming, B. & Pretzer, J. (1990). Cognitive–behavioral approaches to personality disorders. In M. Hersen, R. M. Eisler, & P. M. Miller (Eds.), *Progress in behavior modification* (Vol. 25). Newbury Park, CA: Sage.

Freeman, A., Pretzer, J. L., Fleming, B., & Simon, K. M. (1990). *Clinical applications of cognitive therapy.* New York: Plenum Press.

Freidman, C. J., Shear, M. K., & Frances, A. (1987), DSM III personality disorders in panic patients, *Journal of Personality Disorders, 1,* 132–135.

Gasperini, M., Provenza, M., Ronchi, P., Scherillo, P., Bellodi, L., & Smeraldi, E. (1989). Cognitive processes and personality disorders in affective patients. *Journal of Personality Disorders, 3,* 63–71.

Greenberg, D., & Stravynski, A. (1985). Patients who complain of social dysfunction: I. Clinical and demographic features. *Canadian Journal of Psychiatry, 30,* 206–211.

Hollon, S. D., & Kendall, P. C. (1980). Cognitive self-statement in depression: Development of an automatic thoughts questionnaire. *Cognitive Therapy and Research, 4,* 383–395.

Hurlburt, R. T., Leach, B. C., & Saltman, S. (1984). Random sampling of thought and mood. *Cognitive Therapy and Research, 8,* 263–276.

Isen, A. M. (1984). Toward understanding the role of affect in cognition. In R. S. Wyer & T. K. Skrull (Eds.), *Handbook of social cognition.* Hillsdale, NJ: Erlbaum.

Kellner, R. (1986). Personality disorders. *Psychotherapy and Psychosomatics, 46,* 58–66.

Kendall, P. C., & Hollon, S. D. (1981). Assessing self-referent speech: Methods in the measurement of self-statements. In P. C. Kendall & S. D. Hollon (Eds.), *Assessment strategies for cognitive behavioral interventions.* New York: Academic Press.

Klinger, E. (1978). Modes of normal conscious flow. In K. S. Pope & J. L. Singer (Eds.), *The stream of consciousness: Scientific investigation into the flow of human experience.* New York: Plenum Press.

Linehan, M. M. (1987a). Dialectical behavior therapy in groups: Treating borderline personality disorders and suicidal behavior. In C. M. Brody (Ed.), *Women in groups*. New York: Springer.

Linehan, M. M. (1987b). Dialectical Behavioral Therapy: A cognitive behavioral approach to parasuicide. *Journal of Personality Disorders, 1,* 328–333.

Linehan, M. M. (1987c). Commentaries on "The inner experience of the borderline self-mutilator": A cognitive behavioral approach. *Journal of Personality Disorders, 1,* 328–333.

Linehan, M. M., Armstrong, H. E., Allmon, D. J., Suarez, A., & Miller, M. L. (1988). *Comprehensive behavioral treatment for suicidal behaviors and borderline personality disorder. II: Treatment retention and one year follow-up of patient use of medical and psychological resources.* Unpublished manuscript, University of Washington, Department of Psychology, Seattle.

Linehan, M. M., Armstrong, H. E., Suarez, A., & Allmon, D. J. (1988). *Comprehensive behavioral treatment for suicidal behaviors and borderline personality disorder: I. Outcome.* Unpublished manuscript, University of Washington, Department of Psychology, Seattle.

Liotti, G. (1992). Egocentrism and the cognitive psychotherapy of personality disorders. *Journal of Cognitive Psychotherapy: An International Quarterly, 6,* 43–58.

Lockwood, G. (1992). Psychoanalysis and the cognitive therapy of personality disorders. *Journal of Cognitive Psychotherapy: An International Quarterly, 6,* 25–42.

Lockwood, G., & Young, J. (1992). Introduction: Cognitive therapy for personality disorders. *Journal of Cognitive Psychotherapy: An International Quarterly, 6,* 5–10.

Luborsky, L., McLellan, A. T., Woody, G. E., O'Brien, C. P., & Auerbach, A. (1985). Therapist success and its determinants. *Archives of General Psychiatry, 42,* 602–611.

Mahoney, M. J. (1974). *Cognition and behavior modification.* Cambridge, MA: Ballinger.

Mahoney, M. J. (1977). Some applied issues in self-monitoring. In J. D. Cone & R. P. Hawkins (Eds.), *Behavioral assessment: New directions in clinical psychology*. New York: Brunner/Mazel.

Marlatt, G. A., & Gordon, J. M. (Eds.). (1985). *Relapse prevention: Maintainence strategies in the treatment of addictive behaviors.* New York: Guilford Press.

Matthews, G. R., & Antes, J. R. (1992). Visual attention and depression: Cognitive biases in the eye fixations of the dysphoric and the nondepressed. *Cognitive Therapy and Research, 16,* 359–371.

Mavissakalian, M., & Hamman, M. S. (1987). DSM-III personality disorder in agoraphobia: II. Changes with treatment. *Comprehensive Psychiatry, 28,* 356–361.

Mays, D. T. (1985). Behavior therapy with borderline personality disorders: One clinician's perspective. In D. T. Mays & C. M. Franks (Eds.), *Negative outcome in psychotherapy and what to do about it*. New York: Springer.

Mays, D. T., & Franks, C. M. (1985). Negative outcome: What to do about it. In D. T. Mays & C. M. Franks (Eds.), *Negative outcome in psychotherapy and what to do about it*. New York: Springer.

McNally, R. J., Riemann, B. C.,& Kim, E. (1990). Selective processing of threat cues in panic disorder. *Behaviour Research and Therapy, 28,* 407–412.

Merluzzi, T. V., Glass, C. R., & Genest, M. (Eds.). (1981). *Cognitive assessment.* New York: Guilford Press.

O'Leary, K. M., Cowdry, R. W., Gardner, D. L., Leibenluft, E., Lucas, P. B., & deJong-Meyer, R. (1991). Dysfunctional attitudes in borderline personality disorder. *Journal of Personality Disorders, 5,* 233–242.

Overholser, J. C. (1991). Categorical assessment of the dependent personality disorder in depressed in-patients. *Journal of Personality Disorders, 5,* 243–255.

Padesky, C. A. (1986, September). *Personality disorders: Cognitive therapy into the 90's.* Paper presented at the Second International Conference on Cognitive Psychotherapy, Umeå, Sweden.

Padesky, C. A. (1988). Schema-focused CT: Comments and questions. *International Cognitive Therapy Newsletter, 4,* pp. 5, 7.

Parks, C. W., Jr., & Hollon, S. D. (1988). Cognitive assessment. In A. S. Bellack & M. Hersen (Eds.), *Behavioral assessment: A practical handbook.* New York: Pergamon Press.

Persons, J. B. (1991). *Cognitive therapy in practice: A case formulation approach.* New York: Norton.

Persons, J. B., Burns, B. D., & Perloff, J. M. (1988). Predictors of drop-out and outcome in cognitive therapy for depression in a private practice setting. *Cognitive Therapy and Research, 12,* 557–575.

Pretzer, J. L. (1983, August). *Borderline personality disorder: Too complex for cognitive-behavioral approaches?* Paper presented at the meeting of the American Psychological Association, Anaheim, CA. (ERIC Document Reproduction Service No. ED 243 007)

Pretzer, J. L. (1985, November). *Paranoid personality disorder: A cognitive view.* Paper presented at the meeting of the Association for the Advancement of Behavior Therapy, Houston, TX.

Pretzer, J. L. (1988). Paranoid personality disorder: A cognitive view. *International Cognitive Therapy Newsletter, 4,* 4, 10–12.

Pretzer, J. L. (1992). *Towards a cognitive typology of personality disorders.* Unpublished manuscript.

Pretzer, J. L., Beck, A. T., & Newman, C. F. (1990). Stress and stress management: A cognitive view. *Journal of Cognitive Psychotherapy: An International Quarterly, 3,* 163–179.

Pretzer, J. L., & Fleming, B. M. (1990). Cognitive-behavioral treatment of personality disorders. *Behavior Therapist, 12,* 105–109.

Rosenbaum, M. (1980). A schedule for assessing self-control behaviors: Preliminary findings. *Behavior Therapy, 11,* 109–121.

Rothstein, M. M., & Vallis, T. M. (1991). The application of cognitive therapy to patients with personality disorders. In T. M. Vallis, J. L. Howes, & P. C. Miller (Eds.), *The challenge of cognitive therapy: Applications to nontraditional populations.* New York: Plenum Press.

Safran, J. D., & McMain, S. (1992). A cognitive–interpersonal approach to the treatment of personality disorders. *Journal of Cognitive Psychotherapy: An International Quarterly, 6,* 59–68.

Scott, W. B. (1992, February). *Self-schema in an individual diagnosed as having multiple personality disorder.* Paper presented at the meeting of the Cleveland Area Behavior Therapy Association, Cleveland, OH.

Simon, K. M. (1983, August). *Cognitive therapy with compulsive patients: Replacing rigidity with structure.* Paper presented at the meeting of the American Psychological Association, Anaheim, CA.

Simon, K. M. (1985, November). *Cognitive therapy of the passive–aggressive personality.* Paper presented at the meeting of the Association–for Advancement of Behavior Therapy, Houston, TX.

Simon, K. M., & Fleming, B. M. (1985). Beck's cognitive therapy of depression: Treatment and outcome. In R. M. Turner & L. M. Ascher (Eds.), *Evaluating behavior therapy outcome.* New York: Springer.

Stangl, D., Pfohl, B., Zimmerman, M., Bowers, W., & Carenthal, C. (1985). A structured interview for the DSM-III personality disorders: A preliminary report. *Archives of General Psychiatry, 42,* 591–596.

Stephens, J. H., & Parks, S. L. (1981). Behavior therapy of personality disorders. In J. R. Lion (Ed.), *Personality disorders: Diagnosis and management* (2nd ed.). Baltimore: Williams & Wilkins.

Stravynski, A., Marks, I., & Yule, W. (1982). Social skills problems in neurotic outpatients: Social skills training with and without cognitive modification. *Archives of General Psychiatry, 39,* 1378–1385.

Taylor, S., & Rachman, S. J. (1991). Fear of sadness. *Journal of Anxiety Disorders, 5,* 375–381.

Taylor, S., & Rachman, S. J. (1992). Fear and avoidance of aversive affective states: Dimensions and causal relations. *Journal of Anxiety Disorders, 6,* 15–25.

Turkat, I. D. (1990). *The personality disorders: A psychological approach to clinical management.* New York: Pergamon.

Turkat, I. D., & Maisto, S. A. (1985). Personality disorders: Application of the experimental method to the formulation and modification of personality disorders. In D. H. Barlow (Ed.), *Clinical handbook of psychological disorders: A step-by-step treatment manual.* New York: Guilford Press.

Turner, R. M. (1986, March). *The bio-social-learning approach to the assessment and treatment of borderline personality disorder.* Paper presented at the Carrier Foundation Behavioral Medicine Update Symposium, Belle Meade, NJ.

Turner, R. M. (1987). The effects of personality disorder diagnosis on the outcome of social anxiety symptom reduction. *Journal of Personality Disorders, 1,* 136–143.

Turner, S. M., Bidel, D. C., Borden, J. W., Stanley, M. A., & Jacob, R. G. (1991). Social phobia: Axis I and Axis II correlates. *Journal of Abnormal Psychology, 100,* 102–106.

Turner, S. M., & Hersen, M. (1981). Disorders of social behavior: A behavioral approach to personality disorders. In S. M. Turner, K. S. Calhoun, & H. E. Adams (Eds.), *Handbook of clinical behavior therapy.* New York: Wiley.

Watkins, P. C., Mathews, A., Williamson, D. A., & Fuller, R. D. (1992). Mood-congruent memory in depression: Emotional priming or elaboration? *Journal of Abnormal Psychology, 101,* 581–586.

Weisman, A. N., & Beck, A. T. (1978). *Development and validation of the dys-*

functional attitude scale: A preliminary investigation. Paper presented at the annual meeting of the American Educational Research Association, Toronto, Canada.

Woody, G. E., McLellan, A. T., Luborsky, L., & O'Brien, C. P. (1985). Sociopathy and psychotherapy outcome. *Archives of General Psychiatry, 42,* 1081–1086.

Young, J. E. (1983, August). *Borderline personality: Cognitive theory and treatment.* Paper presented at the annual meeting of the American Psychological Association, Anaheim, CA.

Young, J. (1987). *Schema-focused cognitive therapy for personality disorders.* Unpublished manuscript.

Young, J. (1990). *Cognitive therapy for personality disorders: A schema-focused approach.* Sarasota, FL: Professional Resource Exchange.

Young, J. E., & Lindemann, M. D. (1992). An integrative schema-focused model for personality disorders. *Journal of Cognitive Psychotherapy: An International Quarterly, 6,* 11–24.

Young, J., & Swift, W. (1988). Schema-focused cognitive therapy for personality disorders: Part I. *International Cognitive Therapy Newsletter, 4,* 5, 13–14.

3

A Psychoanalytic Theory of Personality Disorders

OTTO F. KERNBERG

CATEGORICAL VERSUS DIMENSIONAL MODELS OF PERSONALITY DISORDERS

Why is it important to attempt to formulate a psychoanalytic view of the etiology, structure, and mutual relations of the personality disorders? First, it is necessary to do so because of advances in the psychoanalytic understanding of particular types of personality disorders, their diagnosis, treatment, and prognosis, and their high prevalence. Second, it is necessary because major controversies continue in psychological and psychiatric research dealing with these disorders, which an exploration from a psychoanalytic viewpoint might possibly help to resolve. I am referring to such controversies as (1) whether categorical or dimensional criteria should be used for classifying these disorders, (2) the relative influence of genetic and constitutional, psychodynamic, and psychosocial determinants of these disorders, and, most importantly, (3) the relationship between descriptive or surface behavior and underlying biological and psychological structures.

A major problem is the understanding of the psychopathology of these disorders, that is, how the various behavioral characteristics of any particular personality disorder relate to each other and to their particular predisposing and causative factors. Empirical researchers studying specific personality disorders (such as the borderline personality disorder, the narcissistic personality disorder, the antisocial personality disorder) have attempted to pinpoint their etiological factors, but they have repeatedly found that multiple factors appear to combine in the background of any particular personality disorder, without a clear answer to how these factors relate to each other in codetermining a specific type of psychopathology (Marziali, 1992; Paris, 1994; Steinberg, Trestman, & Siever, 1994; Stone, 1993a, 1993b).

Researchers proceeding with a dimensional model usually carry out complex factor analyses of a great number of behavioral traits, leading to specific factors or a few overriding behavioral characteristics that, in different combinations, would seem to characterize the particular personality disorders described by clinicians (Benjamin, 1992, 1993; Costa & Widiger, 1994; Widiger & Frances 1994; Widiger, Trull, Clarkin, Sanderson & Costa, 1994). This approach links particular behaviors and lends itself to establishing a general theory, which in turn integrates the major dimensions arrived at by statistical analyses. These dimensions, however, tend to have rather general relations to any particular personality disorder and, so far, seem to have been of little use for clinical purposes. (One notable exception may prove to be Benjamin's [1992, 1993] "structural analysis of social behavior [SASB]" a model strongly influenced by contemporary psychoanalytic thinking.)

A currently well-known dimensional model, the five-factor model, has synthesized numerous factor analyses into the proposal that Neuroticism, Extroversion, Openness, Agreeableness, and Conscientiousness constitute basic factors that may describe all "officially" accepted personality disorders in DSM-IV (American Psychiatric Association, 1994; Costa & Widiger, 1994; Widiger et al., 1994). The problem, I believe, is whether these are really fundamental determinants of the organization of the normal personality or even of the personality disorders. An "equalization" of these character traits seems strange when applied to the subtleties of the clinical features of specific personality constellations. To develop factorial profiles for each personality disorder on the basis of those five factors has an eerie quality of unreality for the experienced clinician.

Those researchers who are inclined to maintain a categorical approach to personality disorders, usually clinical psychiatrists motivated to find specific disease entities, tend to proceed differently. They study the clinically prevalent constellations of pathological personality traits, carry out empirical research regarding the validity and reliability of the corresponding clinical diagnoses, attempt to achieve a clear differentiation between personality disorders, and, of course, keep in mind the clinical relevance of their approaches (Akhtar, 1992; Stone, 1993a). This approach, pursued in DSM-III (American Psychiatric Association, 1980) and DSM-IV, has helped to clarify—or at least to permit the clinical psychiatrist to become better acquainted with—some frequently seen personality disorders. The approach has been plagued, however, by the high degree of comorbidity of the severe types of personality disorders, and by the unfortunate politicalization of decision making, by committee, of what personality disorders to include and exclude in the official DSM system, and under what labels (Jonas & Pope, 1992; Kernberg, 1992; Oldham, 1994). For this reason, a common personality disorder such as the hysterical personality disorder has remained excluded, whereas the depressive–masochistic personality disorder, excluded under DSM-III, has now reemerged under the heading "depressive personality disorder" in the appendix of DSM-IV, but shorn of its masochistic component (previously "tolerated" in DSM-III-R (American Psychiatric Association, 1987) under the then still politically correct title of "self-defeating" personality disorder) (Kernberg, 1992).

A major problem of both categorical and dimensional classification systems, in my view, has been the tendency to anchor the empirical research too closely to surface behavior, behavior that may serve very different functions according to the underlying personality structures. Thus, for example, what is seen as social timidity, social phobia, or inhibition, and may contribute to a diagnosis of either a schizoid or an avoidant personality, may in fact reflect the cautiousness of a deeply paranoid individual, or the fear of exposure of a narcissistically grandiose individual, or a reaction formation against exhibitionistic tendencies in a hysterical individual. A related problem is the necessary dependency, in large-scale research efforts, on standardized inquiries or questionnaires that tend to be responded to, in part, according to the social values of particular personality traits: for example, to be excessively conscientious has a more desirable value than being irresponsible, to be generous a higher value than being envious, and so forth. Our very diagnostic instruments need much further elaboration and may even have contributed to some of our problems.

It is far from my intention to suggest that a psychoanalytic exploration will resolve all existing problems. I cannot at this point, present a satisfactory, integrated psychoanalytic model of classification of personality disorders. For psychoanalytically oriented research has also been limited by the difficulty in assessing abnormal personality traits outside the clinical situation, the enormous difficulties inherent in carrying out research on the psychoanalytic situation itself, and the controversies that have developed, within contemporary psychoanalysis, regarding the treatment approaches to some personality disorders, such as, for example, the borderline and the narcissistic personalities.

A psychoanalytic study of patients with personality disorders undergoing psychoanalytic treatment, however, allows us to observe the relationships (1) among the patient's pathological personality traits, (2) between surface behavior and underlying psychic structure, (3) between various constellations of pathological behavior patterns as they change in the course of treatment, (4) between motivation of behavior and psychic structure, and (5) between changes in the patient's behavior and shifts in dominant transference patterns.

In fact, the possibility of jointly evaluating a patient's motivation, intrapsychic structure, and therapeutic change provides important information regarding the origins, functions, and mechanisms of these therapeutic changes in patients with personality disorders.

In addition, the observation of infant–caregiver interactions from a psychoanalytic perspective, the study of the effects of early trauma on the development of psychological functioning from such a perspective, and efforts to link these observations with the study of early development from behavioral and biological perspectives should mutually enrich these fields. Perhaps even more importantly, the psychoanalytic approach to personality disorders permits, I believe, the development of particular techniques to deal with the specific transferences of these disorders and obtain significant characterological change as a consequence of shifts in transference patterns, a clinical observation that still needs to be grounded in empirical research. In this connection, some of the subtle aspects of the differential diagnosis of the personality disorders facilitated by a psychoanalytic approach permit us to establish prognostic indicators, such as the differentiation between the narcissistic personality disorder, the malignant narcissism syndrome, and the antisocial personality proper (Bursten, 1989; Hare, 1986; Kernberg, 1989; Stone, 1990).

TEMPERAMENT, CHARACTER, AND THE STRUCTURE OF THE NORMAL PERSONALITY

To begin, I shall refer to temperament and character as crucial aspects of personality. Temperament refers to the constitutionally given and largely genetically determined, inborn disposition to particular reactions to environmental stimuli, particularly to the intensity, rhythm, and thresholds of affective responses. I consider affective responses, particularly under conditions of peak affect states, crucial determinants of the organization of the personality. Inborn thresholds regarding the activation of both positive, pleasurable, rewarding, and negative, painful, aggressive affects represent, I believe, the most important bridge between biological and psychological determinants of the personality (Kernberg, 1994). Temperament also includes inborn dispositions to cognitive organization and to motor behavior, such as, for example, the hormonal-, particularly testosterone-derived differences in cognitive functions and aspects of gender role identity that differentiate male and female behavior patterns. Regarding the etiology of personality disorders, however, the affective aspects of temperament appear as of fundamental importance.

Cloninger (Cloninger, Svrakic, & Przybeck, 1993) related particular neurochemical systems to temperamental dispositions he called "novelty seeking," "harm avoidance," "reward dependence," and "persistence," offering one such avenue. I should add, however, that I question Cloninger's direct translations of such dispositions into the specific types of personality disorders of the DSM-IV classification system. Torgersen, on the basis of his twin studies of genetic and environmental influences on the development of personality disorders (1985, 1994), found genetic influences significant only for the schizotypal personality disorder; for practical purposes, they are significantly related to normal personality characteristics but have very little relationship with specific personality disorders.

In addition to temperament, character is another major component of personality. Character refers to the particular dynamic organization of behavior patterns of each individual that reflect the overall degree and level of organization of such patterns. While academic psychology differentiates character from personality, the clinically relevant terminology of character pathology, character neurosis, and neurotic character refer to the same conditions, also referred to as personality trait and personality pattern disturbances in earlier DSM classifications, and to the personality disorders in DSM-III and DSM-IV. From a psychoanalytic perspective, I propose that character refers to the behavioral manifestations of ego identity, while the subjective aspects of ego identity, that is, the integration of the self concept and of the concept of significant others are the intrapsychic structures that determine the dynamic organization of character. Character also includes all the behavioral aspects of what in psychoanalytic terminology is called ego functions and ego structures.

From a psychoanalytic viewpoint, the personality is codetermined by temperament and character, but also by an additional intrapsychic structure, the superego. The integration of value systems, the moral and ethical dimension of the personality—from a psychoanalytic viewpoint, the integration of the various layers of the superego—are an important component of the total personality. Personality itself, then, may be considered the dynamic integration of all behavior patterns derived from temperament, character, and internalized value systems (Kernberg, 1976, 1980). In addition, the dynamic unconscious or the id constitutes the dominant, and potentially conflictive, motivational system of the personality. The extent to which sublimatory integration of id impulses into ego and superego functions has taken place reflects the normally adaptive potential of the personality.

I shall now present my proposed psychoanalytic model for the classification of personality disorders, incorporating significant contributions to this particular approach from other psychoanalytic researchers and theoreticians such as Salman Akhtar (1989, 1992), Rainer Krause (Krause, 1988; Krause & Lutolf, 1988), Michael Stone (1980, 1990, 1993a), and Vamik Volkan (1976, 1987). The normal personality is characterized, first of all, by an integrated concept of the self and an integrated concept of significant others. These structural characteristics, jointly called ego identity (Erikson, 1956; Jacobson, 1964) are reflected in an internal sense and an external appearance of self-coherence and are a fundamental precondition for normal self-esteem, self-enjoyment, and zest for life. An integrated view of one's self assures the capacity for a realization of one's desires, capacities, and long-range commitments. An integrated view of significant others guarantees the capacity for an appropriate evaluation of others, empathy, and an emotional investment in others that implies a capacity for mature dependency while maintaining a consistent sense of autonomy as well.

A second structural characteristic of the normal personality, largely derived from and an expression of ego identity, is the presence of ego strength, particularly reflected in a broad spectrum of affect dispositions, capacity for affect and impulse control, and the capacity for sublimation in work and values (also contributed to importantly by superego integration). Consistency, persistence, and creativity in work as well as in interpersonal relations are also largely derived from normal ego identity, as are the capacity for trust, reciprocity, and commitment to others, also importantly codetermined by superego functions (Kernberg, 1975).

A third aspect of the normal personality is an integrated and mature superego, representing an internalization of value systems that is stable, depersonificated, abstract, and individualized, and not excessively dependent on unconscious infantile prohibitions. Such a superego structure is reflected in a sense of personal responsibility, a capacity for realistic self-criticism, integrity as well as flexibility in dealing with the ethical aspects of decision making, a commitment to standards, values, and ideals, as well as the contribution to such aforementioned ego functions as reciprocity, trust, and investment in depth.

A fourth aspect of the normal personality is an appropriate and satisfactory management of libidinal and aggressive impulses. It involves the capacity for a full expression of sensual and sexual needs integrated with tenderness and emotional commitment to a loved other, and a normal degree of idealization of the other and the relationship. Here, clearly, a freedom of sexual expression is integrated with ego identity and the ego ideal. In regard to aggression, a normal personality structure includes capacity for sublimation in the form of self-assertion, for withstanding attacks without excessive reaction, a capacity to react protectively, and to avoid turning aggression against the self. Again, ego and superego functions contribute to such an equilibrium.

Underlying these aspects of the normal personality—recently summarized in a set of scales of psychological capacities by Wallerstein (1991)—are significant structural and dynamic preconditions. The structural preconditions refer to the developmental processes by which the earliest internalization of interactions with significant others—that is, of object relations—leads to the completion of a series of successive steps that transform these internalized object relations into the normal ego identity I have described. I am referring here to the sequence of internalization of object relations into the early ego that start with the symbiotic phase described by Mahler (Mahler & Furer, 1968; Mahler, Pine, & Bergman, 1975)—in my view, the internalization of fused self- and object representations under the dominance of a positive or negative peak affect state that leads to "all-good" and "all-bad" fused self and object representations. Such states of symbiotic fusion alternate with other states of internalization of differentiated self and object representations under conditions of low affect activation, that will provide ordinary internalized models of interaction between self and others, while the initially fused internalized object relations under conditions of peak affect states will lead to the basic structures of the dynamic unconscious, the id. My definition of the id characterizes it as the sum total of repressed, dissociated and projected, consciously unacceptable, internalized object relations under conditions of peak affect states. Libido and aggression are the hierarchically supraordinate motivational systems representing the integration of, respectively, positive or rewarding and negative or aversive peak affect states (Kernberg, 1992, 1994).

At a second stage of ego development, again under conditions of peak affect states, a gradual differentiation occurs between self and object representations under conditions of all-good and all-bad interactions, which lead to internal units constituted by self-representation–object representation–dominant affect. In my view, these units constitute the basic structures of the original ego–id matrix that characterizes the stage of separation–individuation described by Mahler.

Eventually, under normal conditions, in a third stage of development, all-good and all-bad representations of self are integrated into an integrated concept of the self that tolerates a realistic view of self as potentially imbued with both loving and hating impulses. A parallel integration occurs of representations of significant others into combined all-good/all-bad representations of each of the important persons in the child's life, mostly parental figures but also siblings. These developments determine the capacity for experiencing integrated, ambivalent relationships with others, in contrast to splitting object relationships into idealized and persecutory ones. This marks the stage of object constancy or of total internalized object relations in contrast to the earlier stage of separation–individuation in which mutually split-off, part object relations dominated psychic experience. Normal ego identity, as defined, constitutes the core of the integrated ego, now differentiated by repressive barriers from both superego and id.

This psychoanalytic model thus includes a developmental series of consecutive psychic structures. It starts with the parallel development of realistic object relations under low affect activation and symbiotic object relations under conditions of peak affect activation. These are followed by the phase of separation–individuation, which is characterized by continuous growth of realistic relations under low affective conditions but significant splitting operations and related defensive mechanisms under activation of intense affect states. This finally leads to the phase of object constancy in which a more realistic integrated concept of self and of significant others evolves in the context of ego identity, and, at the same time, repression eliminates from consciousness the more extreme manifestations of sexual and aggressive impulses that can no longer be tolerated under the effect of the integration of the normal superego.

This structural and developmental model also conceives of the superego as constituted by successive layers of internalized self and object representations (Jacobson, 1964; Kernberg, 1984). A first layer of all-bad, ''persecutory'' internalized object relations reflects a demanding and prohibitive, primitive morality as experienced by the child when environmental demands and prohibitions run against the expression of aggressive, dependent, and sexual impulses. A second layer of superego precursors is constituted by the ideal representations of self and others reflecting early childhood ideals that promise the assurance of love and dependency if the child lives up to them. The mutual toning down of the earliest, persecutory level and the later idealizing level of superego functions and the corresponding decrease in the tendency to reproject these superego precursors then brings about the capacity for internalizing more realistic, toned down, demands and prohibitions from the parental figures, leading to the third layer of the superego corresponding to the ego's stage of object constancy. The integrative processes of the ego facilitate, in fact, this parallel development of the superego. An integrated superego, as we have seen, in turn strengthens the capacity for object relatedness as well as autonomy: An internalized value system makes the individual less dependent on external confirmation or behavior control, while it facilitates a deeper commitment to relationships with others. In short, autonomy and independence and a capacity for mature dependence go hand in hand.

Having thus summarized my model of the development of the psychic apparatus that derives the structures of id, ego, and superego from successive levels of internalization, differentiation, and integration of object relations, I now turn to the dynamic aspect of this development, the motivational factors underlying these structuralized developments, in other words, an ego psychology object relations theory of drives.

THE MOTIVATIONAL ASPECTS OF PERSONALITY ORGANIZATION: AFFECTS AND DRIVES

As I mentioned earlier, I consider the drives of libido and aggression as the hierarchically supraordinate integration of corresponding pleasurable and rewarding, and painful and aversive affect states (Kernberg, 1992, 1994). Affects are instinctive components of human behavior, that is, inborn dispositions common to all individuals of the human species. They emerge in the early stages of development and are gradually organized into drives as they are activated as part of early object relations. Gratifying, rewarding, pleasurable affects are integrated as libido as an overarching drive, and painful, aversive, negative affects are integrated as aggression as an overarching drive. Affects as inborn, constitutionally and genetically determined modes of reaction are triggered first by physiological and bodily experiences and then gradually in the context of the development of object relations.

Rage represents the core affect of aggression as a drive, and the vicissitudes of rage explain, in my view, the origins of hatred and envy—the dominant affects of severe personality disorders—as well as of normal anger and irritability. Similarly, the affect of sexual excitement constitutes the core affect of libido. Sexual excitement slowly and gradually crystallizes out of the primitive affect of elation. The early sensual responses to intimate bodily contact dominate the development of libido in parallel to that of aggression.

Krause (1988) has proposed that affects constitute a phylogeneti-cally recent biological system evolved in mammals as a way for the infant animal to signal emergency needs to its mother, corresponding to a parallel inborn capacity of the mother to read and respond to the infant's affective signals, thus protecting the early development of the dependent infant mammal. This instinctive system reaches increasing complexity and dominance in controlling the social behavior of higher mammals, particularly primates.

Affectively driven development of object relations—in other words, real and fantasied interpersonal interactions that are internalized as a complex world of self and object representations in the context of affective interactions—I propose, constitute the determinants of un-conscious mental life and of the structure of the psychic apparatus. Affects, in short, are both the building blocks of the drives and the signals of the activation of drives in the context of the activation of a particular internalized object relation, as typically expressed in the transference developments during psychoanalysis and psychoanalytic psychotherapy.

In contrast to other contemporary psychoanalytic object relations theories, I have argued that we still need a theory of drives, because a theory of motivation based on affects alone would unnecessarily com-plicate the analysis of the transference relationship to the dominant objects of infancy and childhood. There are multiple positive and nega-tive affects expressed toward the same significant others, and an af-fect theory placing motives on affects only would fail to take into consideration the developmental lines of libidinal and aggressive striv-ings organizing the history of past internalized object relations that we have been able to clarify in the context of psychoanalytic exploration.

I believe this theory of motivation permits us to account for the concept of inborn dispositions to excessive or inadequate affect acti-vation, thereby doing justice to the genetic and constitutional varia-tions of intensity of drives reflected, for example, in the intensity, rhythm, and thresholds of affect activation commonly designated as temperament. This theory equally permits us to incorporate the effects of physical pain, psychic trauma, and severe disturbances in early ob-ject relations as contributing to intensifying aggression as a drive by triggering intense negative affects. In short, I believe the theory does justice to Freud's (1915) statement that drives occupy an intermediate realm between the physical and the psychic realms.

Recent studies of alteration in neurotransmitter systems in severe personality disorders, particularly in the borderline personality disor-der, although still tentative and open to varying interpretations, point to the possibility that neurotransmitters are related to specific distor-tions in affect activation (Stone, 1993a, 1993b). Abnormalities in the adrenergic and cholinergic systems, for example, may be related to general affective instability; deficits in the dopaminergic system may be related to a disposition toward transient psychotic symptoms in borderline patients; impulsive, aggressive, self-destructive behavior may be facilitated by a lowered function of the serotonergic system (deVegvar, Siever, & Trestman, 1994; Steinberg et al., 1994; Stone, 1993a, 1993b; van Reekum, Links, & Fedorov, 1994; Yehuda, Southwick, Penn, & Giller, 1994). In general, genetic dispositions to temperamental variations in affect activation would seem to be mediated by alterations in neurotransmitter systems, providing a potential link between the biological determinants of affective response and the psychological triggers of specific affects.

These aspects of inborn dispositions to the activation of aggression mediated by the activation of aggressive affect states are complementary to the now well-established findings that structured aggressive behavior in infants may derive from early, severe, chronic physical pain, and that habitual aggressive teasing interactions with mother are followed by similar behaviors of infants, as we know from the work of Galenson (1986) and Fraiberg (1983). Grossman's convincing arguments (1986, 1991) in favor of the direct transformation of chronic intense pain into aggression provide a theoretical context for the earlier observations of the battered-child syndrome. The impressive findings of the prevalence of physical and sexual abuse in the history of borderline patients confirmed by investigators both here and abroad (Marziali, 1992; Perry & Herman, 1993; van der Kolk, Hostetler, Herron, & Fisler, 1994) provide additional evidence of the influence of trauma on the development of severe manifestations of aggression.

I am stressing the importance of this model for our understanding of the pathology of aggression because the exploration of severe personality disorders consistently finds the presence of pathological aggression predominating. One key dynamic of the normal personality is the dominance of libidinal strivings over aggressive ones. Drive neutralization, according to my formulation, implies the integration of libidinally and aggressively invested, originally split, idealized and persecutory internalized object relations, a process that leads from the state of separation–individuation to that of object constancy, and culminates in integrated concepts of the self and of significant others and the integration of derivative affect states from the aggressive and libidinal series into the toned-down, discrete, elaborated, and complex affect disposition of the phase of object constancy.

While a central motivational aspect of severe personality disorders is the development of inordinate aggression and the related psychopathology of aggressive affect expression, the dominant pathology of the less severe personality disorders, which, in contrast to border-line personality organization (the severe personality disorders), I have called "neurotic personality organization" (Kernberg, 1975, 1976, 1980, 1984), is the pathology of libido or of sexuality. This field includes particularly the hysterical, the obsessive–compulsive, and the depressive-masochistic personalities, although it is most evident in the hysterical personality disorder (Kernberg, 1984). Although these three are all frequent personality disorders in outpatient practice, only the obsessive-compulsive personality is included in DSM-IV's (American Psychiatric Association, 1994) main list. The depressive–masochistic personality disorder is partly included in the DSM-IV appendix (American Psychiatric Association, 1994), shorn of its masochistic components (these were included in the appendix of DSM-III [American Psychiatric Association, 1980]). The hysterical personality was included in DSM-II (American Psychiatric Association, 1968) (and, one hopes, will be rediscovered in DSM-V—institutional politics permitting). In these disorders, in the context of the achievement of object constancy, an integrated superego, a well-developed ego identity, and an advanced level of defensive operations centering around repression, the typical pathology of sexual inhibition, oedipalization of object relations, and acting out of unconscious guilt over infantile sexual impulses dominate the pathological personality traits. In contrast, sexuality is usually "coopted" by aggression in borderline personality organization, that is, sexual behavior and interaction are intimately condensed with aggressive aims, which severely limits or distorts sexual intimacy, love relations, and fosters the abnormal development of paraphilias with their heightened condensation of sexual and aggressive aims.

An early classification of personality disorders stemming from Freud (1908, 1931) and Abraham (1920, 1921–1925) described oral, anal, and genital characters, a classification that in practice has gradually been abandoned because psychoanalytic exploration found that severe personality disorders present pathological condensations of conflicts from all of these stages. The classification proposed by Freud and Abraham seems of value when limited to the less severe constellations of these disorders (Kernberg, 1976). At the same time, however, their description of the relationship among oral conflicts, pathological dependency, a tendency toward depression, and self-directed aggression is eminently relevant for personality disorders along the entire developmental spectrum and can be observed most specifically in the depressive–masochistic personality (Kernberg, 1992). This personality disorder, while reflecting an advanced level of neurotic personality organization, transports, so to speak, an oral constellation of conflicts in a relatively unmodified fashion into the oedipal realm. Similarly, anal conflicts are most clearly observable in the obsessive–compulsive personality disorder, that, in parallel to the depressive–masochistic one, transports anal conflicts into the context of the oedipal conflicts of object constancy. Yet, anal conflicts are also relevant along the entire spectrum of personality disorders.

Fenichel (1945) attempted a psychoanalytic classification of character constellations into sublimatory and reactive types, the reactive types including avoidance (phobias) and opposition (reaction formations). He then went on to classify personality disorders or character pathology into pathological behavior toward the id (oral, anal, and phallic conflicts), toward the superego (moral masochism, psychopathy, acting out), and toward external objects (pathological inhibitions, pathological jealousy, pseudohypersexuality). This classification also was abandoned in practice, mainly because it became evident that all character pathology presents simultaneously pathological behavior toward these psychic structures.

A PSYCHOANALYTIC MODEL OF NOSOLOGY

My own classification of personality disorders centers on the dimension of severity (Kernberg, 1976). Severity ranges from (1) psychotic personality organization, (2) borderline personality organization, to (3) neurotic personality organization (see Figure 3.1).

Psychotic Personality Organization

"Psychotic personality organization" is characterized by lack of integration of the concept of self and significant others, that is, identity diffusion, a predominance of primitive defensive operations centering around splitting and loss of reality testing. The defensive operations of splitting and its derivatives (projective identification, denial, primitive idealization, omnipotence, omnipotent control, devaluation) have as a basic function to maintain separate the idealized and persecutory internalized object relations derived from the early developmental phases predating object constancy—that is, when aggressively determined internalizations strongly dominate the internal world of object relations, in order to prevent the overwhelming control or destruction of ideal object relations by aggressively infiltrated ones. This primitive constellation of defensive operations centering around splitting thus attempts to protect the capacity to depend on good objects and escape from terrifying aggression. This basic function of the primitive constellation of defensive operations actually dominates most clearly

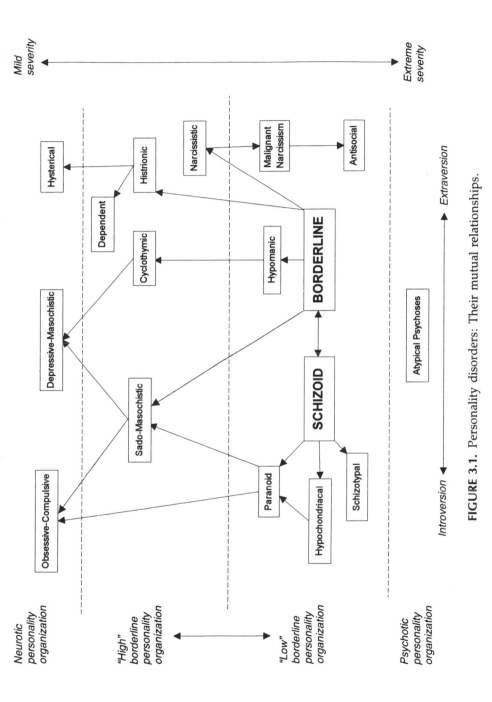

FIGURE 3.1. Personality disorders: Their mutual relationships.

in the borderline personality organization, while an additional, most primitve function of these mechanisms in the case of psychotic personality organization is to compensate for the loss of reality testing in these patients.

Reality testing refers to the capacity to differentiate self from nonself, intrapsychic from external stimuli, and to maintain empathy with ordinary social criteria of reality, all of which are typically lost in the psychoses and manifested particularly in hallucinations and delusions (Kernberg, 1976, 1984). The loss of reality testing reflects the lack of differentiation between self and object representations under conditions of peak affect states, that is, a structural persistence of the symbiotic stage of development, its pathological hypertrophy, so to speak. The primitive defenses centering aound splitting attempt to protect these patients from the chaos in all object relations derived from their loss of ego boundaries in intense relationships with others. All patients with psychotic personality organization really represent atypical forms of psychosis. Therefore, strictly speaking, psychotic personality organization represents an exclusion criterion for the personality disorders in a clinical sense.

Borderline Personality Organization

''Borderline personality organization'' is also characterized by identity diffusion and the same predominance of primitive defensive operations centering on splitting, but it is distinguished by the presence of good reality testing, reflecting the differentiation between self and object representations in the idealized and persecutory sector, characteristic of the separation–individuation phase (Kernberg, 1975). Actually, this category includes all the severe personality disorders in clinical practice. Typical personality disorders included here are the borderline personality disorder, the schizoid and schizotypal personality disorders, the paranoid personality disorder, the hypomanic personality disorder, hypochondriasis (a syndrome that has many characteristics of a personality disorder proper), the narcissistic personality disorder (including the malignant narcissism syndrome [Kernberg, 1992]), and the antisocial personality disorder.

All these patients present identity diffusion, the manifestations of primitive defensive operations, and varying degrees of superego deterioration (antisocial behavior). A particular group of patients typically suffer from significant disorganization of the superego, namely, the narcissistic personality disorder, the malignant narcissism syndrome, and the antisocial personality disorder.

All the personality disorders within the borderline spectrum present, because of identity diffusion, severe distortions in their interpersonal relations—particularly problems in intimate relations with others, lack of consistent goals in terms of commitment to work or profession, uncertainty and lack of direction in their lives in many areas, and varying degrees of pathology in their sexual life. They often present an incapacity to integrate tenderness and sexual feelings, and they may show a chaotic sexual life with multiple polymorphous perverse infantile tendencies. The most severe cases, however, may present with a generalized inhibition of all sexual responses as a consequence of a lack of sufficient activation of sensuous responses in the early relation with the caregiver, an overwhelming predominance of aggression that interferes with sensuality (rather than even recruiting it for aggressive aims). All these patients also evince nonspecific manifestations of ego weakness, that is, lack of anxiety tolerance, of impulse control, and of sublimatory functioning in terms of an incapacity for consistency, persistence, and creativity in work.

A particular group of personality disorders present the characteristics of borderline personality organization, but these patients are able to maintain more satisfactory social adaptation, and are usually more effective in obtaining some degree of intimacy in object relations and in integrating sexual and tender impulses. Thus, in spite of presenting identity diffusion, they also evince sufficient nonconflictual development of some ego functions, superego integration, and a benign cycle of intimate involvements, capacity for dependency gratification, and a better adaptation to work that make for significant quantitative differences. They constitute what might be called a "higher level" of borderline personality organization or an intermediate level of personality disorder. This group includes the cyclothymic personality, the sadomasochistic personality, the infantile or histrionic personality, and the dependent personalities, as well as some better-functioning narcissistic personality disorders.

Neurotic Personality Organization

The next level of personality disorder, namely, "neurotic personality organization," is characterized by normal ego identity and the related capacity for object relations in depth, ego strength reflected in anxiety tolerance, impulse control, sublimatory functioning, effectiveness and creativity in work, and a capacity for sexual love and emotional intimacy disrupted only by unconscious guilt feelings reflected in specific pathological patterns of interaction in relation to sexual intimacy. This group includes the hysterical personality, the depressive–masochistic personality, the obsessive personality, and many so-called "avoidant personality disorders," in other words, the "phobic character" of psy-choanalytic literature (which, in my view, remains a problematic enti-ty). As mentioned before, significant social inhibition or phobias may be found in several different types of personality disorder, and the un-derlying hysterical character structure typical for the "phobic person-ality" as described in early psychoanalytic literature only applies to some cases.

DEVELOPMENTAL, STRUCTURAL, AND MOTIVATIONAL CONTINUITIES

Having thus classified personality disorders in terms of their severity, let us now examine particular continuities within this field that estab-lish a psychopathologically linked network, one might say, of related personality disorders (see Figure 3.1). The borderline personality dis-order and the schizoid personality disorder may be described as the simplest form of personality disorders, reflecting a fixation at the level of separation–individuation, with the "purest" expression of the gener-al characteristics of borderline personality organization. Fairbairn (1954), in fact, described the schizoid personality as the prototype of all per-sonality disorders and provided an understanding of the psy-chodynamics of these patients unsurpassed to this day. He described the splitting operations separating "good" and "bad" internalized ob-ject relations, the self and object representation dyads of the split-off object relations, the consequent impoverishment of interpersonal re-lations, and their replacement by a defensive hypertrophy of fantasy life. The borderline personality disorder presents similar dynamic characteristics—but with an expression of this pathology in impulsive interactions in the interpersonal field in contrast to the expression of the pathology in the patient's fantasy life and social withdrawal in the schizoid personality (Akhtar, 1992; Stone, 1994).

In the course of psychoanalytic exploration, the apparent lack of affect display of the schizoid personality turns out to reflect severe split-ting operations, to the extent of fragmentation of the patients' affec-tive experience, which "empties out" their interpersonal life, while their internalized object relations have split off characteristics similar to those of the typical borderline patient (Kernberg, 1975). In contrast, the borderline personality disorder patient's intrapsychic life is enact-ed in his interpersonal patterns, very often replacing any self-awareness by means of driven, repetitive behavior patterns. The borderline pa-tient thus evinces the typical triad of identity diffusion, primitivity of affect display (affect storms), and lack of impulse control. It may well be that the descriptive differences between the schizoid and border-line disorders reflect a temperamental dimension, namely, that of ex-troversion and introversion, one of the important temperamental factors that emerges under different names in various models of clas-sification.

The schizotypal personality represents the most severe form of schi-zoid personality disorder, while the paranoid personality reflects an increase of aggression in comparison to the schizoid personality dis-order, with a dominance of projective mechanisms and a defensive self idealization related to the efforts to control an external world of per-secutory figures. If splitting per se dominates in the borderline and schizoid personality disorders, projective identification dominates in the paranoid personality disorder. The hypochondriacal syndrome reflects a projection of persecutory objects into the interior of the body; hypochondriacal personalities usually also show strong paranoid and schizoid characteristics.

The borderline personality proper presents an intensity of affect activation and lack of affect control that also suggests the presence of a temperamental factor; but the integration of aggressive and libidinal affects obtained in the course of treatment often brings about a remark-able toning down and modulation of affect response. The increase of impulse control and affect tolerance resulting during treatment illus-trates that splitting mechanisms are central in that pathology (over-coming splitting, that is, integrating mutually split affects, leads to their integration, toning down, and maturation). The hypomanic personal-ity disorder, in contrast, appears to include a pathology of affect acti-vation that points to temperamental predisposition, which probably also holds true for its milder form, the cyclothymic personality.

Borderline personality disorders presenting intense aggression may evolve into the sadomasochistic personality disorder. If a disposition to strong sadomasochism becomes incorporated into or controlled by a relatively healthy superego structure (which also incorporates a depressive potential into a disposition to guiltladen responses) and ego identity is achieved, the conditions for a depressive–masochistic per-sonality disorder are also present. The depressive–masochistic person-ality may be considered the highest level of two developmental lines that go from the borderline personality through the sadomasochistic to the depressive–masochistic on the one hand, and from the hypo-manic through the cyclothymic personality disorders to the depres-sive–masochistic one, on the other. This entire area of personality dis-orders thus reflects the internalization of object relations under condi-tions of abnormal affective development or affect control.

When severe inborn disposition to aggressive reactions, early trau-

ma, severe pathology of early object relations, physical illness, and/or
sexual and physical abuse intensify the dominance of aggression in
the personality structure, a particular pathology of aggression may develop that includes, as we have already seen, the paranoid personality, hypochondriasis, sadomasochism and that may also characterize
a subgroup of the narcissistic personality disorder.

The narcissistic personality disorder is of particular interest because,
in contrast to the clear indication of identity diffusion of all other personality disorders included in borderline personality organization, in
the narcissistic personality, a lack of integration of the concept of significant others goes hand in hand with an integrated, but pathological, grandiose self. This pathological grandiose self replaces the
underlying lack of integration of a normal self (Akhtar, 1989; Plakun,
1989; Ronningstam & Gunderson, 1989). In the course of psychoanalytic treatment or psychoanalytic psychotherapy, we may observe the
dissolution of this pathological grandiose self and the reemergence of
the typical structure of identity diffusion of borderline personality organization before a new integration of normal ego identity can take
place.

In the narcissistic personality, the pathological grandiose self ab-
sorbs both real and idealized self and object representations into an
unrealistically idealized concept of self, with a parallel impoverishment
of idealized superego structures, a predominance of persecutory superego precursors, the reprojection of these persecutory superego
precursors (as a protection against excessive, pathological guilt), and
a consequent weakening of the later, more integrated superego functions (Kernberg, 1975, 1984, 1992). The narcissistic personality, therefore, often presents some degree of antisocial behavior.

When intense pathology of aggression dominates in a narcissistic
personality structure, the pathological grandiose self may become infiltrated by ego syntonic aggression, with the development of a gran-
diosity combined with ruthlessness, sadism, or hatred that translates
into the malignant narcissism syndrome, that is, a combination of narcissistic personality, antisocial behavior, ego syntonic aggression, and
paranoid tendencies. This syndrome, I have proposed, is intermediate between the narcissistic personality disorder and the antisocial personality disorder proper, in which a total absence or deterioration of
superego functioning has occurred (Kernberg, 1992). The antisocial personality disorder (Akhtar, 1992; Bursten, 1989; Hare, 1986; Kernberg,
1984) usually reveals, in psychoanalytic exploration, severe underlying paranoid trends, together with a total incapacity for any nonexploitive investment in significant others. The total absence of the
capacity for guilt feelings, of any concern for self and others, the in-

capacity to identify with any moral or ethical value in self or others, and an incapacity to project a dimension of personal future characterize this personality disorder, thus differentiating it from the less severe syndrome of malignant narcissism, in which some commitment to others and a capacity for authentic guilt feelings are still present. The extent to which nonexploitive object relations—the capacity for significant investment in others—are still present and the extent to which antisocial behaviors dominate are the most important prognostic indicators for any psychotherapeutic approach to the personality disorders (Kernberg, 1975; Stone, 1990).

At a higher level of development, the obsessive–compulsive personality may be conceived as one in which inordinate aggression has been neutralized by its absorption into a well-integrated, but excessively sadistic superego, leading to the perfectionism, self-doubts, and chronic need to control the environment as well as the self that are characteristic of this personality disorder. There are cases, however, where this neutralization of aggression is incomplete, the severity of aggression determines regressive features of this personality disorder, and transitional cases with mixed obsessive, paranoid, and schizoid features can be found that maintain a borderline personality organization in spite of the presence of significant obsessive–compulsive personality features.

While the infantile or histrionic personality disorder is a milder form of the borderline personality disorder and still within the borderline spectrum, the hysterical personality disorder represents a higher-level type of the infantile or histrionic personality disorder within the neurotic spectrum of personality organization. In the hysterical personality, the emotional lability, extroversion, dependent, and exhibitionistic traits of the histrionic personality are restricted to the sexual realm, while these patients are able to have normally deep, mature, committed, and differentiated object relations in other areas. In addition, in contrast to the sexual "freedom" of the typical infantile personality, the hysterical personality often presents a combination of pseudo-hypersexuality and sexual inhibition, with a particular differentiation of the relationships to men and women that contrasts with the nonspecific orientation toward both genders of the infantile or histrionic personality (Kernberg, 1992).

The depressive–masochistic personality disorder (Kernberg, 1992), the highest level outcome of the pathology of depressive affect as well as that of sadomasochism characteristic of a dominance of aggression in primitive object relations, presents not only a well-integrated superego (as in all other personalities with neurotic personality organization), but an extremely punitive superego. This superego predisposes the patient to self-defeating behavior and reflects an unconscious need to suffer as an expiation for guilt feelings or a precondition for sexual pleasure, a reflection of the oedipal dynamics characterizing this spectrum of personality disorders. The excessive dependency and easy sense of frustration of these patients go hand in hand with their "faulty metabolism" of aggression, where depression ensues when an aggressive response would have been appropriate, and an excessive aggressive response to the frustration of their dependency needs may rapidly turn into a renewed depressive response as a consequence of excessive guilt feelings.

FURTHER CONSIDERATIONS ON IMPLICATIONS OF THIS CLASSIFICATION

This classification combines a structural and developmental concept of the psychic apparatus based upon a theory of internalized object relations that permits classifying personality disorders according to the severity of the pathology, the extent to which the pathology is dominated by aggression, the extent to which pathological affective dispositions influence personality development, the effect of the development of a pathological grandiose self structure, and the potential influence of a temperamental disposition to extroversion/introversion. In a combined analysis of the vicissitudes of instinctual conflicts between love and aggression, and of the development of ego and superego structures, this classification permits us to differentiate as well as relate the different pathological personalities to each other.

This classification also illuminates the advantages of combining categorical and dimensional criteria. There are clearly developmental factors relating several personality disorders to each other, particularly along an axis of severity. Figure 3.1 summarizes the relationships among the various personality disorders outlined in what follows. Thus, a developmental line links the borderline, the hypomanic, the cyclothymic, and the depressive–masochistic personality disorders. Another developmental line links the borderline, the histrionic or infantile, the dependent, and the hysterical personality disorders. Still another developmental line links, in complex ways, the schizoid, schizotypal, paranoid, and hypochondriacal personality disorders, and, at a higher developmental level the obsessive–compulsive personality disorder. And finally, a developmental line links the antisocial personality, the malignant narcissism syndrome, and the narcissistic personality disorder (the latter, in turn, containing a broad spectrum of severity). Further relationships of all prevalent personality disorders are indicated in Figure 3.1.

In my view, the vicissitudes of internalized object relations and the development of affective responses emerge as basic components of a contemporary psychoanalytic approach to the personality disorders. I have already stressed why the concept of drives as supraordinate integration of the corresponding series of aggressive and libidinal affects is important in spelling out an overall developmental and structural model. At the same time, the developmental vicissitudes of internalized object relations permit us to deepen our understanding of these patients' affective responses.

Affects always include a cognitive component, a subjective experience of a highly pleasurable or unpleasurable nature, neurovegetative discharge phenomena, psychomotor activation, and, very crucially, a distinctive pattern of facial expression that, originally, serves a communicative function directed to the caregiver. The cognitive aspect of affective responses, in turn, always reflects the relationship between a self representation and an object representation, which facilitates the diagnosis of the activated object relationship in each affect state that emerges in the therapeutic relationship.

One crucial advantage of the proposed classification of personality disorders is that the underlying structural concepts permit an immediate translation of the patient's affect states into the object relationship activated in the transference and a "reading" of this transference in terms of the activation of a relationship that typically alternates in the projection of self and object representations. The more severe the patient's pathology, the easier the patient may project either his self representation or his object representation onto the therapist while enacting the reciprocal object or self representation, which helps to clarify, in the middle of intense affect activation, the nature of the relationship and permits, by gradual interpretation of these developments in the transference, an integration of the patient's previously split off representations of self and significant others. This conceptualization, therefore, has direct implications for the therapeutic approach to personality disorders. The final section of this study describes a psychoanalytic psychotherapy derived from this conceptual framework and developed by our research group on borderline personality organization (Kernberg, Selzer, Koenigsberg, Carr, & Appelbaum, 1989).

This classification also helps to clarify the vicissitudes of the development of the sexual and aggressive drives. From the initial response of rage as a basic affect develops the structured affect of hatred as the central affect state in severe personality disorders, and hatred, in turn, may take the forms of conscious or unconscious envy, or an inordinate need for revenge that will color the corresponding transference developments. Similarly, regarding the sexual response, the psychoanalytic understanding of the internalized object relations activated in sexual fantasy and experience facilitates the diagnosis and treatment of abnormal condensations of sexual excitement and hatred such as in the perversions or paraphilias, and the inhibitions of sexuality and restrictions in the sexual responsiveness derived from its absorption in the patient's conflicts around internalized object relations.

The unconscious identification of the patient with the role of victim and victimizer in cases of severe trauma, physical, and sexual abuse can also be better diagnosed, understood, and worked through in the transference and countertransference with patients suffering from these conditions in the light of the theory of internalized object relations that underlies this classification; and the understanding of the structural determinants of pathological narcissism makes it possible to resolve the apparent incapacity of narcissistic patients to develop differentiated transference reactions, in parallel to their severe distortions of object relations in general.

Psychoanalytic exploration has been central in providing us with present day knowledge about the characteristics of the personality disorders: the hysterical personality, the obsessive–compulsive personality, the narcissistic personality, the borderline personality, and the schizoid personality have received their most detailed and sensitive descriptions by contributors within the psychoanalytic field. At this point, in addition to the ongoing contributions to further diagnostic refinements and, particularly, therapeutic approaches to the personality disorders, psychoanalysis has an important task in exploring the relationship between psychoanalytic formulations and the findings within the related fields of developmental psychology, clinical psychiatry, affect theory, and neurobiology in order to link its findings with those stemming from these disciplines.

In what follows, I present an overview of the application of my ego-psychology–object relations theory to the psychoanalysis and psychoanalytic psychotherapy of the personality disorders.

PSYCHOANALYSIS AND PSYCHOANALYTIC PSYCHOTHERAPY OF PERSONALITY DISORDERS

A General Therapeutic Frame

The analysis of the transference is a central concern in my general technical approach. Transference analysis consists in analyzing the reactivations in the here-and-now of past internalized object relations. This process constitutes, at the same time, the analysis of the component structures of ego, superego, and id and their intra- and interstructural conflicts. I conceive of internalized object relations as reflecting not actual object relations from the past but, rather, a combination of realistic and fantasied—and often highly distorted—internalizations of such past object relations and defenses against them under the effects of instinctual drive derivatives. In other words, I see a dynamic tension between the here-and-now, which reflects intrapsychic structure, and the there-and-then unconscious psychogenetic determinants derived from the patient's past developmental history.

The basic contribution of object relations theory to the analysis of the transference is to expand the frame of reference within which transference manifestations are explored, so that the increasing complexities of transference regression in patients with deep levels of psychopathology may be understood and interpreted. Transference interpretation differs according to the nature of the patient's psychopathology. In practice, the transference of patients with a neurotic personality organization can be understood as the unconscious repetition in the here-and-now of pathogenic relations from the past—more concretely, the enactment of an aspect of the patient's unconscious infantile self in relating to (also unconscious) infantile representations of the parental objects.

Patients with neurotic personality organization present well-integrated superego, ego, and id structures. Within the psychoanalytic situation, the analysis of resistances brings about the activation in the transference, first, of relatively global characteristics of these structures and, later, of the internalized object relations of which these are composed. The analysis of drive derivatives occurs in the context of the analysis of the relation of the patient's infantile self to significant parental objects as projected onto the therapist.

The fact that neurotic patients regress to a relatively integrated although repressed unconscious infantile self that relates to relatively integrated although unconscious representations of the parental objects makes such transferences fairly easy to understand and to interpret: it is the unconscious relationship to the parents of the past, including realistic and fantasied aspects of such relations and the defenses against them, that is activated in the transference. The unconscious aspect of the infantile self carries with it a concrete wish reflecting a drive derivative directed to such parental objects and a fantasied fear about the dangers involved in expressing this wish. What ego psychology–object relations theory stresses is that even in these comparatively "simple" transference enactments, the activation is always of basic dyadic units of a self representation and an object representation linked by a certain affect, and these units reflect either the defensive or the impulsive aspects of the conflict. More precisely, an unconscious fantasy that reflects an impulse–defense organization is typically activated first in the form of the object relation representing the defensive side of the conflict and only later by the object relation reflecting the impulsive side of the conflict (Kernberg, 1976, 1980, 1984).

What makes the analysis of internalized object relations in the transference of patients with severe personality disorders more complex (but also permits the clarification of such complexity) is the development of the defensive primitive dissociation or splitting of internalized object relations (Kernberg, 1975, 1992). In these patients, the tolerance of ambivalence characteristic of higher-level neurotic object relations is replaced by a defensive disintegration of the representations of self and objects into libidinally and aggressively invested part-object relations. The more realistic or more easily understandable past object relations of neurotic personality organization are replaced by highly unrealistic, sharply idealized, or sharply aggressivized or persecutory self and object representations that cannot immediately be traced to actual or fantasied relationships of the past.

What is activated here are either highly idealized part-object relations under the impact of intense, diffuse, overwhelming affect states of an ecstatic nature or equally intense, but painful and frightening, primitive affect states that signal the activation of aggressive or persecutory relations between self and object. We can recognize the nonintegrated nature of the internalized object relations by the patient's disposition to rapid reversals of the enactment of the role of self and object representations. Simultaneously, the patient may project a complementary self or object representation onto the therapist; this, together with the intensity of affect activation, leads to apparently chaotic transference developments. These rapid oscillations, as well as the sharp dissociation between loving and hating aspects of the relation to the same object, may be further complicated by defensive condensations of several object relations under the impact of the same primitive affect, so that, for example, combined father–mother images confusingly condense the aggressively perceived aspects of father and mother. Idealized or devalued aspects of the self similarly condense various levels of past experiences.

An object relations frame of reference permits the therapist to understand and organize what looks like complete chaos so that he/she can clarify the various condensed part-object relations in the transference, bringing about an integration of self and object representations, which leads to the more advanced neurotic type of transference.

The general principles of transference interpretation in the treatment of borderline personality organization include the following tasks

(Kernberg, 1984): (1) to diagnose the dominant object relation within the overall chaotic transference situation; (2) to clarify which is the self representation and which is the object representation of this internalized object relation and the dominant affect linking them; and (3) to interpretively connect this primitive dominant object relation with its split-off opposite.

The patient with borderline personality organization shows a predominance of preoedipal conflicts and psychic representations of preoedipal conflicts condensed with representations of the oedipal phase. Conflicts are not so much repressed as expressed in mutually dissociated ego states reflecting the primitive defense of splitting. The activation of primitive object relations that predate the consolidation of ego, superego, and id is manifest in the transference as apparently chaotic affect states; these, as has been outlined before, have to be analyzed in sequential steps. The interpretation of primitive transferences of borderline patients brings about a transformation of part-object relations into total object relations, of primitive transferences (largely reflecting stages of development that predate object constancy) into the advanced transferences of the oedipal phase.

At severe levels of psychopathology, splitting mechanisms permit the contradictory aspects of intrapsychic conflicts to remain at least partially conscious in the form of primitive transferences. Patients with neurotic personality organization, in contrast, present impulse–defense configurations that contain specific unconscious wishes reflecting sexual and aggressive drive derivatives embedded in unconscious fantasies relating to the oedipal objects. In these patients, we find relatively less distortion of both the self representations relating to these objects and the representations of the oedipal objects themselves. Therefore the difference between past pathogenic experiences and their transformation into currently structured unconscious dispositions is not as great as in the primitive transferences found in patients with borderline personality organization.

I assume that in all cases the transference is dynamically unconscious in the sense that, because of either repression or splitting, the patient unconsciously distorts the current experience because of his fixation to pathogenic conflicts with a significant internalized object of the past. The major task is to bring the unconscious transference meanings in the here-and-now into full consciousness by means of interpretation. This is the first stage in analyzing the relation between the unconscious present and the unconscious past.

What is enacted in the transference is never a simple repetition of the patient's actual past experiences. I agree with Melanie Klein's (1952) proposal that the transference derives from a combination of real and fantasied experiences of the past and defenses against both. This is another way of saying that the relationship between psychic reality and objective reality always remains ambiguous: The more severe the patient's psychopathology and the more distorted his/her intrapsychic structural organization, the more indirect is the relationship of current structure, genetic reconstruction, and the developmental origins.

The Treatment of Patients with Borderline Personality Organization

On the basis of all these formulations, we (Kernberg et al., 1989; Clarkin et al., 1992; Kernberg, 1993) have constructed a theory of psychodynamic treatment that derives from the theory of psychoanalytic technique and modifies this technique in the light of a general strategy geared to the resolution of the specific disturbances of borderline patients. The basic objective of this psychodynamic psychotherapy is the diagnosis and psychotherapeutic resolution of the syndrome of identity diffusion, and, in the process, resolution of (1) primitive defensive operations characteristic of these patients and (2) transformation of their primitive internalized "part-object" relationships into "total" object relationships characteristic of more advanced, neurotic and normal functioning individuals.

Primitive internalized object relations are constituted by part-self representations relating to part-object representations in the context of a primitive, all-good or all-bad, affect state, and they are part-object relations precisely because the representation of self and the representation of object have been split into an idealized and persecutory component—in contrast to the normal integration of good or loving and bad or hateful representations of self and significant others. These primitive or part-object relations emerge in the treatment situation in the form of primitive transferences characterized by the activation of such self and object representations and their corresponding affect as a transference "unit" enacted defensively against an opposite primitive transference unit under completely opposite affect valence or dominance.

STRATEGIES OF THE TREATMENT

In essence, the *psychotherapeutic strategy* in the psychodynamic treatment of borderline patients consists of a three step procedure:

1. Step 1 is the diagnosis of an emerging primitive part-object relationship in the transference and the interpretative analysis of the

dominant unconscious fantasy structure that corresponds to this particular transference activation. For example, the therapist may point out to the patient that their momentary relationship resembles that of a sadistic prison guard and a paralyzed, frightened victim.

2. Step 2 of this strategy is to identify the self and the object representation of this particular primitive transference and the typically oscillating or alternating attribution of self and object representation by the patient to himself and to the therapist. For example, the therapist may point out, in expanding the previous intervention, that it is as if the patient experienced him/herself as a frightened, paralyzed victim while attributing to the therapist the behavior of a sadistic prison guard. Later on, in the same session, the therapist may point out to the patient that, by now, the situation has become reversed in that the patient behaves like a sadistic prison guard while the therapist has been placed in the role of the patient as a frightened victim.

3. Step 3 of this interpretative intervention would be delineating the linkage between the particular object relationship activated in the transference and an entirely opposite one activated at other times but constituting the split-off, idealized counterpart to this particular, persecutory object relationship. For example, if at other times the patient has experienced the therapist as a perfect, all-giving mother, while the patient experiences him/herself as a satisfied, happy, loved baby who is the exclusive objective of mother's attention, the therapist might point out that the persecutory prison guard is really a bad, frustrating, teasing, and rejecting mother. At the same time, the victim is an enraged baby who wants to take revenge but is afraid of being destroyed because of the projection of his/her own rage onto mother. The therapist might add that this terrible mother–infant relationship is kept completely separate from the idealized relationship out of the fear of contaminating the idealized one with the persecutory one, and of the destruction of all hope that, in spite of the rageful, revengeful attacks on the bad mother, the relationship with the ideal mother might be recovered.

The successful integration of mutually dissociated or split-off, all-good and all-bad, primitive object relations in the transference includes the integration not only of the corresponding self and object representations but also of primitive affects. The integration of intense, polarized affects leads, over time, to affect modulation, to an increase in the capacity for affect control, to a heightened capacity for empathy with both self and others, and a corresponding deepening and maturing of all object relations.

This psychotherapeutic strategy also involves a particular modification of three basic tools derived from standard psychoanalytic technique. First, the strategy involves "interpretation," that is, the establishment of hypotheses about unconscious determinants of the patient's behavior as the major technical tool of the treatment. In contrast to standard psychoanalysis, however, interpretation here involves mostly the preliminary phases of interpretive interventions, that is, a systematic "clarification" of the patient's subjective experience, the tactful "confrontation" of the meanings of those aspects of his/her subjective experience, verbal communication, nonverbal behavior and total interaction with the therapist that express further aspects of the transference, and a restriction of the unconscious aspects of interpretation to the *unconscious meanings in the "here and now" only*. In contrast to standard psychoanalysis, where interpretation centers on unconscious meanings both in the "here and now" and the "there and then" of the unconscious past, in the psychodynamic psychotherapy of borderline patients, psychodynamic interpretations of the unconscious past are reserved to relatively advanced stages of the treatment. At these later stages, the integration of primitive transferences has transformed primitive into advance transferences (more characteristics of neurotic functioning, and more directly reflective of actual experiences from the past).

Another difference with standard psychoanalysis is given by the modification of "transference analysis," in each session, derived from the therapist's ongoing attention to (1) the long range treatment goals with any particular patient and (2) the dominant, current conflicts in the patient's life outside the sessions. In order that the treatment not gratify excessively the patient's transference—thus undermining the patient's initial motivation and treatment goals objectives, the therapist him/herself has to keep in touch with long-range treatment goals. Also, in order to prevent splitting off of external reality from the treatment situation—and severe acting out expressed by such dissociation between external reality and the treatment hours—transference interpretation has to be linked closely to the present realities in the patient's life. In short, then, in contrast to psychoanalysis (where a systematic focus on the transference is a major treatment strategy), in the psychodynamic psychotherapy of borderline patients, transference analysis is modified by attention to initial treatment goals and current external reality.

Third, insofar as interpretations require a position of "technical neutrality" (the therapist's equidistance from the forces in mutual conflict in the patient's mind), technical neutrality is an important aspect of the psychodynamic psychotherapy of borderline patients—as well as of standard psychoanalysis. However, given the severe acting out of borderline patients inside and outside the treatment hours, technical neutrality may have to be limited by indispensable structuring (limit setting) of the treatment situation, which (at least temporarily) reduces technical neutrality and requires its reinstatement by means of interpretations of the reasons for which the therapist moved away from a position of technical neutrality. All these considerations summarize the essential elements of the psychodynamic psychotherapy of borderline patients.

The strategy also determines a set of "tactical considerations" regarding the interventions in each treatment hour that give a particular coloring to this psychotherapy that differentiates it from both standard psychoanalysis and from supportive psychotherapy derived from psychoanalytic theory. In contrast to supportive psychotherapy, the therapist refrains, as much as possible, from technical interventions such as affective and cognitive support, guidance and advice giving, direct environmental intervention, and any other technical maneuver that would reduce technical neutrality—with the exception of necessary structuring or limit setting in or outside the treatment hours. In supportive psychotherapy, transferences are utilized for enhancing the therapeutic alliance, patient compliance, or symptom resolution. In contrast, in psychodynamic treatment, both positive and negative transferences are interpreted (with the exception of milder aspects of the positive transference, which may be left untouched, particularly in early stages of the treatment, in order to foster the therapeutic alliance). Our treatment approach includes a systematic effort to interpret primitive idealizations of the therapist because of their counterpart to dissociated primitive negative transferences.

In each session, it is important to assess the patient's capacity to differentiate fantasy from reality and to carry out interpretation of unconscious meanings only after the confirmation of commonly shared views of reality on the part of the patient and therapist. This may require consistent and tactful confrontation of the patient with immediate reality before interpreting its unconscious meaning. The patient's attribution of fantastic meanings to the therapist's interpretive interventions also needs to be clarified and interpreted. It is important to assess secondary gain of severe symptoms and behaviors, to interpret such secondary gain, and, if necessary, reduce or eliminate it by limit setting, with the corresponding need to reassess and interpret any slippage of technical neutrality. The analysis of unconscious sexual conflicts must include the analysis of contamination of sexuality with aggression in order to help the patient to free his/her sexual behavior from the control by aggressive impulses.

Another crucial aspect of tactical interventions is the need to interpret primitive defenses systematically as they emerge in each hour: The interpretation of primitive defenses tends to strengthen reality testing and overall ego functioning. In contrast to older conceptions of primitive defenses, these do not "strengthen" the frail ego of the borderline patient but are the very cause of chronic ego weakness. Interpretation of primitive defenses is a major tool for increasing ego strength and reality testing and facilitates the interpretation of primitive transferences.

Given the strong tendencies toward acting out on the part of borderline patients, dangerous complications in their treatment may derive from their characterologically based, "nondepressive" suicidal attempts, drug abuse, self-mutilating and other self-destructive behaviors, and aggressive behaviors that may be life threatening to themselves and others. An important aspect of each session, and not just a part of the overall structuring of the treatment, is the assessment of whether there are emergency situations that require immediate interventions. On the basis of our general treatment strategy and experience in the treatment of severely ill borderline patients, we have constructed the following set of priorities of intervention that reflect the need to assess, diagnose, and treat these and other complications.

A threat of imminent suicidal or homicidal behavior has the highest priority in each session. If there seem to be immediate threats to the continuity of the treatment, these constitute the second highest priority that needs to be taken up by the therapist. If the patient appears to be communicating in deceptive or dishonest ways, this constitutes the third highest priority: Psychodynamic psychotherapy demands honest communication between patient and therapist and, by the same token, the interpretation of the transferential meanings that underlie the patient's dishonesty or deceptiveness. In more general terms, "psychopathic" transferences must take precedence, in terms of their interpretive management, over "paranoid" ones, and paranoid transferences, in turn, over less severely distorting transferences ("depressive" transferences). Acting out in the sessions as well as outside the session constitutes the next highest priority, already signaled in our earlier statement that transference analysis must include the consideration of dominant conflicts outside the hours.

With these priorities considered, the therapist may then concentrate fully on the analysis of the transference along the lines outlined before. There are times when the dominant affects in the hours are linked with developments outside the hours: That is, "affective dominance" may not always center in the transference, and if that is so, affective dominance determines the focus of the therapist's attention—with an awareness that affect-laden conflicts outside the treatment situation also may have transferential implications that may become clearer and dominant later on.

These considerations summarize the psychotherapeutic approach derived from a psychoanalytic theory regarding the origin, development, and structure of the severe personality disorders, that is, borderline personality organization. The synthesis of this therapeutic approach in the form of a manual of technique (Kernberg et al., 1989) is the basis of an empirical research thrust presently in progress.

REFERENCES

Abraham, K. (1920). Manifestations of the female castration complex. In *Selected papers on psycho-analysis* (pp. 338–369). London: Hogarth Press, 1927.

Abraham, K. (1921–1925). Psycho-analytical studies on character formation. In *Selected papers on psycho-analysis* (pp. 370–417). London: Hogarth Press, 1927.

Akhtar, S. (1989). Narcissistic personality disorder: Descriptive features and differential diagnosis. In O. F. Kernberg (Ed.), *Narcissistic personality disorder: Psychiatric clinics of North America* (pp. 505–530). Philadelphia: Saunders.

Akhtar, S. (1992). *Broken structures.* Northvale, NJ: Jason Aronson.

American Psychiatric Association. (1968). *Diagnostic and statistical manual of mental disorders* (2nd ed.). Washington, DC: Author.

American Psychiatric Association. (1980). *Diagnostic and statistical manual of mental disorders* (3rd ed.). Washington, DC: Author.

American Psychiatric Association. (1987). *Diagnostic and statistical manual of mental disorders* (3rd ed., rev.). Washington, DC: Author.

American Psychiatric Association. (1994). *Diagnostic and statistical manual of mental disorders* (4th ed.). Washington, DC: Author.

Benjamin, L. S. (1992). An interpersonal approach to the diagnosis of borderline personality disorder. In J. F. Clarkin, E. Marziali, & H. Munroe-Blum (Eds.), *Borderline personality disorder* (pp. 161–198). New York: Guilford Press.

Benjamin, L. S. (1993). *Interpersonal diagnosis and treatment of personality disorders.* New York: Guilford Press.

Bursten, B. (1989). The relationship between narcissistic and antisocial personalities. In O. F. Kernberg (Ed.), *Narcissistic personality disorder: Psychiatric clinics of North America* (pp. 571–584). Philadelphia: Saunders.

Clarkin, J. F., Koenigsberg, H., Yeomans, F., Selzer, M., Kernberg, P., & Kernberg, O. F. (1992). Psychodynamic psychotherapy of the borderline patient. In J. F. Clarkin, E. Marziali, & H. Munroe-Blum (Eds.), *Borderline personality disorder* (pp. 268–287). New York: Guilford Press.

Cloninger, C. R., Svrakic, D. M., & Przybeck, T. R. (1993). A psychobiological model of temperament and character. *Archives of General Psychiatry, 50,* 975–990.

Costa, P. T., & Widiger, T. A. (1994). Introduction. In P. T. Costa & T. Widger

(Eds.), *Personality disorders and the five-factor model of personality* (pp. 1–10). Washington, DC: American Psychological Association.

deVegvar, M. L., Siever, L. J., & Trestman, R. L. (1994). Impulsivity and serotonin in borderline personality disorder. In K. R. Silk (Ed.), *Biological and neurobehavioral studies of borderline personality disorder* (pp. 23–40). Washington, DC: American Psychiatric Press.

Erikson, E. H. (1956). The problem of ego identity. *Journal of the American Psychoanalytic Association, 4,* 56–121.

Fairbairn, W. (1954). *An object-relations theory of the personality.* New York: Basic Books.

Fenichel, O. (1945). *The psychoanalytic theory of neurosis.* New York: Norton.

Fraiberg, A. (1983). Pathological defenses in infancy. *Psychoanalytic Quarterly, 60,* 612–635.

Freud, S. (1908). Character and anal erotism. *Standard Edition, 9,* 167–175.

Freud, S. (1915). Instincts and their vicissitudes. *Standard Edition, 14,* 109–140.

Freud, S. (1931). Libidinal types. *Standard Edition, 21,* 215–220.

Galenson, E. (1986). Some thoughts about infant psychopathology and aggressive development. *International Review of Psycho-Analysis, 13,* 349–354.

Grossman, W. (1986). Notes on masochism: A discussion of the history and development of a psychoanalytic concept 1. *Psychoanalytic Quarterly, 55,* 379–413.

Grossman, W. (1991). Pain, aggression, fantasy, and concepts of sadomasochism. *Psychoanalytic Quarterly, 60,* 22–52.

Hare, R. D. (1986). Twenty years of experience with the Cleckley psychopath. In W. H. Reid, D. Dorr, J. I. Walker, & J. W. Bonner III (Eds.), *Unmasking the psychopath* (pp. 3–27). New York: Norton.

Jacobson, E. (1964). *The self and object world.* New York: International Universities Press.

Jonas, J. M., & Pope, H. G. (1992). Axis I comorbidity of borderline personality disorder: Clinical implications. In J. F. Clarkin, E. Marziali, & H. Munroe-Blum (Eds.), *Borderline personality disorder* (pp. 149–160). New York: Guilford Press.

Kernberg, O. F. (1975). *Borderline conditions and pathological narcissism.* New York: Jason Aronson.

Kernberg, O. F. (1976). *Object relations theory and clinical psychoanalysis.* New York: Jason Aronson.

Kernberg, O. F. (1980). *Internal world and external reality: Object relations theory applied.* New York: Jason Aronson.

Kernberg, O. F. (1984). *Severe personality disorders: Psychotherapeutic strategies.* New Haven: Yale University Press.

Kernberg, O. F. (1989). The narcissistic personality disorder and the differential diagnosis of antisocial behavior. In O. F. Kernberg (Ed.), *Narcissistic personality disorder: Psychiatric clinics of North America* (pp. 553–570). Philadelphia: Saunders.

Kernberg, O. F. (1992). *Aggression in personality disorder and perversions.* New Haven: Yale University Press.

Kernberg, O. F. (1993). The psychotherapeutic treatment of borderline patients.

In J. Paris (Ed.), *Borderline personality disorder* (pp. 261–284). Washington, DC: American Psychiatric Press.

Kernberg, O. F. (1994). Aggression, trauma, and hatred in the treatment of borderline patients. In I. Share (Ed.), *Borderline personality disorder: The psychiatric clinics of North America* (pp. 701–714). Philadelphia: Saunders.

Kernberg, O. F., Selzer, M. A., Koenigsberg, H. W., Carr, A. C., & Appelbaum, A. H. (1989). *Psychodynamic psychotherapy of borderline patients.* New York: Basic Books.

Klein, M. (1952). The origins of transference. In *Envy and gratitude* (pp. 48–56). New York: Basic Books, 1957.

Krause, R. (1988). Eine Taxonomie der Affekte und ihre Anwendung auf das Verständnis der frühen Störungen. *Psychotherapie und Medizinische Psychologie, 38,* 77–86.

Krause, R., & Lutolf, P. (1988). Facial indicators of transference processes in psychoanalytical treatment. In H. Dahl & H. Kachele (Eds.), *Psychoanalytic process research strategies* (pp. 257–272). Heidelberg: Springer.

Mahler, M., & Furer, M. (1968). *On human symbiosis and the vicissitudes of individuation.* New York: International Universities Press.

Mahler, M., Pine, F., & Bergman, A. (1975). *The psychological birth of the human infant.* New York: Basic Books.

Marziali, E. (1992). The etiology of borderline personality disorder: Developmental factors. In J. F. Clarkin, E. Marziali, & H. Munroe-Blum (Eds.), *Borderline personality disorder* (pp. 27–44). New York: Guilford Press.

Oldham, J. M. (1994). Personality disorders. *Journal of the American Medical Association, 272,* 1770–1776.

Paris, J. (1994). *Borderline personality disorder.* Washington, DC: American Psychiatric Press.

Perry, J. C., & Herman, J. L. (1993). Trauma and defense in the etiology of borderline personality disorder. In J. Paris (Ed.), *Borderline personality disorder* (pp. 123–140). Washington, DC: American Psychiatric Press.

Plakun, E. (1989). Narcissistic personality disorder: A validity study and comparison to borderline personality disorder. In O. F. Kernberg (Ed.), *Narcissistic personality disorder: Psychiatric clinics of North America* (pp. 603–620). Philadelphia: Saunders.

Ronningstam, E., & Gunderson, J. (1989). Descriptive studies on narcissistic personality disorder. In O. F. Kernberg (Ed.), *Narcissistic personality disorder: Psychiatric clinics of North America* (pp. 585–602). Philadelphia: Saunders.

Steinberg, B. J., Trestman, R. L., & Siever, L. J. (1994). The cholinergic and noradrenergic neurotransmitter systems and affective instability in borderline personality disorder. In R. Silk (Ed.), *Biological and neurobehavioral studies of borderline personality disorder* (pp. 41–62). Washington, DC: American Psychiatric Press.

Stone, M. (1980). *The borderline syndromes.* New York: McGraw-Hill.

Stone, M. (1990). *The fate of borderline patients.* New York: Guilford Press.

Stone, M. (1993a). *Abnormalities of personality.* New York: Norton.

Stone, M. (1993b). Etiology of borderline personality disorder: Psychobiological factors contributing to an underlying irritability. In J. Paris (Ed.), *Borderline personality disorder* (pp. 87–102). Washington, DC: American Psychiatric Press.

Stone, M. (1994). Characterologic subtypes of the borderline personality disorder: With a note on prognostic factors. In I. Share (Ed.), *Borderline personality disorder: The psychiatric clinics of North America* (pp. 773–784). Philadelphia: Saunders.

Torgersen, A. M. (1985). Temperamental differences in infants and 6-year-old children: A follow-up study of twins. In J. Strelalau, F. H. Farley, & A. Gale (Eds.), *The biological basis of personality and behavior: Theories, measurement, techniques, and development* (pp. 227–239). Washington, DC: Hemisphere.

Torgersen, A. M. (1994, June). *Genetics of personality disorder.* Paper presented at the First European Congress on Disorders of Personality, Nijmegen, The Netherlands.

van der Kolk, B. A., Hostetler, A., Herron, N., & Fisler, R. E. (1994). Trauma and the development of borderline personality disorder. In I. Share (Ed.), *Borderline personality disorder: The psychiatric clinics of North America* (pp. 715–730). Philadelphia: Saunders.

van Reekum, R., Links, P. S., & Fedorov, C. (1994). Impulsivity in borderline personality disorder. In K. R. Silk (Ed.), *Biological and neurobehavioral studies of borderline personality disorder* (pp. 11–22). Washington, DC: American Psychiatric Press.

Volkan, V. (1976). *Primitive internalized object relations.* New York: International Universities Press.

Volkan, V. (1987). *Six steps in the treatment of borderline personality organization.* Northvale, NJ: Jason Aronson.

Wallerstein, R. (1991). *Scales of psychological capacity.* Unpublished manuscript.

Widiger, T. A., & Frances, A. J. (1994). Toward a dimensional model for the personality disorders. In P. T. Costa & T. Widiger (Eds.), *Personality disorders and the five-factor model of personality* (pp. 19–40). Washington, DC: American Psychological Association.

Widiger, T. A., Trull, T. J., Clarkin, J. F., Sanderson, C., & Costa, P. T., Jr. (1994). A description of the DSM-III-R and DSM-IV personality disorders with the five-factor model of personality. In P. T. Costa & T. Widiger (Eds.), *Personality disorders and the five-factor model of personality* (pp. 41–56). Washington, DC: American Psychological Association.

Yehuda, R., Southwick, S. M., Perry, B. D., & Giller, E. L. (1994). Peripheral catecholamine alterations in borderline personality disorder. In R. Silk (Ed.), *Biological and neurobehavioral studies of borderline personality disorder* (pp. 63–90). Washington, DC: American Psychiatric Press.

4

An Interpersonal Theory of Personality Disorders

LORNA SMITH BENJAMIN

The first draft of the model for Structural Analysis of Social Behavior (SASB; Benjamin, 1974) emerged in the late 1960s. The news had been dominated by reports of atrocities from the Vietnam war, so it was easy to agree with those who hold that "primitive basics" underlay much of human social interaction. Freud and his psychoanalytic colleagues led the way to understanding with his emphasis on the primitive features of human interaction. He insisted that sexuality and, later, aggression provide the basic energy for human interaction (Freud, 1896). Adler (1955) added the idea that there is a primary drive for power or superiority. Mahler (1968) marked the importance of differentiation, that is, of separate psychological "territory."

Each of these aspects—sexuality, aggression, dominance, and separate territory—is described by a pole of the SASB model. Combinations of the four basics describe many "higher" interpersonal and intrapsychic positions. The SASB descriptions can be applied to both "personality" and interpersonal "situation." The purpose of the SASB model is to provide methods and concepts to make interpersonal and intrapsychic process more amenable to scientific study. It can apply to parent–child interactions; therapy process in individual, group, or marital settings; peer–peer interactions; boss–employee interactions, and more. Although the method can be used in a range of contexts, my own personal interest has been to develop the SASB model for use in psychotherapy. It has seemed important to be able to assess what people talk about most in that context, namely, their relationships with themselves and important other people. Appropriate methods of measuring these interpersonal and intrapsychic factors should yield data that can enhance efficacy in treatment and prevention of mental disorder.

Figure 4.1 summarizes the SASB research program. The first step was to develop and validate the SASB model (and relevant variations), associated theory, and measuring instruments. These include (1) the Intrex questionnaires, which provide ratings by self and others; (2) the SASB coding system, which provides objective observer ratings of videotapes of a wide variety of interactions: therapist–client, parent–child, peer–peer, husband–wife, employer–employee, teacher–student, and more; and (3) Software that generates a number of parameters that summarize and characterize the data gathered by questionnaire and by the coding system.[1]

The next step was to apply the model and measurement techniques to clinical problems in diagnosis and treatment. Relevant diagnosis is an essential first step in treatment planning. One must know what is normal and what can go wrong before one can attempt to "correct" things through psychotherapy. Once the assessment is made, models and methods should help organize treatment planning, direct interventions, and evaluate the outcomes. They also should have preventive implications. The most comprehensive effort using SASB was summarized in my book, *Interpersonal Diagnosis and Treatment of Personality Disorders* (Benjamin, 1993b, the second edition of which is Benjamin, 1996). The SASB model was used to describe DSM-III-R and DSM-IV personality disorders, to infer prototypical developmental histories, to anticipate transference problems, and to prescribe specific

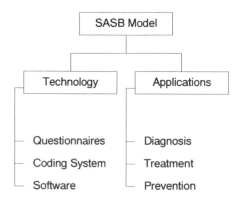

FIGURE 4.1. Summary of SASB projects.

interpersonal psychosocial treatment interventions. Applications to prevention are less well developed. However, a longitudinal prospective study of interactions between depressed mothers and their infants has attempted to apply the SASB model and technology to the problem of prevention of mental disorders. Illustrative preliminary data from that project are presented.

This chapter begins with a review of the features of the SASB model and the technology that it offers for measurement of object relations. "Object relations theory concerns itself with how individuals develop in relation to the people around them. Internalizing and externalizing relationships, attachment and separation, introjection and projection, and transmuting internalization are the key issues in development" (Hamilton, 1989, p. 1552). After a discussion of models, methods, applications, and their validity, there is an extended discussion of future plans. These center on the vexing question of why individuals with personality disorder are so unresponsive to usual and customary forms of psychotherapeutic intervention. As a clinician, I am convinced that individuals with personality disorder can be quite responsive to certain forms of psychotherapy. The question is how to operationalize explanations, procedures, and outcomes and demonstrate efficacy. I believe a good answer lies in using SASB-based concepts and methods to operationalize and test hypotheses about the unconscious attachments that maintain the maladaptive patterns of personality disorder. This chapter provides a summary of the theory and methods that will be used in that effort.

THE SASB MODEL

The full SASB model appears in Figure 4.2, and the most user-friendly version, called the simplified cluster model, appears in Figure 4.3. The SASB model has a long intellectual heritage that includes Sigmund Freud (1896), Henry Murray (1938), and Harry Stack Sullivan (1953). Freud exposed the profound importance of childhood learning and the role of the unconscious. Murray and Sullivan moved Freud's ideas in a clearly interpersonal direction. Timothy Leary (1957), Earl Schaefer (1965), and others then proposed that circumplex models of social interaction can be used to describe important aspects of these clinical theories. The SASB circumplex model combines structural features from the Leary and the Schaefer versions. Its applications lean heavily on clinical wisdom from Freud and Sullivan. The structure and history of the SASB model have been detailed elsewhere (e.g., Benjamin, 1974, 1984, 1993b). In Benjamin (1994b) there is an extended discus-

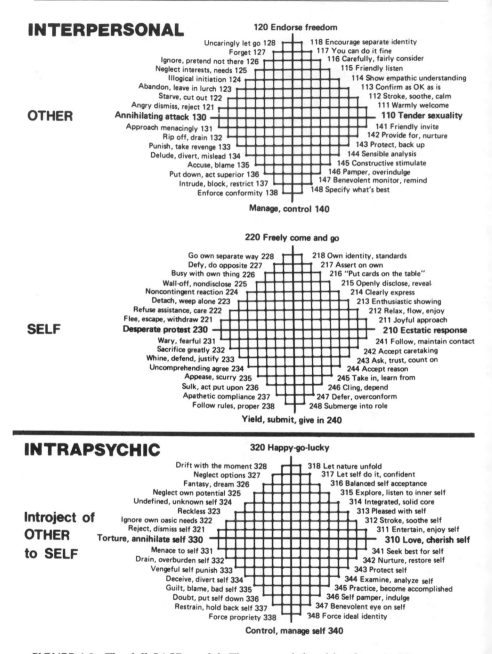

FIGURE 4.2. The full SASB model. The space defined by the primitive axes can be divided up into infinitely many components. The full model is the most detailed version available. From Benjamin (1979a). Copyright 1979 by the William Alanson White Psychiatric Foundation. Reprinted by permission.

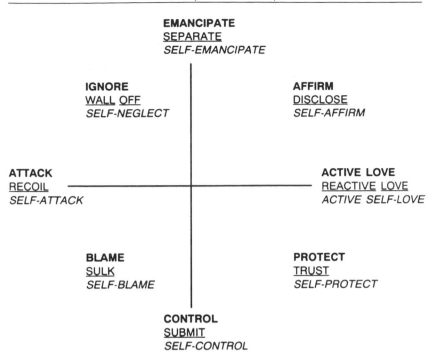

FIGURE 4.3. The simplified cluster SASB model. The points shown on the full model in Figure 4.2 can be grouped to provide a simpler version. The horizontal axis runs from hate to love, and the vertical axis from enmeshment to differentiation. The three types of focus are represented by different styles of print. Complementarity is shown by adjacent **BOLD** and <u>UNDERLINED</u> points. Introjection is shown by adjacent **BOLD** and *ITALICIZED* points. From Benjamin (1993b). Copyright 1993 by The Guilford Press. Reprinted by permission.

sion of how SASB compares to the Leary-based circumplex models in the ability to describe clinical problems (symptoms, diagnoses).

All circumplex models arrange categories in a circle defined by two underlying axes or dimensions. The several versions of the SASB model are built on the same underlying axes: affiliation (aggression vs. sexuality) and interdependence (dominance/submission vs. independence). These underlying axes provide the components for many other interpersonal and intrapsychic positions. For example, consider parents who go on vacation and leave their young children at home unattended. Their behavior could be SASB-coded as *123, Abandon, leave in lurch* on the full model (located at about 10 o'clock on Figure 4.2). It would be called **IGNORE** on the simplified cluster model (the same location, Figure 4.3). These particular SASB codes reflect the fact that such parental behavior is both hostile and separate.

On the horizontal axes of the SASB model, murder represents maximum attack and is opposed by sexuality, the point of maximum affiliation. The reader might object that sexual behavior is not always loving.
He or she would be right; sexual behavior itself can be coded anywhere
on the SASB model, depending on the context. For example, rather
than maximal affection, sexual behavior can instead represent ATTACK,
or SUBMIT or WALL OFF or SELF-NEGLECT, or more. Nonetheless, pure
sexuality is proposed to be the point of maximal friendliness. It is
represented by the points ACTIVE LOVE/REACTIVE-LOVE/ACTIVE SELF-LOVE
on the simplified SASB model of Figure 4.3. In that form, sexuality
is neutral with respect to the dimension of dominance/submission versus independence. Space and power are shared equally. There is no
hostility. The fact that people often combine sexuality with other interpersonal agendas does not preclude its definition in the pure form
as maximally intense friendliness.

The SASB model shares with all other circumplex models the idea
that love and hate should be placed on a horizontal axis. All circumplex models also include the Adlerian perspective by providing a node
for dominance. The widely cited Leary version (e.g., Wiggins, 1982;
Kiesler, 1983) places submission opposite dominance on the vertical
axis of a single surface. The SASB model, by contrast, places submission on a separate surface or domain, at a place that matches dominance
exactly (i.e., at the 6 o'clock position on Figures 4.2 and 4.3). The SASB
use of emancipation opposite dominance follows Schaefer's (1965) lead.
The implication of this change is that submission goes with or complements dominance. Submission does not, as hypothesized by the
Leary-based circumplex models, oppose dominance. The SASB model
provides that if one person is dominant and the other is submissive,
they are in a harmonious, not an opposing, relationship.

The SASB model places CONTROL opposite EMANCIPATE. It adds
separate space to the enmeshed space already defined by the traditional Leary-based models. By adding a domain for separateness, the
SASB model articulates both enmeshed (CONTROL/SUBMIT) and differentiated (EMANCIPATE/SEPARATE) parts of interpersonal space. People
who go and let others go their separate ways are highly differentiated. By contrast, people who insist on controlling others or who allow
themselves to be controlled are very enmeshed; they do not have a
separate identity. The SASB model's ability to define differentiated
space is vitally important to describing both normal and psychopathological personalities. The "traditional" Leary-based circumplexes do
not define space that is independent.

There are three different circumplexes in the SASB model. They
differ in attentional focus. In all three domains, the two axes; love–

hate and enmeshment–differentiation, provide the component dimensions. In Figure 4.2, the three types of focus are shown on separate surfaces, and in Figure 4.3, they appear as different types of print. Parent-like behavior is represented by the top section of the full model (Figure 4.2) and by the **bold print** in the simplified model (Figure 4.3). Parent-like behavior is matched by child-like behavior, shown by the middle section of the full model (Figure 4.2) and by the underlined print in the simplified model (Figure 4.3). Finally, introjected behavior is shown by the bottom section of the full model (Figure 4.2) and by the *italicized* print in the simplified model (Figure 4.3). The vertical axes differ for the three types of focus. If the focus is on other, the vertical axis runs, as described above, from CONTROL to EMANCIPATE. If the focus is on self, the vertical axis ranges from SUBMIT to SEPARATE. And if introjection is the domain, the vertical axis goes from *SELF-CONTROL* to *SELF-EMANCIPATE*.

Dissecting Events by SASB Coding

The steps to follow when dissecting an event in terms of the underlying dimensions of the SASB model are illustrated. Consider the example of the vacationing parents who left their children unattended:

1. Determine who is to be coded (referent *X*) in relation to whom (referent *Y*). *X* = the parents and *Y* = the children. Code from the perspective of *X*.

2. Determine the attentional focus. Transitive action, attention that is directed from one person (*X*) to another (*Y*), is called focus on other. Once *X* and *Y* have been identified, the coder knows that if the transaction is about *Y*, the focus is on other. *When the transaction is about what* X *is doing to, for or about* Y, *the focus is on other.* Here, the concern is about what the parents (*X*) are doing (or failing to do) to, for or about the children.

Intransitive reaction, attention that is on the self in reaction to another, is called focus on self. *When* X *is concerned about what* Y *is going to do to, for, or about* X, *the focus is on self.* In the case of the vacationing parents, the children who are left unattended likely would be coded in terms of what the parents do (or don't do) about the self. Following the suggestion of Sullivan (1953), transitive action that is turned inward upon the self is called introjection. If the event is not interpersonal, and if *X* acts upon *X*, the event is an introjection.

3. Determine the degrees of friendliness or hostility that are marked by the horizontal axes of the models. Points to the right are

progressively more friendly as they approach the sexuality pole. Points to the left are progressively more hostile as they approach the murderous pole.

4. Determine the degrees of enmeshment/differentiation that are marked by the vertical axes of the model. Points in the upward direction are progressively more independent or differentiated, and points in the downward direction are progressively more enmeshed. The names of the poles are different for the three types of attentional focus. For example, the point of maximal transitive enmeshment is CONTROL, and the position of maximal intransitive enmeshment is SUBMIT.

5. Combine the judgments to find the SASB category that best applies. For example, the vacationing parents are transitive and hostile and independent in relation to the children they left unattended at home. This puts them in the region of IGNORE on the simplified version of the cluster model. The children's intransitive reaction might match the parents in hostility and independence and place them at WALL OFF. If they copy the parents and treat themselves as they have been treated, the children might internalize the parental neglect as SELF-NEGLECT.

The Predictive Principles

The predictive principles can suggest what may have antedated and what may follow a given interpersonal event. The main predictive principles are complementarity, introjection, similarity, opposition, and antithesis.

Complementarity

Two individuals are in complementary positions if their focus is on the same person and if their behaviors can be coded at the same position in interpersonal space. The first person must be focused on other while the second person is focused on the self. In the vacationing parents example, the children would complement the parental IGNORE if they took the position WALL OFF that was suggested in step 5 above. In the full model of Figure 4.2, the complement of *123, Abandon, leave in lurch* is shown as *223, Detach, weep alone.*

Introjection

Introjection is shown whenever an individual treats him- or herself as he or she has been treated by important others. In the example above, the parental IGNORE was introjected as *SELF-NEGLECT.* On the full model, the parental *123, Abandon, leave in lurch* would be introjected to yield the position *323, Reckless.* If the parents don't care about them, the children will not care about themselves.

Similarity

Similarity is shown whenever an individual copies or acts like someone else. A more familiar clinical term for this pattern is identification. Children who grew up in an atmosphere characterized by parental IG-NORE are more likely to do the same to their own children. They identify with and are similar to their own parents.

Opposition

Opposition is shown at 180° angles on the SASB models. The opposite for the vacationing parents is, for example, PROTECT on the simplified model; it is *143, Protect, back up* on the full model. The opposite of the children's WALL OFF is TRUST on the simplified model. The opposite of their *223, Detach, weep alone* is *243, Ask, trust, count on* in the full model.

Antithesis

The complement of an opposite is an antithesis. The antithesis of IG-NORE is TRUST. Through the principle of complementarity, the antithesis pulls for the opposite of any given position. For example, to the extent that children show the sweet dependency marked by the point TRUST, neglectful parents are less likely to IGNORE them. The parents are more likely to provide the opposite, namely, PROTECT. In short, the principle of antithesis helps trusting children draw parents who might be inclined to neglect them into a more protective role. Their neediness "pulls" for caregiving, though success is not guaranteed. Nonetheless, the childrens' chances of eliciting what they need is increased when they show the antithesis of IGNORE.

In the present example of the negligent parents, and in subsequent examples throughout the chapter, the reader is encouraged to get the "ballpark" description using the simplified cluster model of Figure 4.3. This can be enriched by appeal to the full model of Figure 4.2. For example, it is argued that the parental vacation can be generally described by the simplified model as IGNORE. The long-term expected reactions of the children are WALL OFF and *SELF-NEGLECT.* The full-model version of these trends is as follows. The negligent parents are likely to show the following behaviors: *128, Uncaringly let go; 127, Forget; 126, Ignore, pretend not there; 125, Neglect interests, needs; 124, Illogical initiation; 123,*

Abandon, leave in lurch; 122, *Starve, cut out;* and 121, *Angry dismiss, re-ject.* The children are likely to complement with 228, *Go own separate way;* 227, *Defy, do opposite;* 226, *Busy with own thing;* 225, *Wall-off, non-disclose;* 224, *Noncontingent reaction;* 223, *Detach, weep alone;* 222, *Refuse assistance, care;* or 221, *Flee, escape, withdraw.* Their expected self con-cept would be 328, *Drift with the moment;* 327, *Neglect options;* 326, *Fan-tasy, dream;* 325, *Neglect own potential;* 324, *Undefined, unknown self;* 323, *Reckless;* 322, *Ignore own basic needs;* and 321, *Reject, dismiss self.*

It is not yet clear when one principle rather than another is invoked. However, clear connections between childhood social learning and adult personality can often be found in terms of just a few of these principles. The most common connections are: (1) the adult personal-ity identifies with (similarity) the original parental position; (2) the adult personality continues to show a position that is complementary to the parental position (recapitulation); (3) the adult personality treats the self as did the parents (introjection). Less often, children show the op-posite and/or the antithesis of the original positions.

The example of vacationing parents shows how daily transactions can be described by SASB codes. If they are repeated over context and time, these microevents can set the character. Normal infants and tod-dlers show a brief period of detachment (WALL OFF) after separation from parents even if it increases their distress (SELF-NEGLECT). But the breach is healed quickly after the reunion. On the other hand, if per-ceived parental neglect is sustained by characteristic and long-lasting actual neglect, the detachment and self-neglect can become a trait. In sum, if the negligent vacation taking is representative of the parent-ing behaviors, the children's reactions would become traits. These astonishingly simple and direct connections, combined with inherit-ed temperament, assure that personality "runs in families."

METHODS OF GENERATING DATA
IN TERMS OF THE SASB MODEL

The clinician who is working "on line" can do informal SASB coding of the therapy process and content. Process codes help the therapist remain precisely and consistently aware of transference phenomena. Content codes of the stories told by the patient can help the therapist identify the basic patterns characteristic of the personality and guide the exploration of the quintessential issues.

For example, an individual with borderline personality disorder (BPD) is characterized (Benjamin, 1993b, Chap. 5) by a baseline pat-tern of demanding dependency (TRUST and **CONTROL** or **BLAME**). She might use this process to tell a story of incestual, somewhat loving, but also painful sexual abuse history (ACTIVE LOVE plus CONTROL plus ATTACK). Her demanding dependency calls for the therapist to complement her presentation with PROTECT and SUBMIT. If the therapist is unaware of this process, he or she is likely to resent the BPD's control (e.g., I will kill myself if you are not warm and loving enough). It is easy to react with subtle if not overt hostility, which the BPD will detect immediately. Then, she will ATTACK the therapist for not caring, and the process may degrade from there. By contrast, the therapist who is fully aware of the transference pull for deferent nurturance and the reasons for it is much more likely to remain differentiated. He or she can then be more appropriately supportive in the effort to help the BPD build her own personal strength.

In addition to such informal "on-line" use of SASB coding, there are methods to more rigorously turn interpersonal and intrapsychic events into data. Patients rating the Intrex questionnaires provide formal estimates of their views of themselves and others. Internal and test–retest estimates of reliability are usually .80 or better. In addition, objective observers can generate reliable codes of videotapes and transcripts of key interactions. These assessments can be between the patient and important other people such as parents, spouse, children, therapist, peers, and so on. Because both self-ratings and objective observations are in the same (SASB) metric, the two perspectives (self-description, objective observer rating) can be compared.

Sometimes discrepancies between self- and observer ratings are clinically important. For example, Humes and Humphrey (1994) showed that parents with a drug-dependent adolescent described themselves as more friendly to this daughter than did objective observers. One obvious clinical implication is that the family fight about the daughter needs to be dealt with more directly and, one hopes, more effectively.

Intrex Questionnaires

The long-form Intrex questionnaires provide one item for each of the points on the full SASB model. Some items that would describe the vacationing but neglectful parents are *123, Abandon, leave in lurch* (just when P is needed most, P abandons C, leaves C alone with trouble), *124, Illogical initiation* (P ignores the facts and offers C unbelievable nonsense and craziness), *125, Neglect interests, needs* (P neglects C, C's interests, needs), and *126, Ignore, pretend not there* (P just doesn't notice or pay any attention to C at all). Such long form items provide detailed sampling of a given region of interpersonal space. In this example, the space is characterized by hostile differentiation.

The Intrex short form provides only one item for each of the points on the simplified model. For example, there is only one item to sample the entire region of hostile differentiation involving parent-like focus: IGNORE 1 (Without giving it a second thought, P uncaringly ignores, neglects, abandons C). There are two versions of the short form, so the investigator who would like to add a second sampling of the region can add short form version 2. The item from that version for the parent-like hostile differentiation, IGNORE, is: "Without giving it a thought, P carelessly forgets O, leaves him/her out of important things."

Using either the short or the long form, the clinician or researcher typically samples selected relationships. An important feature of the SASB technology for assessing personality is that the patient's view of important other people is considered as explicitly as are the ratings of the self. Many assessment instruments ask the rater to describe him- or herself (an "I" form). The Sullivanian perspective demands assessment of "He and She" or "They" as well. This perspective builds the opportunity for the clinician to *assess distortions in perception of others* as well as *of the self in response to others.* Of course, a perception can be defined as a distortion only if it disagrees with the perspective generated by reliable objective observers. Distortion often may be attributed to the patient. However, distortion should sometimes be attributed to other family members. Different perspectives can be compared and contrasted by having different raters complete the questionnaires or by comparing questionnaire ratings with observer codes of actual interactions. The focus on interpersonal and intrapsychic interaction makes the SASB technology appropriate for assessment and treatment of the person within his or her social system. It also can be used to assess and treat systems themselves, as in family or group therapy (e.g., MacKenzie, 1990; Humphrey & Benjamin, 1986).

To illustrate the use of the questionnaires, consider the following short form results for a woman who has been in psychotherapy for 3½ years. For demonstration cases like this, the criteria for selection attempt to assure that the problem patterns are unlikely to remit spontaneously. This woman's chief complaints of depression, anxiety, and generalized dissatisfaction with self and others had been in place for more than 10 years. There were five previous failed therapies. Her initial presentation has been summarized elsewhere (Benjamin, 1993a). Figure 4.4 shows the Intrex short form ratings of her best and her worst introject states at the beginning of therapy. A glance at the figure shows that, at her best, she was "luke-warm" to herself, and her ratings on the friendly side ranged from 15 to 50 points below the norm. At worst, she was very hostile to herself, giving unusually high ratings to the

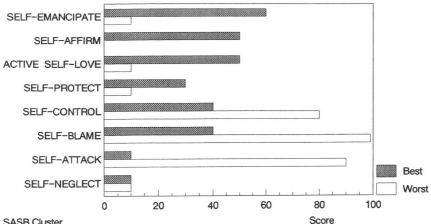

SASB Cluster   Score

FIGURE 4.4. The patient's introject at best and worst at start of therapy as measured by the Intrex questionnaire. Ratings of herself at worst suggest that her self-concept was organized around model point SELF-BLAME. At best, she was much friendlier to herself, although there still was a strong tendency to SELF-BLAME. The Intrex profiles help assess object relations and assist with treatment planning.

items representing points: SELF-ATTACK and SELF-NEGLECT. Figure 4.5 compares the patient's worst introject at the beginning of therapy and 3½ years later. The reduction in self-attack is striking. However, she still is self-blaming and shows too much self-neglect. She does not yet enjoy enough self affirmation and self-protection to be classified as fully recovered. This basis of this conclusion is developed more fully in a later section called Defining normality and setting therapy goals.[2]

Table 4.1 presents the formal parameters used to characterize profiles like those shown in Figures 4.4 and 4.5. Let "object relations" now be defined as the individual's SASB codable interpersonal and intrapsychic representations of him or herself and important others. If that definition is granted, then Table 4.1 summarizes some of this patient's object relations in terms of the SASB model. The left-hand side of the table presents the standard group of Intrex ratings, which were made at the beginning of therapy. These include introject in the best and worst states, relationship with significant other person in the best and worst states, relationship with mother as remembered for ages 5–10, relationship with father as remembered for ages 5–10, and parental marital relationship as remembered for ages 5–10. Each interpersonal relationship is broken down into four eight-point groups. These are: (1) he/she focuses on me; (2) he/she reacts to me; (3) I focus on him/her; (4) I react to him/her. The right-hand side of Table 4.1 presents

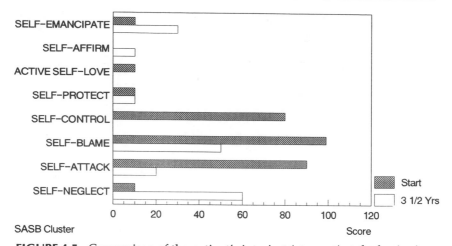

FIGURE 4.5. Comparison of the patient's introject (at worst) at the beginning of therapy and 3½ years later. The centering on *SELF-BLAME*, noted in Figure 4.4, had been broken up and reduced. However, her tendency to *SELF-NEGLECT* remained problematic. Profiles can show changes in object relations during therapy.

ratings made 3½ years after the start of therapy. The standard series was rated as usual. Two other relationships were added: the therapist and an important former lover.

The summary parameters are called pattern coefficients. They are product–moment correlations between actual cluster scores (e.g., the values shown in Figures 4.4 and 4.5) and various theoretical scores. The theoretical predictions are based on cosine curves that describe a circle centered at various points on the model. Other predictions are defined by orthogonal polynomials that describe additional systematic patterns possible among a set of eight cluster points. Some of the theoretical curves can reasonably be said to represent attack (or recoil), and others control (or submission). In Table 4.1, the entries in the columns labeled **ATTACK**/RECOIL or **CONTROL**/SUBMIT display the largest of two or three possible values. If the domain is parent-like or transitive, the control/submit pattern coefficient describes the degree of control. If the domain is child-like or intransitive, the control/submit pattern coefficient describes the degree of submission.

Table 4.1 shows a correlation of .908 between the patient's ratings of her introject at worst and the best-fitting theoretical curves representing **ATTACK**. At her worst, the patient was centered on self-attack when she started therapy. The value .908 is marked with an asterisk, as are all entries in the table that equal or exceed .81. That value was identified as significant at the .05 level by Monte Carlo methods providing

TABLE 4.1. Interpersonal and Intrapsychic Changes Described by Pattern Coefficients

Relationship	Start			3½ years later		
	ATTACK/RECOIL	CONTROL/SUBMIT	CONFLICT	ATTACK/RECOIL	CONTROL/SUBMIT	CONFLICT
1. Introject at best	-.626	.349	.331	-.259	-.148	.432
2. Introject at worst	.908*	.620	-.193	.703	-.716	.244
3. Husband focuses on me at best	-.865*	-.370	-.177	-.837*	-.829*	.276
4. Husband reacts to me at best	-.929*	.605	.234	-.873*	-.565	.241
5. I focus on husband at best	-.963*	-.648*	.124	-.821*	.444	.222
6. I react to husband at best	-.929*	.819*	.098	-.936*	-.772	.163
7. Husband focuses on me at worst	-.492	-.894	.451	-.532	-.893*	.363
8. Husband reacts to me at worst	-.355	-.961	.237	-.656	-.638*	.436
9. I focus on husband at worst	-.779	.659	.319	-.874*	-.638	.310
10. I react to husband at worst	.305	.631	.564	-.716	.674	.494
11. Mother focused on me	.305	.631	.564	.722	.664	.571
12. Mother reacted to me	.318	-.643	.468	.417	.557	.384
13. I focused on mother	-.805*	-.750	.329	-.448	-.638*	.563
14. I reacted to mother	.831*	.767	.368	.793	.487	.316
15. Father focused on me	-.714	.387	.407	-.170	.486	.543
16. Father reacted to me	-.876*	-.664	.093³	-.873*	-.570	-.328
17. I focused on father	-.853*	-.598	.213	-.817*	-.390	.233
18. I reacted to father	-.778	.935*	.222	-.575	.912*	.280
19. Mother focused on father	.256	-.194	.662	.180	.370	.764
20. Mother reacted to father	.404	.380	.622	.904*	.554	.321
21. Father focused on mother	.265	-.145	.606	.169	-.165	.470
22. Father reacted to mother	.884*	-.815*	-.135	.422	-.397	-.511
23. Therapist focuses on me				-.819*	.444	.231
24. Therapist reacts to me				-.874*	-.551	.213
25. I focus on therapist				-.910*	-.603	.194
26. I react to therapist				-.870*	.413	-.213
27. Old lover focused on me at best				-.355	.201	.689
28. Old lover reacted to be at best				-.905*	-.410	.087
29. I focused on old lover at best				-.615	-.473	.545
30. I reacted to old lover at best				-.983*	.695	.070
31. Old lover focused on me at worst				.556	-.247	-.269
32. Old lover reacted to me at worst				-.494	-.547	.613
33. I focused on old lover at worst				.446	-.466	-.278
34. I reacted to old lover at worst				.651	.480	-.409

Note. Values that equal or exceed .81 are marked with an asterisk.

contexts for both the English (Benjamin, 1988) and the German language translations (Davies-Osterkamp, Hartkamp, & Junkert, 1993). When profiles for individual patients are interpreted, less strict value of .71 serves as a subjectively meaningful boundary. It accounts for at least half the variance. If the Attack (ATK) coefficient is .71 or more, the relationship can be called attacking, and the label usually has face validity in the opinion of the rater. More detailed explanations of pattern coefficients and their attributes are available (Benjamin, 1984, 1988; Benjamin & Wonderlich, 1994).

Table 4.1 shows that assessment by SASB questionnaires yields numbers that describe the sampled relationships in terms of the two axes of the SASB model. Positive attack coefficients describe hostile relationships, and negative attack coefficients describe friendly ones. Positive control or submission (CON/SUB) coefficients describe enmeshed relationships, and negative control coefficients describe a pattern of differentiation. At the start of therapy, this patient was clearly submissive to her husband at her best (.819). He reciprocated, being responsive to her influence too (.605). However, at his worst, he changed dramatically to become maximally separate from her (−.961). Indeed, a few months after therapy started, he abruptly left. He later returned, wanting to reconcile, but the patient was not willing to resume the relationship.

The third parameter is a conflict coefficient (CFL) that reflects the degree to which a given domain has endorsements centering on opposite poles. The highest conflict coefficients identified at the start of therapy in this case were in the perceived parental relationship. Figure 4.6 shows the conflicted profiles for the complementary set: father focused on mother (.606) and mother reacted to father (.622). These positive conflict coefficients reflect opposing endorsements on the vertical axes and therefore suggest an intimacy/distance conflict. Negative conflict coefficients would reflect opposing endorsements on the horizontal axis and suggest an attachment conflict. In the relationship shown in Figure 4.6, the father was characterized by both CONTROL and IGNORE behavior in relation to the mother. In other words, his focus on his wife involved both enmeshment and differentiation. The figure shows that the mother also was conflicted in her response to her husband. She matched her husband's ambivalence on the dimension of enmeshment (SUBMIT and SULK) versus differentiation (SEPARATE). Her conflicted position in the intransitive domain was complementary to the her husband's conflicted position in the transitive domain. They showed complementarity in an intimacy/distance[3] conflict. The patient's view was that even though the parents clearly disliked one another, they grimly stayed together out of a sense of duty and propriety. The conflict coefficients shown in Table 4.1 reflect their ambivalence.

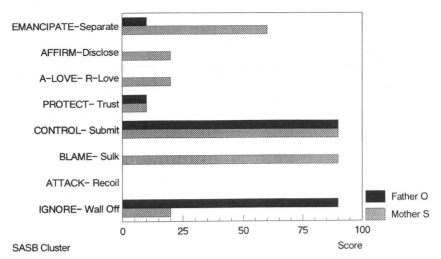

FIGURE 4.6. The patient's view of her parents' marriage when she was aged 5–10. The father showed strong opposing tendencies of **CONTROL** and **IGNORE**, while the mother complemented these conflicting messages with the opposing positions of <u>SUBMIT</u> and <u>SEPARATE</u>. The pattern coefficients can quantify as well as qualitatively describe conflict.

Additional "hot spots" in the patient's object relations are shown in Table 4.1. At the start of therapy, she felt that her relationship with her husband was generally friendly, even at worst. However, the marital relationship was marked by differences in their respective positions on the intimacy distance dimension, discussed above. For example, at worst, she attempted to control him, but he was highly autonomous. By contrast to the friendly relationship with her husband, the patient saw her mother as hostile (attack = .684 when focused on the patient) and somewhat controlling (control = .728). In addition to showing hostile enmeshment, the mother also neglected the patient (conflict = .564). The patient's relationship with her father was less conflicted. She saw him as friendly (attack = −.714) and moderately controlling (control = .387). She matched his warmth (attack = −.778) and strongly deferred to him (submit = .935).

The right-hand side of Table 4.1 summarizes comparable data generated 3½ years later. Inspection of that part of the table shows that her view of herself and her parents during childhood remained quite stable over the 3½-year period. She consistently recalled hostile enmeshment with her mother and friendly dependency on her father. It probably is not coincidental that the patient's husband showed the complete opposite (180° away on the SASB model) of hostile enmeshment. Instead of being hostile and controlling, her husband was markedly friendly and highly independent.

The patient's view of the relationship with the therapist was characterized by friendliness (attack ranged from − .819 to − .910) and moderate autonomy. Except for her reaction to the therapist, which is mildly submissive (.413), the control/submit coefficients ranged from − .44 to − .60, indicating a moderate degrees of autonomy in most aspects of the therapy relationship. A relationship characterized by friendly autonomy is optimally comfortable (Benjamin, 1994a; Henry, 1994). A current description of this pattern is "autonomy within connectedness" (Berlin & Johnson, 1989; Gilligan, 1977). The average of the conflict coefficients for the relationship with the therapist was .212, and the average conflict in all the other relationships was .384. The relationship with the therapist was less conflicted than any other that was assessed.

In addition to graphical profiles (Figures 4.4–4.6), pattern coefficients (Table 4.1), a single two-space map of all relationships can be generated. Figure 4.7 provides an example. Each relationship is summarized by four sets of affiliation (AF) and autonomy (AU) scores (he/she focuses, he/she reacts; I focus, I react). A weighted affiliation or autonomy score is a sum of the cross-products of each cluster score with a weight, divided by the number of cross-products. Affiliation weights are maximized at the friendliness pole and minimized at the attack pole. Autonomy weights are maximized at the differentiation pole and minimized at the enmeshment pole. Although conflict is obscured completely, this method does have the advantage of providing a one-page map of the rater's interpersonal space. Figure 4.7 provides an affiliation/autonomy map of the data shown on the right-hand side of Table 4.1.

Figure 4.7 shows that the patient's relationships with her father and her husband were benevolent. They were located in the friendly part of interpersonal space, and both allowed autonomy. The figure also shows that her mother was engaged in hostile control, and as a child, the patient showed resentful compliance to that control (M to c). When assuming the parent-like role, the patient was friendly to her mother and gave her autonomy (C to m). Scores for the ex-lover place him quite close to the mother (P,M and p,m). The patient herself said as she returned this set of ratings, "I noticed while filling this out how similar he [ex-lover] was to Momma."

Clinical assessment shows that the patient's view was that her father hated her mother and all women. For much of her young life, she had been "on his side" and hated women too—until she became old enough to realize she was one. Then she felt totally betrayed and confused. Her solution, in effect, was to resign her identity as a woman—indeed, as a human being. Her anger at and detachment from society at large and herself in particular was marked.[4]

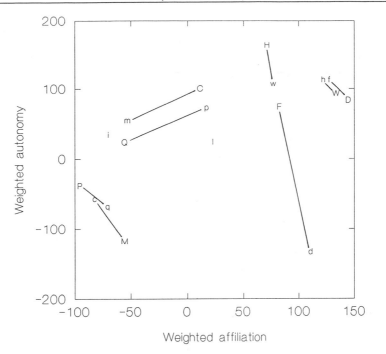

FIGURE 4.7. Two-dimensional representation of the patient's object relations 3½ years after therapy started. Her ex-lover was very much like her mother, while her husband was more like her father. Capital letters indicate transitive focus on another person while lower-case letters show intransitive reaction by self (except for the symbols I, which represents Introject at best, and i, which represents introject at worst). M,m = mother, C,c = patient with mother; F,f = father; D,d = patient with father; H,h = husband at best; W,w = patient with husband at best; P,p = ex-lover at worst; Q,q = patient with ex-lover at worst.

In addition to characterizing the various relationships in a single picture, the 2-dimensional maps visually mark similarities, complementarities, and introjections. Consider the patient's complementarity in relation to her mother's focus on her. The line (distance) between the theoretically complementary symbols M and c is quite short. With her father, the comparable complementary combination (parent focuses, child reacts) is not so short (line F to d). Still, distances within complementary sets tended to be smaller (M to c; m to C; P to q; Q to p; H to w; W to h). Distances between sets were likely to be large (e.g, Mother and father were widely discrepant, as shown by MF and cd). The relationships with ex-lover and husband also were like night and day (Pq and Hw).

The introject at worst (i) was close in space to the location of her relationship with her mother. Introject at best (I) was closer to the location for her relationship with father and husband. It is reasonable to speculate that she was under the influence of internalizations from her mother when at her worst. The benevolent input from her father and husband was more influential when she was at her best.

In sum, the three different ways of characterizing the questionnaire ratings are: (1) profiles based on cluster scores, (2) pattern coefficients that summarize the relations among cluster scores, and (3) plots in a two-space with weighted affiliation and autonomy scores. Each has advantages and disadvantages. Briefly, the profiles show most directly how the relationship is experienced. They are easily used for conventional between-group comparisons using repeated-measures MANOVA. Such profiles are familiar to most researchers who use profile measures such as the MMPI, MCMI, SCL-90-R, and the like.

The pattern coefficients are especially useful at the level of $n = 1$ because they quantify a relationship in terms that patients and clinicians can understand (attacking, controlling, conflicted). It is easy to compare ratings within an individual set like the two shown in Table 4.1. For example, at the start of therapy, it is clear that the patient saw her father as engaging in more friendly focus ($-.714$) than her mother (.684). The pattern coefficients are especially important when using the short form because they summarize information within a set of eight independently rated points. This gives more psychometric power and construct validity than would the use of unrelated individual scores. Most assessment methods would look to an additive score to assess an attribute (e.g., hostility). The pattern coefficient method considers the point of interest (ATTACK) plus its relation to all others in the set. For an ATTACK coefficient to be highly positive, the hostile points must receive high endorsements, and the friendly points must receive low endorsements. In addition, points theoretically in between must receive moderate endorsements. If any of these conditions fails, the magnitude of the pattern coefficient cannot be very large. The pattern coefficient represents a theoretically precise relationship among a set of eight numbers. Moreover, each of the points on an SASB profile is independently rated. No cluster score has any a priori dependence on any other. This independence makes more remarkable the order within profiles that is quantified by the pattern coefficients. Such procedural independence is not characteristic of the widely used MMPI, for example, which has item overlap among scales.

This unfamiliar feature, that a number specifically assesses relations among all endorsements within the set, has yielded an unusual and unexpected result. Pattern coefficient data consistently suggest that interpersonal relationships are seen in dichotomous terms: as friendly or hostile; as controlling or freeing; as submissive or independent.

Interpersonal perceptions may be categorical. Unfortunately, there are few familiar statistical procedures for handling data that are so clearly distributed bimodally (see Benjamin & Wonderlich, 1994, for an extended discussion of this problem). Actual ratings have pattern coefficients that are bimodally distributed, whereas randomly generated ratings do not.

The Objective Observer Coding System

Profiles

The process of coding videotapes of interactions has been described in manuals (Benjamin, Giat, & Estroff, 1981; Grawe-Gerber & Benjamin, 1989; Humphrey & Benjamin, 1989). These codes can yield data comparable to those available from questionnaires. Codings can be summarized as profiles like those shown in Figures 4.4–4.6; by pattern coefficients like those of Table 4.1; and by maps based on weighted affiliation and autonomy scores like Figure 4.7. In addition, the objective observer codes can be submitted to simple one-step sequential analysis and Markov chain analysis. Some of these features will be illustrated using the SASB codes of the interactions between a depressed mother and her 19-month-old toddler. Data were obtained during the second reunion after separation from the mother according to protocol in the Ainsworth "Strange Situation." (Ainsworth, Blehar, Waters, & Wall, 1978).[5]

Figure 4.8 shows the profiles for mother and baby during the second reunion. By far, this mother's most frequent response to her baby was to protect and nurture him. She also showed some CONTROL, BLAME and IGNORE codes, suggesting coercion and miscuing. The baby complemented her nurturance with a relatively large percentage of complementary behaviors coded as TRUST. He also showed an unusually high frequency of behaviors coded as SULK and RECOIL. These relatively high levels of hostile reaction suggest disrupted attachment.

The pattern coefficients for the data in Figure 4.8 suggest that the mother was somewhat friendly (ATK = −.22), and likely to give mixed messages on the control dimension (CON only = .40, but CFL = .54). The baby was minimally friendly (ATK = −.16), submissive (.37), and unusually conflicted about attachment (CFL = −.48). The weighted affiliation, autonomy vectors (AF, AU) suggest that the dyad was "luke warm" and only mildly enmeshed (mother's AF = 17.44, AU = −28.07; baby's AF = 10.40, AU = −29.72). The (AF, AU) vectors suggest that the relationship was highly complementary. Overall, the baby matched the mother's position, and vice versa. The correlation between

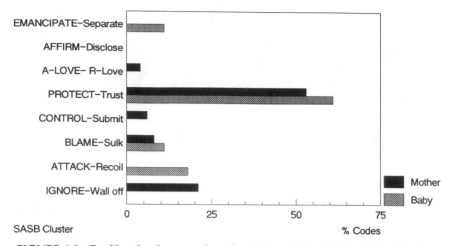

FIGURE 4.8. Profile of a depressed mother interacting with her baby during reunion after the second separation in the Strange Situation protocol. They were complementary in that she was protective, and the baby trusting. However, he also showed some disruption of attachment with his unusual response of RECOIL. A product–moment correlation of .82 between the two profiles estimates their complementarity.

the mother's focus on the baby and his reaction to her (eight cluster points) was .82. The distance (Pythagorean distance on AF, AU) was only 7.23; They were very close.

Sequences

The SASB software provides a method for testing the relevance of sequence. Figure 4.9 shows the one-step progression of mother to baby, and Figure 4.10 shows the sequences from baby to mother. To simplify the presentation, the figures include only proportions greater than .30, the arbitrary but conventional number for noting loadings in factor analyses.

Figure 4.9 shows that the baby typically responded to a variety of maternal initiations (**IGNORE, BLAME, CONTROL, PROTECT**) with TRUST. When he responded with other positions, such as RECOIL or SULK, it followed her coercion (**CONTROL**) or miscuing (**IGNORE**). Figure 4.10 shows that the mother had a very strong tendency to nurture or **PROTECT**, no matter what the baby did. The exception was when he RECOILed, which she then ignored.

Figures 4.9 and 4.10 also demonstrate that the mother's behaviors occurred mostly on the transitive surface, while the baby's were plotted on the intransitive surface. This is a confirmation of the definitions

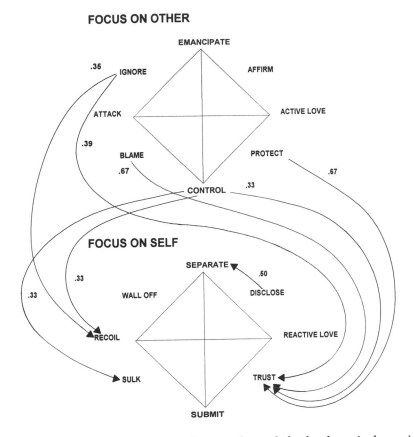

FIGURE 4.9. One-step transitions from mother to baby for the pair shown in Figure 4.8. He had a strong tendency to TRUST no matter what she did first. If he reacted in a hostile way, it was in response to his mother's CONTROL or IGNORE. One-step probabilities permit analysis of sequencing in the development of psychopathology.

of transitive focus as prototypically parent-like and of intransitive focus as prototypically child-like.

Figures 4.11 and 4.12 respectively show the transition probabilities for mother and baby, using Markov chain analysis (see Benjamin, 1979b; 1986b). Figure 4.11 shows that whatever her initial state, the mother is highly likely to move toward PROTECT. Figure 4.12 shows that the baby moves toward friendly dependency (TRUST) even when he starts from positions of alienation (RECOIL and SEPARATE). The Markov chaining data show that SASB-based complementarity theory can be confirmed for transitional states (Figures 4.11 and 4.12) as well as for profiles (Figure 4.8).

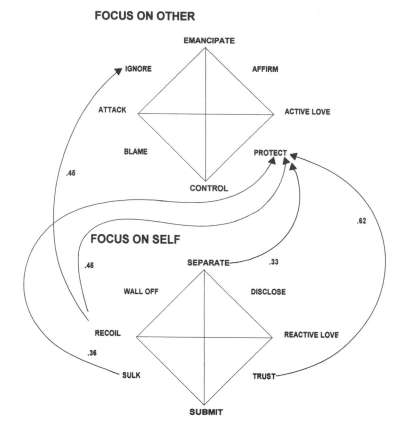

FIGURE 4.10. One-step transitions from baby to mother for the pair shown in Figures 4.8 and 4.9. She had a strong tendency to **PROTECT**, no matter what he did. If she reacted in a hostile way, it was in response to his <u>RECOIL</u>.

The cross-sectional and sequential analyses suggest that this relationship was characterized by a complementary relation: mother **PRO-TECT**; baby <u>TRUST</u>. If the videotapes are viewed with an uncritical eye, there is no "abuse," and the relationship is basically friendly. However, many observers are troubled by the exchanges. It is not clear what is wrong, but "something is different." The problems are suggested by the palpable but not very frequent presence of behaviors with hostile codes: mother: **BLAME, IGNORE,** and baby <u>RECOIL</u>, <u>WALL OFF</u>. It should be noted that many mothers, including those in the control group in this sample, showed some of these hostile behaviors under this high-ly stressful protocol. Analyses of group results are not yet complete. Early scans suggest that critical differences between depressed and

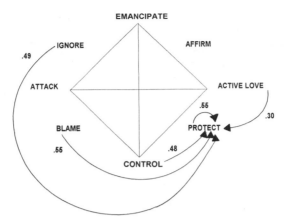

FIGURE 4.11. Transition matrix for the mother shown in Figure 4.8. The position to which she was most likely to move was PROTECT.

nondepressed mothers are not going to appear simply in terms of warmth or supportiveness versus rejection or hostility. Nor are they in dominance *versus* submission. Rather, they are mostly to be found in the sequential analyses and in the analyses of complexity. Examples are given below.

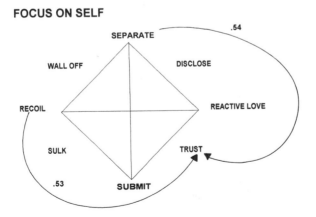

FIGURE 4.12. Transition matrix for the baby shown in Figure 4.8. The position to which he was most likely to move was TRUST, and this complements his mother's transition to **PROTECT**.

Analysis of Complexity

The quality of the differences detected by SASB-based analysis of complexity of communication is illustrated by excerpts from the reunion of this dyad. This transcript was made by an undergraduate student blind to the hypotheses of the study and to the SASB coding system.

The baby was extremely distressed by the second separation and continued to cry hard as she picked him up and carried him about the room (RECOIL). Very shortly after reunion, she took him toward the one-way observation mirror and pointed at their reflection:

MOTHER: "See, lookit" (**PROTECT**; this appears to be an attempt to nurture).

MOTHER: "Look at that." She turns and points. She looks back at her child (**PROTECT**).

BABY: Continue sobbing (RECOIL).

MOTHER: "They don't want to see you crying." She wipes her child's face (**ACTIVE LOVE** plus **CONTROL** plus **IGNORE**).

MOTHER: Looking at her child, she says: "Dry your tears. Go ahead." She pushes his hand away and squeezes her child's nose (**CONTROL** plus **ACTIVE LOVE** plus **IGNORE**).

BABY: He squeals, then rubs his face (SULK; *SELF-PROTECT*).

MOTHER: She grabs a tissue and puts it to her child's nose. She says, "Look up. Blow" (**CONTROL**).

BABY: Starts to cry (RECOIL).

MOTHER: She blows through her nose while looking at her child (**PROTECT**).

BABY: He continues to cry while pushing his mother's hand away (RECOIL plus SEPARATE).

MOTHER: She says, "Blow." She puts the tissue to her own nose and blows into it, more or less "in his face" (**PROTECT** plus **BLAME** plus **IGNORE**; this triple code reflects the increasing anger and apparent mockery in her voice; she still is trying to "help him," and she still is miscuing).

BABY: He looks at his mother, then puts both of his hands to his nose. He still is crying (TRUST plus RECOIL; the baby accepts her suggestion, but his distress continues).

After the nose blowing is completed, the mother begins to try to interest the baby in various toys in the room; he looks and responds

(TRUST), with varying degrees of accompanying distress (SULK or RECOIL) or resistance (SEPARATE). He gradually calms and accepts (TRUST) her showing of various pictures (kittens, Sesame Street figures).

The codes of this brief exchange show that the mother was nurturant and warm (PROTECT). However, she also conveys that he should shape up and not be upset (CONTROL). She does not cue appropriately on him (IGNORE), and offers input about the environment that is incorrect or, at best, irrelevant ("They don't want to see you cry").

The summary analysis of the complexity between this dyad was striking. Sixteen percent of the mother's and 18% of the baby's communications were complex. There were a relatively large number of triple codes from the mother (6.8%). Both mother and baby showed complex codes that mixed clearly warm with clearly hostile messages. The SASB software can separate these mixed forms of complex codes from those that are completely friendly (loving joshing); and those that are completely hostile (nothing confusing about the intent). Group results will be reported elsewhere.

In speculating about the meaning of the complexity of communication between this mother and infant, one notes that the mother's triple codes have the elements of Bateson's "double bind." This pattern has been described as a "triple blocker"[6] (Humphrey & Benjamin, 1986). The prediction would be that if this infant stays with this mother, and if she continues this mode of mothering, he will be very confused about the meaning of warmth and helpfulness. He will be unable to label his own affect accurately or to know how others see him. He will understand that there are very definite expectations for how he should behave and feel and that these will not necessarily relate to how he actually does feel. His sense of self and his ability to read cues correctly about himself, his situation, and others' views of him is likely to be compromised. It is not clear whether this would be associated with depression or worse (e.g., schizophrenia). Such analyses on a large sample, pursued longitudinally, could fairly test the Bateson hypothesis. The SASB model and technology are capable of operationalizing subtleties of mother–infant interaction in ways that relate directly to fairly complex but unconfirmed developmental theories about adult psychopathology.

REVIEW OF THE EVIDENCE FOR VALIDITY OF THE SASB MODEL AND ITS APPLICATIONS TO THE DIAGNOSIS AND TREATMENT OF PERSONALITY DISORDER

The SASB model, questionnaires, coding system, and software have been used by others in a variety of research contexts. These reports are relevant to many of the methodological concerns the editor asks authors to discuss. A list of such studies can be obtained from me. The present chapter is confined to my own work with the SASB model and technology.

A primary methodological concern is the question of validity of the SASB models and methods. According to the American Psychological Association (1985), there are three types of validity: (1) content, (2) criterion-related (concurrent and predictive), and (3) construct validity. Very briefly, (1) content validity has to do with whether the measure or theory assesses what it claims to assess. If the judgment is informal, as in the opinion of the reader, face validity[7] is established. Content validity is more than face validity; it must be established by formal ratings. (2) Criterion-related validity is subdivided into two forms: concurrent validity and predictive validity. Concurrent validity is manifest when the measure bears a meaningful relationship to other measures that already have established validity in the domain in question. Predictive validity is established when the theory can foretell findings. (3) Construct validity requires that the theory be able to generate an infinite number of operations that can confirm or disconfirm the theory. "Evidence of construct validity is not found in a single study; rather, judgments of construct validity are based upon an accumulation of research results" (American Psychiatric Association, 1974, p. 30).

Content validity is subject to the flaws inherent in finding consensus. Anything that is established by vote can be overturned by finding new and different voters. Concurrent validity is handy for satisfying editors but constrains progress because new ideas necessarily are tied to old ones. Predictive validity also is constrained by the validity of the measures it predicts. Construct validity has the disadvantage of being difficult to define and difficult to establish. It requires that there be an infinitude of predictions that can be tested by experiment and that can cover every challenge. I believe that a viable clinical theory must have strong construct validity. Moreover, if there is construct validity, the other types of validity follow. Further detail on the very important topic of construct validity is available in a classic paper by MacCorquedale and Meehl (1948). A survey of the relationship of the SASB model and its clinical applications and these various types of validity follows.

Content Validity

The SASB Model, Questionnaires, and Coding System

If the reader thinks the presentation of the SASB model and the technology as illustrated in Figures 4.1 to 4.12 makes sense, then those components have face validity. Formal tests of content validity have established that judges unfamiliar with SASB would describe the questionnaire items in terms of the predicted underlying theoretical dimensions. The dimensional ratings procedure (Benjamin, 1988, 1994a) provided that undergraduate students rate each SASB item on scales respectively representing the theoretical underlying dimensions (focus; love–hate; enmeshment–differentiation). Average ratings for each item were then used to reconstruct the model. For example, the items representing the point AFFIRM were assigned values by the naive students. Group results suggested that the items did reflect focus on another person, moderate degrees of friendliness, and moderate amounts of freedom giving. These judgments appropriately placed AFFIRM at approximately 1:30 o'clock on Figure 4.3. The process was repeated for each point of the model. The result was a reasonable facsimile of the cluster version of the SASB model. This dimensional ratings procedure formally established the content validity of the SASB items.

The Application to DSM Personality Disorders

Face validity could be established by reader reaction to the descriptions of the diagnoses as they appear in Benjamin (1993b.) A formal survey of randomly selected clinician readers would be required to establish content validity.

Criterion-Related Validity: Concurrent Validity

The SASB Model

The SASB model is different from the Leary-based circumplex models in several major ways. Among the five biggest differences is: (1) the dimension of focus. Also, (2) the domain of differentiation is included. (3) There is an explicit way to link interpersonal with intrapsychic events. (4) The SASB model is applied to specific relationships (spouse, parents, children and more), whereas the "traditional" Leary-based circumplexes are used as trait measures. (5) Finally, the SASB assesses the individual's view of others (he, she, they) as well as of the self (I).

Figure 4.13 presents a formal test of concurrent validity between a representative SASB measure (rater with significant other at best) and the traditional circumplex as represented by Wiggins's IAS-R. Product–moment correlations between the two circumplexes, using this sample of 174 psychiatric inpatients, are suggestive but not impres-

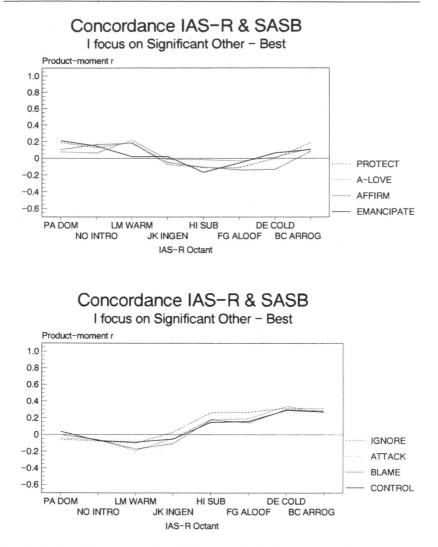

FIGURE 4.13. Concurrent validity between the ICL as assessed by Wiggins's IAS-R and the SASB. PA, Ambitious, Dominant; NO, Gregarious, Extroverted; LM, Warm, Agreeable; JK, Unassuming, Ingenuous; HI, Lazy, Submissive; FG, Aloof, Introverted; DE, Cold, Quarrelsome; BC, Arrogant, Calculating. The general trend for friendly points to correlate with friendly points is there, but overall concordance is weak.

sive. There is modest circumplex ordering, especially in the lower part of Figure 4.13. The range in magnitude of r is small. Positive correlations do appear when friendly SASB items are related to friendly IAS-R items (PA, NO, LM, JK) and when hostile SASB items are compared to hostile IAS-R items (HI, FG, DE, BC).[8] The relatively weak concurrent validity suggests that although both models are based on circumplex logic, they are only distantly related. This is not surprising, given the rather large theoretical discrepancies about the structure and usage of these two circumplex models. If the SASB were to be dismissed because of its poor correspondence to the more traditional circumplex, there would be no room for going beyond what the traditional circumplex can do.

The Application to DSM Personality Disorders

The Wisconsin Personality Inventory (WISPI; Klein et al., 1983) presents items that correspond directly to the items of Axis II of DSM-III-R and DSM-IV (American Psychiatric Association, 1987, 1994). The WISPI was written to makes sense of the perspective of the rater and to incorporate the interpersonal contextual cues outlined by Benjamin (1993b). The entire formulation was based on SASB codes of DSM criteria and case illustrations. To illustrate, consider DSM-IV item 5 for borderline personality disorder: "Recurrent suicidal threats, gestures, or behavior, or self-mutilating behavior." The corresponding WISPI item is: "I like to be intimate with people, and if I sense any rejection, I deliberately hurt myself by doing something like cutting or burning myself. Then I feel better." Unlike DSM, which describes "objective" behavior, this WISPI statement is written to the phenomenology of the rater. It includes a likely interpersonal stimulus to the behavior as well as its consequence. The addition of interpersonal context helps "explain" the self-mutilating behavior and therefore enhances the likelihood it will be endorsed (only) by those to whom it is appropriate.

Concurrent validity would be shown by agreement with diagnoses made by other methods (e.g., the SCID-II interviewing method, the PDE examination, the PDQ self-rating scales). Again, the problem is that concurrent validity assumes that the measures used as the standard are acceptable. Measures that improve the standard necessarily will deviate from it and show "poor" concurrent validity. For Axis II diagnoses, agreement among the different methods is notably poor (Klein, 1988; Fiedler, 1995).

Criterion-Related Validity: Predictive Validity

The SASB Model

The predictive principles of complementarity, introjection, similarity, and antithesis mark the strongest tests of predictive validity of the SASB model. Formal analyses of the predictive principles are presented below under the heading of construct validity.

The Application to DSM Personality Disorders

The SASB-based analysis of the DSM definitions of personality disorders (Benjamin, 1993b) includes predictions about the developmental histories of individuals with the respective disorders. The SASB-based analysis of personality disorder provides detail about how to be accurate in making differential diagnoses. If appropriately narrowed by this method, the resulting diagnoses predict specific and different developmental histories for individuals with the respective disorders. A formal research plan to test those predictions is to be drawn. Briefly, researchers will use the recommended interviewing method (Benjamin, 1993b, Chap. 4) with personality-disordered inpatients. Diagnoses will be based on traditional DSM measures (e.g., SCID-II) as well as on Benjamin's (1993b) view of the Axis II disorders. Developmental history will be explored. Objective raters will assess the degree to which the predicted social learning experiences were present in the history. The expected connection between developmental history and diagnosis, if confirmed, will have important implications for prevention and treatment.

Construct Validity

The SASB Model

Construct validity has been central to the SASB-based research program. As suggested above, if construct validity is sound, the other types follow easily. The proof is trivial: content, concurrent, and predictive validity are subsets of the infinitude of operations that a valid construct must generate. Because the meaning of a valid construct can never be exhausted, one can never finish testing construct validity. For the present context, a few representative tests of the validity of the structure and predictive principles of the SASB model are presented.

Tests of the construct validity of the structure of the SASB model itself have included factor analyses of rater responses to the Intrex items, circumplex analyses, and tests of internal consistency. Examples of validating factor analyses appeared in Benjamin (1974, 1994a). In brief, the predicted underlying factors do consistently emerge, and factor loadings can be used to generate reasonable facsimiles of the model. The factor-analytic reconstructions of raters' views affirm the hypothetical structure of interpersonal space.

Reconstructions of the SASB model based on the dimensional ratings method are different. They confirm the hypothetical structure in terms of the *opinions* of raters inspecting the content of the SASB items. Judgment of the structure of the items (dimensional ratings) is different from judgment of how well the items apply to the self (factor analyses of interpersonal histories). The dimensional ratings represent content as well as construct validity. They have generally yielded good reconstructions of the model (Benjamin, 1988).

Figure 4.14 presents an example of a form of circumplex analysis that confirms the hypothetical structure. The data in Figure 4.14 are from 173 psychiatric inpatients rating their view of their significant other person, focusing on them at best. The figure shows product–moment correlations among the scores assigned to items assessing the eight clusters in the transitive domain. Consider the correlations for each of the clusters with PROTECT, shown at the top of Figure 4.14. The correlation of PROTECT with itself necessarily is 1.00. The figure shows that the clusters on either side of PROTECT, namely CONTROL and AC-TIVE LOVE, have large and positive correlations with it. Clusters theoretically further away from PROTECT have progressively lower correlations with it. The smallest (largest negative) correlation is with its opposite, IGNORE. This pattern of high positive correlations with theoretically adjacent points and high negative patterns with theoretically opposite points defines circumplex order. The order with respect to the polar points EMANCIPATE and CONTROL was less than ideal, but this is not surprising because inpatients typically have adjustment difficulties marked by enmeshment/differentiation struggles. However, the point EMANCIPATE did correlate most strongly with the adjacent clusters, AFFIRM and IGNORE. It also showed a small correlation with CONTROL, its theoretical opposite.

Another way of establishing circumplex order is to use cluster analysis. In Figure 4.15, the data from Figure 4.14 are shown as a (simple linkage) cluster analysis. The biggest subdivision (on the far right) is friendly (ACTIVE LOVE, PROTECT, AFFIRM, plus EMANCIPATE) versus hostile (IGNORE, ATTACK, BLAME, plus CONTROL). At the finest subdivisional level (at the far left), the clusters appear in almost exact theoretical order. Clusters 3 and 4 are interchanged, but otherwise, the arrangement is exactly as predicted: clusters are in the order 1, 2, 4,

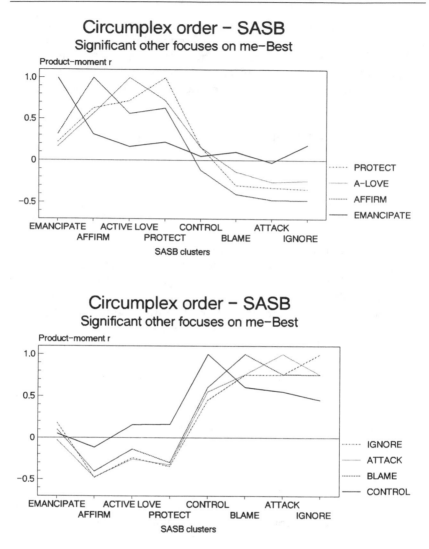

FIGURE 4.14. Circumplex order within the SASB ratings of the significant other person chosen for rating by psychiatric inpatients. For most points, the circumplex order is quite strong. Circumplex order of this magnitude is obtained for most perspectives (self, other), state (best, worst), situations (with significant others, parents, others), and samples (inpatients, outpatients, normals). This contributes to construct validity.

Tree diagram

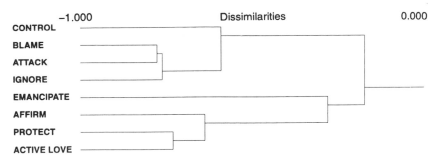

FIGURE 4.15. Cluster analysis of the data shown in Figure 4.14. This method of analysis also strongly confirms the circumplex order.

3, 5, 6, 7, 8. This ordering shows that data within this set have good circumplex order. Similar results are found for most sets of eight clusters, whether they are of rater views of others (Figure 4.14) or of self (Figure 4.13). The hypothetical structure proposed by the SASB model applies to social perceptions of self and others.

Figure 4.16 illustrates one of many ways of testing the principle of complementarity. It is from the data set already discussed for Figures 4.8 to 4.12. Figure 4.16 shows that the most common sequence is: Mother PROTECTs and baby complements with TRUST. The finding may be considered robust, since the two independent groups showed the same trends. One group consisted of mothers who had been identified as depressed when the study began a year before ($n = 41$). The second group consisted of mothers who were matched on socioeconomic variables by not-depressed controls ($n = 29$). The matching of complementary points also was excellent when the sequential tally was reversed: baby to mother. By far, mothers exhibited PROTECT most often in response to baby's TRUST. Complementarity works both ways: parent to child and child to parent.

Studies of complementarity using the traditional circumplex have been equivocal (e.g., Orford, 1986; Tracey, 1994). One problem has been that the traditional interpersonal circles fail to define differentiated space, and so they are capable of defining complementarity only in enmeshed space. Another problem with trait studies of complementarity is that it not always appropriate or expected. Recommended applications of the SASB assess a number of possible other correspondences including introjection, similarity, and antithesis. Complemen-

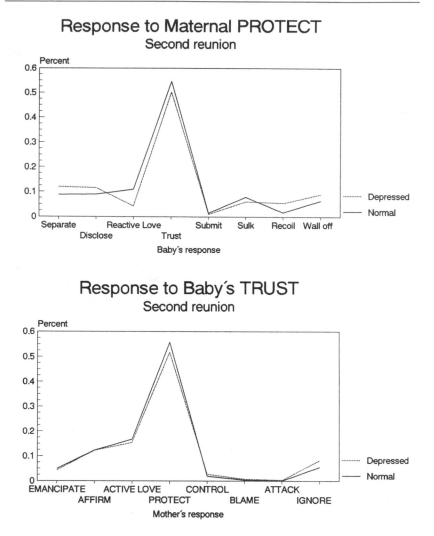

FIGURE 4.16. Group profiles for the depressed mother sample. The babies of depressed mothers showed significantly less REACTIVE LOVE, suggesting a weaker attachment. Otherwise, the cross-sectional profiles were quite similar during this highly stressful laboratory test of attachment.

tarity is only one possible predictable way of matching interacting individuals.

Figure 4.17 provides an example of the failure of complementarity in the same data set that provided excellent complementarity in the domain of friendly enmeshment. In the context of the second reunion, mothers and infants did not show complementarity when the issue was differentiation. If the mother showed behaviors coded as EMANCIPATE (e.g., "Want to go play with the toys now?"), the normal babies would often complement with SEPARATE (top of Figure 4.17). However, they also were likely to show TRUST, probably reflecting lingering insecurity from their very recent separation stress. In sum, the normal babies did show complementarity in relation to their mother's attempts to get back to "business as usual." But they also showed a nearly antithetical tendency[9] in the same setting, probably because of their temporary insecurity. Their antithetical response theoretically should "draw" more PROTECTion from the mother. If they were indeed insecure at the moment, the position was highly adaptive. In sum, two trends were going on with the normal babies in this setting: a complementary match to the message to go play again and a tendency to draw for more reassurance. The data suggest that the state of the babies with nondepressed mothers was somewhat unstable after the second reunion.

The depressed babies were different: they did not show palpable complementarity to maternal EMANCIPATion. They were devoted almost exclusively to drawing for PROTECTion with their position of TRUST. One might conclude that they were more dependent and did not have the security required for comfortable separation represented by the point SEPARATE.[10]

The bottom part of Figure 4.17 suggests that the depressed mothers pulled for enmeshment. When babies made an attempt to SEPARATE, the depressed mothers were highly likely to provide a friendly antithesis, PROTECT. By contrast, normal mothers were more likely to let the baby go if he or she initiated SEPARATion. Still, normals did retain a slight tendency to show PROTECT following this separation stress.

In sum, the group data show that both depressed and normal mothers and babies show strong complementarity in the form of PROTECT and TRUST. Complementarity was less apparent if the interpersonal issue was differentiation. If one member of the dyad started to separate, the other was likely to try to bring the other back with PROTECT (mothers) or TRUST (babies). This tendency was much greater for the depressed mothers. Differences between groups in this regard were statistically significant.

One of the many implications of construct validity is that a valid

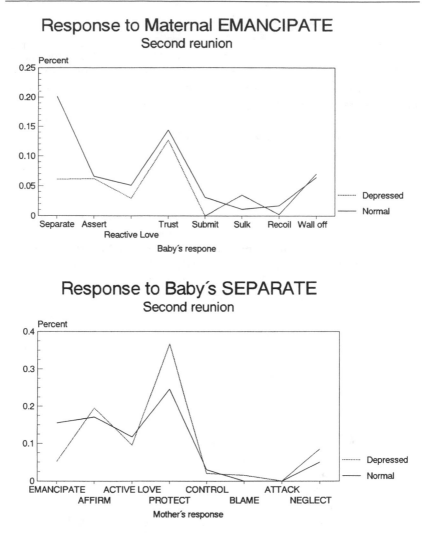

FIGURE 4.17. One-step transitions in the sample of depressed and normal mothers and their babies. Normal infants and mothers showed a significantly greater ability to complement each other when the issue was differentiation (**EMANCIPATE**/SEPARATE). Mothers in the depressed group and their infants were more likely to resist separation and instead to show **PROTECT**/TRUST.

construct will suggest revisions of and additions to itself. For example, the SASB model, which is a construct that describes interpersonal and intrapsychic behaviors, should have parallels in the domains of affect and cognitive style. The reasoning is that the primitive basics used to construct the model appeared in an evolutionary context. If these behavioral propensities were needed for survival, it would make sense that the affective and cognitive systems would support them. For example, the affects and cognitive styles that go with CONTROL should support behaviors that will implement dominance. The affects and cognitive styles that go with SUBMIT should support submissive behaviors. Each of the behaviors described by the SASB model should show predictable correlations with affect and cognition.

Early versions of Structural Analysis of Affective Behavior (SAAB) and Structural Analysis of Cognitive Behavior (SACB) appeared in Benjamin (1986a). The recent version is shown here as Table 4.2. These parallel models have not been validated, but examples of how they might be applied appear below in the discussion of comorbidity between depression and certain personality disorders.

The Application to DSM Personality Disorders

Tests of the model's applications to interpersonal diagnosis and treatment are emerging slowly over time and context. The SASB-based analyses of DSM descriptions of personality disorder make many predictions that can be confirmed or disconfirmed by readers, informally in their clinical practices and formally in their research. There are clear, refutable statements about interpersonal history, about expected transference reactions, and about treatment interventions. The implications for prevention are apparent. Comorbidity (between Axis I and Axis II) is explained by invoking the idea that specific affects and cognitive style accompany the social behaviors described by the SASB model (Benjamin, 1974, 1986a, in press). Drawing on the observations of Blatt (1974), Seligman (1975), and others, I have named personality disorders that are more likely to be accompanied by depression. These have SASB-coded "base rates" that include submissiveness and/or self-criticism. Moore (1995) confirmed that prediction by showing strong correlations between depression scores on the SCL-90-R and theoretically selected personality disorder scores on the Morey (1988) MMPI scales. The specific personality disorders that are characterized by SELF-BLAME and SELF-ATTACK (Benjamin, 1993b, p. 394) are borderline, narcissistic, histrionic, dependent, obsessive–compulsive, passive–aggressive, and avoidant. According to the helplessness/self-criticism formula, these would be likely to show "comorbid" depression[11]

**TABLE 4.2. Hypothetical Parallels between Behaviors
(Described by the SASB Model), Affect, and Cognition**

SASB behaviors	Affective parallels	Cognitive parallels
EMANCIPATE	Indifferent	Broad scan
AFFIRM	Sympathetic	Balanced
ACTIVE LOVE	Cherishing	Expect continuity
PROTECT	Comforting	Rational
CONTROL	Energized	Sharp focus
BLAME	Arrogant	Judgmental
ATTACK	Vengeful	Terminating
IGNORE	Rejecting	Illogical
SEPARATE	Unconcerned	Immune
DISCLOSE	Confident	Honest
REACTIVE LOVE	Merry, joyful	Open
TRUST	Hopeful	Agreeable
SUBMIT	Helpless	Deferential
SULK	Humiliated	Constricted
RECOIL	Panicked	Closed
WALL OFF	Hopeless	Incoherent

Note. From Benjamin (1986a, pp. 632–633). Copyright 1986 by The Guilford Press. Adapted by permission.

Shea, Glass, Pilkonis, Watkins, and Docherty (1987) reported that
depression is more likely in avoidant, dependent, and obsessive–
compulsive disordered outpatients. Pilkonis and Frank (1988) obtained
the same results. Pfohl, Stangl, and Zimmerman (1984) reported on
the most frequent comorbidity between depression and personality
disorder in an inpatient sample. It was with borderline, histrionic, and
dependent personality disorders. These theoretical predictions about
comorbidity, accompanied by the independent empirical observations of others, contribute to the construct validity of the SASB-based
interpretations of personality disorder and the problem of "comorbidity."

Informal documentation of the construct validity of the SASB-based
treatment recommendations is available through clinician narratives.
Sheffield (1994) provides a single documented case illustration of the
helpfulness of the approach. More formal documentation is planned
in a clinic that will accept only well-entrenched "intractable" cases of
personality disorder. Process studies, including SASB codes of therapy content and process plus adherence measures, will attempt to specify whether the choices of interventions conform to prediction.

The most difficult challenge is to operationalize and test for the
presence of the unconscious wishes and fears that organize and main-

tain the personality disorders. Yet this centrally important issue must be addressed if individuals with personality disorder are to be more effectively helped to change. The balance of this chapter is devoted to sketches of theory and methods that might be used to assess these hypothetical "drivers" of personality.

FUTURE THEORETICAL DEVELOPMENT: IMPORTANT PERSONS AND THEIR INTERNALIZED REPRESENTATIONS AND EFFECTIVE TREATMENT

Background: Attachment Theory

The psychoanalyst John Bowlby (1969) developed what is now known as "attachment theory." Grounded in ethology (see Tinbergen, 1951), attachment theory is of quintessential relevance to object relations theory, a modern branch of psychoanalysis (Greenberg & Mitchell, 1983). I believe the arguments of Bowlby and some of the object relations analysts may be summarized, revised, and tested by appeal to the SASB model. Psychoanalysts Greenberg and Mitchell (1983, pp. 2–3) note that personality is reflected in terms of the interactions one has with oneself and others. Because the SASB model is specifically designed to assess interactions with self and others, it offers a promising way to assess object relations. An example was given in Figure 4.7 and Table 4.1.

The linkages among the literatures of primatology, developmental psychology, and object relations theory can be made explicit using the SASB model. The following theoretical summary emerges: Patterns of personality are shaped by temperament interacting with experiences with important others, most especially those who were present during critical early periods of development. Humans are preprogrammed to attach to those who care for them when they are most vulnerable. This process begins at birth. Reflexes in the neonate facilitate hanging on to the mother. Three reflexes: the startle, the grasp, and the strong propensity for ventral contact assure that attachment can take place because they facilitate proximity to the mother. Once in the vicinity of the mother, the rooting, placing, and sucking reflex chain increases the likelihood of nursing. As the infant matures, the following reflexes, which in the human are visual at first, help the infant stay within the protective orb of the parent. These attachment reflexes have clear adaptive value.

In addition to the need to maintain proximity, the infant has an "opposing" need for independence that becomes stronger as it gets older. Bowlby noted that the ability to separate paradoxically is dependent on having a secure attachment. As the child matures and finds its way separately from the parent, attachment behaviors are no longer apparent except under conditions of stress. When challenged, the child seeks contact with the attachment object to renew security. These patterns were summarized by Ainsworth et al. (1978), who subjected Bowlby's ideas to experimental test. A *securely attached* child is confident that his/her parenting figure will be responsive, available, comforting, and protective, particularly under stress. The security allows the child to explore the environment and develop his/her own abilities as a separate person. SASB codes for the parent of a securely attached child are PROTECT, which appropriately moves to EMANCIPATE. The SASB codes for the securely attached child are TRUST, moving appropriately to SEPARATE.

These ideas about the role of secure attachment in the development of "normality" have been supported by studies in monkeys (Harlow & Harlow, 1962) and by a large research literature in humans. An SASB-based review of representative studies of attachment is offered by Florsheim, Henry, and Benjamin (1996). Recently, Kraemer proposed that the quality of the attachment relationship also affects the infant primate's neurochemistry (Kraemer, Ebert, Lake, & McKinney, 1989; Kraemer, 1992). A slightly different but clearly related literature in social psychology has explored the impact of "attachment styles" on adult personality, especially in love relationships (e.g., Hazen & Shaver, 1994). Attachment also has been related to psychopathology (Teti, Gelfand, Messinger, & Isabella, 1995).

Bowlby further suggested that attachment experiences shape personality as the child takes in representations of the caregivers. The child retains them as "internal working models" (Bowlby, 1969, p. 81). These working models organize the child's social perceptions and responses. Bowbly (1977) applied his attachment theory specifically to psychopathology:

> Attachment theory [is] a way of conceptualizing the propensity of human beings to make strong affectional bonds to particular others and of explaining the many forms of emotional distress and personality disturbance, including anxiety, anger, depression, and emotional detachment, to which unwilling separation and loss give rise. Though it incorporates much psychoanalytic thinking, many of its principles derive from ethology, cognitive psychology, and control theory. (p. 201)

> Exploratory activity is of great importance in its own right, enabling a person or an animal to build up a coherent picture of environmental features which may at any time become of importance for survival. Children and other young creatures are notoriously curious and inquiring,

which commonly leads them to move away from their attachment figure. In this sense, exploratory behavior is antithetical to attachment behavior. In healthy individuals the two kinds of behavior normally alternate. The behavior of parents, and of anyone else in the care-giving role, is complementary to attachment behavior. The roles of the caregiver are first to be available and responsive as and when wanted and, secondly, to intervene judiciously should the child or older person who is being cared for be heading for trouble. Not only is it a key role, but there is substantial evidence that how it is discharged by a person's parents determines in great degree whether or not he grows up to be mentally healthy. . . . The main variable to which I draw attention is the extent to which a child's parents (a) provide him with a secure base, and (b) encourage him to explore from it. (p. 206)

In the psychoanalytic literature such a person is said to have a strong ego; and he may be described as showing "basic trust" (Erikson, 1950), "mature dependence" (Fairbairn, 1952) or as having "introjected a good object" (Klein, 1948). In terms of attachment theory he is described as having built up a representational model of himself as being both able to help himself and as worthy of being helped should difficulties arise. (p. 204)

Bowlby emphasized that good attachment is a prerequisite to healthy independence. He noted that a "good" attachment object is consistently protective but also permits exploration of the world and the development of competence. The child takes in the experience with the parent and develops an internal working model of the relationship. The model provides the security *and permission* (italics added) needed to reach out. Some years later, Bretherton (1985) commented on the impact of Bowlby's ideas:

In summary, Bowlby's most significant conceptual contributions to attachment theory are (1) that the attachment system may be regarded as a behavioral and, I would add, ideational control system with its own distinct motivation (distinct from systems regulating sexual and feeding behavior) and (2) that individual differences in the functioning of that system appear to be closely tied to an individual's working model of self, others, and the world. *The manner in which early patterns of interaction with attachment figures come to be organized into more trait-like interactional styles is not yet completely clear* [italics added]. That attachment patterns established in infancy play a significant role in the patterning of the personality was proposed not only by Bowlby (1973) but also by Ainsworth (1967), Hinde (1982), Main et al. (1985), Ricks (1985), and Sroufe and Fleeson (in press). (Bretherton, 1985, p. 14)

Bretherton noted that Bowlby had not clearly delineated exactly how attachment affects working models and personality. In this chapter, there is an attempt to answer Bretherton's query. Connections between SASB codes of the relationship with the attachment object and the internal working models, as well as the relation between the models and the personality will be drawn.

Important Persons and Their Internalized Representations (IPIRs)

Definition of IPIRs and Psychic Proximity

I have suggested (Benjamin, 1994b) that internal working models be called important persons and their internalized representations. The construct of IPIRs borrows from Bowlby the idea that mental events are primarily interpersonal in nature and are shaped importantly by early experiences with caregivers and others. The concept of an IPIR differs from psychoanalytic descriptions of internal working models in that the description of an IPIR must be specific enough to be SASB codable. If it is SASB codable, the IPIR has been described in terms of the underlying components: sexuality, aggression, power, and territory. The construct of IPIRs also invokes three specific SASB-codable mechanisms to be described in the next section. These mechanisms are directly relevant to Bretherton's query. They specifically connect the child's relationship with the early attachment object to the patterns of adult personality.

There are three ways to connect SASB codes of an individual's IPIRs to SASB codes of his/her experiences with important others (usually caregivers, otherwise called "attachment objects"). These connecting mechanisms are (1) identification, (2) recapitulation, and (3) introjection. They respectively invoke the SASB predictive principles of similarity, complementarity and introjection.

1. The process of *identification* is easy to see in young children. When there is imitation, the SASB codes of the attachment object and the individual's characteristic patterns are the same. For example, behavioral observations would show that a well-PROTECTed child becomes a PROTECTive person. Children with nurturant models will become protective of others. The theoretical explanation of this sequence is that the attachment object PROTECTs the child, the IPIR becomes PROTECTive, and the child imitates the IPIR as he/she PROTECTs others across time and context.[12] The construct of an IPIR can account for persons who can help others during crisis situations while other people are following the rule of "every man for himself." Presumably such a helpful person identifies with the IPIR and cares for others as would the IPIR.[13]

2. The principle of *recapitulation*[14] is observed when the child reacts as if the attachment object were present. When there is internalization, the child's behavior *complements* the IPIR (and the attachment object's prototypic position for that situation). For example, the PROTECTed child is a TRUSTing person across time and context. The theoretical explanation of this sequence is that the attachment object PROTECTs the child, the IPIR becomes PROTECTive, and the child complements that PROTECTion with TRUST. He/she is secure in the faith built by experience with the attachment object. He/she expects to be treated well. This benevolent expectation can prevail even under threatening circumstances. The normal individual, however, can read cues well enough to become suspicious when it is indicated. That is because the benevolent attachment object and the associated IPIR have supported the development of competence as well as trust. The benevolent attachment object and the associated IPIR have struck a balance in the dialectic of protecting and letting go.

3. The principle of *introjection* is observed when the child treats him/herself as did the attachment object. The behavioral observations would show that the PROTECTed child *SELF-PROTECTs*. The theoretical explanation of this sequence is that the attachment object PROTECTs the child, the IPIR PROTECTs the child, and the child imitates the IPIR's treatment as he or she *SELF-PROTECTs* over time and context. The construct of an IPIR can account, for example, for a situation in which one person is self-protective and everyone else is reckless. Consider the teen who has had too much to drink but decides to take a taxi home rather than ride with her inebriated friends. Presumably that teen has a protective IPIR that can prevail despite group norms.

In all three cases, the internal working model, the IPIR, is like the attachment object. All three mechanisms invoke a form of copying, a basic primate propensity.[15] Accordingly, the three copy processes differ only in directional focus. The differences parallel the three focus domains of the SASB models. If there has been identification, the person acts like the IPIR (and the attachment object). The principle of similarity is invoked. If there is internalization, the person reacts to the "present" IPIR as if it were the antecedent attachment object. The principle of complementarity to the IPIR (and the attachment object) is invoked. If there is introjection, the person treats him- or herself as does the IPIR (and as did the attachment object).

Just as there can be more than one caregiver, there can be more than one IPIR. It will be important to identify variables that affect who becomes an IPIR and whether there is identification, recapitulation, and/or introjection. The best present guess draws from Kagan's findings (reviewed under the heading "identification" in Mussen, Conger, & Kagan, 1971) that dominance (CONTROL) and warmth (ACTIVE LOVE) facilitate identification in children.

Assume that dominance and warmth are required to form an IPIR. According to the SASB model, those two nodes combine to yield PRO-TECT, the position that characterizes prototypic caregivers or "attachment objects." PROTECT is complemented by TRUST, the prototypic position for the secure child. One working hypothesis is that a person who is likely to become internalized as an IPIR must be seen by the child as a source of PROTECTion. More potent attachment objects also show the more intense behaviors described by the poles around this point: CONTROL and ACTIVE LOVE,[16] the variables that enhance imitation.

If parental behaviors described by the points PROTECT, CONTROL, and ACTIVE LOVE are central to the formation of IPIRs, it is appropriate to consider more exactly what comprises these behaviors. Inspection of the simplified SASB model in Figure 4.3 shows that the point midway between CONTROL and ACTIVE LOVE is PROTECT. Detail on that midpoint is provided by the Intrex long form items 143, Protect, back up (P lovingly looks after C's interests and takes steps to protect O; P actively backs C up), 144, Sensible analysis (with much kindness and good sense, P figures out and explains things to C), 145, Constructive stimulate (P gets C interested and teaches C how to understand and do things), and 146, Pamper, overindulge (P pays close attention to C so P can figure out all of C's needs and take care of everything). The boundaries between SASB clusters are arbitrary, and it is important to note that the item in cluster ACTIVE LOVE that is closest to PROTECT is 142, Provide for, nurture (P provides for, nurtures, takes care of C). This item probably should be included in the group that characterizes prototypical attachment objects.

An operational definition of behaviors most likely to generate an IPIR is that they should receive high levels of endorsement of those SASB items that combine dominance and warmth. In addition, behaviors coded in the pure CONTROL cluster and also the ACTIVE LOVE cluster probably also help to create lasting IPIRs. Data to test these guesses could be generated by Intrex questionnaire ratings or by SASB codes of patient's narratives or of videotapes of interactions between the patient and important others. Most probable candidates to become IPIRs are the mother, father, older siblings, and other adults living in the home such as stepparents or grandparents. In exploring who becomes an IPIR, it will also be important to assess the interaction of dominance and warmth with the gender of the attachment object and child.

This analysis provides a theory (the hypothetical construct of IPIRs) and a methodology (SASB coding of deep tracking interviews described in Benjamin, 1993b; ratings on the SASB Intrex questionnaires) to connect the relationship with the attachment object and the adult patterns of personality. The construct of IPIRs is testable and refutable because of the high degree of specificity. In addition, the hypotheses about the mechanisms for connecting early relationships and adult patterns of personality also can be tested and confirmed or rejected. SASB coding of patient narratives or ratings on the SASB questionnaire[17] provide preliminary supporting data. The most helpful interview material is generated by the "deep tracking" method described in Benjamin (1993b, Chap. 4). Longitudinal prospective studies of representative interactions between important others and the child would provide a more definitive data set.

Normal Personality

I have suggested (Benjamin, 1994b), as has Henry (1994), that normal personalities operate from a baseline characterized by SASB codes in the so-called attachment group (AG). These are **AFFIRM**/DISCLOSE/ *SELF-AFFIRM*; **ACTIVE LOVE**/REACTIVE LOVE/*ACTIVE SELF-LOVE*; and **PROTECT**/ TRUST/*SELF-PROTECT*. These normal behaviors reflect clear friendliness and moderate degrees of differentiation and enmeshment. They describe optimal attachment to the caregivers. The parenting received by a normal person would be coded mostly within the AG. The IPIRs generated by a normal parent would also be coded within the AG. These are "good" IPIRs reflecting good attachment. The behaviors generated and supported by these IPIRs would also fall within the AG. These are "normal" behaviors in the ideal sense, and they define the ideal therapy goals. The normal person's behaviors would be organized and maintained by wishes to maintain good relations with the good IPIRs. A normal person would wish to continue to receive love from (AG) and to avoid attack by or rejection from the good IPIRs.

The affects that parallel AG behaviors are shown in Table 4.2. These feelings are very pleasant and help maintain AG behaviors. Infants, children, and adults naturally seek conditions that will make them feel confident, merry, joyful, and hopeful. Table 4.2 suggests that these behaviors and affects are accompanied by effective cognitive styles including honesty, openness, agreeableness, balance, and rationality.

A normal person will fear events that are described in opposite terms. Figure 4.3 shows that the behaviors opposite the AG are **BLAME**/ SULK/*SELF-BLAME*; **ATTACK**/RECOIL/*SELF-ATTACK*; and **IGNORE**/WALL OFF/ *SELF-NEGLECT*. These are the disaffiliative or disrupted attachment group

(DAG). The parallel models sketched in Table 4.2 suggest that DAG behaviors will be associated with specific unpleasant affects (e.g., humiliation, panic, hopelessness, arrogance, vengefulness, and rejection) and specific cognitive styles (e.g., constricted, closed, incoherent, illogical, and judgmental). In addition to fearing DAG from the benevolent IPIRs, normal individuals also fear loss of AG from these IPIRs.

A "good enough" parent typically shows behaviors that can be coded in the AG. Sometimes it is necessary for the good parent to engage in behaviors that are not friendly and not moderate in enmeshment or independence. For example, limit setting, coded as CONTROL, is required for normal development. CONTROL also enhances IPIR formation. Limit-setting behaviors are not warm, and they are not moderate on the enmeshment/differentiation dimension. A normal parent also will occasionally show behaviors coded as BLAME, IGNORE, WALL OFF, and SULK. These clearly hostile behaviors are normative if they are relatively infrequent and occur only in a context in which specific child behaviors should be discouraged on behalf of the child's growth and development. Examples of such problem behaviors would include running in the street, hitting or biting others, use of obscene language, and so on. A certain amount of hostile control (BLAME = "No. That is wrong") or time-outs (IGNORE, restricted to situation and short in duration) are required to assure normal socialization. A normal child, accustomed to parental behaviors coded in the AG (and showing secure attachment), will find DAG parental behaviors to be very aversive. He or she will fear them and will behave in ways that will help avoid them.

Normal parenting behavior changes as the child matures. For example, parental CONTROL decreases and parental behaviors coded as EMANCIPATE, increase. ACTIVE LOVE and REACTIVE LOVE decrease somewhat to prepare the child for the transition to sexual bonding with an age mate. The fact that adolescents can be so annoying to parents happens to facilitate the needed letting go.

In addition to requiring baseline AG behaviors, normality requires a balance of focus. In a normal parent–child relationship, a balance of focus evolves as the child matures. At first, the parent's behaviors are exclusively in the parent-like domain, and the child's behaviors are in the child-like domain. This idea has been confirmed in parent–child data sets (e.g., Benjamin, 1974; Benjamin & Gelfand, 1992). The parent becomes progressively less characterized by AG behaviors coded on the parent-like surface. Normally the parent shows more behaviors coded on the child-like surface as the child matures. For example, the parent increasingly begins to DISCLOSE to and TRUST the normal child. Naturally these behaviors are confined to appropriate social role. The normal parent does not disclose intimate details about his or her sexual life, for example. But the normal parent does disclose affect relevant to the child ("I am mad about this"; "I am happy you found what you wanted"; "I am tired and distracted"). If the parent provides realistic feedback as well as guidance, the child can learn that he/she is not the center of the universe. He/she also gets to really know the parent. Similarly, if the parent TRUSTs appropriately ("I really need your help with this"), the maturing child can learn that he/she is competent and can provide valued services too.

If focus in the parent–child relationship is not balanced by the end of adolescence, the child is not balanced. When the parent focuses exclusively on the child, the parent does not have a self as far as the child knows, then narcissism is encouraged. On the other hand, when the parent focuses exclusively on him- or herself, the child can become "parentified." The needy parent elicits caregiving from the child as the principle of complementarity demands. Too much or too little parental focus on self can then seriously compromise the child's sense of self. Either imbalance of focus can lead to major psychopathology in the child.

Why Do Hostile and "Unrewarding" Attachment Objects Become IPIRs?

A particularly difficult question is *why* do hostile and neglectful parents, ones who do not consistently provide the child with such basic "reinforcements" as food or shelter or comfort, still become IPIRs? I suggest that the child imitates the attachment object in one of the three ways just described to achieve *psychic proximity.* Psychic proximity is the mental equivalent of reunion with the mother after separation stress. Mental "contact" with the attachment object via psychic proximity is reassuring and invokes the pleasant affects and cognitions associated with "good attachment." The (unconscious) reasoning in relation to the IPIR (and the original attachment object) is "I'll follow the patterns of our relationship so that I can maintain psychic proximity to you." Psychic proximity provides an "intrapsychic hug." Psychic proximity provides reunion with the "source," the IPIR.

Psychic proximity is coded within the AG. The focal point is at REACTIVE LOVE on the child-like surface of the SASB model. The adjacent points, TRUST and DISCLOSE also describe attachment. They implement psychic proximity to the IPIR. Psychic proximity fulfills the organizing wish to receive love from the IPIR. Acting like the IPIR, acting as if the IPIR were present, or treating the self as would the IPIR can bring psychic proximity.

The need for psychic proximity to the IPIR increases under stress, just as the infant seeks the parent when stressed. Challenges to the family loyalties represented by the IPIRs probably also increase the need for psychic proximity, just as the departure of the mother will cause the infant to follow and cling. Activation of the IPIR in response to stress resolves more quickly in those who have a secure attachment. This parallels the observation that more secure infants settle more quickly after reunion with the parent. The infantile prototype was documented earlier in this chapter in Figures 4.9 to 4.12. Children of depressed mothers were less well attached and less able to separate after stress. The inference is that their emerging IPIRs continued to say, as did their attachment object, "Let me PROTECT you." By contrast, the normal child is able to begin to internalize the message: "It's all right now. Find out what is out there if you like. I'll be here if you need me" (PROTECT, AFFIRM, EMANCIPATE, PROTECT). The dance between holding and letting go is there for the normals.

If the early attachment objects show many behaviors characterized as DAG, the child will imitate, internalize, and introject these. The parent prone to ATTACK the child will encourage the child to ATTACK others, to SELF-ATTACK, and to RECOIL from others as if they are ready to ATTACK. This child's IPIR is coded in the DAG group. The concept of psychic proximity can be invoked to support the argument that "every psychopathology is a gift of love (Benjamin, 1993a)." The child still seeks AG from the IPIR, even if it means engaging in behaviors characterized as DAG. Recall that when stressed, the individual activates the IPIR by acting out the patterns it organizes, and DAG behaviors are what has been copied to form a malovelent IPIR. Still, the motivation for the DAG behaviors is to receive AG from the malevolent IPIR. If the original attachment object was a "monster" (e.g., shows baseline ATTACK), the child may become a "monster" (ATTACK) or a victim. He/she recapitulates DAG behaviors in order to receive the ACTIVE LOVE of the IPIR.

Seasoned clinicians (and parents) will quickly note that some children who are raised without violence nonetheless become violent. Sometimes this phenomenon is simply a case of failure to set limits. Many parents mistakenly hold the "empty tank theory of development." If you give the child enough love, he/she will thrive. Needs must be fulfilled; frustration must be avoided at all costs. The satisfied child will become a satisfied adult. Unfortunately the empty tank theory fails to include the crucial variable of dominance. The parents who invoke this approach usually are very warm but submissive to their children. Without the dominance factor, the parental IPIR is weak, and the child does not have a mechanism for self-regulation. He/she helplessly flies into blind rages whenever the world does not obey. And then there is depression as it dawns on the child that the world will simply not come around to serve as expected. Even while providing a physically safe and nurturing environment, the parent who fails to add the node of interpersonal dominance to warmth fails to offer psychological PROTECTion. That child cannot *SELF-PROTECT*, is insecure, and is unable to comfortably learn the dance between trust and exploring the world.

There are other ways that children can become violent even though no violence is apparent within the family. Occasional episodes of parental violence can set the template for violence in the child. The parent need not show many behaviors in the DAG group for the IPIR and the child to imitate them. Unfortunately, learning about hostility is extremely potent. The primate will learn to associate specific experiences with danger and hostility very easily. For example, a baby monkey needs only to observe the mother's fear of a specific venomous snake once, and he/she has the avoidance lesson for a lifetime (Jay, 1965). Survival is assisted if the developing primate is greatly affected by negative affect in the attachment object.

When the attachment object itself is the source of danger, the evolutionary mechanisms run amok. If the protective adult also represents danger him- or herself, there is great confusion. In this case, the infant is to look to the source of danger for protection from that danger. Yet infants do. This was startlingly clear to me while I was a graduate student at the Wisconsin Primate Laboratory. As I was studying thumb-sucking in monkeys, my major professor, Harry Harlow, and some of his other students were trying to create a "rejecting" monkey mother. They made diabolical devices that included having a huggable cylinder that unpredictably projected sharp spikes, and another that sometimes would spring loose and violently throw the baby across the cage. The infants with these violent mothers clung even more tenaciously to them than did baby monkeys who had the famous stable and "effective" terry-cloth mothers (Harlow & Harlow, 1962). One might reason that the tendency to cling to a protective "parent" is enhanced when there is danger, irrespective of the source of the danger. Infants do not have the cognitive skill to make an informed decision whether it is a good idea to attach to the parent or not. In short, even when the parent–infant relationship is contaminated by DAG behaviors (spikes, throwing), the attachment still takes place. Abused children still show AG behaviors in relation to the parent. In face of the danger, the source of which the infant does not comprehend, it is adaptive for the infant to seek the affects associated with the AG, such as comfort, confidence, hope.

Once the pattern of looking to a parent for protection from the danger that the parent him- or herself represents is in place, the child is attached to a malevolent (DAG) IPIR. The child's anxiety only increases the need to maintain proximity and try to elicit parental behaviors that will support the needed behaviors and affects. The child exhibits the three types of copying of parental DAG behaviors. But he or she still seeks AG from the malevolent IPIR. The child continues to seek proximity, just as the hapless laboratory monkey clings to the terry-cloth cylinder that keeps on spiking and throwing him/her violently.

This analysis shows that the primate consistently seeks AG, even though violence begets violence, or more specifically, DAG begets DAG. The personality-disordered individual, the one whose baseline behaviors are outside the normal AG range, seeks AG through psychic proximity to a malevolent IPIR. Because DAG is what the IPIR modeled and supported, the child's behavior is codable in the DAG. You only know what you only know. As cognition develops further, the child's unconscious reasoning becomes: DAG is what the IPIR "wants." If the parent attacks the child, that must be a good thing to do. Consequently, the child attacks others or the self.

Sometimes the quest for love through aggression is in relation to someone else. For example, the terrorist murders hundreds of innocent unarmed civilians for the love of his sect leader. His behavior is violent while his motivation is for ACTIVE LOVE and AFFIRMation. The perpetrator of mayhem seeks AFFIRM, ACTIVE LOVE, PROTECT from a powerful "attachment figure." These approving gods are, as my friend and colleague Marjorie Klein says, "The Big IPIRs." Incomprehensible hostility and cruelty always are justified in the mind of the perpetrator. Hitler wanted to "save" the human race. Jeffrey Dahmer, who sexually assaulted, killed, and cannibalized his victims, allegedly wanted to be "closer" to them. In Bosnia–Herzegovina today, in untold numbers of vicious attacks on defenseless civilians, grieved ancestors are avenged and presumably will approve of and love the perpetrators.

Some patients may declare that they hate the original attachment object (and implicitly, the derivative IPIR). But I have repeatedly found that underneath all the fury is a wish for reconciliation and love. No matter how badly abused they have been, people hang on (usually unconsciously) to the hope that if they do "right," the IPIR ultimately will relent and show approval, acceptance, and love. When allegiance to an IPIR defines "right" in terms of the DAG, the possibility of personality change in the AG direction is slim. Some examples of how destructive behaviors can be seen as gifts of love follow in a subsequent section on case examples.

In my introduction to the subject of IPIRs (Benjamin, 1994b), I suggested that antisocial personality disorder (ASP) might be the one exception to the argument that every psychopathology is a gift of love. However, I recently interviewed a "hard-core" ASP with this question in mind. His responses suggest that perhaps there should be no exclusions to the argument. This violent, seemingly uncaring, self-justified, and self-seeking man was deeply identified with his grotesquely abusive grandfather. His early hurt at the rejection and cruelty from his grandfather was easy to see. His ASP patterns rather directly resembled his grandfather's unfair, unpredictable, extremely harsh tactics. His autonomy was an understandable defense. It could be argued that his antisocial patterns were an attempt to be like his grandfather. The theory of psychic proximity would hold that his imitation of his grandfather was a form of attachment.

The concepts of IPIR and psychic proximity also can explain how attachment drives wishes for revenge, punishment, hostile triumph, and restitution. To be sure, aggression is "hardwired" in the primate. But hostility is better dealt with as a moderator of intimacy and distance than as a primary energy. If the patient is angry, it is important to learn its interpersonal purpose and to address those purposes directly. For example, if the anger is to enhance hostile enmeshment with a destructive IPIR, it is not a good idea for the therapist to facilitate that anger. On the other hand, if the anger represents outrage and a wish to distance, enhancing it can be very therapeutic. Anger is not a source of energy that must be disposed of one way or another. If there is no need for control or distance, there is no anger.

Experience convinces me of the universal goodness of babies and the positive power of their attachment. The simple truth is that babies are not born hostile. They are born helpless, armed only with incredibly appealing "sign stimuli" (Tinbergen, 1951) and a set of reflexes that facilitate attachment. They also have a special cry that typically will bother adults greatly. A normal adult will try to stop that cry by attempting to meet the infant's needs. A normal mother also will find relief from breast pain (and sometimes sexual pleasure) in the process of nursing. These contingencies help bond the infant and mother. On the other hand, an inadequate parent may respond to the cries and needs with hostility. If so, the process of constructing a hostile IPIR and generating a hostile character is under way. In short, normal processes facilitate AG. If the individual turns toward DAG, it is because normal attachment was not supported.

Defenses

Defenses enhance wishes or reduce fears. Everyone, normal or pathological, wishes to receive AG from the IPIR. Fears are to avoid receiving DAG from (or losing AG from) the IPIR. If defenses are normal,
they are in relation to a benevolent IPIR (coded as AG). Normal wishes for AG enhance interpersonal and intrapsychic behaviors that also
are coded in the AG group. If the defenses are pathological, they are
in relation to a malevolent IPIR (coded as DAG). They enhance interpersonal and intrapsychic behaviors that are hostile and coded in the
DAG group.

Defenses support either normal (AG) or pathological behaviors
(DAG) by distorting in one of three ways. (1) There is distortion of
the individual's perception (input). (2) There is an inappropriate
response to the input. (3) The links among the domains of behavior,
affect, and cognition are impaired. In Table 4.3, 17 well-recognized
defenses are classified in terms of these three groups (see also Benjamin, 1994b).

1. Defenses that distort incoming information include projection,
splitting, idealization, and devaluation. All defenses in this group
properly link cognition, affect, and behavior. There is a problem with
input. For idealization, devaluation, and splitting, the cognitive
problem is that views are polarized to extremes. Idealization supports
normative friendly behaviors (AG), but devaluation supports hostile
behaviors (DAG). Splitting supports both DAG and AG; one person
or aspect of the psyche is seen as AG, and the other as DAG. Projection does not necessarily involve polarization of power, but it does attribute the perceiver's own patterns to others.

2. Defenses that permit accurate input but transform the response
to it include displacement, acting out, sublimation, compensation,
regression, and undoing. Affect and behavior are properly linked
in this group. For some of them (displacement, acting out, sublimation), the distortion appears in the choice of situation where the
response is given. For others (compensation, regression, undoing),
the distortion of response appears in the pattern of behavior that is
chosen.

3. Defenses that primarily block awareness of patterns or of links
among them include repression, somatization, denial, intellectualization, lying, dissociation, and isolation. Somatization, denial, and intellectualization alter awareness, but more importantly, they block links
to and between affect and behavior. The defense of lying unlinks behavior from cognition and affect but awareness is unimpaired. The

TABLE 4.3. Mechanisms of Defense

| | System | | |
Defense	Cognition (C)	Affect (A)	Behavior (B)
Transform input			
Projection	Sees pattern in others (DAG)	Linked to C,B	Linked to C,A
Splitting	Views are polarized (AG, DAG)	Linked to C,B	Linked to C,A
Idealization	Views are polarized (AG)	Linked to C,B	Linked to C,A
Devaluation	Views are polarized (DAG)	Linked to C,B	Linked to C,A
Transform response			
Displacement	Aware	Linked to B	Change situation (DAG)
Acting out	Not aware	Linked to B	Change situation (DAG)
Sublimation	Aware or not	Linked to B	Change situation (AG)
Compensation	Aware or not	Linked to B	Substitute pattern (AG)
Regression	Aware or not	Linked to B	Use earlier pattern (DAG)
Undoing	Aware or not	Linked to B	Reverse pattern (AG, DAG)
Block awareness of pattern or of links			
Repression	Not aware	Linked to B	Linked to A
Somatization	Not aware	No links	No links
Denial	Aware, not focused	No links	No links
Intellectualization	Aware, focused	No links	No links
Lying	Aware	Linked to C	No links
Dissociation	Aware only in state	Linked in state	Linked in state
Isolation	Aware only in situation	Linked in situation	Linked in situation

defense of repression leaves affect and behavior linked, but they are not connected to cognition. Dissociation leaves all links intact in a specific state, but isolation leaves links intact only in a specific situation. Outside a specific state or situation, the input is inaccessible during dissociation and isolation.

The analysis presented in Table 4.3 shows why the therapy approach of "uncovering" is appropriate when the defenses of repression and somatization prevail. If awareness of important events is compromised, it is difficult for the individual to respond appropriately to them. Bringing the events to awareness should help *if the behavior associated with the defenses is maladaptive.* On the other hand, it is important to add that if the defenses successfully support AG behaviors, they should be left intact.

It is important to remember that because SASB coding identifies complex behaviors, one can avoid the error of considering "pseudo-friendliness" to be normal. Defenses that support pseudo-AG behaviors should not stand. An angry person who denies his or her rage and puts on false smiles and gladness would draw complex codes, and the falseness needs to be addressed. Consider the situation: "Hello! So *glad* to *see* you," said when the underlying wish, context and affect (nonverbal cues) are more consistent with the message: "Better it should be in a casket." In this case, the SASB code would be AFFIRM or perhaps REACTIVE LOVE for the words and smile, and ATTACK or BLAME for the underlying affect and cognition. The superficial message is in the AG, but the underlying one is in the DAG. In this case, the defense of denial should be addressed even if the individual is trying to present AG behaviors.

The analysis of Table 4.3 also shows that in cases where defenses are associated with DAG behaviors, the therapy approach of facilitating discovery and expression of affect can be helpful. Expression of affect should be relevant when the DAG patient is using defenses that cut off affect from other systems (e.g., somatization, denial, or intellectualization). Discovering feelings and linking them appropriately to the input and response is indicated. Suppose a man is furious at his wife for flirting with the neighbor. However, instead of addressing the matter directly, he gets a headache. The SASB code of this event might be: IGNORE plus SULK plus SELF-NEGLECT. The exact codes cannot be determined without talking to the man and assessing the full dimensionality of his view and response. His somatization defense should be approached with the goal of uncovering, clarifying, and addressing the anger at his wife.

On the other hand, Table 4.3 also implies that such popular expressive therapy techniques may at times be inappropriate. For example, consider a patient who is showing the defense of projection. Suppose he "sees" that his wife is angry with him, when in fact he is angry with her (projection). Suppose also that he is not aware that his anger stems from his need to control her. An "expressive" therapy that helps him respond to her perceived "anger" would only enable his defense of projection. Facilitation of his own "reactive" feelings of anger at his wife wouldn't help either. His affect is already well developed and linked in relation to his distortions of input. Foam bats and yells of rage would be irrelevant at best. Rather than "getting out his anger," the therapy should work on his distorted view of his wife and of the fear that overwhelms him when he can't control her. Then, the relation of all this to his IPIRs and early attachment objects needs exploration. When he has an accurate picture of his own functioning, he will be in a better position to respond appropriately to his wife.

This analysis of defenses is different from the classical psychoanalytic view of defenses in many ways. I noted elsewhere that the present perspective on defenses can explain

> maladaptive behavior that is normal (the generous and honest child in the street culture); adaptive behavior that is pathological (the devoted Satanic cult member); abnormal behavior that does not involve distorted perceptions (the sensitive paranoid); normal behavior that involves distorted perception (the loving child who ignores or immediately forgets his mother's outrageous behavior, thereby preserving attachment; the terminally ill cancer patient who maintains a cheerful attitude and therefore survives longer). (Benjamin, 1994b, p. 76)

In sum, defenses, like bacteria, are not necessarily undesirable. Clinician response to them must depend on a careful understanding of the nature and function of the defense in the light of the overall interpersonal diagnosis and treatment plan. Defenses that support friendly IPIRs and constructive attitudes toward self and others need little attention. As these defenses encourage AG behaviors, the individual will help build and maintain an environment that returns AG behaviors. Normality (AG) will be reinforced, and the individual will stabilize in a constructive interpersonal and intrapsychic position with pleasant affects and cognitions (AG). On the other hand, defenses that support hostile IPIRs might better be challenged. If not, the associated DAG behaviors will only draw more DAG with associated affects and cognitions that are psychopathological. Psychotherapy that facilitates AG and discourages DAG will have better outcomes and put the patient in a position to receive better support from his or her social environment. "What goes around, comes around." Complementarity prevails whether the domain is AG or DAG.

Therapy Implications

The present theory of how and why seemingly "maladaptive" patterns in the adult are sustained by IPIRs has definite treatment implications. A current project is to write a treatment manual that details and illustrates the implications of the foregoing analysis. The most central problem is how to access and change the relationship with the IPIRs. This requires a very broad range of techniques and can profitably draw on wisdom from nearly every school of psychotherapy.

Optimal treatment consistently implements one or more of five steps. These steps can be implemented through a wide variety of approaches from different schools. But every intervention should be evaluated as correct or not, depending on whether it conforms to the following:

1. Consistently implement a pattern of collaboration between the therapist and the patient against "it," the maladaptive patterns.
2. Help the patient learn about intrapsychic patterns along with their associated affects and cognitions. Help the patient learn about where the patterns came from and what they are for (how they were adaptive at one time).
3. Block maladaptive patterns (DAG, especially life-threatening and other seriously damaging actions).
4. Enable the will to change (help change the relationship with the IPIR). If there is to be behavior change during psychotherapy, the individual's relationship with the unconscious organizers must be brought to light and renegotiated. This is accomplished by recognizing one's patterns and their relationship to the early attachment objects (insight). Then the person must in one way or another *decide* whether to detach (give up old wishes and fears) in favor of new and better attachments and ways of being. Differentiation from and letting go of the IPIRs often involve grief. In effect, there has to be a psychological funeral for the patient's hopes that the IPIR will start providing unadulterated AG. Differentiation does not mean that the IPIR is "exorcised." That is probably not possible. Differentiation means that the enmeshment with the IPIR is terminated, and a contract for peaceful coexistence is signed. Sometimes the IPIR is transformed and becomes more benevolent and exhibits more AG. In any case, the IPIR does not "die."
5. Learn new more adaptive and appropriate patterns (AG). When ancient wishes and fears in relation to the IPIR are given up, the relationships with the attachment objects in their current life can improve. New learning can take place if the need for proximity to the old IPIRs on the old terms has been changed. Usual and customary therapy techniques, especially behavior therapy, work very well with personality disorders after differentiation has taken place. The "now what" phase opens

the patient to new ideas on how to do things differently and better. The therapy relationship offers some better ways of relating, but that must be supplanted by other alliances in the patient's environment (marital, filial, colleagial).

Therapist intentions are irrelevant in evaluating effectiveness. Interventions are evaluated in terms of their outcome, their immediate impact on the patient. The question is, was one of the five steps implemented (correct) or not (an error)? For example, if the therapist attempts to teach a new pattern and the collaborative relationship deteriorates, the intervention was incorrect. If the therapist attempts to block a maladaptive pattern and the patient acts out anyway, it is a therapy error. Therapist errors are inevitable; the goal is to minimize, not to eliminate them.

I hasten to add that this "bottom line rule" does not mean the therapist is responsible for whatever the patient does or does not do. The model specifies that the patient is a learner. The therapist is only the coach/teacher. The patient's ability, energy level, genetically set envelope of talent, and will to change are extremely important. Still, the coach must optimize the setting and the learning conditions to give the patient a fair chance. The "bottom line rule" does not let the patient off the existential hook. The "bottom line" rule only keeps the therapist aware that learning can be optimized if the teacher remains alert and active while also being supportive and tolerant. The needed balance between "acceptance" and "change" that is so well articulated by Linehan (1993) is vital to good therapy process.

In the next section, case examples show how patients with very destructive personality disorders are organized by a wish for love from and fear of rejection or punishment from their IPIRs. Specific treatment suggestions illustrate key ways that the five steps might be implemented.

Three Case Examples of How Attachment to IPIRs Organizes Pathological Personality

Each of the examples represents a "difficult case" that had not responded to conventional approaches and that was suspected of having an Axis II complication. They are summarized briefly, and selected features of the case formulation show (1) how the presenting symptoms can be "explained" in terms of early social learning and continuing attachment to IPIRs and (2) that highly focused treatment suggestions can stem from the present interpersonal/developmental diagnosis.

Case 1. Dependent Personality Disorder

The first example is so straightforward that the reader may wonder if it is a "hypothetical." Nonetheless, the case is presented with no alterations except as needed to protect confidentiality. Moreover, the therapy focus before hospitalization had been concentrating on the patient's alleged sexual abuse. The therapy model that had been used was the familiar one of encouraging the patient to express affect about abuse, to confront the abuser, and to receive support for the associated stress. The present analysis suggests that "usual and customary" approach was not focused on the key issue.

The patient suffered from major depression, anxiety, and panic attacks. The precipitating event for hospitalization was the sentencing of an uncle to jail for sexually molesting some family members. The patient, along with other family members, had been active in the trial that resulted in his conviction. In the past year, she had become essentially nonfunctional as a wife and mother. Household work and child care were handled by her husband, who also worked outside the home. The patient's mother worried about her and frequently called and came over to give support.

Since the sentencing, the patient had been troubled with guilt about the conviction and sentencing of her (maternal) uncle, with whom her mother was very close. She also had been arguing with her husband about money. The problem was that the patient spent more than he could earn. The patient and her mother were spending much time together going shopping, out to lunch, and traveling. The patient would ask her mother for permission to do things and says she wanted her mother "to tell me what to do." Recently, she reported that her mother had been "getting after me for asking her." The children were having trouble receiving passing grades in school and had been diagnosed as "learning disabled." The patient herself seemed to function in the lower range of normal intelligence.

Late on the night of this hospitalization, the patient had decided to cut herself with a knife, but "it was not sharp enough." Just as she was wondering how to succeed at cutting herself, her mother telephoned, "sensing" something was wrong. There was an exchange of calls involving the mother's recommendation that the patient tell her husband, who "did not get up (from bed) right away." The patient kept trying to cut herself and failing and ended up lying on the couch sobbing: "I can't handle this. I want my mommy." Finally, the mother arrived and held the patient to calm her, and the mother and husband conveyed the patient to the hospital.

After the birth of each of four children, the patient had been hospitalized for postpartum depression. During the first hospitalization, her depression was so severe that she had to be treated by electroconvulsive therapy. She then could not get out of bed for a month. Things improved when a distant relative came to help out. While hospitalized that first time, the patient said she heard other women discuss their abuse problems and realized she had been "tickled inappropriately" by this uncle. She was not particularly close to him but remembers she "did not want to be around him." Once she had a "flashback" of an incident she could not discuss; but, she noted, much worse things happened to the others. She provided the following account of one of her treatment experiences at the hospital:

> My group therapist wanted me to get angry about what happened and express it. I thought I had done good. But the group therapist hoped I would get angry enough to stand up and yell. The group talked to me before. They suggested what to do. How to sit. How to appear in control of myself. How not to be a victim. I did something I am not proud of. I was really feeling intimidated and stuck with that mock confrontation. So I took my cousin's story and told her story as if it was my story. I lied. I felt really bad about that. I felt pressured and that I did not have enough to say. And I felt criticized for not getting angry enough. I thought I did good.

It is important to know that this uncle was a "favorite son," and the grandparents had defended him to the end. All members who testified against him, including the patient's mother, were now written out of their will. The patient's mother was a "dutiful daughter" who served the others in the family despite being criticized a great deal. She had been highly ambivalent about the trial and conviction.

The patient met many of the DSM-III-R criteria for dependent personality disorder (DPD). (1) She was unable to make everyday decisions without advice and reassurance of her mother and husband. (2) She needed them to make important decisions. (3) She agreed with others even when she thought they were wrong. "I say yes when I think my mother needs it, even when I don't understand or care." (6) She was upset when she was alone without help from her mother or husband. (8) She could not imagine surviving without her mother and husband. (9) She said she "can't handle criticism."

The patient also met the SASB-based interpersonal definition for DPD: "The baseline position is of marked submissiveness to a dominant other person who is supposed to provide unending nurturance and guidance. The wish is to maintain connection to that person even if it means tolerating abuse. The DPD believes that he or she is instrumentally incompetent, and this means that he or she cannot survive without the dominant other person'' (Benjamin, 1993b, p. 226).

The patient showed a necessary descriptor: "Submissiveness stemming from a sense of instrumental inadequacy.'' She did not meet the exclusionary descriptors that I recommend (Benjamin, 1993b) for DPD. These are long-term comfort with autonomy, transitive demands for nurturance, intimacy only if the situation is safe, insistence that others submit, and scorn for authority.

Her interpersonal history also included the conditions that I have hypothesized will shape a dependent personality. There was a wonderful infancy with excellent nurturance. The nurturance did not stop in time for the patient to practice autonomy and competence. She had a poor self-concept by default. Failing to learn how to do things for herself, she felt inadequate. For example, she noted she could not even express anger or cut on her wrists like the other patients. She felt criticized by peers and others for her lack of competence.

The patient's most powerful IPIR was, of course, her mother. The husband was a stand-in who served the same interpersonal purposes. Both were best characterized by the SASB code PROTECT. The patient had internalized her mother and maintained the complementary position of TRUST in relation to the mother, husband, and health care system. She had internalized BLAME concerning her inadequacy. Her organizing wish was to be PROTECTed by her dominant others, and her worst fear was to lose them (IGNORE).

Therapy, then, should focus on the enmeshment with the mother. The mother was deeply upset about the conviction of her brother but refused therapy for herself. The mother's anxiety and her symbiosis with the patient are adequate to account for the patient's anxiety about the uncle's conviction. Rather than attribute her distress primarily to her alleged sexual abuse, treatment planning might follow the five steps.

1. The first task would be to elicit collaboration against her pattern of helpless dependency. The focus on the alleged sexual abuse seemed to enhance her sense of helplessness and inadequacy. In this patient's world, the husband and mother, not the sexually abusive uncle, were central. She agreed that there should be a family conference that would try to change her relationship with her husband and mother. Though she said she would not like it, she thought the husband and mother should "pay attention" when she was coping better instead of when she was inadequate. She also agreed that her upset about the uncle's sentence really represented worry about her mother. It made sense to her to try to develop a separate and strong self.

2. Learning about her dependency, its roots, and its costs might help her to recognize the pattern and begin to change her self-talk from "I can't" to "I'll try." If the mother and husband could learn to reward strength building rather than weakness, change would come faster. A key element of this treatment plan would be to teach all of them the principles of operant conditioning using social reinforcers. For example, the patient could use these ideas in managing the children so that she could then feel better about herself as a mother and wife.

With training from husband and mother (guided by the therapist), the patient could begin to take pride at first in small, and then later in greater accomplishments. Her own diagnosis, "I can't cope," was correct. The long-term solution to that problem was to help her learn to cope. This would be more possible if she had the permission and assistance of the key figures who had heretofore enabled her inadequacy.

3. Her emerging identity as a patient, including attempts to be like the others by cutting herself, was a problem. This could be blocked by minimizing contact with other patients and by concentrating on the goal of building a positive alternative identity. A new can-do identity should be the explicit goal.

4. The will to change would be, as always, the most difficult issue. The patient would be prone to agree with the interviewer and therapist because of her dependent orientation. The therapist would need to be vigilant in blocking "obedience" and nurturing assertiveness in therapy process. As the patient succeeds in asserting during therapy process, she might generalize to the relationships with her husband and mother. Their perspectives would be important. If their identities were invested in her neediness, change would be harder. These questions of who wants what from whom would need exploration and negotiation during family sessions.

5. From the beginning of this treatment, learning new patterns would be a central focus. As is usually true for dependent personality, the IPIRs usually are present in the patient's current life and can be worked with directly. Husband, mother, and the patient probably also could benefit from learning better communication and negotiating skills. If the therapy can help the sources of the IPIRs learn new patterns, it can provide a faster means for the patient to form a new identity. That new self-concept should be associated with changed behaviors, affects, and cognitions.

Case 2: Borderline Personality Disorder

Unlike the first example, here is a case wherein sexual abuse was indeed central to the disorder. The sexual abuse had breathtakingly direct

connections to rather bizarre symptoms. The patient was actively suicidal and homicidal. She had assaulted staff seriously, and they were
understandably frustrated and angry with and afraid of her. Her chart
comprised several volumes, and her suicide attempts were many. Most
extraordinary was her proclivity for swallowing large objects such as
markers, pencils, nails, and most recently, a glass. She had multiple
surgeries to remove these objects, and sometimes the swallowing was
life threatening. The surgeons advised that she be told not to do that!
The patient explained that swallowing relieved her stress. She felt better
afterwards. All categories of psychotropic medication had failed to provide any change or relief. A variety of behavioral programs had failed
to control the swallowing, self-mutilations, suicidality, or assaults on
staff. The patient was strapped to a gurney cart during the consultative interview. She had developed a special relationship with a staff
therapist. Her last swallowing episode took place while he was on vacation, and recently he had been transferred to another service. The
patient was very upset by this loss.

This person's developmental history would make even the most
seasoned clinician cry. Some of the staff who observed the interview
did. The patient's parents were divorced when she was about 3. The
subsequent stepfather and mother were both physically abusive to the
patient and her siblings. The patient says she was kicked, hit, slapped,
and thrown against the walls. These punishments would be for anything, like leaving a light on, getting the house dirty. "No matter what
I did, they were not happy." If her stepfather found one dirty dish,
he would empty all of the cupboards, and the patient would have to
wash everything all over. The parental fights were frequent and very
violent. The patient sometimes tried to protect her mother. Once, after the stepfather shot the patient's beloved cat in front of her and then
approached her with the gun, she grabbed a knife and lunged at him.
Then she ran away, and when she returned after 3 days, nobody said
a word. It was as if nothing had ever happened.

The patient does have some positive memories about this man.
She notes that he took her and her brother fishing and gave her things
at Christmas. Sexual abuse included touching her with his hands, beginning "real nice" and ending violently. Eventually the patient told
her mother about these sexual encounters with her stepfather. The parents had a discussion about it, and the episodes ended without
comment.

The patient's biological father also had a major impact. When she
was quite young, he introduced her to alcohol and drugs. For example, at about age 11, they made brownies with pot, and the patient
ate them at will. From the earliest visitations until the patient was age

23, her biological father would orally rape her. Sometimes, if she refused, he would take a needle and inject her with drugs. When she was "out of it," he would proceed to use her sexually. Intercourse was added to oral rape as she matured. The oral rapes were singularly traumatic because he was adamant that she swallow the semen. If she refused to swallow, he would order her to do so. If she still refused, he would put his hand over her mouth or a pillow over her head, permitting her to breathe only after she swallowed. After a while, the patient discovered she could swallow and purge, and then "he wouldn't win." But after he figured out that she was vomiting the semen back up, he "did it again." This time, he made her swallow and sit still in front of him until enough time had lapsed that she could not vomit it back up. The patient felt angry and humiliated. Yet her father told her: "This is my way of showing you I love you."

The thought of these episodes now makes her sick to her stomach. The father did not do this to the other children. The patient was selected because she was the youngest and "he wanted me to." As she told the story during this interview, she was sure that the staff would think very badly of her for participating in such activity. She believed she was a bad person for not having done something to stop it. Actually, when she was 16 or 17, she says she began to resist, but he said: "You know you want it, you enjoy it; just do it." She felt that was partly true, and that there was no way she could get out of it. The rapes stopped when the patient told her crisis worker at age 23. Her father was taken to court, convicted, and sent to jail. She has not seen him since. She says she is angry for what he did, but still loves him "because he is my dad."

The patient had polysubstance abuse and met each of the criteria for borderline personality disorder (BPD). (1) she was very upset to be left alone; (2) she said that she was very intense in her relationships; (3) she was not clear about who she was and who she wanted to be; (4) she said she was reckless and impulsive in ways that were self-damaging; (5) she displayed frequent self-mutilating and suicidal behaviors; (6) she said that her moods are unstable; (7) she often felt empty; (8) her displays of anger were frequent, unmodulated, and intense; and (9) she said that she was "paranoid" that people will hurt her. The patient functioned from a baseline position of coercive dependency, was sensitive to abandonment, and sabotaged herself when there were signs of success.

This patient clearly met the DSM criteria for BPD. She also met the interpersonal diagnostic criteria for BPD outlined in Benjamin (1993b).

There is a morbid fear of abandonment and a wish for protective nurturance, preferably received by constant physical proximity to the rescuer (lover or caregiver). The baseline position is friendly dependency on a nurturer, which becomes hostile control if the caregiver or lover fails to deliver enough (and there never is enough). There is a belief that the provider secretly if not overtly likes dependency and neediness, and a vicious introject attacks the self if there are signs of happiness or success. (Benjamin, 1993b, p. 117)

She also showed the necessary descriptors: (1) fear of abandonment handled by transitive coercion of protection and nurturance; (2) self-sabotage following happiness or success. She dreaded being discharged from the hospital, and she forced the staff to keep her there. Her self-sabotage occurred blatantly to coerce protection. Alternatively, it was a response to any successes that might suggest she was ready for discharge. The patient did not show the exclusionary condition for BPD: she was not able to tolerate aloneness on a long-term basis.

Her developmental history was also as predicted: (1) family life was chaotic, and so was hers; (2) she had traumatic abandonment experiences, including incest, that directly modeled the interpersonal and intrapsychic patterns of her self-abuse; (3) self-definition and signs of attachment were attacked and destroyed; and (4) sickness elicited nurturance. Her total disability and violence provided the hostile care she understood and needed.

Highlights of the five steps that should be included in the treatment plan include the following:

1. Collaborate with the patient to resist "it," the will to replay the family scenario of hostile enmeshment. Help build an observing ego by encouraging her to reflect on her feelings and wishes when she is tempted to act out her angry feelings. Help her learn that alternative serve her better than loyalties to old patterns and IPIRs. Show tolerance and acceptance of regressions while facilitating new learning.

2. Help her learn about the connections between her patterns of suicidality, homicidality, and severe self-abuse and her learning within the family. Refer to that learning when she threatens to become violent toward self or others. Try to help her learn to recognize what triggers the wish to attack. Teach her that anger usually serves a wish to control (be intimate) or to distance, and help her learn better alternatives.

3. Work toward containing aggression by collaboration rather than by physical restraint. Set clear, fair, and agreed-upon limits and contingencies. Avoid staff splitting. Give privileges contingent on a specific

interval of adequate self-control. Anticipate and collaborate to structure moments where she is vulnerable to acting out.

4. Mobilize the will to change by showing understanding and empathy for her choices, given her history. Help her consider whether she truly wishes to keep her relationship with her IPIRs "going" in this most destructive way. Help her learn to identify anger in service of differentiation from the destructive IPIRs. Help her learn to avoid attacking others in service of attachment to IPIRs. Consider using her sisters as current figures who might support the will to recovery. Try to assign one central therapist would could become a first draft of a better attachment figure. The therapist should be only a transitional object, not a permanent IPIR. Help her decide to give up the identity as professional patient.

5. New patterns can be learned as she understands the basis of her old ones. Teach her anger's role in managing distance and intimacy. Support everything that suggests growing personal strength. Teach her better self-talk. Help her begin to explore vocational options if she should decide to progress to the point of being discharged. If she finds an important relationship, she will need much support and new learning about patterns of intimacy.

Case 3: Obsessive–Compulsive Personality Disorder

I choose another case of extreme violence to test the limits of the idea: "Every psychopathology is a gift of love." This married man in his 40s had a problem with "meanness." He was admitted to the hospital 6 months after he had punched his wife so hard that he ruptured her large intestine during a fight. She was taken to the hospital and was clinically dead on arrival. However, she survived, and the couple decided to keep the truth about the cause of the injury a secret. Eventually, the patient "fessed up" to his boss and to his wife's parents. On the advice of her therapist, his wife insisted he enter the hospital for treatment, lest he hurt her again. He declared. "I feel like a killer. If somebody gets in my face, my space, there is no warning, and I strike back. It is not a matter of whether I will kill someone. Only when." He also had symptoms of depression. In the hospital he was put on nearly every class of drugs including antidepressants, antipsychotics, lithium, and anxiolytics.

During the consultative interview, it became clear that the fight was precipitated by the wife's son. The stepson swore at his mother, and the patient thought that behavior was unacceptable. The wife defended her son, and the couple started fighting. His wife had a habit of taunting him about things he did wrong. As the fight escalated, the patient turned to walk away to avoid acting on his temper. His wife followed and grabbed him. He whirled around and struck her as hard as he could with the back of his fist. He hit her in a vulnerable place, and the blow ruptured her intestine.

The developmental history casts a sensible light on the precipitating episode. The patient was abandoned at an early age. He and his siblings lived with the maternal grandparents, who were extremely strict. The most severe punishments came from the grandfather. If all work was not completed properly, or if there was some other infraction, "it was group punishment time." They had to line up, and the grandfather would beat them each in turn. He would repeat the whole process until somebody "fessed up." The guilty party would get a "double dose," and the rest would "slink off."

During the beatings, the grandfather would sometimes "work with old heavy leather gloves" because they stung more. He would hit wherever he could. He often caught the children with the back of his fist as he lashed out in all directions. The patient "wanted to give him some of his own medicine." Yet, he always respected the grandfather because "he was the adult." As the patient grew larger in his teen years, the grandfather would taunt: "You want to try me you little SOB?" But the patient could not disobey "the unwritten law" that children must respect their parents.

For many years, the patient was taunted by his younger sister. She would "sit and pick, tease and demean" him. She "knew what strings to pull." She was the first person he ever hit, and the incident was a blind rage against her picking. Whenever he hit his sister, his grandparents would punish him severely. He felt that the sister liked to bait him and get him in trouble. The patient had a flashback to these episodes with his sister on the day that he ruptured his wife's intestine.

In high school, the patient did well, but the grandparents never acknowledged his work. He was not permitted to attend sporting or social events, and ultimately, he rebelled. There were disputes with the grandparents and the authorities, and eventually he was kicked out of both the home and the school. He lived in the streets for a while and then ended up living with a sympathetic relative. Despite the alienation, the patient lent his grandfather some money when the need arose. He remained attached to his grandfather, who at the time of hospitalization was dying of kidney failure. The patient had recently visited the grandfather and tried to reconcile. He said he "picked his brains about childhood" and had "written a lot of this information down." The patient noted that the grandfather had only been doing to the children what had been done to him.

Although the patient seemed quite paranoid at the beginning of the interview, the more appropriate Axis II label was obsessive–compulsive personality disorder (OCD). (1) He agreed he was a perfectionist. He explained that in his shop everything was arranged very carefully, and if things are not in their place, he becomes upset. (2) He said he "lives by lists." They do not interfere with function, however. Instead, they help him stay organized. (3) He insists that others do things his way to be sure they are done right. Alternatively, he just does it himself. (4) He works excessively, including going to work on weekends without pay. He finds it difficult to play. (5) He delays decision making to be sure he has the right approach. To illustrate, he explained it recently took weeks to get a sidewalk poured. He had to check on every possible aspect. (6) The patient says he used to be extremely rigid morally. He was a church "fanatic." Recently, he says, he has become less judgmental. (7) He finds it is extremely hard to express affection. His wife needs to be touched and to hear him say "I love you," but he cannot do this.

The patient fits the interpersonal diagnostic description for obsessive–compulsive personality disorder presented in Benjamin (1993b, p. 247). "There is a fear of making a mistake or being accused of being imperfect. The quest for order yields a baseline interpersonal position of blaming and inconsiderate control of others. The OCD's control alternates with blind obedience to authority or principle. There is excessive self-discipline as well as restraint of feelings, harsh self-criticism, and neglect of the self."

He showed the necessary criteria of unreasonable control of others and devotion to perfection. His ideas of how his wife's son should act, of proper parenting, were very clear to him. His conscience was harsh. His confession to his boss was quite risky. However, he was such a good worker that the boss was more than supportive of his attempts to help himself. The patient did not meet any of the exclusionary conditions for OCD. He did not show irresponsible behaviors, emotional excesses or contempt for authority.

His developmental history also consistent with that described for OCD–personality disorder. (1) The grandparents implemented relentless coercion to perform, be correct, and follow the rules, regardless of personal cost. He imitated those paradigms in relation to himself and others. (2) He was judged a "horrible child" and punished for being imperfect. (3) Rules were implemented without personal involvement. This earnest young man was kicked out of the home to live on the streets for irreverence and for disobeying curfew.

Highlights of a treatment plan that implements the five steps would be the following:

1. Help him reconsider his self-definition as a killer and commit to changing his identification with the violent grandfather. Treat regressive thoughts as "the enemy" and nurture an alliance to resist acting on them.

2. Continue the exploration of connections among current problem patterns and early learning. Most central are the issues of aggressive father figures, taunting females, and grief over lost parents.

3. Monitor for the possibility of child abuse, emphasizing prevention and disclosing the need to report. It will be important to remember that uncovering of materials related to these themes will be painful and may temporarily increase the possibility of violent acting out. The patient and therapist will need to collaborate to anticipate and develop specific alternative responses to the tendency to regress and attack in moments of stress.

4. Therapy should center on the grandfather's IPIR. The key to curbing the patient's violence is in helping him differentiate from the grandfather IPIR. If he no longer needs to show his love for the grandfather by being like him, he could move on to patterns that the patient might consciously prefer to live. To the extent that he is angry with his grandfather, he may be able to learn to inhibit his violent reflexes. He might be helped to practice and ingrain self-talk of the form: "Wait a minute! I am not going to be like him now." Simultaneous teaching of constructive alternative responses to coercion and humiliation also would be important. ·

5. Important new learning could take place in couple's therapy. The wife might be helped to find ways other than taunting to approach her husband. The couple could use help with behavioral management of her son. The patient needs to learn softer alternatives to his present approach of administering catastrophic punishment or of leaving.

FUTURE EMPIRICAL DEVELOPMENTS

In the next 5 years or so, I hope to be able to start a clinic that provides low-cost, high-quality long-term treatment for patients with long-standing personality disorder. Patients will need to agree to participate in research protocols. Then, I hope to achieve at least five goals:

1. Show that students can learn to conduct interviews that permit clear SASB-codable formulations of the presentation. Show that students can learn to account for the symptomatology in terms of the developmental principles described and illustrated in this paper.

2. Show that blind coders can reliably identify DSM Axis II diag-

noses as they are modified by the rules of interpersonal context described in Benjamin (1993b) and illustrated in this chapter. Compare these to DSM-IV diagnoses obtained by structured interview (e.g., SCID-II).

3. Develop and test a treatment manual as well as adherence scales that implement the diagnostic and treatment principles (Benjamin, 1993b) and illustrated further in this chapter.

4. Show that treatments are more effective if they stay closer to the "white heat of relevance" defined by the SASB coded interpersonal developmental analysis and the associated five treatment steps.

5. More precisely codify the means of identifying and assessing IPIRs and defenses as they are defined in this chapter. The present approach relies heavily on the idea of attachment to destructive IPIRs as an explanation of psychopathology. The theory is clear, and it is not difficult to implement clinically. However, more rigorous assessment of IPIRs and the associated wishes is needed. I will begin by asking student interviewers to be sure to elicit clear SASB-codable statements of wishes and fears in relation to likely IPIRs. Then blind raters should code the patient's relationship with the IPIRs as well as the patient's key interpersonal and intrapsychic patterns. Subsequent operationalized correspondence (product–moment r) between the codes of the relationship with the IPIRs and the key problem patterns may (or may not) confirm the predictions. The codes of the relationship with the IPIR and of the problem patterns should be the same (identification), complementary or opposite (recapitulation), and/or introjective (introjection). Another approach might be to identify IPIRs and have patients rate their wishes and fears in relation to the IPIRs on the SASB questionnaires. These could be compared to patient and/or informant ratings of the patient when in the problem state.

These straightforward assessments are dependent on penetrating the patient's defenses. For some reason, the SASB-directed "deep tracking" interview used in inpatient consultative cases bypasses defenses temporarily. Patients often discuss issues for the first time. I cannot explain why this happens, though staff often exclaim that there is much new "information." It is not that I "implant" these ideas. All the material for the dynamic formulation is in terms of the patient's own words and images, and it has to be directly affirmed by the patient. I always discuss what I am going to put in the report with the patient. They are free to look at it if they wish. The most difficult moments always come when IPIRs are discussed. For example, patients 2 and 3 declared they hated their abusers but agreed that they still loved and hoped to reconcile. Each also indicated he/she hated to admit it but reflected carefully on the question. Typically, people say things like, "It could be," "I never thought I would say this, but . . . ," "He *is* my father, and I do love him," and so on.

The material that makes these formulations so clear is not obstructed by defenses. Yet I know that defenses exist. Perhaps there is a waxing and waning of distortions in input, response, and linkages. Perhaps the variables that affect the these shifts can be known. Perhaps the deep tracking interview encourages the waning rather than the waxing of defenses. Maybe the experience of being accurately tracked on topics of quintessential relevance encourages trust and self-examination. Perhaps the interviewer summaries of what has been said and the linking of patterns stimulate the patient's desire to push further and learn more.

Even though defenses typically do not interfere much with the deep tracking interview process, I often see evidence of defenses after the interview. For example, I routinely warn staff to put people on high suicide watch after I have talked to someone suicidal about the organizing IPIR. My reasoning is that the "betrayal" of the IPIR may make the patient anxious. Self-destructiveness is a well practiced way to appease angry IPIRs.

Passive–aggressive people sometimes report that they feel abused and exploited by the presence of students during the deep tracking consultative interview. This is consistent with their experience that caregivers take more than they give. This is a defense of devaluation, and it serves the unconscious wish that defaulting caregivers relent and offer restitution for their failings.

Patients from most diagnostic categories often forget what was said during the deep tracking interview. They show defenses of denial, repression, intellectualization, and isolation. These defenses serve to protect the love of the IPIR. That seems to be required when the interviewer explicitly discusses the need for differentiation from the IPIR. Splitting is another defense that can be seen after these interviews. Sometimes I am reported to be the "good guy"; sometimes the "bad one." This occurs most often in patients who have identified one parent as good and the other as bad. Fitting me into that pattern preserves the family rules and helps keep things as they were.

I conclude that I don't really know why defenses are not a problem during the deep tracking consultative inpatient interviews. It would be nice to understand that better. If ways could be found to prevent the appearance of defenses after the interview, the constructive impact could be greater. The present way of analyzing cases can be implemented effectively only if the referring therapist chooses to apply it slowly over time.

SUMMARY

This chapter reviewed the history of the SASB model and associated technology. The model provides that the "primitive" basics of sexuality, aggression, power, and territory can be combined to describe a variety of interpersonal and intrapsychic events. The SASB questionnaires, coding system, and software can quantify object relations in terms of the SASB model. A valid and reliable interpersonal and intrapsychic description of a case can be obtained by using SASB Intrex questionnaires and/or the SASB coding system.

Objective tests of traditionally accepted principles of psychopathology can be tested by SASB coding of key interactions. The example of mother–infant interactions in depressed and normal populations was offered to illustrate the technology and to show the validity of some SASB predictive principles. It also provided data directly relevant to the main thesis that attachment is central to the formation of normal and abnormal personality. Then I noted that the SASB analysis of DSM definitions can help sharpen the Axis II definitions and reduce the overlap among the categories. The SASB analyses of the DSM personality disorders also provide specific developmental hypotheses that have clear psychosocial treatment implications. These applications were addressed at length in Benjamin (1993b).

Following guidelines from the editor, I addressed three types of validity (content, criterion, and construct) with respect to the model and the diagnostic and treatment applications. The technology is quite well validated, and the diagnostic applications in relation to the DSM are clearly articulated. Exposition of treatment principles is now the focus. The biggest challenge to the application of the SASB technology to personality is how to explain the widely recognized persistence and intractability of maladaptive patterns of personality. The proposed resolution lies in two new concepts: the IPIR and psychic proximity. A summary of the working hypotheses is this.

The primate's strong early propensity to attach provides the organizing template for personality. The individual copies the attachment objects in at least three different ways (identification, recapitulation, and introjection) to create internal working models of the attachment relationships. I have named the internal working models IPIRs (important people and their internalized representations). Long past the time of intimate contact with the attachment objects, the adult seeks to receive the "love" of their representatives, the IPIRs. The adult also tries to avoid rejection by or attack from or by IPIRs.

The adult activates patterns associated with the IPIRs at times of stress. The reason for activating the IPIRs is that they bring "psychic proximity." Behaving as you did with the attachment object brings you closer. This psychic proximity is the adult vestige of the child going to the parent for cradling and calming. Individuals with personality disorder behave in their familiar maladaptive ways to seek the love (AG; SASB codes indicating warmth and moderate degrees of enmeshment/differentiation) and avoid the wrath (DAG; SASB codes indicating hostility and moderate degrees of enmeshment/differentiation) of their IPIRs. There was a discussion of normality and of defenses. In brief, SASB behaviors coded in the AG define normality and can be used in setting therapy goals. Defenses support the relationship with the IPIRs (i.e., they support the IPIRs' perceived rules for granting AG).

This construct of IPIRs can be tested and refuted. SASB codes can describe the original attachment relationship and the resultant IPIRs. For example, the perspective of the IPIR can be elicited (and coded) by questions like: "What would your father say if he were here listening to you today?" SASB codes also can describe the associated patterns in the adult personality. SASB predictive principles (similarity, complementarity, introjection) can articulate the connections among the original attachment objects, the IPIRs, and the adult patterns. By invoking the concept of psychic proximity, and by using SASB-based codes to characterize the relationships, the present analysis clarifies how early attachment learning is manifest in the adult personality. It explains what is reinforcing about "maladaptive" patterns.

If the patterns of disorder are sustained by relationship with the IPIRs, it follows that successful therapy with individuals with personality disorders must renegotiate their relationships with the IPIRs. When the relationship with the IPIRs is the central focus of psychotherapy, significant change can take place. But rarely are IPIRs and the concept of psychic proximity the direct focus of therapy. Sometimes they are implicitly addressed (e.g., when an otherwise hopelessly antisocial adolescent is deeply changed by a warm relationship with an admired "tough guy"). If these were more systematic focus on the relationship with the IPIRs, personality disorders would be less "intractable."

The conclusion is that if "every psychopathology is a gift of love," then every psychotherapy must facilitate (benign) differentiation from the underlying attachments before there can be constructive change. I provide three clinical examples. An SASB-coded reading of attachment to the IPIRs combined with the notion of psychic proximity might provide the Rosetta stone for effective psychotherapy with personality-disordered individuals.

ACKNOWLEDGMENTS

I would like to thank the patient who provided the data for Figures 4.4–4.7. For Figures 4.8–4.17, thanks are due Donna Gelfand and Douglas Teti, who shared their data base on depressed and nondepressed mothers with infants. Karen Callaway and Kelly Schloredt supervised the making of transcripts and SASB coded the mother–infant interactions. Callaway's dissertation will explore complementarity in that data base. Support for the SASB analyses of the Gelfand–Teti data bank was provided by a grant from the Research Network I of the MacArthur Foundation, D. Kupfer, Director. Marjorie Klein provided helpful comments on an earlier version of this chapter.

NOTES

1. This intellectual property has been gifted to the University of Utah and is available to qualified users through Intrex at the Department of Psychology, University of Utah, Salt Lake City, UT 84112.

2. Therapy termination is ideal when the patient shows baseline behaviors in the AG group, defined subsequently.

3. Intimacy is described by the SASB model as shared interpersonal space. It can be hostile or friendly. Differentiation is the opposite of intimacy, and it, too, can be hostile or friendly.

4. Her responses to the Wisconsin Personality Inventory (WISPI; Klein et al., 1993) suggested that the Axis II label Avoidant Personality Disorder would be appropriate.

5. The Strange Situation data were generated by Donna Gelfand and Douglas Teti, who were supported by a grant from the National Institute of Mental Health (e.g., Gelfand, Teti, & Fox, 1992). The SASB analyses of the Gelfand–Teti data were supported by a grant to the author from the Research Network I of the MacArthur Foundation, D. Kupfer, Director. Thanks are expressed to the MacArthur Foundation and to Professors Gelfand and Teti for their willingness to share these valuable videotapes.

6. More than one SASB code can be ascribed to a transaction. The provision for multiple codes allows the system to describe an infinite number of psychological events, including some that are quite complex. For example, consider the classical "double bind" first described by Bateson, Jackson, Haley, and Weakland (1956): A schizophrenic man greeted his mother with a warm hug. She shrank back, and, cuing on her withdrawal, her son drew back too. Whereupon she said: "What's the matter? Don't you love me any more?" Such "double-binding" events can be described by three distinct components from the SASB model: (1) the theme of love and affection (ACTIVE LOVE or AFFIRM), (2) coercion, i.e., the demand that the world be seen as defined by the speaker (CONTROL or BLAME), and (3) the fact that the listener is asked to ignore his or her own reality testing, including the fact that what just happened, happened (IGNORE). In sum, the "double bind" as described by this example from

Bateson is a complex code that includes the components ACTIVE LOVE + CONTROL + IGNORE.

7. The American Psychological Association (1974, p. 29) dismissed face validity as irrelevant except perhaps as a factor that may "improve public relations." To the contrary, I believe that face validity is a good idea. Measures should "make sense" to the reasonable reader.

8. The scale on Figure 4.13 is set the same as Figure 4.14 to allow the reader to see easily that circumplex order within the SASB data set is very strong (as is the circumplex order within the IAS-R set of ratings), while circumplex concordance between the SASB and the IAS-R is comparatively weak.

9. TRUST is adjacent to the exact antithesis, SUBMIT.

10. Covariance corrections for the mothers' current depressive state as measured by the Beck Depression Inventory (BDI) did not change these trends.

11. It is important to note that depression, like fever, arises by different routes.

12. Identification is not the same as parentification, described below.

13. This is not the only way to account for such heroism.

14. In Benjamin (1994b), where I introduced the idea of IPIRs, I called this second process *internalization*. I have since decided it is better to call it *recapitulation* and to use the word, *internalization,* as a more general term that describes all three copy processes.

15. Benjamin and Friedrich (1991) speculated on how the SASB model could be combined with current theories of parallel data processing to describe the neurology of mental processing of social images. These ideas could be adapted to describe hypothetical neurological parallels for the IPIR.

16. Intensity is defined qualitatively by the SASB model. The poles describe the primitive basics, and these are the most intense. Points between the poles are more "higher level" and less intense.

17. The question of whether patient perceptions reflect what actually happened has many ramifications in different contexts. In interviews, I consistently try to get SASB-codable examples of patient reports. For example, the claim "my mother didn't give me enough attention" might truly reflect IGNORE on the part of the mother. Alternatively it might reflect SULK and BLAME on the part of the patient. Still another possibility is that the statement reflects TRUST in a health care provider who has suggested this was the problem. I believe that specific SASB-codable examples will clarify and convey the dimensionality of the actual transactions. Concordance can be assessed by SASB-codable behaviors and statements subsequently shown in family sessions. The question of whether ratings on the Intrex questionnaires do or should agree with behavioral codes is fascinating. Sometimes discrepancies are the main clinical point (e.g., Humes & Humphrey, 1994).

REFERENCES

Adler, A. (1955). Individual psychology, its assumptions and its results. In C. Thompson, M. Mazer, & E. Witenberg (Eds.), *An outline of psychoanalysis* (pp. 283–297). New York: Modern Library.

Ainsworth, A. D. F., Blehar, M. C., Waters, E., & Wall, S. (1978). *Patterns of attachment.* Hillsdale, NJ: Erlebaum.

American Psychiatric Association. (1987). *Diagnostic and statistical manual of mental disorders* (3rd ed., rev.). Washington, DC: Author.

American Psychiatric Association. (1994). *Diagnostic and statistical manual of mental disorders* (4th ed.). Washington, DC: Author.

American Psychological Association. (1985). *Standards for educational and psychological testing.* Washington, DC: Author.

Bateson, G., Jackson, D. D., Haley, J., & Weakland, J. (1956). Toward a theory of schizophrenia. *Behavioral Science, 1,* 251–264.

Benjamin, L. S. (1974). Structural analysis of social behavior. *Psychological Review, 81,* 392–425.

Benjamin, L. S. (1979a). Structural analysis of differentiation failure. *Psychiatry, 42,* 1–23.

Benjamin, L. S. (1979b). Use of Structural Analysis of Social Behavior (SASB) and Markov chains to study dyadic interactions. *Journal of Abnormal Psychology, 88,* 303–319.

Benjamin, L. S. (1984). Principles of prediction using Structural Analysis of Social Behavior. In R. A. Zucker, J. Aronoff, & A. J. Rabin (Eds.), *Personality and the prediction of behavior* (pp. 121–172). New York: Academic Press.

Benjamin, L. S. (1986a). Adding social and intrapsychic descriptors to Axis I of DSM-III. In T. Millon & G. Klerman (Eds.), *Contemporary directions in psychopathology* (pp. 599–638). New York: Guilford Press.

Benjamin, L. S. (1986b). Operational definition and measurement of dynamics shown in the stream of free associations. *Psychiatry: Interpersonal and Biological Processes, 49,* 104–129.

Benjamin, L. S. (1988). *Short form intrex users' manual.* Salt Lake City: University of Utah.

Benjamin, L. S. (1993a). Every psychopathology is a gift of love. *Psychotherapy Research, 3,* 1–24.

Benjamin, L. S. (1993b). *Interpersonal diagnosis and treatment of personality disorders.* New York: Guilford Press.

Benjamin, L. S. (1994a). SASB: A bridge between personality theory and clinical psychology. *Psychological Inquiry, 5,* 273–316.

Benjamin, L. S. (1994b). Good defenses make good neighbors. In H. R. Conte & R. Plutchik (Eds.), *Ego defenses: Theory and measurement* (pp. 38–78). New York: Wiley.

Benjamin, L. S. (1996). *Interpersonal diagnosis and treatment of personality disorders* (2nd ed.). New York: Guilford Press.

Benjamin, L. S. (in press). Psychosocial factors in the development of personality disorders. In R. Cloninger (Ed.), *Personality and psychopathology.* Washington, DC: American Psychiatric Press.

Benjamin, L. S., & Friedrich, F. J. (1991). Contributions of Structural Analysis of Social Behavior (SASB) to the bridge between cognitive science and a science of object relations. In M. J. Horowitz (Ed.), *Person schemas and maladaptive behavior* (pp. 379–412). Chicago: University of Chicago Press.

Benjamin, L. S., & Gelfand, D. (1992). *Possible transmission of patterns of depression from mothers to infants.* Progress report to the MacArthur Foundation, Research Network, I. D. Kupfer, Director.

Benjamin, L. S., Giat, L., & Estroff, S. E. (1981). *Manual for coding social interaction in terms of structural analysis of social behavior.* Unpublished manuscript, Department of Psychology, University of Utah, Salt Lake City.

Benjamin, L. S., & Wonderlich, S. (1994). Social perceptions and borderline personality disorder: The relationship to mood disorders. *Journal of Abnormal Personality, 103,* 610–624.

Berlin, S., & Johnson, C. (1989). Woman and autonomy: Using Structural Analysis of Social Behavior to find autonomy within connections. *Psychiatry: Interpersonal and Biological Processes, 52,* 79–95.

Blatt, S. J. (1974). Levels of object representation in anaclitic and introjective depression. *Psychoanalytic Study of the Child, 29,* 107–157.

Bowlby, J. (1969). *Attachment and loss: Vol. I. Attachment.* London: Tavistock Institute of Human Relations.

Bowlby, J. (1977). The making and breaking of affectional bonds. *British Journal of Psychiatry, 130,* 201–210; 421–431.

Bretherton, I. (1985). Attachment theory: retrospect and prospect. *Monographs of the Society for Research in Child Development, 50*(1–2, Serial No. 209), 3–35.

Davies-Osterkamp, S., Hartkamp, N., & Junkert, B. (1993). Die Intrex-Kurzform. In W. Tress (Ed.), *SASB: Die Strukturale Analyse Sozialen Verhaltens* (pp. 156–218). Heidelberg: R. Asanger.

Fiedler, P. (1995). *Zum Stellenwert der Komorbiditatsforschung fur die Verhaltenstherapie.* Paper presented to the conference on Personlichkeitsstorungen. Diagnostik und Psychotherapie, sponsored by the University of Heidelberg, Bad Durkheim.

Florsheim, P., Henry, W., & Benjamin, L. S. (1996). Integrating individual and interpersonal approaches to diagnosis: The Structural Analysis of Social Behavior and attachment theory. In F. Kaslow (Ed.), *Handbook of relational diagnosis.* New York: Wiley.

Freud, S. (1896). Heredity and the etiology of the neuroses. In J. Riviere (Trans.), *Sigmund Freud collected papers* (Vol. 1). New York: Basic Books, 1959.

Gelfand, D. M., Teti, D. M., & Fox, C. E. R. (1992). Sources of parenting stress for depressed and nondepressed mothers of infants. *Journal of Clinical Child Psychology, 21,* 262–272.

Gilligan, C. (1977). In a different voice: Women's conceptions of self and of morality. *Harvard Educational Review, 47,* 481–517.

Grawe-Gerber, M., & Benjamin, L. S. (1989). *Structural Analysis of Social Behavior (SASB). Coding manual for psychotherapy research* (Research Report from the Department of Psychology). Bern: University of Bern.

Greenberg, J. R., & Mitchell, S. A. (1983). *Object relations in psychoanalytic theory.* Cambridge, MA: Harvard University Press.

Hamilton, N. G. (1989). A critical review of object relations theory. *American Journal of Psychiatry, 146,* 1552–1560.

Harlow, H. F., & Harlow, M. K. (1962). Social deprivation in monkeys. *Scientific American, 203,* 136–146.

Hazen, C., & Shaver, P. R. (1994). Deeper into attachment theory. *Psychological Inquiry, 5,* 68–79.

Henry, W. P. (1994). Differentiating normal and abnormal personality: An interpersonal apporoach based on the Structural Analysis of Social Behavior. In S. Stack & M. Lorr (Eds.), *Differentiating normal and abnormal personality* (pp. 316–340). New York: Springer.

Humes, D. L., & Humphrey, L. L. (1994). A multimethod analysis of families with a polydrug-dependent or normal adolescent daughter. *Journal of Abnormal Psychology, 103,* 676–685.

Humphrey, L. L., & Benjamin, L. S. (1986). Using Structural Analysis of Social Behavior to assess critical but elusive family processes: A new solution to an old problem. *American Psychologist, 41,* 979–989.

Humphrey, L. L., & Benjamin, L. S. (1989). *An observational coding system for use with structural analysis of social behavior: the training manual.* Unpublished manuscript, Northwestern Medical School, Chicago.

Jay, P. (1965). The common langur of North India. In I. DeVore (Ed.), *Primate behavior: Field studies of monkeys and apes.* New York: Holt, Rinehart & Winston.

Kiesler, D. J. (1983). The 1982 interpersonal circle: A taxonomy for complementarity in human transactions. *Psychological Review, 90,* 185–214.

Klein, M. H. (1983, Spring). Issues in the assessment of personality disorders. *Journal of Personality Disorders* (Suppl.), 18–33.

Klein, M. K., Benjamin, L. S., Rosenfeld, R., Treece, C., Husted, J., & Greist, J. (1993). The Wisconsin Personality Disorders Inventory: I. Development, reliability, and validity. *Journal of Personality Disorders, 7,* 285–303.

Kraemer, G. W. (1992). A psychobiological theory of attachment. *Behavioral and Brain Sciences, 14,* 1–28.

Kraemer, G. W., Ebert, M. H., Lake, C. R., & McKinney, W. T. (1989). A longitudinal study of the effects of different rearing environments on cerebrospinal fluid norepinephrine and biogenic amine metabolites in rhesus monkeys. *Neuropsychopharmacolgy, 2,* 175–189.

Leary, T. (1957). *Interpersonal diagnosis of personality: A functional theory and methodology for personality evaluation.* New York: Ronald Press.

Linehan, M. (1993). *Cognitive-behavioral treatment of borderline personality disorder.* New York: Guilford Press.

MacCorquedale, K., & Meehl, P. E. (1948). On a distinction between hypothetical constructs and intervening variables. *Psychological Review, 55,* 95–107.

MacKenzie, K. R. (1990). *Time limited group psychotherapy.* Washington, DC: American Psychiatric Press.

Mahler, M. (1968). *On human symbiosis and the vicissitudes of individuation.* New York: International Universities Press.

Moore, A. (1995). *Personality disorder and depression: A theoretical and empirical analysis of comorbidity.* Master's thesis, University of Utah, Salt Lake City.

Morey, L. C. (1988). *The MMPI Personality Disorder Scales: A manual and guide to interpretation.* Unpublished manuscript, Vanderbilt University, Nashville, TN.

Murray, H. A. (1938). *Explorations in personality.* New York: Oxford Press.

Mussen, P. H., Conger, J. J., & Kagan, J. (1971). *Child dvelopment and personality* (3rd ed.). New York: Harper & Row.

Orford, J. (1986). The rules of interpersonal complementarity: Does hostility beget hostility and dominance, submission? *Psychological Review, 93,* 365–377.

Pfohl, B., Stangl, D., & Zimmerman, M. (1984). The implications of DSM-III personality disorders for patients with major depression. *Journal of Affective Disorders, 7,* 309–318.

Pilkonis, P. A., & Frank, E. (1988). Personality pathology in recurrent depression: Nature, prevalence, and relationship to treatment response. *American Journal of Psychiatry, 145,* 435–441.

Schaefer, E. S. (1965). Configurational analysis of children's reports of parent behavior. *Journal of Consulting Psychology, 29,* 552–557.

Seligman, M. (1975). *Helplessness: On depression, development and death.* San Francisco: W. H. Freeman.

Shea, M. T., Glass, D. R., Pilkonis, P. A., Watkins, J., & Docherty, J. P. (1987). *Journal of Personality Disorders, 1,* 27–42.

Sheffield, M. (1994). *Therapy comprehensive exam.* Unpublished thesis, Brigham Young University, Provo, UT.

Sullivan, H. S. (1953). *The interpersonal theory of psychiatry.* New York: Norton.

Teti, D. M., Gelfand, D. M., Messinger, D. S., & Isabella, R. (1995). Maternal depression and the quality of early attachment: an examination of infants, preschoolers, and their mothers. *Developmental Psychology, 31,* 364–376.

Tinbergen, N. (1951). *The study of instinct.* Oxford: Clarendon Press.

Tracey, T. J. (1994) An examination of complementarity of interpersonal behavior. *Journal of Personality and Social Psychology, 67,* 864–878.

Wiggins, J. S. (1982). Circumplex models of interpersonal behavior in clinical psychology. In P. C. Kendall & J. N. Butcher (Eds.), *Handbook of research methods in clinical psychology* (pp. 183–221). New York: Wiley.

5

An Evolutionary Theory of Personality Disorders

THEODORE MILLON
ROGER D. DAVIS

There are those who contend that the major traditions of psychology and psychiatry have, for too long now, been doctrinaire in their assumptions. These critics claim that theories that focus their attention on only one level of data cannot help but generate formulations that are limited by their narrow preconceptions; moreover, their findings must, inevitably, be incompatible with the simple fact that psychological processes are multidetermined and multidimensional in expression. In rebuttal, those who endorse a single-level approach assert that theories that seek to encompass this totality will sink in a sea of data that can be neither charted conceptually nor navigated methodologically. Clearly, those who undertake to propose "integrative theories" are faced with the formidable task, not only of exposing the inadequacies of single-level theories, but of providing a convincing alternative that is both comprehensive and systematic. The reader must judge whether integrative theorists possess the intellectual skills and analytic powers necessary, not only to penetrate the vast labyrinths of man's mind and behavior, but to chart these intricate pathways in a manner that is both conceptually clear and methodologically testable.

Fortunately, ours is a time of rapid scientific and clinical advances, a time that seems optimal for ventures designed to generate new ideas and syntheses. The intersection between the study of "personality," "psychopathology," and "normality" is one of these spheres of significant academic activity and clinical responsibility. Theoretical formulations that bridge these intersections would represent a major and valued intellectual step, but to limit our focus to contemporary research models that address these junctions directly may lead us to overlook the solid footings provided by our field's historic thinkers (such as Freud and Jung), as well as our more mature sciences (such as physics and evolutionary biology). By our failing to coordinate propositions and constructs to principles and laws established by these intellectual giants and advanced disciplines, the different domains comprising our subject will continue to float on their own, so to speak, unconnected to other realms and, hence, requiring that we return to the important task of synthesis another day.

In this chapter, we go beyond current conceptual and research boundaries in personology and incorporate the contributions of past theorists as well as those of our more firmly grounded "adjacent" sciences. Not only may such steps bear new conceptual fruits, but they may provide a foundation that can undergird and guide our own discipline's explorations. Much of psychology as a whole remains adrift, divorced from broader spheres of scientific knowledge, isolated from deeper and more fundamental, if not universal, principles. As the history of psychology amply illustrates, the propositions of our science are not in themselves sufficient to orient its development in a consistent and focused fashion. Consequently, psychology has built a patchwork quilt of dissonant concepts and diverse data domains. Preoccupied with but a small part of the larger pie, or fearing accusations of reductionism, we have failed to draw on the rich possibilities that may be found in both historic and adjacent realms of scholarly pursuit. With few exceptions, cohering concepts that would connect current topics to those of the past have not been developed. We seem repeatedly trapped in (obsessed with?) contemporary fads and horizontal refinements. A search for integrative schemas and cohesive constructs that will link us to relevant observations and laws in other fields of contemporary science is also needed. The goal—albeit a rather "grandiose" one—is to refashion our patchwork quilt into a well-tailored and cohesive tapestry that interweaves the diverse forms in which nature expresses itself.

There is no better sphere within the psychological sciences to undertake such a synthesis than the subject matter of personology, the study of persons. Persons are the only organically integrated system in the psychological domain, evolved through the millennia and inherently created from birth as natural entities, rather than culture-bound and experience-derived gestalts. The intrinsic cohesion of persons is not merely a rhetorical construction but an authentic substantive unity. Personologic features may be differentiated into normal or pathological, and may be partitioned conceptually for pragmatic or scientific purposes, but they are segments of an inseparable biopsychosocial entity.

PHILOSOPHICAL PERSPECTIVES AND ISSUES

The "grand" psychological theories of the 1920s and 1930s failed to fulfill their promise. Moreover, there have been few unifying proposals these past decades. Confidence that integrative schemas in realms such as personality or learning could be fashioned by the convergence of a few basic psychological variables gave way as a feasible aspiration by the 1960s. A hesitant conservatism, either antitheoretical or proempirical in character, gained sway, illustrated in personality by the growth of the "anticonsistency" and "anticoherency" movements, both of which impugned the validity of personality—the first its constancy over place and time, and the second its internal consonance. Fortunately, the pendulum has again begun to swing the other way. What began haltingly has become a reemergence of the integrative mindset, tentative proposals of an "ecumenical" nature that seek to bridge diverse psychological methods and processes. The dislodging of behavioral concretism, the rebirth of cognitive science, and the growth of therapeutic eclecticism, illustrate this encouraging shift.

At this juncture in the history of personality, we must go beyond current conceptual boundaries in order to explore more carefully reasoned, as well as "intuitive," hypotheses. We are not arguing that different spheres of scientific inquiry should be equated, nor are we seeking a single, overarching conceptual system encompassing biology, psychology, and sociology (Millon, 1983). Arguing in favor of establishing explicit links between these domains calls neither for a reductionistic philosophy, a belief in substantive identicality, or efforts to so fashion such links by formal logic. Rather, one should aspire to their substantive concordance, empirical consistency, conceptual interfacing, convergent dialogues, and mutual enlightenment.

Essential Elements of a Clinical Science

Integrative consonance such as that described is not an aspiration limited to ostensibly diverse sciences but is a worthy goal within each science as well. Particularly relevant in this regard are efforts that seek to coordinate the often separate structural and functional domains that comprise a clinical science, namely: its theories, the classification system it has formulated, the diagnostic tools it employs, and the therapeutic techniques it implements. Rather than developing independently and being left to stand in an autonomous and largely unconnected manner, a truly mature clinical science will embody explicit: (1) *theories*, that is, explanatory and heuristic conceptual schemas that are consistent with established knowledge in both its own and related sciences, and from which reasonably accurate propositions concerning pathological conditions can be both deduced and understood, enabling thereby the development of a formal (2) *nosology*, that is, a taxonomic classification of disorders that has been derived logically from the theory, and is arranged to provide a cohesive organization within which its major categories can readily be grouped and differentiated, permitting thereby the development of coordinated (3) *instruments*, tools that are empirically grounded and sufficiently sensitive quantitatively to enable the theory's propositions and hypotheses to be adequately investigated and evaluated, and the constructs comprising its nosology to be readily identified (diagnosed) and measured (dimensionalized), specifying therefrom target areas for (4) *interventions* or strategies and techniques of therapy, designed in accord with the theory and oriented to modify problematic clinical characteristics consonant with professional standards and social responsibilities.

A few words should be said at the outset concerning the undergirding framework used to structure the personology model presented herein. Bipolar or dimensional schemas are almost universally present in the literature; the earliest may be traced to ancient religions, notably in the Chinese *I Ching* texts and the Hebrew *Kabala*. More modern, though equally speculative bipolar systems, have been proposed by keen and broadly informed observers, such as Freud and Jung, or by empirically well-grounded and dimensionally oriented methodologists, such as Raymond Cattell and Hans Eysenck. Each of their proposals fascinates either by virtue of their intriguing portrayals or by the compelling power of their "data" or logic. For the present authors, however, all failed in their quest for the ultimate character of human nature in that their conceptions float, so to speak, above the foundations built by contemporary physical and biological sciences. Formulas of a psychological nature must not only coordinate with, but be anchored firmly to observations derived specifically from modern principles of physical and biological evolution.

The polarity model presented in this chapter is grounded in such modern principles, from which a deeper and clearer understanding may be obtained concerning the nature of both normal and pathological functioning. In essence, it seeks to explicate the structure and styles of personality with reference to "deficient," "imbalanced," or "conflicted" modes of ecological adaptation and reproductive strategy. Some readers will judge these conjectures persuasive; a few will consider them "interesting" but essentially unconfirmable; still others will find little of merit in them. Whatever one's appraisal, the theoretical model that follows may best be approached in the spirit in which it was formulated—an effort to bring together observations from different domains of science in the hope that principles derived in adjacent fields can lead to a clearer understanding of their neighbors.

How Do We Conceive Personality and Personality Disorders?

The word "personality" derives from the Greek *persona* and originally represented the theatrical mask used by dramatic players. Its meaning has changed through history. As a mask assumed by an actor, it suggested a pretense of appearance, that is, the possession of traits other than those that actually characterized the individual behind the mask. In time, the term *persona* lost its connotation of pretense and illusion and began to represent not the mask, but the real person, his or her apparent, explicit, and manifest features. The third and final meaning that the term "personality" acquired delves "beneath" the surface impression of the person and turns the spotlight on the inner, less revealed, and hidden psychological qualities of the individual. Thus, through history the term has shifted from meaning external illusion to surface reality, to opaque or veiled inner traits, the meaning that comes closest to contemporary use. Personality is seen today as a complex and highly contextualized pattern of deeply embedded psychological characteristics that cannot be eradicated easily, characteristics that express themselves automatically in most facets of functioning. Intrinsic and pervasive, they emerge from a complicated matrix of biological dispositions and experiential learnings and comprise the individual's distinctive pattern of perceiving, feeling, thinking, and coping. Personality is not a potpourri of unrelated perceptions, thoughts, and behaviors but a tightly knit organization of attitudes, habits, and emotions. Although we may start in life with more or less random and diverse feelings and reactions, repetitive sequences of experiences to which we are exposed narrow our repertoire to particular behavioral strategies that become prepotent and characterize our personally distinctive way of coping with others and relating to ourselves.

Such a conception of personality breaks the long-entrenched habit of conceiving of personality as a substance, and of personality disorders as diseases, that is, as "foreign" entities or lesions that intrude insidiously within the person and undermine his/her so-called normal functions. The archaic notion that all mental disorders represent external intrusions or internal disease processes is an offshoot of prescientific ideas such as demons or spirits that ostensibly "possess" or cast spells on the person. The role of infectious agents and anatomical lesions in physical medicine has reawakened this archaic view. Of course we no longer see demons, but many still see some alien or malevolent force as invading or unsettling the patient's otherwise healthy status. This view is an appealing simplification to the layman, who can attribute his/her irrationalities to some intrusive or upsetting agent. It also has its appeal to the less sophisticated clinician, for it enables him/her to believe that the insidious intruder can be identified, hunted down, and destroyed. Accordingly, we will use the highly prejudicial phrase "personality disorders" only when required by clarity or the rules of construction, preferring the more apt "clinical personality patterns."

The naive "intrusive disease" model carries little weight among modern-day medical and behavioral scientists. Given our increasing awareness of the complex nature of both health and disease, we now recognize, for example, that most disorders, physical and psychological, result from a dynamic and changing interplay between individuals' capacities to cope and the environment within which they live. The patients' overall constitutional makeup is what serves as the substrate that inclines them to resist or to succumb to potentially troublesome environmental forces. To illustrate: infectious viruses and bacteria proliferate within the environment; it is the person's immunological defenses that determine whether or not these microbes will take hold, spread, and, ultimately, be experienced as illness. Individuals with robust immune activity will counteract the usual range of infectious microbes with ease, whereas those with weakened immune capacities will be vulnerable, fail to handle these "intrusions," and quickly succumb.

Psychic pathology should be conceived as reflecting the same interactive contextual pattern. Here, however, it is not the immunological defenses but the individual's personality pattern—that is, coping skills and adaptive flexibilities—that will determine whether or not the person will master or succumb to the psychosocial environment. Just as physical ill health is likely to be less a matter of some alien virus than it is a dysfunction in the body's capacity to deal with infectious agents, so too is psychological ill health likely to be less a product of some intrusive psychic strain than it is a dysfunction in the personality's capacity to cope with life's difficulties. Viewed this way, the structure and characteristics of personality, normal or abnormal, become the foundation for the individual's capacity to function in a mentally healthy or ill way.

Following our biological–evolutionary analogy, we may say that personality and the environment are best conceptualized as a system. Hierarchical integration and self-regulation are essential characteristics of this system, and both form fundamental themes for this chapter. The personality system is hierarchical because it includes multiple levels of organization—biological, psychological, familial, social, and cultural—each of which builds on the level below in order to secure a measure of emergent complexity and functional autonomy. The personality system is self-regulating because it is the essential substrate involved in maintaining the psychic equilibrium of person against psychosocial stressors of uncertain origin and magnitude.

Taxonomic Issues

No issue concerning either normal or clinical personality functioning has raised deeper or more persistent epistemological questions than those related to classification. The present chapter touches on a few of these questions, but it cannot undertake a thorough examination of the deeper and more problematic philosophical issues involved in the elements of the subject. A complex network of purposes and a correspondingly varied set of contexts and methods, both pragmatic and theoretical, bear on the efficacy and utility of a categorical or dimensional schema.

Further complicating any discussion of personality taxonomy is the fact that the fundamental issues involved cohere only loosely. Factor analysis, for example, produces exclusively dimensional models. Theoretical deductive methods and etiological speculations, on the other hand, may give rise to either dimensional or categorical systems: Not every antisocial, low on conscientiousness in the archempirical five-factor model, for example, need be equally bereft of libidinal investment in the object relations sphere. Note that although both of these conceptions can be modeled as a continuum, they derive from nearly opposite epistemic sources, the more observational–empirical versus the highly inferential–speculative. In general, we might say that taxonomies can be either (1) dimensional, categorical, or synthetically prototypal in structure, (2) observationally (casually or statistically) or theoretically (etiologically or deductively) generated, and (3) manifest or latent with regard to their level of application (descriptive or explanatory). Twelve cells could be generated by crossing these ''taxonomic polarities,'' but it is by no means apparent that each cell is represented in nature by a classification system of equal internal consistency and utility.

In fact, the question can be asked if personality taxonomy is even possible at all. The issue here concerns the nagging nomothetic ver-

sus idiographic issue and degree to which the ideas we carve out of
nature are inherently contextualized. Do persons share important commonalities, such that these can be fruitfully organized and coupled to
a therapeutic agenda? Or, are human beings so intrinsically contextualized and unique that the logic of each individual intervention can
ultimately follow only from an understanding of the person on his/her
"own terms," so that taxonomy must be either impossible or preten-
tiously imposed?

Organization and Conceptualization of the Data of Normal and Clinical Personality

In our own explorations, we first broach the structural questions: How
can we best conceptualize and organize the clinical data that comprise
normal and clinical personality? Clearly, personality characteristics express themselves in a variety of ways. Not only are they complex, but
they can be approached at different levels and can be viewed from
many frames of reference. For example, behaviorally, personality can
be conceived as complicated response patterns to environmental stimuli. At a phenomenological level, they can be understood as experiences
of joy or anguish. Approached physiologically, they can be analyzed
as sequences of complex neural and chemical activity. And intrapsychically, they can be inferred as unconscious processes that enable the
person to enhance life or to defend against anxiety and conflict.

Given these diverse possibilities, we can readily understand why
both normal and pathological states or processes may be classified in
terms of any of several data levels we may wish to focus on and any
of a variety of attributes we may wish to identify and explain. Beyond
this, each data level lends itself to a number of specific concepts and
categories, the usefulness of which must be gauged by their ability to
help solve the particular problems and purposes for which they were
created. That the subject matter of personality is inherently diverse,
complex, contextualized, and multidetermined is precisely the reason
why we must not narrow the data comprising a conceptual scheme
to one level or one approach. Each source and each orientation has
a legitimate and potentially fruitful contribution to make. It should be
clear from these considerations that no single classification of personality traits or disorders will "carve nature at its joints," that is, is an
inevitable representation of the "real world." Rather, our classifications are, at best, interim tools for advancing knowledge and facilitating scientific or clinical goals. They serve to organize our scientific work
in a logical manner and function as explanatory propositions to give
meaning to our clinical experiences.

Moreover, the subject areas that subdivide the natural world differ in the degree to which their phenomena are inherently differentiated and organized. Some areas are "naturally" more articulated and quantifiable than others. To illustrate: Although physics is highly probabilistic in many of its most recondite spheres, the features of our everyday physical world are highly ordered and predictable. Theories in this latter realm (e.g., mechanics, electricity) serve largely to *uncover* the lawful relationships that do, in fact, exist in nature; it was the task of turn-of-the-century physicists to fashion a network of constructs that faithfully mirrored the universal nature of the phenomena they studied. By contrast, probabilistic realms of quantum analysis (e.g., short-lived elementary particles) or systems of recent evolutionary development (e.g., human interactions) are inherently weakly organized and highly contextualized, lacking either articulated or invariant connections among their constituent elements.

In knowledge domains that relate to these less-ordered spheres of nature (the "softer" sciences), classifiers and theorists sometimes find it necessary to *impose* a modestly arbitrary measure of systematization; in so doing, they construct a degree of clarity and coherence that is not fully consonant with the "naturally" unsettled and indeterminate character of their subject. Rather than equivocate strategically, or succumb to the "futility of it all," noble or pretentious statistical or theoretical efforts are made to arrange and categorize these inexact and probabilistic elements so that they simulate a degree of precision and order transcending that which they intrinsically possess. To illustrate: In fields such as economics and psychopathology, categories and classifications are, in considerable measure, splendid fictions, compelling notions, or austere formulas devised to give coherence to their *inherently imprecise* subjects.

Let us ask again: Are conceptual definition and classification possible in organizing the data of normal and clinical personality? Can these most fundamental of scientific activities be achieved in subjects that are inherently inexact, of only modest levels of intrinsic order, and ones in which even the very slightest variations in context or antecedent conditions—often of a minor or random character—produce highly divergent outcomes (Bandura, 1982)? Because this "looseness" within the network of variables in normality and psychopathology is unavoidable, are there any grounds for believing that such endeavors could prove more than illusory? Persuasive answers to this question of a more philosophical nature must be bypassed in this all-too-concise chapter; those who wish to pursue this line of analysis would gain much by reading, among others, Pap (1953), Hempel (1965), and Meehl (1978).

Categories and Dimensions

Important differences separate medical from psychological traditions in their approach to classifying their primary subject domains. Psychology's substantive realms have been approached with considerable success by employing methods of dimensional analysis and quantitative differentiation (e.g., intelligence measures, aptitude levels, trait magnitudes, etc.). By contrast, medicine has made its greatest progress by increasing its accuracy in identifying and categorizing discrete "disease" entities. The issue separating these two historic approaches as it relates to the subject domain of normal and abnormal personality may best be stated in the form of a question: Should personality be conceived and organized as a series of dimensional traits that combine to form a unique profile for each individual, or should certain central characteristics be selected to exemplify and categorize personality types found commonly in clinical populations?

The view that personality *pathology* might best be conceived as dimensional traits has only recently begun to be taken as a serious alternative to the more classic categorical approach. Certain trait dimensions have been proposed in the past as relevant to these disorders (e.g., dominance–submission, extraversion–introversion, and rigidity–flexibility), but these have not been translated into the full range of personality syndromes. Some traits have been formulated so that one extreme of a dimension differs significantly from the other in terms of their clinical implications; an example here would be emotional stability versus emotional vulnerability. Other traits are psychologically curvilinear such that both extremes have negative implications; an example of this would be found in an activity dimension such as listlessness versus restlessness.

Despite their seeming advantages and recent advocates, dimensional systems have not taken strong root in the formal diagnosis of clinical personality patterns. Numerous complications and limitations have been noted in the literature. Foremost among these is the fact that there is little agreement among dimensional theorists concerning the number of traits necessary to represent personality and psychopathology. Historically, for example, Menninger (1963) contended that a single dimension would suffice; Eysenck (1960) asserts that three are needed. Recent models, most notably the five-factor model (FFM) (Costa & McCrae, 1990; Goldberg, 1990; Norman, 1963), have begun to achieve a modest level of consensus. Even among those who have studied and developed the so-called lexical model, however, there are disagreements.

Another problem here is that theorists may "invent" dimensions in accord with their expectations rather than "discovering" them as if they were intrinsic to nature, merely awaiting scientific detection. The number of traits or factors required to assess personality may not be determined by the ability of our research to disclose some inherent truth but rather by predilections for conceiving the studies we undertake and organizing the data they generate (Kline & Barrett, 1983; Millon, 1990).

Categorical or prototypal models appear to have been the preferred schema for representing both clinical syndromes and clinical personality patterns. Note, however, that most contemporary categories neither imply nor are constructed to be all-or-none typologies. Although singling out and giving prominence to certain features of behavior, they do not overlook the others but merely assign them lesser significance. The process of assigning centrality or relative dominance to particular characteristics distinguishes a schema of categories from one composed of trait dimensions. Conceived in this manner, a type simply becomes a superordinate category that subsumes and integrates psychologically covariant traits.

There are, of course, objections to the use of categorical typologies in personality. They contribute to the fallacious belief that syndromes of abnormality are discrete entities, even medical "diseases," when, in fact, they are merely concepts that help focus and coordinate observations. Numerous classifications have been formulated in the past century, and one may question whether any system is worth utilizing if there is so little consensus among categorists themselves. Is it possible to conclude from this review that categorical or dimensional schemas are potentially the more useful for personality classifications? An illuminating answer may have been provided by Cattell, who wrote: "The description by attributes [traits] and the description by types must be considered face and obverse of the same descriptive system. Any object whatever can be defined either by listing measurements for it on a set of [trait] attributes or by sequestering it to a particular named [type] category" (1970, p. 40).

In effect, Cattell has concluded that the issue of choosing between dimensional traits and categorical types is both naive and specious since they are two sides of the same coin. The essential distinction to be made between these models is that of comprehensiveness. Types are higher-order syntheses of lower-order dimensional traits: They encompass a wider scope of generality. For certain purposes it may be useful to narrow attention to specific traits; in other circumstances a more inclusive level of integration may be appropriate (Grove & Tellegen, 1991). Whatever one's verdict, there is little doubt that categorical schemas must be operationalized in terms of lower-order diagnostic attributes.

The question then is: How should the clinical personologic constructs be organized to best meet diagnostic and therapeutic purposes? We will address this question in the assessment section of this paper, advocating a position termed prototypal domain traits.

Theoretical and Empirical Issues: Manifest and Latent Taxa

The elements that comprise a classification system are called taxa (singular: taxon); they may be differentiated in a number of different ways. What may be labeled as "manifest taxa" involve classes that are based on observable or phenotypic commonalities (e.g., overt behaviors). "Latent taxa" pertain to groupings formed on the basis of abstract mathematical derivations (factor or cluster analysis) or the propositional deductions of a theory, each of which ostensibly represents the presence of genotypic commonalities (e.g., etiological origins or constitutional dispositions).

Manifest—Observational and Mathematically Inductive Personologic Taxa

For the greater part of history, taxonomies of both normal and abnormal persons were formed on the basis of systematic observation, the witnessing of repetitive patterns of behavior and emotion among a small number of carefully studied persons or patients. Etiological hypotheses were generated to give meaning to these patterns of covariance (e.g., Hippocrates anchored differences in observed temperament to his humoral theory, and Kraepelin distinguished two major categories of severe pathology, dementia praecox and manic–depressive disease, in terms of their ostensive divergent prognostic course). The elements comprising these theoretical notions were post hoc, however, imposed after the fact on prior observational data, rather than serving as a generative source for taxonomic categories. The most recent example of a clinical taxonomy, one tied explicitly to phenomenal observation and constructed by intention to both atheoretical and nonquantitative, is, of course, DSM. Spitzer, chairperson of the Task Force, stated in the DSM-III manual (American Psychiatric Association, 1980) that "clinicians can agree on the identification of mental disorders on the basis of their clinical manifestations without agreeing on how the disturbances came about" (p. 7).

Personologic taxonomies can be generated in two ways. The polar distinction between manifest taxa, at the one end, and latent taxa, at the other, represents in part a broader epistemological dichotomy that exists between those who prefer to employ data derived from observational–inductive contexts versus those who prefer to draw their ideas from more theoretical–deductive sources. A parallel distinction was first drawn by Aristotle when he sought to contrast the understanding of disease with reference to knowledge of latent principles—which ostensibly deals with all instances of a disease, however diverse—versus direct observational knowledge, which deals presumably only with specific and individual instances. To Aristotle, knowledge based on direct experience alone represented a more primitive type of knowledge than that informed by mathematics or conceptual theory which could, through the application of principles, explain not only why a particular disease occurs, but illuminate commonalities among seemingly diverse ailments.

Inasmuch as manifest taxa stem from the observations and inferences of, for example, clinical diagnosticians, they comprise, in circular fashion, the very qualities that clinicians are likely to see and deduce. Classes so constructed will not only direct future observers to focus on and to mirror these same taxa in their patients, but they may lead future nosologists away from potentially more useful constructs with which to fathom less obvious patterns of attribute covariation, perhaps based on etiological speculation. In large measure, observationally based taxa gain their import and prominence by virtue of consensus and authority. Cumulative experience and habit are crystallized and subsequently confirmed by official bodies such as the various DSM committees (Millon, 1986). Specified criteria are denoted and articulated, acquiring definitional, if not stipulative powers, at least in the eyes of those who come to accept the manifest attributes selected as infallible taxonomic indicators.

In addition to the perspicacious but fallible eye of the trained observer, who comes to the taxonomic task with preconceptions and biases, there exist several families of multivariate techniques (e.g., factor analysis, multidimensional scaling, and cluster analysis), which, by virtue of their formal rigor and theoretical innocence, easily surpass the sensitivity of the observer in their inexorable search for patterns of attribute covariation.

Factor analysis is perhaps the most widely used of these multivariate techniques, and as such, it deserves brief commentary. Although "factor analysis" itself is a generic term encompassing a family of numerical procedures, all essentially seek to reveal an underlying structure by identifying factors that account for the covariation of observed variables. Linear combinations of these variables are extracted to accumulate as much of the variance of the original data set as possible. The resulting data-reductive variates present a parsimonious representation of the data set while offering near-criterion level performance.

Factors derived in this manner are usually rotated after their initial mathematical extraction in order to increase their psychological interpretability.

One factor model of personality, the five-factor model, has gained extensive academic publicity. The "Big Five" were originally extracted by a lexical approach, which assumes that "most of the socially relevant and interpersonally salient personality characteristics have become encoded in the natural language" (John, 1990, p. 67). According to Digman (1990), the five-factor model has been replicated across multiple data sources, in children and adults, and in several different languages. Indeed, the model is usually put forward on the strength of its convergent validity.

Despite the ostensively productive lines of investigation that factorial techniques have demonstrated, several concerns continue to be raised concerning the viability of factor analysis as an instrument of conceptualization at a genotypic or latent level. Thus, early in its application, Kendell (1975) reported that skepticism in the field remains high, "largely because of the variety of different factor solutions that can be obtained from a single set of data and the lack of any satisfactory objective criterion for preferring one of these to the others. The number of factors obtained and their loadings are often affected considerably by relatively small changes in the size or composition of the subject sample, or in the range of tests employed" (p. 108). Sprock and Blashfield (1984) concluded that "deciding when to stop the process of selecting the number of factors, rotating the solutions, and interpreting the factors are all highly subjective and at the discretion of the user. Therefore, many distrust the results" (p. 108).

In addition to these methodological caveats, a number of conceptual forewarnings must be kept in mind regarding the structural implications of these mathematical approaches. Content alone is an insufficient basis on which to establish a taxonomy. Moreover, as is known among those involved in the development of psychometric instruments (Loevinger, 1957; Millon, 1977, 1986), a reasonable degree of "fidelity" should exist between the pattern of relationships among the scales of a test and its structural model of normality or pathology. Let us consider: The root-metaphor underlying the personality construct is integration, that personality forms an integrated system. A cardinal characteristic of systems is that one element of the system constrains what can exist elsewhere. The dimensions of the five-factor model, however, have been deliberately constructed to be orthogonal or independent. An individual's score on one dimension does *not* constrain the score obtained on any other. Thus the methodology of orthogonal extraction methods appears incommensurate with the epistemology of the personality construct.

Concerns may also be raised with regard to the sufficiency of ordinary language descriptors. Although the ordinary-language lexical hypothesis may indeed be valid for interpersonally salient descriptors, is it valid for more scientific-language descriptors? Judgments can converge without being correct in the sense of yielding anything beyond surface impressions. Perhaps an example from another descriptive domain would illustrate the potentially trivial nature of the five-factor model for both science and clinical work. Let us gather the responses of a wide range of subjects from every culture and language to a comprehensive set of descriptive terms of human physical (not psychological) characteristics. How many and what factors would be likely to emerge? Our guess is that five or six highly loaded dimensions (traits) would be identified and replicated—namely, sex (male to female), race (black to white), age (young to old), height (short to tall), physique (thin to heavy), and appearance (beautiful to ugly). Despite its convergence across cultures and languages, would this finding be of value in anything but the most superficial characterizations? Might it signify nothing but the usual limits of human cognition (e.g., George Miller's Seven—plus or minus two)? Have these surface distinctions not caused us great social difficulties, notably gross racial and sex discrimination?

Related to this is a concern which regards the utility of inductive mathematical techniques in "Kuhnian situations." Just as the manifest taxa which stem from the observations of clinical diagnosticians comprise in a tautalogical fashion the qualities clinicians are likely to see, mathematically generated taxa in the lexical tradition draw upon characteristics likely to be considered salient by normal persons. This objection gets at the periodic reconceptualization of personality according to new theoretical perspectives, with the consequent introduction of new terms which, as Hempel (1965, p. 140) said, "have a distinct meaning and function only in the context of [the] corresponding theory." The progress of "normal science" relies on successive refinements of that which already exists, rather than the transformations of the whole gestalt of scientific knowledge that accompanies scientific revolutions. Because inductive mathematical–statistical procedures cull from preexisting constructs their covariate attribute patterns, they are well-suited to normal science refinements, but they cannot be suited to scientific revolutions and cannot effect these revolutions on their own. Consequently, any inductive methodology, while capable perhaps of refining knowledge, cannot be forward looking in the manner required for scientific revolutions. The distillation of current constructs is an essentially static rather than dynamic approach. Recall that the lexical approach assumes that the essential dimensions of personality are *already* in the normal lexicon.

Hence, despite its popularity with many a distinguished psychometrician, the psychological composition of factorial structures is far from universally accepted. Not only do few personologic or psychopathologic entities give evidence of factorial "purity" or attribute independence, but factorial solutions tend to be antithetical to the predominant polythetic structure and overlapping relationships that exist among normal personalities and clinical conditions. Neither personologic nor syndromic taxa consist of entirely homogeneous and discrete attributes. Rather, taxa are comprised of diffuse and complex characteristics that share many attributes in common, factorially derived or otherwise. Consistent with the basic organizational–dynamic thesis of the systems concept, the meaning of these attributes is transformed by the context in which they exist. Although major depression is experienced by both narcissistic and dependent personalities, they are very different depressions, different by virtue of the systems in which they are embedded. Similarly, personalities may share single traits whose functional significance varies as a function of the overall organization of the personality.

This is not the chapter or setting for such purposes, but it should be noted in passing that other equally astute and productive investigators have registered a measure of dissent from both the sufficiency of scope of the "Big Five," and its adequacy as a latent explicator of the personality disorders (Benjamin, 1993; Carson, 1993; Davis & Millon, 1993). Beyond these skeptics of the fruitfulness of the FFM are those who question the wisdom of employing latent mathematical methods at all. In his usual perspicacious manner, Kendell's comment of more than a decade ago (1975), upon reviewing the preceding 20-year period, may be judged by some as no less apt today than it was then:

> Looking back on the various studies published in the last twenty years it is clear that many investigators, clinicians and statisticians, have had a naive, almost Baconian, attitude to the statistical techniques they were employing, putting in all data at their disposal on the assumption that the computer would sort out the relevant from the irrelevant and expose the underlying principles and regularities, and assuming all that was required of them was to collect the data assiduously beforehand.
>
> Moreover, any statistician worth his salt is likely to be able, by judicious choice of patients and items, and of factoring or clustering procedures, to produce more or less what he wants to. (p. 118)

Latent Theoretical Personologic Taxa

In the early stages of knowledge, conceptual categories rely invariably on observed similarities among phenomena (Tversky, 1977). As knowledge advances, overt similarities are discovered to be an insufficient, if not false basis for cohering categories and imbuing them with scientific meaning (Smith & Medin, 1981). As Hempel (1965) and Quine (1977) have pointed out, it is theory that provides the glue that holds concepts together and gives them both their scientific and clinical relevance. In his discussion of classificatory concepts, Hempel wrote (1965):

> The development of a scientific discipline may often be said to proceed from an initial "natural history" stage . . . to subsequent more and more "theoretical stages . . . The vocabulary required in the early stages of this development will be largely observational. . . . The shift toward theoretical systematization is marked by the introduction of new, "theoretical" terms . . . more or less removed from the level of directly observable things and events. . . .
>
>   These terms have a distinct meaning and function only in the context of a corresponding theory. (pp. 139–140)

Theory, when properly fashioned, ultimately provides more simplicity and clarity than unintegrated and scattered information. As effectively argued by contemporary philosophers of science (Hempel, 1965; Quine, 1961), unrelated knowledge and techniques, especially those based on surface similarities, are a sign of a primitive science. All natural sciences have organizing principles that not only create order but also provide the basis for generating hypotheses and stimulating new knowledge. A good theory not only summarizes and incorporates extant knowledge but is heuristic in that it originates and develops new observations and new methods.

What are the essential elements that distinguish between a true science and explanatory schema and one that provides a mere descriptive summary of known observations and inferences? Simply stated, the answer lies in its power to generate concepts, propositions, and observations other than those used to construct it. This generative power is what Hempel meant by the "systematic import" of a science. He contrasted what are familiarly known as "natural" (theoretically guided, deductively based) and "artificial" (conceptually barren, similarity based) scientific systems.

Despite the utility of theory, doubts have arisen when introducing theory into the study of personology. Given our intuitive ability to "sense" the correctness of a psychological insight or speculation, theoretical efforts that impose structure or formalize these insights into a scientific system are likely to be perceived not only as cumbersome and intrusive but alien as well. This discomfiture and resistance does not arise in fields such as particle physics, where everyday observations are not readily available and where innovative insights are few and far between. In such subject domains, scientists are not only quite comfortable, but turn readily to deductive theory as a means of helping them explicate and coordinate knowledge. It is paradoxical but true and unfortunate that psychologists learn their subject quite well merely by observing the ordinary events of life. As a consequence of this ease, they may shy away from the "obscure and complicating" yet often fertile and systematizing powers inherent in formal theory, especially theories other than those learned in their student days.

Despite the shortcomings of historic and contemporary theoretical schemas, systematizing principles and abstract concepts can "facilitate a deeper seeing, a more penetrating vision that goes beyond superficial appearances to the order underlying them" (Bowers, 1977, p. 130). For example, pre-Darwinian taxonomists such as Linnaeus limited themselves to "apparent" similarities and differences among animals as a means of constructing their categories. Darwin was not "seduced" by appearances. Rather, he sought to understand the principles by which overt features came about. His classifications were based not only on keenly observed descriptive qualities but on genuinely explanatory ones.

However, ostensibly toward the end of pragmatic sobriety, those of an antitheory bias have sought to persuade the profession of the failings of premature formalization, warning us that we cannot arrive at the future we yearn for by lifting our science by its own bootstraps. To them, there is no way to traverse the road other sciences have traveled without paying the dues of an arduous program of empirical research. Formalized axiomatics, they say, must await the accumulation of "hard" evidence that is simply not yet in. Shortcutting the route with ill-timed theoretical systematics, such as a latent taxonomy, will lead us down primrose paths, preoccupying our attentions as we wind fruitlessly through endless detours, each of which could be averted by holding fast to an empirical philosophy or a clinical methodology.

AN UNDERGIRDING EVOLUTIONARY FRAMEWORK

No one argues against the view that theories that float, so to speak, on their own, unconcerned with the empirical domain or clinical knowledge, should be seen as the fatuous achievements they are and the travesty they may make of the virtues of a truly coherent nosological system. Formal theory should not be "pushed" far beyond the data, and its derivations should be linked at all points to established clinical observations. As I have written elsewhere (Millon, 1987a), structurally weak theories make it impossible to derive systematic and logical nosologies; this results in conflicting derivations and circular reasoning. Most nosological theories of psychopathology have generated brilliant deductions and insights, but few of these ideas can be attributed to their structure, the precision of their concepts, or their formal procedures for hypothesis derivation. Here, of course, is where the concepts and laws of adjacent sciences may come into play, providing models of structure and derivation, as well as substantive theories and data that may undergird and parallel the principles and observations of one's own field.

The role of evolution is most clearly grasped when it is paired with the principles of ecology. So conceived, the procession of evolution represents a series of serendipitous transformations in the structure of a phenomenon (for example, elementary particle, chemical molecule, living organism) that appear to promote survival in both its current and future environments. Such processions usually stem from the consequences of either random fluctuations (such as mutations) or replicative reformations (for example, recombinant mating) among an infinite number of possibilities—some simpler, others more complex, some more and others less organized, some increasingly specialized and others not. Evolution is defined, then, when these restructurings enable a natural entity (for example, species) or its subsequent variants to survive within present and succeeding ecological milieus. It is the continuity through time of these fluctuations and reformations that comprises the sequence we characterize as evolutionary progression.

In recent times, we have seen the emergence of sociobiology, a new "science" that explores the interface between human social functioning and evolutionary biology (Wilson 1975, 1978). Contemporary formulations by psychologists have likewise proposed the potentials and analyzed the problems involved in cohering evolutionary notions, individual differences, and personality traits (e.g., D. M. Buss, 1984). The common goal among these proposals is not only the desire to apply analogous principles across diverse scientific realms but also to reduce the enormous range of psychological concepts that have proliferated through history; this might be achieved by exploring the power of evolutionary theory to simplify and order previously disparate features. For example, all organisms seek to avoid injury, find nourishment, and reproduce their kind if they are to survive and maintain their populations. Each species displays commonalities in its adaptive or survival style. Within each species, however, there are differences in style and differences in the success with which its various members adapt to the diverse and changing environments they face. In these simplest of terms, "personality" would be employed as a term to represent the more or less distinctive style of adaptive functioning that a particular organism of a species exhibits as its relates to its typical range of environments. "Normal personalities," so conceived, would signify the utilization of species-specific modes of adaptation that are effective in "average or expectable" environments. "Disorders" of personality, so formulated, would represent different styles of maladaptive functioning that can be traced to deficiencies, imbalances, or conflicts in a species to relate to the environment it faces.

A few more words should be said concerning analogies between evolution and ecology, on the one hand, and normal and abnormal personality, on the other. During its life history an organism develops an assemblage of traits that contribute to its individual survival and reproductive success, the two essential components of "fitness" formulated by Darwin. Such assemblages, termed complex adaptations and strategies in the literature of evolutionary ecology, are close biological equivalents to what psychologists and psychiatrists have conceptualized as personality styles. In biology, explanations of a life-history strategy of adaptations refer primarily to biogenic variations among constituent traits, their overall covariance structure, and the nature and ratio of favorable to unfavorable ecological resources that have been available for purposes of extending longevity and optimizing reproduction. Such explanations are not appreciably different from those used to account for the development of normal and pathological personality styles.

Bypassing the usual complications of analogies, a relevant and intriguing parallel may be drawn between the phylogenic evolution of a species genetic composition and the ontogenic development of an individual organism's adaptive strategies (that is, its "personality style"). At any point in time, a species will possess a limited set of genes that serve as trait potentials. Over succeeding generations the frequency distribution of these genes will likely change in their relative proportions depending on how well the traits they undergird contribute to the species "fittedness" within its varying ecological habitats. In a similar fashion, individual organisms begin life with a limited subset of their species' genes and the trait potentials they subserve. Over time the salience of these trait potentials—not the proportion of the genes themselves—will become differentially prominent as the organism interacts with its environments, "learning" from these experiences which of its traits "fit" best, that is, are optimally suited to its ecosystem. In phylogenesis, then, actual gene frequencies change during the generation-to-generation adaptive process, whereas in ontogenesis it is the salience or prominence of gene-based traits that changes as adaptive learning takes place. Parallel evolutionary processes occur, one within the life of a species, the other within the life of an organism. What is seen in the individual organism is a shaping of latent potentials in adaptive and manifest styles of perceiving, feeling, thinking, and acting; these distinctive ways of adaptation, engendered by the interaction of biological endowment and social experience, comprise, in our view, the elements of what is termed personality styles, normal or abnormal. Thus the formative process of a single lifetime parallels gene redistributions among species during their evolutionary history.

If human beings are intrinsically contextualized systems, how is a taxonomy of personality, normal and abnormal, to be derived? Taxonomy, of course, is all in the boundaries. However, some boundaries are better than others, and those that map onto the intrinsic features of a subject domain are best. The threefold method of decomposition that appears to the authors the most fruitful for a taxonomy of personology suggests itself on the basis of the *formal characteristics of organic systems alone*, thus placing not only the content (which will follow shortly), but also the taxonomy's *structural* features on a logical basis. Each of these boundaries provides a way of sectioning what is essentially an organic whole.

The first boundary marks off a system as a distinctive phenomenon. First and foremost, a system must exist. In living systems, this boundary should be looked at as permeable, otherwise the system cannot exchange food and energy, or in the case of self-conscious living systems, information, with its environment. The second boundary marks off current states of the organism from those that may or may not exist in the future. Exchanges of energy and information between a system and its environment occur only across time. In this conception, the essential elements are successively added to arrive at a fully dynamic model: person, person–environment interaction, and finally, person–environment transaction, in which the person–environment system is seen as unfolding serially such that both the person and environment become something other than what would have been dictated by an interaction alone.

Whereas the circular feedback and the serially unfolding character of this dynamic process defies simplification, it does contrast what is required for the validity of a taxonomy embedded in the philosophy of naive realism with one whose root metaphor is integrative. Given the thoroughgoing interconnectedness of persons with their world, all boundaries must be essentially inexact, but they need not be structurally arbitrary. An integrative taxonomy must be judged by its utility in decomposing and recomposing the phenomena of a subject domain, here clinical personality patterns and their associated Axis I disorders. In other words, an integrative taxonomy succeeds only if the parts into which it has broken the world, upon being conceptually resynthesized, leave one with the rather numinous feeling that the dynamic self-referential complexity of the totality somewhat exceeds the capacity of the of mind to grasp. A systems conception succeeds if it puts Humpty Dumpty back together again.

The integrated whole of psychopathology is thus divided into two axes, Axis I and Axis II, according to the vertical or horizontal formal character of the etiologies involved. Axis I may be further divided into levels of organization from which inputs into the various manifestations of classical psychiatric pathology may originate—biochemical, macrobiological, familial, social, and cultural. Following this same scheme, a set of constructs for making divisions within Axis II will be put forward which, significantly, are *not* grounded in any one level of organization. This is a necessary feature of the model, since only a set of constructs *not* anchored in any one level of organization can span all levels of organization in order to be truly integrative and thus commensurate with the epistemology of the personality construct. In the following section, the boundaries that have been set forth are linked to contents, or what we call polarities, derived from their coupling with the principles of evolution. Later in this chapter, we show how these polarities can be used to generate a taxonomy of DSM personality disorders.

Existential Aims: The Pain–Pleasure Polarity

Every system can be conceptualized on its own terms, as a closed system, existing in-and-of itself. The most basic of all motivations, that of existence, has a twofold aspect. The first pertains to the enhancement or enrichment of life, that is, creating or strengthening ecologically survivable organisms. The second is the preservation of life, that is, creating survivability and security by avoiding events that might terminate it. Although we disagree with Freud's concept of a death instinct (Thanatos), we believe he was essentially correct in recognizing that a balanced yet fundamental biological bipolarity exists in nature, a bipolarity that has its parallel in the physical world. As Freud wrote in one of his last works, "The analogy of our two basic instincts extends from the sphere of living things to the pair of opposing forces—attraction and repulsion—which rule the inorganic world" (Freud, 1940, p. 72). Among humans, the former may be seen in life-enhancing acts that enrich existence by what are experientially recorded as "pleasurable" events (positive reinforcers), the latter in life-preserving behaviors oriented to achieve security by repelling or avoiding events that are experientially characterized as "painful" (negative reinforcers). More will be said of these fundamental if not universal mechanisms for countering entropic disintegration in the next section.

Existence is literally a "to-be" or "not-to-be" issue. In the inorganic world, to be is essentially a matter of possessing qualities that distinguish a phenomenon from its surrounding field, that is, of not being in a state of entropy. Among organic beings, to be is a matter of possessing the properties of life as well as being located in ecosystems that facilitate processes that enhance and preserve life, maintaining the integrity of the organism within its surrounding field. In the phenomenological or experiential world of sentient organisms, events that extend life and preserve it correspond largely to metaphorical terms such as pleasure and pain, that is, recognizing and pursuing life-enriching motivations and rewards, on the one hand, and recognizing and eschewing life-threatening emotions and sensations, on the other.

The pleasure–pain bipolarity not only places sensations, motivations, feelings, emotions, moods, and affects on two contrasting dimensions but recognizes that each possesses separate and independent quantitative gradations. That is, events which are attractive, gratifying, rewarding, or positively reinforcing may be experienced as weak or strong, as can those that are aversive, distressful, sad, or negatively reinforcing.

Numerous theories of motivation/emotion over the years have proposed models that refer essentially to affective expressions of this evolutionary bipolarity. Most closely akin in the recent literature are the factor analytic dimensions of positive and negative emotionality described by Tellegen (1985) and his students (Clark & Watson, 1988; Watson & Clark, 1984; Watson & Tellegen, 1985). As noted previously, and as conceived in the pleasure–pain bipolarity, both positive and negative emotions may display the full quantitative range independent of the other; that is, low levels of pleasure are not the same as pain, and vice versa; similarly, high and low levels of positive emotionality may coexist with varying levels of negative emotionality. Several theorists associate levels of intensity with the dimension of arousal/activation. In our judgment, however, the active–passive polarity, to be described more fully shortly, relates to a separate evolution-based polarity.

Although there are many philosophical and metapsychological issues associated with the nature of pain and pleasure as constructs, it is neither our intent nor our task to inquire into them in detail here. That they recur as a polar dimension time and again in diverse psychological domains (for example, learned behaviors, unconscious processes, emotion and motivation, as well as their biological substrates) has been elaborated in another publication (Millon, 1990).

Adaptive Modes: The Active–Passive Polarity

The second basic polar distinction relates to what we have termed the modes of adaptation; it is also framed as a two-part polarity. One may best be characterized as the mode of ecological accommodation, signifying inclinations to passively "fit in," to locate and remain securely anchored in a niche, subject to the vagaries and unpredictabilities of the environment, all acceded to with one crucial proviso: that the elements comprising the surroundings will furnish both the nourishment and the protection needed to sustain existence. Though based on a somewhat simplistic bifurcation among adaptive strategies, this *passive* accommodating mode is one of the two fundamental methods that living organisms have evolved as a means of survival. It represents the core process employed in the evolution of what has come to be designated as the plant kingdom, a stationary, rooted, yet essentially pliant and dependent survival mode. By contrast, the other of the two major modes of adaptation is seen in the lifestyle of the animal kingdom. Here we observe a primary inclination toward ecological modification, an *active* tendency to change or rearrange the elements comprising the larger milieu, to intrude upon otherwise quiescent settings, a versatility in shifting from one niche to another as unpredictability arises, a mobile and interventional mode that actively stirs, maneuvers, yields, and, at the human level, substantially transforms the environment to meet its own survival aims.

Both modes—passive and active—have proven impressively capable of nourishing and preserving life. Whether the polarity sketched is phrased in terms of accommodating versus modifying, passivity versus activity, or plant versus animal, it represents, at the most basic level, the two fundamental modes that organisms have evolved to sustain their existence. This second, modifying–accommodating polarity differs from the first, enhancing–preserving (that concerned with what may be called existential "becoming"), in that it characterizes modes of "being," that is, how what has become endures.

Broadening the active–passive polarity model to encompass human experience, we find that the vast range of behaviors engaged in by humans may fundamentally be grouped in terms of whether initiative is taken in altering and shaping life's events or whether behaviors are reactive to and accommodate those events.

This distinction may be traced back to early notions of Thomas Hobbes who spoke of behavior as a response to the "vital spirits," conceiving humans as passive and helpless animals reacting either to the "appetites" (pursuit of pleasure) or the "aversions" (avoidance of pain). Whether from without (environmental pressures) or from within (biological drives or unconscious determinants), more-or-less traditional and mechanistic theories such as Hobbes's assert that humans are subjected to and have minimal control over forces that compel them to behave as they do. By contrast, organismic theories, reflecting the views of more contemporary thinkers and cultures, dismiss the attitude that humans are essentially passive robots who merely react to external and largely unknown promptings. Rather, they propose that humans actively determine the course of their own behaviors, that they confront life's opportunities and dilemmas, choose what will be done, and even initiate actions that alter the very character of their environments. Both views in our judgment are correct in part; humans are at times actors and at other times reactors. Moreover, it is our contention that significant individual differences of personologic significance are to be found along this activity–passivity dimension. No individual is one or the other but both in varying proportions, a difference relevant to the assessment of personality styles.

Often reflective and deliberate, those who are passively oriented manifest few overt strategies to gain their ends. They display a seeming inertness, a phlegmatic quality, a tendency toward acquiescence, a restrained attitude in which they initiate little to modify events, waiting for the circumstances of their environment to take their course before making accommodations. Some may be temperamentally ill-equipped to rouse or assert themselves; perhaps past experience has deprived them of opportunities to acquire a range of competencies or confidence in their ability to master the events of their environment; equally possible is a naive confidence that things will come their way with little or no effort on their part. From a variety of diverse sources, then, those at the passive end of the polarity appear merely to sustain their existence, engaging in few direct instrumental activities to intercede in life events or to generate change. They seem suspended, quiescent, placid, immobile, restrained, listless, waiting for things to happen and reacting to them only after they occur.

Descriptively, those who are at the active end of the polarity are best characterized by their alertness, vigilance, liveliness, vigor, forcefulness, stimulus-seeking energy, and drive. Some plan strategies and scan alternatives to circumvent obstacles or avoid the distress of punishment, rejection, and anxiety. Others are impulsive, precipitate, excitable, rash, and hasty, seeking to elicit pleasures and rewards. Although specific goals vary and change from time to time, actively aroused individuals seek to alter their lives, to intrude on passing events by energetically and busily modifying the circumstances of their environment.

Much can be said for the survival value of fitting a specific niche well, but no less important are flexibilities for adapting to diverse and unpredictable environments. Here again a distinction, though not a hard and fast one, may be drawn between the accommodating (plant) and the modifying (animal) mode of adaptation, the former more rigidly fixed and constrained by ecological conditions, the latter more broad-ranging and more facile in its scope of maneuverability. As we proceed in evolved complexity to the human species, we cannot help but recognize the almost endless variety of adaptive possibilities that may (and do) arise as secondary derivatives of a large brain possessing an open network of potential interconnections that permit the functions of self-reflection, reasoning, and abstraction. But this takes us beyond this segment of the chapter. The reader may wish to look elsewhere (Millon, 1990) for a fuller discussion of active–passive parallels in wider domains of psychological thought (e.g., the "ego apparatuses" formulated by Hartmann, 1939, or the distinction between classical and operant conditioning in the writings of Skinner, 1938, 1953).

"Normal" or optimal functioning, at least among humans, appears to call for a flexible balance that interweaves both polar extremes. In the first polarity, behaviors encouraging both life enhancement (seeking pleasure) and life preservation (pain avoidance) are likely to be more successful in achieving survival than actions limited to one or the other alone. Similarly, regarding adaptation, modes of functioning that exhibit both ecological accommodation *and* ecological modification are likely to be more successful than either by itself. Here again we put forth two polarities to represent the degrees to which persons balance these two adaptive modes.

Replicatory Strategies: The Self–Other Polarity

Although less profound than the first polarity, which represents the enhancement of order (existence–life–pleasure) and the prevention of disorder (nonexistence–death–pain), or the second polarity, which differentiates the adaptive modes, accommodation (plant-passive) versus those of modification (animal-active), the third polarity, based on distinctions in reproductive strategies (gene replication), is no less fundamental; it contrasts the maximization of reproductive propagation (male–self) from that of the maximization of reproductive nurturance (female–other).

Evolutionary biologists (Cole, 1954; Trivers, 1974; Wilson, 1975) have recorded marked differences among species in both the cycle and pattern of their reproductive behaviors. Of special interest is the ex-treme diversity among and within species in the number of offspring spawned and the consequent nurturing and protective investment the parents make in the survival of their progeny. Designated the *r*-strategy and *K*-strategy in population biology, the former represents a pattern of propagating a vast number of offspring but exhibiting minimal at-tention to their survival; the latter is typified by the production of few progeny followed by considerable effort to assure their survival. Ex-emplifying the *r*-strategy are oysters, which generate some 500 mil-lion eggs annually; the *K*-strategy is found among the great apes, which produce a single offspring every 5 to 6 years.

Of particular note here is Jung's foresight in anticipating this differ-ence in replication style and its fundamental adaptive significance. Quoting Jung:

> There are in nature two fundamentally different modes of adaptation which ensure the continued existence of the living organism. The one consists in a high rate of fertility, with low powers of defense and short duration of life for the single individual; the other consists in equipping the individu-al with numerous means of self-preservation plus a low fertility rate. This biological difference, it seems to me, is not merely analogous to, but the actual foundation of, our two psychological modes of adaptation. Blake's intuition did not err when he described the two classes of men as "prolif-ic" and "devouring." Just as, biologically, the two modes of adaptation work equally well and are successful in their own way, so too with the typical attitudes. The one achieves its end by a multiplicity of relation-ships, the other by monopoly. (1921, pp. 331–332)

Not only do species differ in where they fall on the *r*- to *K*-strategy continuum, but *within* most animal species an important distinction may be drawn between male and female genders. It is this latter differentiation that undergirds what has been termed the self- versus other-oriented polarity, implications of which are briefly elaborated.

Female humans typically produce about 400 eggs in a lifetime, of which no more than 20 to 25 can mature into viable infants. The ener-gy investment expended in gestation, nurturing, and caring for each child, both before and during the years following birth, is extraordi-nary. Not only is the female required to devote much of her energies to bring the fetus to full term, but during this period, she cannot be fertilized again; in contrast, the male is free to mate with numerous females. And should her child fail to survive, the waste in physical and emotional exertion is not only enormous; it amounts to a substan-tial portion of the mother's lifetime reproductive potential. There ap-pears to be good reason, therefore, to encourage a protective and caring inclination on the part of the female, as evident in a sensitivity to cues of distress and a willingness to persist in attending to the needs and nurturing of her offspring.

Although the male discharges tens of millions of sperm on mating, this is but a small investment, given the ease and frequency with which he can repeat the act. On fertilization, his physical and emotional commitment can end with minimal consequences. Although the protective and food-gathering efforts of the male may be lost by an early abandonment of a mother and an offspring or two, much more may be gained by investing energies in pursuits that achieve the wide reproductive spread of his genes. Relative to the female of the species, whose best strategy appears to be the care and comfort of child and kin, that is, the K-strategy, the male is likely to be reproductively more prolific by maximizing self-propagation that is, adopting the r-strategy. To focus primarily on self-replication may diminish the survival probabilities of a few of a male's progeny, but this occasional reproductive loss may be well compensated for by mating with multiple females and thereby producing multiple offspring.

In sum, males tend to be self-oriented as a result of the fact that competition for reproductive resources maximizes the replicatory advantages of their genes. Conversely, females tend to be other-oriented as a result of the fact that their competence in nurturing and protecting their limited progeny maximizes the replicatory advantages of their genes. The consequences of the male's r-strategy are a broad range of what may be seen as self-advancing as opposed to other-promoting behaviors, such as acting in an egotistic, insensitive, inconsiderate, uncaring, and noncommunicative manner. Male relationships thereby exhibit a "vertical" or hierarchical quality, one characterized by dominance of self over others. In contrast, females are more disposed to be other-promoting, affiliative, intimate, empathic, protective, and solicitous (Gilligan, 1982; Rushton, 1985; Wilson, 1978). Female relationships demonstrate a horizontal or even reverse hierarchical quality, one founded on equalitarian transactions, or even priority given to others.

What we have sought in the preceding paragraphs is a theoretical rationale based on concepts derived from evolutionary thinking as a way to account for a frequently studied dimension that contrasts power-oriented, arrogant, impersonal, tough-minded, competitive, ambitious, dominating, and autonomous traits at the one extreme, and love-oriented, altruistic, nurturant, intimate, harmony-seeking, warm, trusting, and cooperative behaviors at the other. These two broad trait realms reflect, we believe, a fundamental bipolarity that exists in nature, one that expresses itself in two contrasting aims of human motivation/emotion. One derives from and is most closely allied with the reproductive strategies available to the male gender, those of self-advancement or what has been termed "individuation," and the second stemming from and connected most centrally to instrumental options of reproduction that prove optimal for those of the female gender, those being strategies of other-promotion, or what we would call "nurturance."

Abstract Processes: The Thinking–Feeling Polarity

The capacity to sort and to recompose, to coordinate and to arrange the symbolic representations of experience into new configurations is, in certain ways, analogous to the random processes of recombinant replication, though they are more focused and intentional: To extend this rhetorical liberty, genetic replication represents the recombinant mechanism underlying the adaptive progression of phylogeny, whereas abstraction represents the recombinant mechanism underlying the cognitive progression of ontogeny. The uses of replication are limited, constrained by the finite potentials inherent in parental genes. In contrast, experiences, internalized and recombined, through cognitive processes are infinite. Over one lifetime, innumerable events of a random, logical, or irrational character transpire, construed and reformulated time and again, some of which proving more, and others less adaptive than their originating circumstances may have called forth. Whereas the actions of most subhuman species derive from successfully evolved genetic programs, activating behaviors of a relatively fixed nature suitable for a modest range of environmental settings, the capabilities of both implicit and intentional abstraction give rise to adaptive competencies that are suited to radically divergent ecological circumstances, circumstances which themselves may be the result of far-reaching acts of symbolic and technological creativity.

DEVELOPMENTAL STAGES

A generative theoretical basis for a taxonomy of personality should also be generative with respect to personality development. In the pages that follow, we briefly link the evolutionary model presented to what we consider to be the origins of personality.

Early Development

The culling of that which we call personality from a universe of possibilities takes place through the addition of successive constraints on system functioning. Each child displays a wide variety of behaviors in the first years of life. Although exhibiting a measure of consistency consonant with his/her constitutional disposition, the way in which the child responds to and copes with the environment tends to be largely spontaneous, changeable, and unpredictable. These seemingly random and capricious behaviors serve an important exploratory function. The child is "trying out" a variety of behavioral alternatives for dealing with his/her environment. Over time the child begins to discern which of these actions enable him/her to achieve his/her desires and avoid discomforts. Endowed with certain capacities, energies, and temperaments, and through experience with parents, sibs, and peers, the child learns to discriminate which activities are both permissible and rewarding, and which are not.

Tracing this sequence over time, it can be seen that a shaping process has taken place in which the child's initial range of diverse behaviors gradually becomes narrowed, selective, and, finally, crystallized into preferred ways of relating to others and coping with this world. These learned behaviors not only persist but are accentuated as a result of being repetitively reinforced by a limited social environment. Given continuity in constitutional equipment and a narrow band of experiences for learning behavioral alternatives, the child acquires a pattern of traits that are deeply etched and difficult to modify. These characteristics comprise his/her personality—that is, ingrained and habitual ways of psychological functioning that emerge from the individual's entire developmental history, and which, over time, come to characterize the child's "style."

Pathology is the result of a totality of influences deriving from multiple levels of organization. The interaction between biological and psychological factors is not unidirectional such that biological determinants always precede and influence the course of learning; the order of effects may be reversed, especially in early development. Biological maturation is dependent on favorable environmental experience, and the development of the biological substrate itself can be disrupted, even totally arrested, by depriving the maturing organism of stimulation at sensitive periods of neurological growth. Nevertheless, there is an intrinsic continuity throughout life. The authors contend that childhood events are more significant to personality formation than later events and that later behaviors are related in a determinant way to early experience. Despite an occasional disjunctiveness in development, there is an orderly and sequential continuity, fostered by mechanisms of self-perpetuation and social reinforcement, that links the past to the present. The characteristics of early development that create the foundations of lifelong continuity are discussed next.

Maturational Plasticity

Deeply embedded behavior patterns may arise as a consequence of psychological experiences that affect developing biological structures so profoundly as to transform them into something substantially different from what they might otherwise have been. Circumstances that exert so profound an effect are usually those experienced during infancy and early childhood, a view that can be traced to the seminal writings of Freud at the turn of the century. The observations of ethologists on the consequences of early stimulation upon adult animal behaviors add substantial evidence for this position (Rakic, 1985, 1988). Experimental work on early developmental periods also has shown that environmental stimulation is crucial to the maturation of psychological functions. In essence, psychological capacities fail to develop fully if their biological substrates are subjected to impoverished stimulation; conversely, these capacities may develop to an excessive degree as a consequence of enriched stimulation (Lipton & Kater, 1989).

Maturation refers to the intricate sequence of ontogenetic development in which initially inchoate bodily structures progressively unfold into specific functional units. Early stages of differentiation precede and overlap with more advanced states such that simpler and more diffuse structures interweave and connect into a complex and integrated network of functions displayed ultimately in the adult organism. It was once believed that the course of maturation from diffusion to differentiation to integration arose exclusively from inexorable forces within the genes. Maturation was thought to evolve according to a preset timetable that unfolded independently of environmental conditions. This view is no longer tenable. Maturation follows an orderly progression, but the developmental sequence and level of ultimate biological function are substantially dependent on environmental stimuli and nutritional supplies. Thus, maturation does not progress in a fixed course leading to a predetermined level but is subject to numerous variations that reflect the character of environmental experience.

The answer to why early experiences are more central to development than later experiences derives in part from the fact that peak periods of structural maturation occur from prenatal stages through the first years of postnatal life. An example may illustrate this point well. In the nervous system, prenatal deficiencies in nutrition will retard the differentiation of gross tissue into separable neural cells; early postnatal deficiencies will deter the proliferation of neural collaterals and their integration. However, deficiencies arising later in life will have but little effect on the development of these neural structures.

Organismic Nutrition

Nutrition should be viewed more broadly than is commonly done in order to understand biological maturation. Nutrition includes not only obvious components, such as food, but additionally what Rapaport has termed "stimulus nutriment" (1958). This concept suggests that the impingement of environmental and psychological stimuli upon the maturing organism has a direct bearing on the chemical composition, ultimate size, and patterns of neural branching within the brain (Lipton & Kater, 1989; Purves & Lichtman, 1985).

The belief that the maturing organism requires periodic psychological nutriments for proper development has led some to suggest that the organism actively seeks an optimum level of stimulation. Thus, just as the infant cries out in search of food when deprived or wails in response to pain, so too may it engage in behaviors that provide it with psychosensory stimulation requisite to maturation (Butler & Rice, 1963; Murphy, 1947). Although infants are restricted largely to stimulation supplied by others, they often engage in what appear to be random exercises that, in effect, furnish them with feedback experiences. In the first months of life, infants can be seen to track auditory and visual stimuli; as they mature further, they grasp incidental objects and then mouth and fondle them. Furthermore, the young of all species display more exploratory and frolicsome behavior than adults. These seemingly "functionless" play activities are not functionless at all; they may be essential to growth, a means of self-stimulation indispensable to the maturation and maintenance of biological capacities (Ainsworth, Behar, Waters, & Wall, 1978; Bowlby, 1969; Bretherton, 1985; Volkmar & Provence, 1990). In sum, unless certain chemicals and structures are activated by environmental stimulation, the biological substrate for a variety of psychological functions may be impaired irrevocably. In turn, deficiencies or abnormalities in functions that normally mature in early life set the stage for progressive constraints on later functioning.

What evidence is there that serious consequences may result from an inadequate supply of early psychological and psychosensory stimulation?

Numerous investigators (e.g., Beach & Jaynes, 1954; Killackey, 1990; Melzack, 1965; Rakic, 1985, 1988; Scott, 1968; Thompson & Schaefer, 1961) have shown that impoverished early environment results in permanent adaptational difficulties. For example, primates reared in isolation tend to be deficient in traits such as emotionality, activity level, social behavior, curiosity, and learning ability. As adult organisms, they possess a reduced capacity to cope with their environments, to discriminate essentials, to devise strategies and manage stress. Comparable results are found among humans. Children reared under unusually severe restrictions, such as in orphanages, evidence deficits in social awareness and reactivity, are impulsive and susceptible to sensorimotor dysfunctions, and display a generally low resistance to stress and disease. These early difficulties have double-barreled effects. Not only is the child hampered by specific deficiencies, but each of them yields to progressive and long-range consequences in that each retards the development of more complex capacities (Ainsworth et al., 1978; Bowlby, 1960; Bretherton, 1985; Volkmar & Provence, 1990).

Conversely, intense levels of early stimulation also appear to have effects, at least in animals. Several investigators have demonstrated that enriched environments in early life resulted in measurable changes in brain chemistry and brain weight. Others have found that early stimulation accelerated the maturation of the pituitary–adrenal system, whereas equivalent later stimulation was ineffective. On the behavioral level, enriched environments in animals enhance problem-solving abilities and the capacity to withstand stress.

More interesting, however, is the possibility that some kinds of overstimulation may produce detrimental effects. Accordingly, excess stimulation would result in overdevelopments in biological substrates that are disruptive to effective psychological functioning. Just as excess food leads to obesity and physical ill health, so too may the psychostimulation of certain neural substrates, such as those subserving emotional reactivity, dispose the organism to overreact to social situations. Thus, when schemas that subserve problematic personality traits become prepotent, they may disrupt what would otherwise be a more balanced pattern of functioning.

Evolutionary Phases

Does the timing of the specific environmental events have any bearing on their effect? The concept of sensitive periods of development states that there are limited time periods during which particular stimuli are necessary for the full maturation of an organism, after which they will have minimal or no effects. Without the requisite stimulation, the organism will suffer various maldevelopments that are irremediable and cannot be compensated for at a later date.

Embryological research suggests that the effects of environmental stimuli on morphological structure are most pronounced when tissue growth is rapid (Killackey, 1990; Rakic, 1985, 1988). The mechanisms that account for the special interaction between stimulation and periods of rapid neural growth are as yet unclear. Psychological stimulation itself promotes a proliferation of neural collaterals, an effect most pronounced when growth potential is greatest. Moreover, early psychological stimulation creates selective growth so that certain collaterals establish particular interneuronal connections to the exclusion of others. In behavioral terms: Once these connections are biologically embedded, the first sets of stimuli that traverse them, especially if pervasive, appear to preempt the circuit, thereby decreasing the chance that subsequent stimuli will co-opt the circuit for other effects. In cognitive terms: once schemas are in place for perceiving objective events in a particular way, these schemas co-opt future interpretations of similar events.

Numerous theorists have proposed, either by intention or inadvertently, developmental schemas based on a concept of sensitive periods. Among these are Heinz Werner (1940), Jean Piaget (1952), and, of course, both Freud (1908) and Erikson (1950). None, however, have presented their notions in terms of evolutionary–neuropsychological growth stages, although G. Stanley Hall (1916) sought to formulate a developmental theory of "recapitulation" anchored to Darwin's model. Although such compound terminology may seem formidible, it is intended to communicate first the fact that personologic developmental constraints derive from the history of human adaptation and second that the ultimate instantiation of these constraints lies in evolutionary principles, whether they be expressed in personality traits, cognitive schemas, or sociocultural customs (Wilson, 1978).

Broadly speaking, there are four "stages" that an individual human organism must pass through and a parallel set of four "tasks" that must be fulfilled to perform adequately in life. The first three pairs of these stages and tasks, and in part the fourth as well, are shared by lower species and may be thought of as recapitulating four phases of *evolution* (Millon, 1990). Each stage and task corresponds to one of the four evolutionary phases: existence, adaptation, replication, and abstraction. Polarities, that is, contrasting functional directions, representing the first three of these phases (pleasure–pain, passive–active, other–self) have been used to construct a theoretically anchored classification of personality styles and disorders, such as described in this text. Such bipolar or dimensional schemes are almost universally present throughout the literatures of mankind, as well as in psychology at large (Millon, 1990). As noted earlier, they may be traced to ancient religions, notably in the Chinese *I Ching* texts and the Hebrew *Kabala*.

In the life of the individual organism, each evolutionary stage is recapitulated and expressed ontogenetically; that is, each individual organism moves through developmental stages that have functional goals related to their respective phase of evolution. Within each stage, every individual acquires personologic dispositions representing a balance ore predilection toward one of the two polarity inclinations; which inclination emerges as dominant over time results from the inextricable and reciprocal interplay of intraorganismic and extraorganismic factors Thus, during early infancy, the primary organismic task is to "continue to exist." Here, evolution has supplied mechanisms that orient the infant toward life-enhancing environments (pleasure) and away from life-threatening ones (pain).

The expression of traits or dispositions acquired in early stages of development may have their expression transformed as later faculties or dispositions develop (Millon, 1969). Temperament is perhaps a classic example. An individual with an active temperament may develop, contingent on contextual factors, into an avoidant or an antisocial personality. The transformation of earlier temperamental characteristics takes the form of what we will call "personologic bifurcations." Thus, if the individual is inclined toward a passive orientation and later learns to be self-directed, a narcissistic style ensues. But if the individual posesses an active orientation and later learns to be self-directed, an antisocial style ensues. Thus, early developing dispositions may undergo "vicissitudes," whereby their meaning in the context of the whole organism is subsequently reformed into more complex personality trait configurations.

As previously noted, the authors believe that the development of personality disorders should be organized in terms of fundamental personologic axes embedded in evolutionary theory. These are discussed below.

Phase 1: Existence

The first phase, existence, concerns the survival of integrative phenomena, whether a nuclear particle, virus, or human being, against the forces of entropic decompensation. Evolutionary mechanisms associated with this stage relate to the processes of *life enhancement* and *life preservation*. The former are concerned with orienting individuals toward improving the quality of life; the later orient indiviudals away from actions or environments that decrease the quality of life, or even jeopardize existence itself. These two superordinate processes have been called "existential aims." At the highest level of abstraction such mechanisms form phenomenologically or metaphorically, a pleasure–pain polarity. Most humans exhibit both processes, those oriented toward enhancing pleasure and avoiding pain. Some individuals, however, appear to be conflicted in regard to existential aims (e.g., the sadistic), whereas others possess deficits in such aims (e.g., the schizoid). In terms of evolutionary–neuropsychological stages (Millon, 1969, 1981, 1990), orientations on the pleasure–pain polarity are set during a "sensory–attachment" developmental stage, the purpose of which is to further mature and selectively refine and focus the largely innate ability to discriminate between pain and pleasure signals.

Phase 2: Adaptation

Everything that exists, exists in an environment. To come into existence as a surviving particle or living creature is but an initial phase. Once an integrated structure exists, it must maintain its existence through exchanges of energy and information with its environment. This second evolutionary phase relates to what we have termed the modes of adaptation; it also is framed as a two-part polarity: a passive orientation, that is, to be "ecologically accommodating" in one's environmental niche versus an active orientation, that is, to be "ecologically modifying" and to intervene in or to alter one's surrounds. These "modes of adaptation" differ from the first phase of evolution in that they relate to how that which has come to exist, endures. In terms of neuropsychological development, this polarity is ontogenetically expressed as the "sensorimotor–autonomy stage," during which the child typically progresses from an earlier, relatively passive style of accommodation to a relatively active style of modifying his or her physical and social environment.

The accommodating–modifying polarity necessarily derives from an expansion of the systems concept. Whereas in the existence phase the system is seen as being mainly intraorganismic in character, the adaptation phase expands the systems concept to its logical progression, from person to person-in-context. Some individuals, those of an active orientation, operate as genuine agencies, tending to modify their environments according to their desires. For these individuals, an active-organism model is appropriate. Other persons, however, seek to accommodate to whatever is offered, or, rather than work to change what exists, seek out new, more hospitable venues when current ones become problematic. For these individuals, a passive-organism model is appropriate.

Phase 3: Replication

Although organisms may be well-adapted to their environments, the existence of any life form is time-limited. To circumvent this limitation, organisms exhibit patterns of the third polarity, "replicatory strategies," by which they leave progeny. These strategies relate to what biologists have referred to as an *r*- or *self*-propagating strategy, at one polar extreme, and a *K*- or *other*-nurturing strategy at the second extreme. Psychologically, the former is disposed toward individually oriented actions that are perceived by others as egotistic, insensitive, inconsiderate, and uncaring; whereas the latter is disposed toward nurturant-oriented actions that are seen as affiliative, intimate, protective, and solicitous (Gilligan, 1982; Rushton, 1985; Wilson, 1978). Like pleasure–pain, the self–other polarity is not unidimensional. Whereas most humans exhibit a reasonable balance between the two polar extremes, some personality disorders are quite conflicted on this polarity, as are the compulsive and negativistic personalities. In terms of neuropsychological growth stages, an individual's orientation toward self and others evolves largely during the "pubertal–gender identity" stage.

As with the passive–active polarity, the self–other bipolarity necessarily derives from an expansion of the systems concept. Whereas with the adaptation phase the system was seen as existing within an environment, here the system is seen as evolving over time. As before, the goal of the organism is its survival of continuance. When expressed across time, however, survival means reproducing, and strategies for doing so.

Phase 4: Abstraction

The reflective capacity to transcend the immediate and concrete, to interrelate and synthesize diversity, to represent events and processes symbolically, to weigh, reason, and anticipate, each signifies a quantum leap in evolution's potential for change and adaptation (Millon, 1990). Once one is emancipated from the real and present, unanticipated possibilities and novel constructions may routinely be created by various styles of abstract processing. It is these capacities that are represented in the neuropsychological stage of "intracortical-integration."

The abstract mind may mirror outer realities, but it reconstructs them in the process, reflectively transforming them into subjective modes of phenomenological reality, rendering external events subject to individualistic designs. Every act of apprehension is transformed by processes of abstract symbolism. Not only are internal and external images emancipated from direct sensory and imaginal realties, allowing them to become entities, but contemporaneous time also loses its immediacy and impact, becoming as much a construction as a substance. Cognitive abstractions bring the past effectively into the present, and their power of anticipation brings the future into the present as well. With past and future embedded in the here and now, humans can encompass, at once not only the totality of our cosmos, but its origins and nature, its evolution, and how these have come to pass. Most impressive of all are the many visions humans have of life's indeterminate future, where no reality as yet exists.

Comment

Because any classification system is a simplification of nature, the most important aspect of a taxonomy is where the boundaries are drawn. We believe our evolutionary system conception, linked to fundamental stages of development, provides the most secure foundation for dissecting the personologic sphere. Accordingly, and in contrast to earlier formulations (e.g., Freud, Piaget, Erikson), it seems more reasonable to us to construct a developmental model based on evolutionary phases and their related neuropsychological stages and tasks rather than on ones oriented to psychosexual or cognitive processes and periods. As noted, part-function models such as the latter two fail to encompass the entire person, are unconnected to the deeper laws of evolutionary progression, and, hence, cannot form either a comprehensive or a firm grounding for a modern developmental theory.

A qualification should be noted before describing the developmental stages derived from the model. First, individuals differ with regard to the degree to which they are constrained at each level of organization. Biologically speaking, children of the same chronological age, for example, often are not comparable in the level and character of their biological capacities. Not only does each infant start life with distinctive neurological, physiochemical, and sensory equipment; each also progresses at his/her own maturational rate toward some ultimate but unknown level of potential. The same is true for constraints of a sociocultural nature.

Second, although we differentiate four seemingly distinct stages of development in the following section, it is important to state at the outset that all four stages and their related primary processes begin in utero and continue throughout life, that is, they proceed simultaneously and overlap throughout the developmental process. For example, the elements that give shape to ''gender identity'' are under way during the sensory–attachment phase, although at a modest level, as the elements that give rise to attachment behaviors continue and extend well into puberty. Stages are differentiated only to bring attention to periods of development when certain processes and tasks are prominent and central. The concept of sensitive periods implies that developmental stages are not exclusionary; rather, they merely demarcate a period in life when certain development potentialities are salient in their maturation and in their receptivity to relevant life experiences.

The characteristics and consequences of the four "overlapping" stages of neuropsychological development are discussed next, as are their roots in the evolutionary phase theory.

Neuropsychological Stages

The four stages of development to be described below parallel the four evolutionary phases discussed previously. Moreover, each evolutionary phase is related to a different stage of ontogenetic development (Millon, 1969). For example, life enhancement–life preservation corresponds to the sensory–attachment stage of development in that the latter represents a period when the young child learns to discriminate between those experiences that are enhancing and those that are threatening.

Stage 1. Sensory—Attachment: The Life Enhancement (Pleasure)–Life Preservation (Pain) Polarity

The first year of life is dominated by sensory processes, functions basic to subsequent development in that they enable the infant to construct some order out of the initial diffusion experienced in the stimulus world, especially that based on distinguishing pleasurable from painful "objects." This period has also been termed that of attachment because infants cannot survive on their own (Fox, Kimmerly, & Schafer, 1991) but must "fasten" themselves to others who will protect, nurture, and stimulate them, that is, provide them with experiences of pleasure rather than those of pain.

Such themes are readily understood through an evolutionary theory of personality development. Whereas evolution has endowed adult humans with the cognitive ability to project future threats and difficulties as well as potential rewards, human infants are comparably impoverished, being as yet without the benefit of the abstract capacities. Evolution has therefore "provided" mechanisms or substrates that orient the child toward those activities or venues that are life-enhancing (pleasure) and away from those that are potentially life-threatening (pain). Existence during this highly vulnerable stage is quite literally a to-be or not-to-be matter.

As noted previously, life-enhancing actions or sensations can be subsumed under the rubric of "pleasure," whereas life-threatening actions or sensations can be subsumed under the metaphorical term "pain." Such a "pleasure–pain polarity" simply recognizes that although the behavioral repertoire of the young child, the operational means, so to speak, may be manifestly diverse, for examples, smiles, coos, stranger anxiety, and primitive reflexes, the end, or "existential aim," is universal and has as its bare minimum the maintenence of life itself. In the normal organism, both pleasure and pain are coordinated toward ontogenetic continuity. However, whether as a result of genetic factors, early experiences, or their interaction, some pathological patterns display aberrations in their orientation toward pleasure or pain. Deficits in the strength of both painful and pleasurable drives, for example, either constitutionally given or experientally derived, are involved in the schizoid pattern, whereas a reversed or conflicted pleasure–pain orientation inclines toward the masochistic or sadistic personality disorders.

Development of Sensory Capacities. The early neonatal period is characterized by undifferentiation. The organism behaves in a diffuse and unintegrated way, and perceptions are unfocused and gross. Accordingly, the orientation of the infant is toward sensations that are proportionately broad and undifferentiated, although increasingly the distinction between pleasure and pain becomes central to subsequent refinements. Freud recognized that the mouth region is a richly endowed receptor system through which neonates establish their first significant relationship to the world, but it is clear that this oral unit is merely the focal point of a more diverse system of sensory capacities for making significant distinctions. Through oral and other tactile contacts, the infant establishes a sense, or "feel," of the environment that evoke pleasurable or painful responses.

According to neuropsychological and evolutionary theories, it would be expected that the amount and quality of tactile stimulation to which the neonate is exposed will contribute significantly to the infant's development as precocities or retardations, depending on the level of stimulation. Moreover, it is likely that the quality and patterning of this stimulation may lead the infant to experience inchoate feelings tentatively drawn against the background of pleasure–pain. These form the phenomenological prototypes of such later-evolving emotions such as fear, joy, sadness, and anger.

Development of Attachment Behaviors. The neonate cannot differentiate between objects and persons; both are experienced simply as stimuli. How does this initial indiscriminateness become progressively refined into specific attachments? For all essential purposes, the infant is helpless and dependent on others to avoid pain and supply its pleasurable needs. Separated from the womb, the neonate has lost its physical attachment to the mother's body and the protection and nurturance that attachment provided; it must turn toward other regions or sources of attachment if it is to survive and obtain nourishment and stimulation for further development (Bowlby, 1969; Gewirtz, 1963; Hinde, 1982; Lamb, Thompson, Gardner, & Estes, 1985; Ribble, 1943; Spitz, 1965). Attachment behaviors may be viewed, albeit figuratively, as an attempt to reestablish the unity lost at birth that enhanced and protected life. In fact, recent investigations show that although initial attachments are transformed across stages of development, they remain important across the lifespan (e.g., Sroufe & Fleeson, 1986). Whether the infant's world is conceptualized as a buzz or a blank slate, it must begin to differentiate venues or objects that further its existential aims, supplying nourishment, preservation, and stimulation from those that diminish, frustrate, or threaten them. These initial relationships, or, "internal representational models" (e.g., Crittenden, 1990), apparently "prepared" by evolution, become the context through which other relationships develop.

Consequences of Impoverishment. A wealth of clinical evidence is available showing that humans deprived of adequate maternal care in infancy display a variety of pathological behaviors. We cannot, of course, design studies to disentangle precisely which of the complex of variables that compromise maternal care account for these irreparable consequences; the lives of babies cannot be manipulated to meet our scientific needs.

However, extensive reviews of the consequences in animals of early stimulus impoverishment show that sensory neural fibers atrophy and cannot be regenerated by subsequent stimulation (Beach & Jaynes, 1954; Riesen, 1961). Inadequate stimulation in any major receptor function usually results in decrements in the capacity to utilize these sensory processes in later life. The profound effects of social isolation have been studied thoroughly and show that deprived monkeys are incapable at maturity of relating to peers, of participating effectively in sexual activity, and of assuming adequate roles as mothers. Abstracting to those substrates and pathways that undergird pleasure–pain, we might expect that such underelaboration, if pervasive, might at the least render emotional discriminations of a more refined or narrow character impossible, or worse, result in the wholesale impoverishment of all affective reactions, as seen in the schizoid pattern.

The potential effects of moderate levels of early sensory impoverishment have been little researched. The reader should note, however, that the degree of sensory impoverishment varies along a gradient or continuum; it is not an all-or-none effect. Children who receive less than an optimum degree of sensory stimulation will be likely to grow up less "sensory-oriented" and less "socially attached" than those who have experienced more (Bowlby, 1952, 1969, 1973; Goldfarb, 1955; Yarrow, 1961). Such variations are especially relevant to the study of personality disorders, which lie on a continuum with normal functioning.

Consequences of Enrichment. Data on the consequences of too much, or enriched, early sensory stimulation are few and far between; researchers have been concerned with the effects of deficit, rather than excess, stimulation.

A not unreasonable hypothesis, however, is that excess stimulation during the sensory–attachment stage would result in overdevelopments among associated neural structures (Rosenzweig et al., 1962); these may lead to oversensitivities that might, in turn, result in potentially maladaptive dominance of sensory functions or pleasurable substrates. Along this same line, Freud hypothesized that excess indulgence at the oral stage was conducive to fixations at that period. Eschewing both oral and fixation notions, the authors propose that excess sensory development in childhood will require a high level of stimulus maintenance in adulthood, as seen in persistent sensory-seeking or pleasure-seeking behaviors. These individuals might be characterized by their repetitive search for excitement and stimulation, their boredom with routine, and their involvement in incidental and momentarily gratifying adventures. Exactly what neural or chemical mechanisms undergird such a stimulus-seeking pattern is a matter for speculation. Whatever the mechanisms may be, it appears plausible both neurologically and clinically that overenriched early stimulation can result in pathological stimulus-seeking behavior, a pattern dominated by relatively capricious and cognitively unelaborated, pleasurable pursuits.

Excess stimulation, especially if anchored exclusively to a parental figure, might result in an overattachment to that parent. This is demonstrated most clearly in the symbiotic child, where an abnormal clinging to the mother and a persistent resistance to stimulation from other sources often result in overwhelming feelings of isolation and panic, as when the child is sent to nursery school or feels "replaced" by a newborn sibling.

Stage 2: Sensorimotor–Autonomy; The Ecologically Accommodating (Passive)–Ecologically Modifying (Active) Polarity

Not until the end of the first year has the infant matured sufficiently to engage in actions independent of parental support. Holding the drinking cup, the first few steps, or a word or two, all signify a growing capacity to act autonomously. As the child develops the functions that characterize this stage, he/she begins to comprehend the attitudes and feelings communicated by stimulative sources. No longer is rough parental handling merely excess stimulation, undistinguished from the playful tossing of an affectionate father; the child now discerns the difference between harshness and good-natured roughhousing.

In the sensiomotor–autonomy stage, the focus shifts from existence in itself to existence within an environment. From an evolutionary perspective, the child in this stage is learning a "mode of adaptation," an "active tendency" to modify its ecological niche versus a "passive tendency" to accomodate to whatever the environment has provided. The former reflects a disposition toward taking the initiative in shaping the course of life events; the latter a disposition to be quiescent, placid, unassertive, to react rather than act, to wait for things to happen, and to accept what is given. In the prior sensory–attachment stage, the infant was in its native mode, so to speak, largely passive, mostly dependent upon parental figures to meet its existential needs. Though the child may have engaged in behaviors, for example, crying, that seemed active by virtue of the arousal they evoked in others, these signals were intended to recruit others in the service of fundamental needs. Here it was parental figures, rather than the child him/herself, who either modified the ecological milieu or sought out a more hospitable one. With the development of autonomous capacities, the young child finds him/herself embedded in an environment, an environment either to be explored and later modified, or feared and accomodated to. The child must "decide" whether to "break out" of dependence on parental figures or to perpetuate this dependent pattern into later years. Whatever alternative is pursued, it is, of course, a matter of degree rather than a yes–no decision.

Undoubtedly important in the child's orientation toward the environment are its attachments. Those children who possess a "secure base" will explore their environments without becoming fearful that their attachment figure cannot be recovered (Ainsworth, 1967). On the other hand, those without such a base tend to remain close to their caretakers, assuming the more passive mode, one likely ultimately to restrict their range of coping resources through decreased or retarded sociocognitive competence (Millon, 1969).

Development of Sensorimotor Capacities. The unorganized movements of the neonate progressively give way to focused muscular activity. As the neural substrate for muscular control unfolds, the aimless motor behavior of the infant is supplanted by focused movements. These newly emergent functions coordinate with sensory capacities to enable the child to explore, manipulate, play, sit, crawl, babble, throw, walk, catch, talk, and otherwise intervene in his/her ecological milieu as desired. The maturing fusion between the substrates of sensory and motor functions is strengthened by the child's exploratory behavior. Manipulative play and the formation of babbling sounds are methods of self-stimulation that facilitate the growth of action-oriented interneuronal connections; the child is building a neural foundation for more complicated and refined skills such as running, handling utensils, controlling sphincter muscles, and articulating precise speech. Children's intrinsic tendency to "entertain" themselves represents a necessary step in establishing capacities that are more substantial than maturation alone would have furnished. Stimulative experiences, either self-provided or provided by relations with others, are requisites for the development of normal, activity-oriented sensorimotor skills. Unless retarded by environmental restrictions, biological handicaps, or insecure attachments, toddlers' growing sensorimotor capacities prepare them to take an active rather than passive role in coping with their environment.

Development of Autonomous Behaviors. Perhaps the most significant aspect of sensorimotor development is that it enables children to begin to take an active stance in doing things for themselves, to influence their environment, to free themselves from domination, and to outgrow the dependencies of their first years. Children become aware of their increasing competence and seek new ventures. Needless to say, conflicts and restrictions arise as they assert themselves (Erikson, 1959; White, 1960). These are seen clearly during toilet training, when youngsters often resist submitting to the demands of their parents. A delicate exchange of power and cunning often ensues. Opportunities arise for the child to actively extract promises or deny wishes; in response, parents may mete out punishments, submit meekly, or shift inconsistently. Important precedents for attitudes toward authority, power, and autonomy are generated during this period of parent–child interaction.

Consequences of Impoverishment. A lack of stimulation of sensorimotor capacities can lead to retardations in functions necessary to the development of autonomy and initiative, leading children to remain within a passive adaptational mode. This is seen most clearly in children of overprotective parents. Spoon-fed, excused from "chores," restrained from exploration, curtailed in friendships, and protected from "danger"—all illustrate controls that restrict growing children's opportunities to exercise their sensorimotor skills and develop the means for autonomous behavior. A self-perpetuating cycle often unfolds. These children may fear abandoning their overlearned dependency upon their parents, since they are ill-equipped to meet other children on the latter's terms. They may become timid and submissive when forced to venture out into the world, likely to avoid the give and take of competition with their peers, and they may seek out older children who will protect them and upon whom they can lean. Here the passive mode that began as dependence on parental figures is continued in the larger social context (Millon, 1969).

Consequences of Enrichment. The consequences of excessive enrichment during the sensorimotor–autonomy stage are found most often in children of excessively lax, permissive, or overindulgent parents. Given free rein with minimal restraint, stimulated to explore and manipulate things to their suiting without guidance or control, these children will often become irresponsibly undisciplined in their behaviors. Their active style compels these children to view the entire ecological milieu as a playground or medium to be modified according to their whims. Carried into the wider social context, these behaviors run up against the desires of other children and the restrictions of less permissive adults. Unless the youngsters are extremely adept, they will find that their actively self-centered and free-wheeling tactics fail miserably. For the few who succeed, however, a pattern of egocentrism, unbridled self-expression, and social arrogance may become dominant. The majority of these youngsters fail to gain acceptance by peers and never quite acquire the flexibility to shift between active and passive styles according to contextual demands. Such children are conspicuous in their lack of the normal give-and-take skills which form the basis of genuine social relationships.

Equally important as a form of enrichment is the intensity of attachments. Children acquire representations about the world, themselves, and others through their interactions with attachment figures (Bowlby, 1969, 1973). Constant concern about a child's welfare may cause that child to view him/herself as an object of frailty, resulting later in a passive style wherein the older child or adult constantly makes bids for others to take the initiative in transforming the environment.

Stage 3. Pubertal–Gender Identity: The Progeny Nurturance (Other)–Individual Propagation (Self) Polarity

Somewhere between the 11th and 15th years, a rather sweeping series of hormonal changes unsettle the psychic state that had been so carefully constructed in preceding years. These changes reflect the on-

set of puberty and the instantiation of sexual and gender-related characteristics that are preparatory for the emergence of the *r*- and *K*-
strategies—strong sexual impulses and adultlike features of anatomy,
voice, and bearing. Erratic moods, changing self-images, reinterpre-
tations of one's views of others, new urges, hopeful expectancies, and
a growing physical and social awkwardness all upset the relative
equanimity of an earlier age. Disruptive as it may be, this turbulent
stage of growth bifurcates and focuses many of the remaining elements
of the youngster's biological potential. It is not only a preparatory phase
for the forthcoming independence from parental direction, but is when
the psychological equivalent of the *r*- and *K*- strategies—self (male) and
other (female) orientations—begin to diverge and then coalesce into
distinct gender roles.

With the unsettling influences of adolescence, both physiological
and social, and the emergence of the individual as a being of genuine
reproductive potential, the *r*- and *K*- strategies begin to take on an implicitly criterial role in the selection of the behaviors of the moment,
as well as future goals, from a universe of implicit alternatives. These
strategies are psychologically expressed, at the highest level of abstraction, in an orientation toward self and an orientation toward others.
Here the male can be prototypically described as more dominant, im-
perial, and acquisitive, and the female more communal, nurturant, and
deferent.

These representations—self, other, and their coordination—are essential to the genesis of the personality system. Both attachment theory and the evolutionary model presented here recognize the
importance of self and other constructs. From an attachment perspective, these constructs represent inchoate interpersonal relationships,
the intricacies of which are made possible by cognitive developments.
No longer is the world an unorganized swirl of events; increasingly,
it is organized around relationships and expectations. While relationships are organic wholes (Sroufe & Fleeson, 1986), within these wholes,
the individual's orientation, that is, his/her expectations about future
states of the relationship and outcomes desired from the relationship,
are oriented toward self and other, and the individual may possess
positive or negative models of each. (Bartholomew & Horowitz, 1991)

Development of Pubertal Maturation. Pubescence is characterized
by the rapidity of body growth, genital maturity, and sexual awareness. A series of transformations take place that are qualitatively different from those developed earlier in childhood. They created an element
of discontinuity from prior experiences, confronting the youngster, not
only with an internal "revolution" of a physiological nature, but also

with a series of psychological tasks that are prompted by emergent sexual feelings. Perhaps more applicable to this stage of life than those that Freud considered paramount in infancy, the emergence of pubertal sexuality is central to the psychic development of the adolescent. Much effort is invested both consciously and unconsciously to incorporate these new bodily impulses into one's sense of self and one's relationship to others. Youngsters must establish a gender identity that incorporates physiological changes and the powerful libidinal feelings with which they are associated. The increase in pubertal libidinal drives requries a reorganization of one's sense of adolescent identity. Developed in a satisfactory manner, the adolescent is enabled to search out relevant extrafamilial love objects.

Development of Gender Identity. Developing a gender identity is not so much acquiring a means for satisfying libidinal impulses as it is a process of refining the youngster's previously diffused and undifferentiated sense of self. This is achieved most effectively by reflecting the admiration of a beloved other. The feedback received in real and fantasized love relationships assists the teenager to revise and define his/her gender-identity. It serves also to clarify and further develop a new self-concept that encompasses relationships with peer companions of both genders, rather than parents or siblings.

Not uncommonly, the definition of one's own gender identity brings forth a rejection of the opposite sex. "They" are treated with derision and contempt. A turning toward the same-sex peer group is of value in defining one's identity, a process that is deeply embedded by a self-conscious selection and alliance of same-sex peers. Pubertal boys avoid girls, belittle them, and strongly reject female sentimentality. Girls turn for affection and support toward their same-sex peers, sharing secrets, intimacies, and erotically tinged fantasies and romances. All these efforts add a psychosocial dimension and gender definition to increasingly powerful pubertal processes.

Consequences of Impoverishment. The goal of the adolescent is in part to achieve a libidinous extrafamilial object, an aim ultimately resulting in a richer and more mature emotional life. As noted, with the onset of puberty, parental identification declines and is replaced by identifications with valued peers, both real friendships and romanticized heroes. The lack of such identifications and role models during adolescence may culminate in imaginary infatuations, unreal and ineffectual substitute for the desirable qualities that usually emerge from everyday personal relationships.

Without direct guidance from their elders, teenagers will be left to their own devices to master the complexities of a varied world, to control intense aggressive and sexual urges that well up within them, to channel their fantasies, and to pursue the goals to which they aspire. They may become victims of their own growth, unable to discipline their impulses or fashion acceptable means for expressing desires. Scattered and unguided, they cannot get hold of a sense of personal identity, a consistent direction and purpose to their existence. They become "other-directed" individuals who vacillate at every turn, overly responsive to fleeting stimuli and shifting from one erratic course to another. Ultimately, without an inner core or anchor to guide their future, they may flounder or stagnate. Deficient gender identifications and inadequate sexual initiations may interfere in significant ways with the development of their emotional maturity.

Borderline personality disorders often characterize this pattern of gender diffusion. The aimlessness and disaffiliation of borderlines from the mainstream of traditional family life may be traced, in part, to the failure of experience to provide a coherent set of gender role models and values around which these individuals can focus their lives and orient themselves toward a meaningful future.

Consequences of Enrichment. In contrast to the problems that arise from a deficiency of gender role models, we frequently observe excessive dependency on peer-group sexual habits and values. Some adolescents who have been ill-disposed to the values of problematic peer groups may find themselves isolated and avoided, if not ridiculed and ostracized. To protect themselves against this discomforting possibility, these teenagers may submerge their identity to fit the roles given them by others. They may adopt gender models that have been explicitly or implicitly established by group customs. They act, dress, use language, and enact their gender roles in terms of peer-group standards.

Not untypically, peer groups provide a formal structure to guide the youngster, with uniforms, rituals, and even specified heroes as imitative models. Such identities, gender and otherwise, are provided by belonging to neighborhood gangs or "hippie" subcultures. Many high school students conform unquestioningly to the sexual standards of their peers in order to be accepted, to be enmeshed in the good feeling of group solidarity, and to boost their sense of identity through identification. In effect, these youngsters have jettisoned parental norms for peer-group norms, and it is these latter norms that foreclose independent thought and feeling. What is seen in these identifications is an increase in narcissism, a posture of arrogance and rebellion, as well as defiance against conventional societal norms.

As the diffusion of earlier bisexual trends give way to a distinct heterosexual orientation, sexuality becomes the most prominent feature of these ''enriched'' youngsters. Many become sensitive, almost exclusively, to erotic stimuli, in contrast to the more global and varied aspect of normal heterosexual relationships. Such adolescents often ''back-off,'' stating that they are worried that they might be getting ''too involved.'' Hence, pubertal maturation in these youngsters may not only intensify their labidinal drives, but it may also increase in equal measure their aggressive/hostile drives. As a consequence of these developments and transfromations, these youngsters may now have developed behaviors that accentuate the stereotypical roles of masculinity and femininity.

Stage 4: Intracortical–Initiative: The Intellectual Reasoning (Thinking)–Affective Resonance (Feeling) Polarity

The intracortical–initiative stage coordinates with the fourth phase of the evolutionary progression, the thinking–feeling polarity. The peak period of neurological maturation for certain psychological functions generally occurs between the ages of 4 and 18 years. The amount and kind of intrapsychic and contextual stimulation at these times of rapid growth will have a strong bearing on the degree to which these functions mature. Thinking and feeling are broad and multifaceted constructs with diverse manifestations. Whereas the focus in the first three stages of development was on the child's existential aims, mode of adaptation, and gender identification, here the focus shifts to the individual as a being-in-time.

Initially, the child must acquire abstract capacities that enable it to transcend the purely concrete reality of the present moment and project the self-as-object into myriad futures contingent upon its own style of action or accomodation. Such capacities are specifically cognitive and emotional, and they may have wide-ranging consequences for the personality system if they fail to cohere as integrated structures, as in the more severe personality disorders, for example, borderline and schizotypal.

What are the capacities that unfold during this stage, and what consequences can be attributed to differences in the quality and intensity of relevant experience?

Development of Intracortical Capacities. Progressively more complex arrangements of neural cells become possible as children advance in maturation. Although these higher-order connections begin in early infancy, they do not form into structures capable of rational foresight and adult-level planning until the youngsters have fully developed their more basic sensorimotor skills and pubertal maturations. With these capacities as a base, they are able to differentiate and arrange the objects of the physical world. As verbal skills unfold, they learn to symbolize concrete objects; soon they are able to manipulate and coordinate these symbols as well as, if not better than, the tangible events themselves. Free of the need to make direct reference to the concrete world, they are able to recall past events and anticipate future ones. As increasingly complex cortical connections are established, higher conceptual abstractions are formulated, enabling the children to transfer, associate, and coordinate these symbols into ideas of finer differentiation, greater intricacy, and broader integration. These internal representations of reality, the product of symbolic thought, the construction of events past, present, and future, take over as the primary elements of the representational world. Especially significant at this period is a fusion between the capacities to think and feel.

Development of Integrative Processes. When the inner world of symbols is mastered, giving objective reality an order and integration, youngsters are able to create some consistency and continuity in their lives. No longer are they buffeted from one mood or action to another by the swirl of changing events; they now have an internal anchor, a nucleus of cognitions that serves as a base and imposes a sense of sameness and continuity upon an otherwise fluid environment. As they grow in their capacity to organize and integrate their world, one configuration becomes increasingly differentiated and begins to predominate. Accrued from experiences with others and their reactions to the child, an image or representation of self-as-object has taken shape. This highest order of abstraction, the sense of individual identity as distinct from others becomes the dominant source of stimuli that guides the youngster's style of behavior. External events no longer have the power they once exerted; the youngster now has an ever-present and stable sphere of internal representations, transformed by rational and emotional reflections, which governs one's course of action and from which events are initiated.

Consequences of Impoverishment. The tasks of integrating a consistent self–other differentiation as well as consolidating the divergencies of though and feeling are not easy in a world of changing events and pluralistic values. From what sources can a genuine balance between reason and emotion be developed?

The institutions that interweave to form the complex fabric of society are implicitly designed to shape the assumptive world of its younger members. Family, school, and church transmit implicit values and explicit rules by which the child is guided in behaving and thinking in a manner consonant with those of others. The youngster not only is subject to cultural pressures but requires them to give direction to his/her proliferating capacities and impulses. Without them, potentials may become overly diffuse and scattered; conversely, too much guidance may narrow the child's potentials and restrict his/her adaptiveness. In either case, the self and other, as well as the relationship of thought and emotion, are no longer expressed in their elaborated and multifaceted forms. Instead are manifested narrowly or rigidly, with the result that the individual lacks the flexibility required to successfully navigate life's social contexts on his/her own. Once basic patterns of thought are shaped during this period, it is difficult to orient them along new pathways.

What are the effects of inadequate or erratic stimulation during the peak years of intracortical integration?

Without direct tuition from elders, youngsters are left to their own devices to master the complexities of a varied world, to control intense urges, to channel fantasies, and to pursue the goals to which they aspire. They may become victims of their own growth, unable to orient their impulses or fashion acceptable means for expressing their desires. Scattered and unguided, they may be unable to construct a sense of internal cohesion or a consistent direction and purpose to their existence. They may vacillate at every turn, overly responsive to fleeting stimuli, shifting from one erratic course to another. Without an inner core or anchor to guide their future, they may flounder or stagnate.

Evidently, the impoverishment of integrative stimuli will have a profound effect. Fortunately, with proper guidance, the "immaturity and irresponsibility" of many adolescents may be salvaged in later years. But for others, the inability to settle down into a consolidated path may become a problem of increasingly severe proportions.

Consequences of Enrichment. The negative consequences of over-enrichment at the fourth stage usually occur when parents are controlling and perfectionistic. The overly trained, overly disciplined, and overly integrated youngsters are given little opportunity to create his/her own destiny. Whether by coercion or enticement, children who, too early, is led to control his/her emergent feelings, to focus his/her thoughts along narrowly defined paths and to follow the prescriptions of parental demands, have been subverted into adopting the identities of others. Whatever individuality he/she may have acquired is drowned in a model of adult orderliness, propriety, and virtue. Such oversocialized and rigid youngsters lack the spontaneity, flexibility, and creativeness we expect of the young; they have been trained to be old men before their time, too narrow in perspective to respond to the excitement, variety, and challenge of new events. Overenrichment at this stage has set them on a restrictive course and has deprived them of the opportunity to become themselves.

Comment. It would be an error to leave this discussion of evolutionary–neuropsychological development with the impression that personality growth is merely a function of stimulation at sensitive maturational periods. Impoverishment and enrichment have their profound effects, but the quality or kind of stimulation the youngster experiences is often of greater importance. The impact of parental harshness or inconsistency, of sibling rivalry or social failure, is more than a matter of stimulus volume and timing. Different dimensions of experience take precedence as the meaning conveyed by the source of stimulation becomes clear to the growing child. This facet of psychogenesis will be considered shortly, as well our discussion of the central tasks that must be undertaken at each of the four sequential stages of development.

Normal psychological process depend on a substrate of orderly neuronal connections. The development of this intricate neural substrate unfolds within the organism in accord with genetically determined mechanisms, but there remain substantial numbers of fibers whose direction of growth is modifiable. To summarize the previous section, it might be said that the basic architecture of the nervous system is laid down in a relatively fixed manner, but refinements in this linkage system do not develop without the aid of additional experiences. Environmental experiences not only activates neural collaterals but alters these structures so as to preempt them for similar subsequent experiences. Thus, early experiences not only construct new neural pathways but, in addition, selectively prepare them to be receptive to later stimuli that are qualitatively similar.

This second consequence of experience, representing the selective lowering of thresholds for the transmission of similar subsequent stimuli, is described in the conceptual language of psychology as learning. It reflects the observation that behaviors that have been subject to prior experience are reactivated with increasing ease. With this second consequence of stimulation, we begin to conceive the nervous system as more than a netwowrk of abstract pathways; it is now viewed as posessing the residues of specific classes of environmental stimuli. These environmentally anchored neural connections interweave to form patterns of perception and behavior that relate to discriminable events in the external world. By including qualitatively discriminable features of the stimulus world within our purview, we shift our attention to observational units that transcend neural mechanisms located strictly within the anatomical limits of the body. It is necessary to represent these complex external–internal relationships in a conceptual language that is broader in scope than that of neurology.

We noted further that there are sensitive periods in the maturation of the nervous system when the effects of stimulation are especially pronounced; these occur at points of rapid neural growth. Stimulus impoverishment at these critical stages leads to an underdevelopment among neural connections; deficit neural development will have long-range deleterious effects, since early growth serves as a prerequisite to the development of subsequent capacities. Comparable complications may arise as a function of stimulus enrichment.

Environmental experiences not only activate the growth of neural collaterals but alter these structures in such ways as to preempt them for similar subsequent experiences. Early stimulus experiences, then, not only construct new neural pathways, but, in addition, selectively prepare these pathways to be receptive to later stimuli that are qualitatively similar. This second consequence of stimulus experience, representing a selective lowering of the threshold for the neural transmission of similar subsequent stimuli, has been described in the conceptual language of psychology as the process of learning; it reflects the observation that perceptions and behaviors that have been subjected to prior experience and training are reactivated with relative ease.

With this second consequence of stimulation in mind, we can begin to speak of the nervous system as more than a network of abstract pathways; it now may be viewed as possessing the residues of *specific* classes of environmental stimuli. These environmentally anchored neural connections interweave to form complex patterns of perception and behavior that relate to discriminable events in the external world. No longer will we be dealing, therefore, with the simple quantitative volume of stimulation; by including qualitatively discriminable features of the stimulus world within our purview, we must begin to shift our attention to observational units that transcend the neural mechanisms of bodily funtion. It now will be necessary to represent these more complex stimulus events in a conceptual language that is broader in scope than that found in neurology.

What conceptual level and units of observation will best enable us to describe and analyze the effects of the *quality* or content of experience?

As noted earlier, the qualitative aspect of stimulation alters the threshold of neural transmission for similar subsequent stimuli. This change in the probability of neural transmission is descriptively similar to the psychological process known as learning; learning often is defined as an increment in the probability that previously experienced stimulus situations will be perceived rapidly and that responses previously associated with them will be elicited.

Both neurological and learning concepts can be utilized to describe changes in response probabilities arising from prior stimulus exposure. But, since learning concepts are formulated in terms of behavior-environment interactions, it would appear reasonable, when discussing the specific properties of qualitatively discriminable stimulus events, to utilize the conceptual language of learning. Moreover, the principles derived from learning theory and research describe subtle features of psychological behavior that cannot begin to be handled intelligently in neurological terms. With the principles and conceptual language of learning, we can formulate precisely our ideas about the effects of qualitatively discriminable stimulus events, that is, differences not only in the magnitude but in the variety and content of the stimulus world as we experience it.

Let us keep in mind that learning concepts and neurological concepts do not represent intrinsically different processes; we are using the former because they have been more finely differentiated and, therefore, are more fruitful tools for formulating notions about qualitatively different stimulus–behavior interactions.

Developmental Tasks

As has been noted in prior sections, experience is likely to have a more profound effect at certain stages in the developmental sequence than at others. This statement reiterates a conviction stated earlier that pronounced environmental influences occur at periods of rapid neurological growth. A further reason for the stage-specific significance of experience is the observation that children are exposed to a succession of social tasks that they are expected to fulfill at different points in the developmental sequence. These stage-specific tasks are timed to coincide with periods of rapid neurological growth (e.g., the training of bladder control is begun when the child possesses the requisite neural equipment for such control; similarly, children are taught to read when intracortical development has advanced sufficiently to enable a measure of consistent success). In short, a reciprocity appears between periods of rapid neurological growth and exposure to related experiences and tasks. To use Erikson's (1950) terms, the child's newly emerging neurological potentials are challenged by a series of "crises" with the environment. Children are especially vulnerable at the critical stages, since experience both shapes their neurological patterns and results in learning a series of fundmental attitudes about themselves and others.

What experiences typically arise at the four neuropsychological stage described earlier, and what are the central attitudes learned during these periods.

In seeking answers to these questions, this discussion turns briefly to the fertile ideas of Freud and Erikson. During the sensory-attachment stage, when pleasure and pain discriminations are central, the critical attitude learned deals with one's "trust of others." The sensorimotor–autonomy stage, when the progression from passive to active modes of adaption occurs, is noted by learning attitudes concering "adaptive confidence." During the pubertal–gender identity stage when the separation between self and other roles is sharpened, we see the development of reasonably distinct "sexual roles." The intracortical–integrative stage, when the coordination between intellectual and affective process develops, may best be characterized by the acquisition of a balance between "reason and emotion." A brief elaboration of these is in order.

Task 1: Developing Trust of Others (Pain–Pleasure Polarity)

Trust may be described as a feeling that one can rely on the affections and support of others. There are few periods of life when an individual is so wholly dependent on the goodwill and care of others than during the relatively helpless state of infancy. Nothing is more crucial to the infant's well-being than the nurturance and protection afforded by his/her caretakers. Through the quality and consistency of this support, deeply ingrained feelings of trust are etched within the child. From the evolutionary model presented earlier, trust and mistrust represent facets of the pleasure and pain constructs, generalized to adaptational venues within the physical environment, such as the nursery, as well as the environment of prototypal social objects. Within the infant's world, of course, trust and mistrust lack their phenomenological and moral dimensions, resembling more global and undifferentiated feelings of soothing calm (pleasure) or tense apprehension (pain) than consciously abstracted states.

Such perceptual indiscriminateness of associations is highly significant. Thus, feelings and expectancies arising from specific experiences become highly generalized and come to characterize the child's image of the entire environment. Because children are unable to make fine discriminations, their early attachments become pervasive and widespread. Nurtured well and given comfort and affection, they will acquire a far-reaching trust of others; they learn that discomfort will be moderated and that others will assist them and provide for their needs. Deprived of warmth and security or handled severely and painfully, they will learn to mistrust their environment, to anticipate further stress, and view others as harsh and undependable. Rather than developing an optimistic and confident attitude toward the future, they will be disposed to withdraw and avoid people for fear that these persons will recreate the discomfort and anguish that were experienced in the past.

Task 2: Acquiring Adaptive Confidence (Active–Passive Polarity)

Children become progressively less dependent on their caretakers during the sensorimotor–autonomy stage. By the second and third years they are ambulatory and possess the power of speech and control over many elements in their environment. They have acquired the manipulative skills to venture forth and test their competence to handle events on their own (White, 1960). In terms of the evolutionary model, this stage concerns the active–passive polarity. Here children struggle to break out of the inherently dependent and passive mode of infancy. Rather than remain a passive receptacle for environmental forces, clay to be molded, they acquire competencies that enlarge their vistas and allow them to become legitimate actors in their environments.

However, subtle, as well as obvious, parental attitudes shape children's confidence in their ability to exercise their competencies. These attitudes markedly influence behavior, since it is not only what the children can do that determines their actions but how they feel about what they can do. The rewards and punishments to which they are exposed and the degree of encouragement and affection surrounding their first performances will contribute to their confidence in themselves. Severe discipline for transgressions, humiliating comments in response to efforts at self-achievement, embarrassment over social awkwardness, deprecations associated with poor school performance, and shame among one's peers as a result of physical inadequacies, all weigh heavily to diminish self-esteem. Faced with rebuffs and ridicule, children learn to doubt their competence and adequacy. Whether they actually possess the skills to handle events is no longer the issue; they simply lack the confidence to try, to venture out or to compete. Believing their efforts will be ineffectual and futile, these children often adopt a passive, wait-and-see attitude toward their environment and their future.

Task 3: Assimilating Sexual Roles (Self–Other Polarity)

The many crushes and infatuations experienced during the pubertal period serve as genuine source of development. Gender roles emerge in significant ways through interaction with others, especially as enacted in peer-group relationships. Adhering to the models of peer behaviors helps the youngster find and evaluate how certain gender roles fit. The high school clique, the neighborhood gang, the athletic team all aid the teenager in discovering his/her gender identity, providing both useful role models and instant social feedback. The "bull" session among boys and the endless phone conversations between girls serve significant goals by providing evaluative feedback as the youngster searches to define him/herself. It is particularly during the time of rapid body changes when genital impulses stimulate sexual fantasies that the adolescent learns to rely on peers as important guides and sounding boards.

Security is found in peer relationships in that youngsters share a code as to what constitutes appropriate gender behaviors. No less important is the mutuality they experience in struggling through the same pubertal issues. The importance of the influence of the peer group is perhaps nowhere more significant than in the realm of sexual behaviors. For the most part, the adolescent finds security in accepting the peer–gender norms as preliminary guides regarding how one can regulate one's impulses, feelings, and sexual inclinations.

Task 4: Balancing Reason and Emotion (Intracortical–Integration Polarity)

The emergence of this final developmental stage—with its capacities for thinking, feeling, evaluating, and planning—leads children to formulate a clear image of themselves as a certain "kind of adult," an identity discernible from others, one capable of having independent judgments and of fashioning the child's own course of action. Healthy children must acquire a coherent system of internalized values that will guide them through a changing and varied environment. They must find their own anchor and compass by which to coordinate both their feelings and ideas about life. Equipped by successful efforts toward autonomy, they will have confidence that they possess a direction in life that is valued by others and one that can safely withstand the buffeting of changing events. In terms of the evolutionary model, such children are capable of integrating their feelings and thoughts, setting their own agendas, and becoming masters of their own fate.

Conversely, if deprived of rewarded achievements and unable to construct a picture of a valued identity, they will lack the means to meet life's tasks rationally and be unable to handle discouraging emotional forces that may arise. In such cases, their identity may come to be defined through the goals and needs of others rather than through self. Without an integrated and consistent integration of thought and feeling, the growing adolescent or adult will flounder from one tentative course to another and be best with amorphous and vague feelings of discontent and uselessness.

PERSONALITY AND PSYCHOPATHOLOGY

A classification system will go awry if its major categories encompass too diverse a range of clinical conditions; there is need to subdivide psychopathology in terms of certain fundamental criteria. For this reason we have stressed an integrative perspective, which differentiates among Axis I disorders and Axis II patterns on the basis of the formal properties of systems alone. Such an innovation distinguishes syndromes that would otherwise be seen as simply lying along side each other, in the same plane so to speak, according to their presumed prototypal etiological pattern, either linear (deriving from one or another level of organization) or circular (possessing a qualitative organization that cuts across and is anchored in all levels of organization).

Clinical Personality Patterns and Classical Psychiatric Disorders

Any conception of clinical personality patterns must distinguish these patterns not only from their more normal variants but also from the classical psychiatric disorders that largely constitute Axis I. As previously noted, personality disorders are not medical illnesses for which some discrete pathogen can be found, or for which exists some underlying unitary cause. The use of such language as "disorder" is indeed unfortunate, for personality disorders are not disorders at all in the medical sense. Instead, personality disorders are best conceptualized as disorders of the entire matrix of the person. Hence, we prefer the terms "pattern" or "style" rather than the intrinsically reifying "disorder." Such a misconception is paradigmatic rather than diagnostic, and tends to nullify the logic of the multiaxial model, encouraging the view that classical clinical syndromes and clinical personality patterns exist alongside each the other in a horizontal relationship. In contrast, the essence of the multiaxial model lies in its *structural* innovation; that is, it has been specifically composed to encourage the view that classical psychiatric disorders have their meaning transformed by the overarching personality patterns in which they are embedded.

The multiaxial model may be more formally represented with the aid of general systems concepts and the idea of levels of organization. *Both axes represent prototypal expressions of systemic dysfunctioning, but the causal nature of the dysfunction is different for each axis.* With the Axis I disorders, etiology flows from one or more levels of organization. Prototypally, these are distinctly vertical pathologies whose manifest symptomatology reflects the interaction of biological, familial, and social inputs. Major depression, for example, may be driven primarily by endogenous biologically depressive substrates, or it may result from and be accompanied by grief following the death of a family member.

The personality disorders, however, do not refer to systemically dysregulating inputs from any one level of organization. Instead, personality disorders are distinctly horizontal patterns that refer to qualitative aspects of organization that cut across all levels of organization and thus have referents in every level of organization. The organization of personality disorders is as integrative as those of so-called normal personalities, which is why personality disorders are so tenacious. Note that these integrative horizontal clinical patterns are sustained by causal pathways that are intrinsically circular or reflexive, whereas Axis I disorders, although often multidetermined, are potentially linear in nature. Note further that all functional and structural domains are assumed to be equipotent in the degree to which they constrain system functioning.

With real individuals, of course, it is seldom so. The behavior of actual persons is highly constrained in some domains (e.g., interpersonally, cognitively) and not at all in others, such that the meaning of each domain is transformed by a gestalt of which it is transactionally a part. Morever, dysregulating inputs from various levels of organization, the classical psychiatric disorders, create systemic reverberations that lend each individual's pathology and adaptive capacity a unique coloration. Each individual thus forms a dynamic organizational or integrated whole that may be decomposed according to separate axes for purposes that are heuristic, rather than real. No one really believes that the individual "exists" as an entity dismembered on separate axes. Thus, although Wilhelm Reich (1945, p. 42) spoke truly when he said that "each individual case entails a definite plan that must be deduced from the [logic of the] case itself," the multiaxial model recognizes that there are certain taxonomic structural boundaries that can and must be established from the formal properties of general systems alone, irrespective of issues of content.

Personality Patterns, Symptom Disorders, and Adjustment Reactions

On a systems basis, we may distinguish three prototypal kinds of disorders, "personality patterns," "symptom disorders," and "adjustment reactions," depending on the source of those constraints that feed into the pathology. Although behavior is always the product of an individual-by-environment transaction at multiple levels of both organism and context, we must nevertheless average over certain elements in order to place in high relief those classes of phenomena that will serve as the structural reference points for our taxonomy.

With personality patterns, behavioral constraints are assumed to lie exclusively within the person. Clinical patterns result when these patterns become dysfunctional in "average or expectable environments" (Hartmann, 1939).

With symptom disorders, referred to since DSM-III as clinical syndromes (American Psychiatric Association, 1980), system constraints are assumed to lie both within the person and environment and to be prototypally equipotent. Conceived as intensifications or disruptions in a patient's characteristic style of functioning, symptom disorders are viewed as a reaction to a situation for which the individual's personality is notably vulnerable. Hysterical conversions and fugue states are dramatic examples of symptom disorders. Symptom disorders occur in response to situations that appear rather trivial or innocuous when viewed objectively. Nevertheless, disordered patients feel and respond in a manner similar to that of persons who face realistically distressing situations. As a consequence, symptom disorders fail to "make sense" and often appear irrational and strangely complicated. To the experienced clinician, however, the response signifies the presence of an unusual vulnerability on the part of the patient; in effect, a seemingly neutral stimulus apparently has touched a painful hidden memory or emotion. Viewed in this manner, symptom disorders arise among individuals encumbered with adverse past experiences. They reflect the upsurge of deeply rooted feelings that press to the surface, override present realities, and become the prime stimulus to which the individual responds. It is this flooding into the present of the reactivated past that gives symptom disorders much of their symbolic, bizarre, and hidden meaning.

At the opposite end of a continuum are the adjustment reactions, defined as highly specific pathological responses that are precipitated by and largely attributable to circumscribed external events. Here constraints are assumed to lie exclusively within the environment—these clinical patterns result when average or expectable persons are faced with situations to which almost anyone would react pathologically, the demise of one's entire family in a natural disaster, for example. In contrast to symptom disorders, adjustment reactions are simple and straightforward. They do not "pass through" a chain of complicated and circuitous transformations before emerging in manifest form. Uncontaminated by the intrusion of distant memories and intrapsychic processes, behavior reactions tend to be rational and understandable in terms of the precipitating stimulus. Isolated from past emotions and from defensive manipulations, they are expressed in an uncomplicated and consistent fashion—unlike symptom disorders, whose features are highly fluid, wax and wane, and take different forms at different times.

We might sum up by saying that traits that comprise personality patterns have an inner momentum and autonomy; they are expressed with or without inducement or external precipitation. In contrast, the responses comprising behavior reactions are stimulus specific; that is, they are linked to external conditions in that they operate independent of the individual's personality and are elicited by events that are "objectively" troublesome. Symptom disorders are similar to behavior reactions in that they are prompted also by external events, but their close connection to personality results in the intrusion of traits and behaviors that complicate what might otherwise be a reaction to the environment within the nonclinical range.

Not surprisingly, the distinctions made in differentiating personality patterns, adjustment reactions, and symptom disorders closely correspond to a related issue in personality theory and research, namely, personality consistency and specificity. Personality patterns are conceived as enduring (stable) and pervasive (consistent) characteristics of behavior, that is, pathological traits that persist over time and are displayed across situations. At the other end of the continuum are the behavior reactions, described as situationally specific, pathological responses induced by the conditions of the environment. Symptom disorders lie between these two and are formulated as pathological phenomena that reflect the interaction of personality vulnerabilities and situational stimuli. In essence, symptom disorders represent the interactionist view concerning the origin of pathological symptoms; behavior reactions reflect the situationist position; and personality patterns correspond to the personologic perspective. By differentiating the major categories of pathology in accord with the threefold schema of patterns, reactions, and disorders, a small step will be taken toward distinguishing syndromes in a manner that parallels the three primary sources of pathogenesis, the individual (personologic), the environment (situational), and their interaction.

In the separation of all of pathology into three classes, one must keep in mind that the *structural* (as opposed to content) validity of a taxonomy that seeks to partition that which is fundamentally an integrative whole depends on the degree to which the putative parts, once reassembled, lend insight and understanding to the whole as it is now seen as a totality. The tripartite scheme explicated above is not a pure heuristic fiction, however. Empirical research shows that individuals differ in the degree to which their behaviors exhibit consistency. Moreover, each individual displays consistency only in certain characteristics; that is, each of us possesses particular traits that are resistant to situational influence and others that can be readily modified. Stated differently, the several characteristics comprised in our personality do not display equal degrees of consistency and stability. Furthermore, the traits that exhibit consistency in one person may not exhibit consistency in others. In general, consistency is found only in traits that are central to the individual's style of functioning. For some, what is of significance is being compliant and agreeable, never differing or having conflict; for another, it may be crucial to keep one's distance from people so as to avoid rejection or the feeling of being humiliated; and for a third, the influential characteristic may be that of asserting one's will and dominating others. Thus, each individual possesses a small and distinct group of primary traits that persist and endure and exhibit a high degree of consistency across situations. These enduring (stable) and pervasive (consistent) characteristics are what we mean when we speak of personality. Going one step further, personality pathology comprises those stable and consistent traits that persist inflexibly, are exhibited inappropriately, and foster vicious circles that perpetuate and intensify already present difficulties.

The terminology and categories since DSM-III are not differentiated in accord with the preceding discussion; the term "disorder" is applied to all clinical syndromes, including those of "personality disorders." Nevertheless, there is reason to reflect further on these distinctions. For the present, we note once more that personality is a concept that represents a network of deeply embedded and broadly exhibited traits that persist over extended periods of time and characterize the individual's distinctive manner of relating to his/her environment. Pathological personalities are distinguished from their normal counterparts by their adaptive inflexibility, their tendency to foster vicious circles, and their tenuous stability under stressful conditions. Our attention turns next to specifying the stable and persistent pathological personality patterns that comprise Axis II of DSM, including those that have been listed in the appendix of DSM-III, DSM-III-R, and DSM-IV. Each personality exhibits distinctive coping strategies that persist inflexibly, are exhibited inappropriately, and foster vicious circles that perpetuate and intensify the prior difficulties. These patterns will be deduced theoretically in a later section.

Normal and Clinical Personality Patterns

Numerous attempts have been made to develop definitive criteria for distinguishing psychological normality from abnormality. Some of these criteria focus on features that characterize the so-called normal, or ideal, state of mental health, as illustrated in the writings of Offer and Sabshin (1974, 1991); others have sought to specify criteria for concepts such as abnormality or psychopathology. The most common criterion employed is a statistical one in which normality is determined by those behaviors that are found most frequently in a social group and pathology or abnormality, by features that are uncommon in that population.

Central to our understanding of normality and abnormality is the recognition that these terms exist as relative concepts; they represent arbitrary points on a continuum or gradient. No sharp line divides normal from pathological behavior. Not only is personality so complex that certain areas of psychological functioning operate normally while others do not, but environmental circumstances change such that behaviors and strategies that prove adaptive at one time fail to do so at another. Moreover, features differentiating normal from abnormal functioning must be extracted from a complex of signs that not only wax and wane but often develop in an insidious and unpredictable manner. Personality disorders, as previously remarked, are not disorders or diseases at all in the medical sense. Rather, personality disorders are reified constructs employed to represent varied styles or patterns in which the personality system functions *maladaptively* in relation to its environment and over time.

The interactional aspect of such a conception is an important one, because it is informed by general systems concepts: Normal persons exhibit flexibility in their transactions with their environment, meaning that their responses or behaviors are appropriate to a given situation and over time. If person and environment are conceptualized as a dynamic system, an intercoupled person–environment unit, then the evolution of the unit through its successive states is said to be subject to constraints that lie both in the person and in the environment. When environmental constraints dominate, the behavior of individuals tends to converge, regardless of their prepotent dispositions: Almost everyone stops when stop lights are red. When environmental constraints are few or not well-defined, however, there is opportunity for flexibility, novelty, and the expression of individual differences in behavior.

Personality traits may be defined as those factors or characteristics that seem to inhere in the person, precisely *because* they pervasively constrain the number, quality, and pattern of states that the organismic–environmental system can assume across time. In other words, at an observational or manifest level, personologic constraints *are* traits. To illustrate: In the absence of constraints, all system states are possible. Such states may be thought of as potentialities, in that, speaking behaviorally, there are as many different future states for the organism as there are responses any such organism can emit. Thus, far from being essential and structurally independent atoms of personality, traits are intrinsically interconnected, representing an inferential shorthand for those system constraints that carve from an infinite universe of possible personologic patterns that unique set of states the organism will probabilistically assume. Thus traits are often described as prepotent dispositions.

Another characteristic of systems is especially relevant to personality disorders. The number of states any system can assume diminishes with the addition of successive constraints. When the person–environment interaction is pervasively constrained by personologic factors, the variability or flexibility of an individual's behavior is no longer appropriate and proportional to what the environment requires. We might say that the interaction is now being *driven* exclusively by the person. When the number of possible system states allowed by the intersection of personologic and environmental constraints approaches zero, when no degrees of freedom remain, no coping maneuver effectively fields environmental challenges, then the immunological function of the individual's personality has been compromised. Such an exhaustion of system states (possibilities) leads to the classically psychiatric Axis I conditions, such as anxiety or depressive disorders; moreover, the probability of these conditions is increased in proportion to the number and quality of constraints on the interaction supplied by the person. The relationship between contextual and personality constraints and Axis I and Axis II pathology is represented in a series of Venn diagrams in Figure 5.1.

When the alternative strategies employed to achieve goals, relate to others, and cope with stress are few in number and rigidly practiced ("adaptive inflexibility"), when habitual perceptions, needs, and behaviors perpetuate and intensify preexisting difficulties ("vicious circles"), and when the person tends to lack resilience under conditions of stress ("tenuous stability"), we speak of a clinically interesting per-

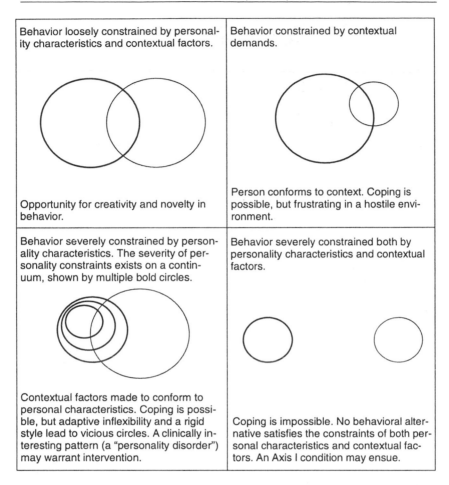

Behavior loosely constrained by personality characteristics and contextual factors.	Behavior constrained by contextual demands.
Opportunity for creativity and novelty in behavior.	Person conforms to context. Coping is possible, but frustrating in a hostile environment.
Behavior severely constrained by personality characteristics. The severity of personality constraints exists on a continuum, shown by multiple bold circles.	Behavior severely constrained both by personality characteristics and contextual factors.
Contextual factors made to conform to personal characteristics. Coping is possible, but adaptive inflexibility and a rigid style lead to vicious circles. A clinically interesting pattern (a "personality disorder") may warrant intervention.	Coping is impossible. No behavioral alternative satisfies the constraints of both personal characteristics and contextual factors. An Axis I condition may ensue.

FIGURE 5.1. Personologic (heavy line) and contextual (light line) constraints and their relationship to Axis I and Axis II pathology.

sonality pattern. Borrowing terminology from the medical model, we may even say that a personality ''disorder'' exists, if we keep in mind that the disorder is an interactional aberration that admits of degrees, shading gently from normality to clinicality, and has at a latent level no single underlying cause or disease pathogen but, instead, is as multidetermined as the personality system itself is multifaceted. These three disorder criteria are intimately related to the clinical personality taxonomy that will be proposed in later paragraphs. Before proceeding to the clinical realm, however, we discuss those criteria we deem significant in appraising normality.

THEORETICALLY DERIVED NORMAL
PERSONALITY CRITERIA

In the following sections we draw upon the first three of the evolutionary polarities described previously. The fourth polarity is also worthy of note and relevant to an understanding of personality traits. However, to include this polarity in the following section will take us somewhat afield in this already overly long chapter. Interested readers may wish to look into the manual for the Millon Index of Personality Styles (MIPS) to review the details of this fourth polarity (Millon, Weiss, Millon, & Davis, 1994).

Aims of Existence: Pain–Pleasure Polarity

An interweaving and shifting balance between the two extremes that comprise the pain–pleasure bipolarity typifies normality. Both of the following criteria should be met in varying degrees as life circumstances require. In essence, a synchronous and coordinated personal style should have developed to answer the question of whether the person should focus on experiencing only the pleasures of life versus concentrating his/her efforts on avoiding its pains.

Life Preservation: Avoiding Danger and Threat

One might assume that a criterion based on the avoidance of psychic or physical pain would be sufficiently self-evident not to require specification. As is well known, debates have arisen in the literature as to whether mental health/normality reflects the absence of mental disorder, being merely the reverse side of the mental illness or abnormality coin. That there is a relationship between health and disease cannot be questioned; the two are intimately connected, conceptually and physically. On the other hand, to define health solely as the absence of disorder will not suffice. As a single criterion among several, however, features of behavior and experience that signify both the lack of (for example, anxiety, depression) and an aversion to (for example, threats to safety and security) pain in its many and diverse forms provide a necessary foundation upon which other, more positively constructed criteria may rest. Substantively, positive normality must comprise elements beyond mere nonnormality or abnormality. And despite the complexities and inconsistencies of personality, from a definitional point of view, normality does preclude nonnormality.

Notable here are the contributions of Maslow (1968, 1970), particularly his hierarchic listing of "needs." Best known are the five funda-

mental needs that lead to self-actualization, the first two of which relate to our evolutionary criterion of life preservation. Included in the
first group are the "physiological" needs such as air, water, food, and
sleep, qualities of the ecosystem essential for survival. Next, and equally
necessary to avoid danger and threat, are what Maslow terms the "safety needs," including the freedom from jeopardy, the security of physical protection and psychic stability, as well as the presence of social
order and interpersonal predictability.

That pathological consequences can ensue from the failure to attend to the realities that portend danger is obvious; the lack of air,
water, and food are not issues of great concern in civilized societies
today, although these are matters of considerable import to environ-
mentalists of the future and to those in contemporary poverty-stricken
nations.

It may be of interest next to record some of the psychic pathologies of personality that can be traced to aberrations in meeting this first
criterion of normality. For example, among those termed avoidant personalities (Millon, 1969, 1981), we see an excessive preoccupation with
threats to one's psychic security, an expectation of and hyperalertness
to the signs of potential rejection that leads these persons to disen-
gage from everyday relationships and pleasures. At the other extreme
of the criterion we see a risk-taking attitude, a proclivity to chance haz-
ards and to endanger one's life and liberty, a behavioral pattern characteristic of those we label antisocial personalities. Here there is little of
the caution and prudence expected in the normality criterion of avoiding danger and threat; rather, we observe its opposite, a rash willingness to put one's safety in jeopardy, to play with fire and throw caution
to the wind.

Life Enhancement: Seeking Rewarding Experiences

At the other end of the "existence polarity" are attitudes and behaviors
designed to foster and enrich life, to generate joy, pleasure, contentment, fulfillment, and thereby strengthen the capacity of the individual
to remain vital and competent physically and psychically. This criterion asserts that existence/survival calls for more than life preservation
alone; beyond pain avoidance is pleasure enhancement.

This criterion asks us to go at least one step further than Freud's
parallel notion that life's motivation is chiefly that of "reducing tensions" (that is, avoiding/minimizing pain), maintaining thereby a
steady state, if you will, a homeostatic balance and inner stability. In
accord with our view of evolution's polarities, we would assert that
normal humans are driven also by the desire to enrich their lives, to

seek invigorating sensations and challenges, to venture and explore, all to the end of magnifying if not escalating the probabilities of both individual viability and species replicability.

Regarding the key instrumental role of "the pleasures," Spencer (1870) put it well more than a century ago: "Pleasures are the correlatives of actions conducive to [organismic] welfare . . . the incentives to life supporting acts" (pp. 279, 284). The view that there exists an organismic striving to expand one's inherent potentialities (as well as those of one's kin and species) has been implicit in the literature for ages. That "the pleasures" may be both sign and vehicle for this realization was recorded even in the ancient writings of the *Talmud,* where it states: "Everyone will have to justify himself in the life hereafter for every failure to enjoy a legitimately offered pleasure in this world" (Jahoda, 1958, p. 45).

Turning to more recent psychological formulations, both Rogers (1963) and Maslow (1968) have proposed concepts akin to the criterion of enhancing pleasure. In his notion of "openness to experience," Rogers asserts that the fully functioning person has no aspect of his/her nature closed off. Such individuals are not only receptive to the experiences that life offers but are able also to use them in expanding all of life's emotions, as well as being open to all forms of personal expression. Along a similar vein, Maslow speaks of the ability to maintain a freshness to experience, to keep up one's capacity to appreciate relationships and events. No matter how often events or persons are encountered, one is neither sated nor bored but is disposed to view them with an ongoing sense of "awe and wonder."

As before, a note or two should be recorded on the pathological consequences of a failure to meet a criterion. These are seen most clearly in the personality disorders labeled schizoid and avoidant. In the former there is a marked hedonic deficiency, stemming either from an inherent deficit in affective substrates or the failure of stimulative experience to develop either or both attachment behaviors or affective capacity (Millon, 1981). Among those designated avoidant personalities, constitutional sensitivities or abusive life experiences have led to an intense attentional sensitivity to psychic pain and a consequent distrust in either the genuineness or durability of the "pleasures," such that these individuals can no longer permit themselves to experience them. Both of these personalities tend to be withdrawn and isolated, joyless and grim, neither seeking nor sharing in the rewards of life.

Modes of Adaptation: Passive–Active Polarity

To maintain their unique structure, differentiated from the larger ecosystem of which they are a part, to be sustained as a discrete entity among other phenomena that comprise their environmental field, requires good fortune and the presence of effective modes of functioning. The vast range of behaviors engaged in by humans may fundamentally be grouped in terms of whether initiative is taken in altering and shaping life's events or whether behaviors are reactive to and accommodate those events.

"Normal" or optimal functioning, at least among humans, appears to call for a flexible balance that interweaves both polar extremes. In the first evolutionary stage, that relating to existence, behaviors encouraging both life enhancement (pleasure) and life preservation (pain avoidance) are likely to be more successful in achieving survival than actions limited to one or the other alone. Similarly, regarding adaptation, modes of functioning that exhibit both ecological accommodation and ecological modification are likely to be more successful than either by itself.

As with the pair of criteria representing the aims of existence, a balance should be achieved between the two criteria comprising modes of adaptation, those related to ecological accommodation and ecological modification, or what we have termed the passive–active polarity. Normality calls for a synchronous and coordinated personal style that weaves a balanced answer to the question of whether one should accept what the fates have brought forth or take the initiative in altering the circumstances of one's life.

Ecological Accommodation: Abiding Hospitable Realities

On first reflection, it would seem to be less than optimal to submit meekly to what life presents, to "adjust" obligingly to one's destiny. As described earlier, however, the evolution of plants is essentially grounded (no pun intended) in environmental accommodation, in an adaptive acquiescence to the ecosystem. Crucial to this adaptive course, however, is the capacity of these surroundings to provide the nourishment and protection requisite to the thriving of a species.

To the extent that the events of life have been and continue to be caring and giving, is it not perhaps wise, from an evolutionary perspective, to accept this good fortune and "let matters be"? This accommodating or passive life philosophy has worked extremely well in sustaining and fostering those complex organisms that comprise the plant kingdom. Hence passivity, the yielding to environmental forces, may be in itself not only unproblematic but, where events and circumstances provide the "pleasures" of life and protect against their "pains," positively adaptive and constructive.

The humanistic psychologist Maslow (1970) states that "self-actualized" individuals accept their nature as it is, despite personal weaknesses and imperfections. Comfortable with themselves and the world around them, they do not seek to change "the water because it is wet, or the rocks because they are hard" (p. 153). They have learned to accept the natural order of things. Passively accepting nature, they need not hide behind false masks or transform others to fit "distorted needs." Accepting themselves without shame or apology, they are equally at peace with the shortcomings of those with whom they live and relate.

Where do we find clinical nonnormality that reflects failures to meet the accommodating/abiding criterion?

One example of an inability to leave things as they are is seen in what DSM-IV terms the histrionic personality disorder. Their persistent and unrelenting manipulation of events is designed to maximize the receipt of attention and favors as well as to avoid social disinterest and disapproval. They show an insatiable if not indiscriminate search for stimulation and approval. Their clever and often artful social behaviors may give the appearance of an inner confidence and self-assurance; but beneath this guise lies a fear that a failure on their part to ensure the receipt of attention will, in short order, result in indifference or rejection, and hence their desperate need for reassurance and repeated signs of approval. Tribute and affection must constantly be replenished and are sought from every interpersonal source. As they are quickly bored and sated, they keep stirring up things, becoming enthusiastic about one activity and then another. There is a restless stimulus-seeking quality in which they cannot leave well enough alone.

At the other end of the polarity are personality disorders that exhibit an excess of passivity, failing thereby to give direction to their own lives. Several Axis II disorders demonstrate this passive style, although their passivity derives from and is expressed in appreciably different ways. Dependents typically are average on the pleasure–pain polarity. Passivity for them stems from deficits in self-confidence and competence, leading to deficits in initiative and autonomous skills as well as a tendency to wait passively while others assume leadership and guide them. Passivity among obsessive–compulsive personalities stems from their fear of acting independently, because of intrapsychic resolutions they have made to quell hidden thoughts and emotions generated by their intense self–other ambivalence. Dreading the possibility of making mistakes or engaging in disapproved behaviors, they became indecisive, immobilized, restrained, and passive. High on pain and low on both pleasure and self, self-defeating personalities operate on the assumption that they dare not expect or deserve to have life go their way; giving up any efforts to achieve a life that accords with their "true" desires, they passively submit to others' wishes, acquiescently accepting their fate. Finally, narcissists, especially high on self and low on others, benignly assume that "good things" will come their way with little or no effort on their part; this passive exploitation of others is a consequence of the unexplored confidence that underlies their self-centered presumptions.

Ecological Modification: Mastering One's Environment

The active end of the bipolarity signifies the taking of initiative in altering and shaping life's events. As stated previously, such persons are best characterized by their alertness, vigilance, liveliness, vigor, and forcefulness, their stimulus-seeking energy and drive.

White (1960), in his concept of effectance, sees it as an intrinsic motive, that activates persons to impose their desires upon environments. De Charms elaborates his theme with reference to man as "Origin" and as "Pawn," constructs akin to the active polarity, on the one hand, and to the passive polarity, on the other. He states this distinction as follows:

> That man is the origin of his behavior means that he is constantly struggling against being confined and constrained by external forces, against being moved like a pawn into situations not of his own choosing. . . . An Origin is a person who perceives his behavior as determined by his own choosing; a Pawn is a person who perceives his behavior as determined by external forces beyond his control. . . . An Origin has strong feelings of personal causation, a feeling that the locus for causation of effects in his environment lies within himself. The feedback that reinforces this feeling comes from changes in his environment that are attributable to personal behavior. This is the crux of personal causation, and it is a powerful motivational force directing future behavior. (1968, pp. 273–274)

In a similar vein, Fromm (1955) proposed a need on the part of man to rise above the roles of passive creatures in an accidental if not random world. To him, humans are driven to transcend the state of merely having been created; instead, humans seek to become the creators, the active shapers of their own destiny. Rising above the passive and accidental nature of existence, humans generate their own purposes and thereby provide themselves with a true basis of freedom.

Strategies of Replication: Other–Self Polarity

If an organism merely duplicates itself prior to death, then its replica is "doomed" to repeat the same fate it suffered. However, if new potentials for extending existence can be fashioned by chance or routine events, then the possibility of achieving a different and conceivably superior outcome may be increased. And it is this co-occurrence of random and recombinant processes that does lead to the prolongation of a species' existence. This third hallmark of evolution's procession also undergirds another of nature's fundamental polarities, that between self and other.

As before, we consider both of the following criteria necessary to the definition and determination of normality. We see no necessary antithesis between the two. Humans can be both self-actualizing and other-encouraging, although most persons are likely to lean toward one or the other side. A balance that coordinates the two provides a satisfactory answer to the question of whether one should be devoted to the support and welfare of others or fashion one's life in accord with one's own needs and desires.

Progeny Nurturance: Constructively Loving Others

As described earlier, recombinant replication achieved by sexual mating entails a balanced though asymmetric parental investment in both the genesis and nurturance of offspring.

Before we turn to some of the indices and views of the self–other polarity, let us be mindful that these conceptually derived extremes do not evince themselves in sharp and distinct gender differences. Such proclivities are matters of degree, not absolutes, resulting not only from the consequences of recombinant "shuffling" and gene "crossing over" but from the influential effects of cultural values and social learning. Consequently, most "normal" individuals exhibit intermediate characteristics on this as well as on the other two polarity sets.

More eloquent proposals related to this criterion have been formulated by the noted psychologists Maslow, Allport, and Fromm.

According to Maslow (1970), once humans' basic safety and security needs are met, they next turn to satisfy the belonging and love needs. Here we establish intimate and caring relationships with significant others in which it is just as important to give love as it is to receive it. Noting the difficulty in satisfying these needs in our unstable and changing modern world, Maslow sees the basis here for the immense popularity of communes and family therapy. These settings are ways to escape the isolation and loneliness that result from our failures to achieve love and belonging.

One of Allport's (1961) criteria of the "mature" personality, which he terms a warm relating of self to others, refers to the capability of displaying intimacy and love for a parent, child, spouse, or close friend. Here the person manifests an authentic oneness with the other and a deep concern for his/her welfare. Beyond one's intimate family and friends, there is an extension of warmth in the mature person to humankind at large, an understanding of the human condition and a kinship with all peoples.

To Fromm (1968), humans are aware of the growing loss of their ties with nature as well as with each other, feeling increasingly separate and alone. Fromm believes humans must pursue new ties with others to replace those that have been lost or can no longer be depended on. To counter the loss of communion with nature, he feels that health requires that we fulfill our need by a brotherliness with mankind, a sense of involvement, concern, and relatedness with the world. And with those with whom ties have been maintained or reestablished, humans must fulfill their other-oriented needs by being vitally concerned with their well-being as well as fostering their growth and productivity.

The pathological consequences of a failure to embrace the polarity criterion of "others" are seen most clearly in the personality disorders termed antisocial and narcissistic. Both personalities exhibit an imbalance in their replication strategy; in this case, however, there is a primary reliance on self rather than others. They have learned that reproductive success as well as maximum pleasure and minimum pain is achieved by turning exclusively to themselves. The tendency to focus on self follows two major lines of development.

In the narcissistic personality, development reflects the acquisition of a self-image of superior worth, learned largely in response to admiring and doting parents. Providing self-rewards is highly gratifying if one values oneself or possesses either a "real" or inflated sense of self-worth. Displaying manifest confidence, arrogance, and an exploitative egocentricity in social contexts, this self-orientation has been termed the passive–independent style in the theory, as the individual "already" has all that is important—him/herself. These individuals blithely assume that others will recognize their specialness. Hence they maintain an air of arrogant self-assurance and, without much thought or even conscious intent, benignly exploit others to their own advantage. Although the tributes of others are both welcome and encouraged, their air of snobbish and pretentious superiority requires little confirmation either through genuine accomplishment or social approval. Their sublime confidence that things will work out well provides them with little incentive to engage in the reciprocal give and take of social life. Those whom the theory characterizes as exhibiting the active-independent orientation resemble the outlook, temperament, and socially unacceptable behaviors of DSM antisocial personality disorder. They act to counter the expectation of pain at the hand of others; this is done by actively engaging in duplicitous or illegal behaviors in which they seek to exploit others for self-gain. Skeptical regarding the motives of others, they desire autonomy and wish revenge for what are felt as past injustices. Many are irresponsible and impulsive, actions they see as justified because they judge others to be unreliable and disloyal. Insensitivity and ruthlessness with others are the primary means they have learned to head off abuse and victimization.

Individual Propagation: Actualizing Self

The converse of progeny nurturance is not reproductive propagation but rather the lack of reproductive nurturance. Thus, to fail to love others constructively does not assure the actualization of one's potentials. Both may and should exist in normal/healthy individuals.

Carl Jung's (1961) concept of individuation shares important features with that of actualization in that any deterrent to becoming the individual one may have become would be detrimental to life. Any imposed "collective standard is a serious check to individuality," injurious to the vitality of the person, a form of "artificial stunting."

Perhaps it my own (T. M.) early mentor, Kurt Goldstein (1939, 1940), who first coined the concept under review with the self-actualization designation. As he phrased it, "There is only one motive by which human activity is set going: the tendency to actualize oneself" (1939, p. 196).

The early views of Jung and Goldstein have been enriched by later theorists, notably Fromm, Perls, Rogers, and Maslow.

Following the views of his forerunners, Maslow (1970) stated that self-actualization is the "supreme development" and use of all our abilities, ultimately becoming what we have the potential to become. Noting that self-actualists often require detachment and solitude, Maslow asserted that such persons are strongly self-centered and self-directed, make up their own mind and reach their own decisions, without the need to gain social approval.

In like manner, Rogers (1963) posited a single, overreaching motive for the normal/healthy person—maintaining, actualizing, and enhancing one's potential. The goal is not that of maintaining a homeostatic balance or a high degree of ease and comfort but, rather, to move forward in becoming what is intrinsic to self and to enhance further that which one has already become. Believing that humans have an innate urge to create, Rogers stated that the most creative product of all is one's own self.

Where do we see failures in the achievement of self-actualization, a giving up of self to gain the approbation of others? One personality disorder may be drawn upon to illustrate forms of self-denial.

Those with dependent personalities have learned that feeling good, secure, confident, and so on—that is, those feelings associated with pleasure or the avoidance of pain—is provided almost exclusively in their relationship with others. Behaviorally, these persons learn early that they themselves do not readily achieve rewarding experiences; the experiences are secured better by leaning on others. They learn not only to turn to others as their source of nurturance and security but to wait passively for others to take the initiative in providing safety and sustenance. Clinically, most are characterized as searching for relationships in which others will reliably furnish affection, protection, and leadership. Lacking both initiative and autonomy, they assume a dependent role in interpersonal relations, accepting what kindness and support they may find and willingly submitting to the wishes of others in order to maintain nurturance and security.

A THEORETICALLY DERIVED TAXONOMY OF CLINICAL PERSONALITY PATTERNS

This section turns to a formulation that employs a set of theoretical concepts for deducing and coordinating personality syndromes. The full scope of this schema has been published by one of us (T. M.) in earlier texts. First identified as a "biosocial-learning theory," it is now cast as an "evolutionary systems theory" (Millon, 1990) as a means of generating the established and recognized personality categories through formal deduction and to show their covariation with other mental disorders.

The three major polarities articulated in this chapter have forerunners in psychological theory that may be traced as far back as the early 1900s. A number of pre-World War I theorists proposed sets of polarities that were used as the foundation for constructing a variety of psychological processes. Although others formulated parallel schemas earlier than he, we illustrate these conceptions with reference to ideas presented by Freud. In 1915, Freud wrote what many consider to be among his most seminal papers, those on metapsychology and, in particular, the section entitled "The Instincts and their Vicissitudes." Speculations that foreshadowed several concepts developed more fully later, both by himself and his disciples, were presented in preliminary form in these papers. Particularly notable is a framework that Freud advanced as central to understanding the "mind"; unfortunately, he never developed his developed his basic system of interlocking polarities as a formal system for conceptualizing psychological patterns of normality and abnormality. These polarities were framed by him as follows:

Our mental life as a whole is governed by three polarities, namely the following antitheses:

Subject (ego)–Object (external world)
Pleasure–Pain
Active–Passive

The three polarities within the mind are connected with one another in various highly significant ways. (1925, pp. 76–77)

We may sum up by saying that the essential feature in the vicissitudes undergone by instincts is their subjection to the influences of the three great polarities that govern mental life. Of these three polarities we might describe that of activity–passivity as the biological, that of the ego–external world as the real, and finally that of pleasure–pain as the economic, respectively. (1915, p. 83)

In reviewing the many theories that have been formulated through the centuries, a reader cannot help but be impressed by both the number and diversity of concepts and types proposed. In fact, one might well be inclined to ask, first, where the catalog of possibilities will end and, second, whether these different frameworks overlap sufficiently to enable the identification of common trends or themes. In response to this second question, we find that theorists, going back to the turn of this century, began to propose a threefold group of dimensions that were used time and again as the raw materials for personality construction. Thus, Freud's "three polarities that govern all of mental life" were "discovered" by theorists both earlier and later than him—in France, Germany, Russia, and other European nations, as well as in the United States. The three dimensions of *active–passive, subject–object* or *self–other,* and *pleasure–pain* were identified either in part or in all their components by Heymans and Wiersma, McDougall, Meumann, Kollarits, Kahn, and others. For example, the subject–object distinction parallels Jung's introversive–extroversive dichotomy; active–passive is the same polarity utilized by Adler and is traceable directly to a major distinction drawn by Aristotle. Clearly, then, a review of the basic ingredients selected for building personality typologies since the turn of the century uncovers an unusual consensus. As noted previously, these same three dimensions were "discovered" once more by one of us (T. M.).

Despite the central role Freud assigned these polarities, he did not capitalize on them as a coordinated system for understanding normal and pathological patterns of human functioning. Although he failed to pursue their potentials, the ingredients Freud formulated for his tripartite polarity schema were drawn upon by his followers for many decades to come, seen prominently in the progressive development from instinct or "drive theory," where pleasure and pain were the major forces, to "ego psychology," where the apparatuses of "activity" and "passivity" were central constructs, and, most recently, to "self psychology" and "object relations" theory, where the self–other polarity is the key issue (Millon, 1990).

Forgotten as a metapsychological speculation by most, the scaffolding comprising these polarities was fashioned anew by the senior of us in the late-1960s (Millon, 1969). Unacquainted with Freud's proposals at the time and employing a biosocial-learning model, Millon constructed a framework similar to Freud's "great polarities that govern all of mental life." Phrased in the terminology of learning concepts, the model comprised three polar dimensions: positive versus negative reinforcement (pleasure–pain); self–other as reinforcement source; and the instrumental styles of active versus passive. At the time, Millon wrote,

> By framing our thinking in terms of what reinforcements the individual is seeking, whether he is looking to find them and how he performs, we may see more simply and more clearly the essential strategies which guide his coping behaviors. These reinforcements [relate to] whether he seeks primarily to achieve positive reinforcements (pleasure) or to avoid negative reinforcements (pain). . . .
>
> Some patients turn to others as their source of reinforcement, whereas some turn primarily to themselves. The distinction [is] between *others* and *self* as the primary reinforcement source.
>
> On what basis can a useful distinction be made among instrumental behaviors? A review of the literature suggests that the behavioral dimension of activity–passivity may prove useful. . . . Active patients [are] busily intent on controlling the circumstances of their environment. . . . Passive patients wait for the circumstances of their environment to take their course reacting to them only after they occur. (1969, pp. 193–195)

Do we find parallels within the disciplines of psychiatry and psychology that correspond to these broad evolutionary polarities?

In addition to the forerunners noted previously, there is a growing group of contemporary scholars whose work relates to these polar dimensions, albeit indirectly and partially. For example, a modern conception anchored to biological foundations has been developed by the distinguished British psychologist Jeffrey Gray (1964, 1973). A three-part model of temperament, matching the three-part polarity model in most regards, has been formulated by the American psychologist Arnold Buss and his associates (Buss & Plomin 1975, 1984). Circumplex formats based on factor analytic studies of mood and arousal that align well with the polarity schema have been published by Russell

(1980) and Tellegen (1985). Deriving inspiration from a sophisticated analysis of neuroanatomical substrates, the highly resourceful American psychiatrist Robert Cloninger (1986, 1987) has developed a threefold schema that is essentially coextensive with major elements of the model's three polarities. Less oriented to biological foundations, recent advances in both interpersonal and psychoanalytic theory have likewise exhibited strong parallels to one or more of the three polar dimensions. Millon presents a detailed review of these and other parallels in a recent book (Millon, 1990).

Using the threefold polarity framework as a foundation (Millon, 1969), a series of personality "coping strategies" were formulated that corresponded in significant detail to each of the "official" personality disorders that were subsequently introduced in DSM-III (American Psychiatric Association, 1980). Coping strategies were viewed as complex forms of instrumental behavior, that is, ways of achieving positive reinforcements and avoiding negative reinforcements. Employing a biosocial learning theory at the time, these strategies reflect what kinds of reinforcements individuals have learned to seek or avoid (pleasure–pain), where individuals look to obtain them (self–others), and how individuals have learned to behave in order to elicit or escape them (active–passive). Eight basic personality patterns and three severe variants were derived by combining the "nature" (positive or pleasure vs. negative or pain), the "source" (self vs. others), and the "instrumental behaviors" (active vs. passive) engaged in to achieve various reinforcements. Describing pathological strategies of behavior in reinforcement terms cast them in a somewhat different language than that utilized in the past.

A major distinction derived from the theoretical model is that people may be differentiated in terms of whether their primary source of reinforcement is within themselves or within others. This distinction corresponds to the "dependent" and "independent" patterns. Dependent personalities have learned that feeling good, secure, confident, and so on—that is, those feelings associated with pleasure or the avoidance of pain—are best provided by others. Behaviorally, these personalities display a strong need for external support and attention; should they be deprived of affection and nurturance, they will experience marked discomfort, if not sadness and anxiety. Independent personality patterns, in contrast, are characterized by a reliance on the self. These individuals have learned that they obtain maximum pleasure and minimum pain if they depend on themselves rather than others. In both dependent and independent patterns, individuals demonstrate a distinct preference as to whether to turn to others or to themselves to gain security and comfort.

Of course, such clear-cut commitments are not made by all personalities. Some, those whom we speak of as "ambivalent," remain unsure as to which way to turn; that is, they are in conflict regarding whether to depend on themselves for reinforcement or on others. Some of these patients vacillate between turning to others in an agreeable conformity one time, and turning to themselves in efforts at independence, the next. Other ambivalent personalities display overt dependence and compliance; beneath these outwardly conforming behaviors, however, are strong desires to assert independent and often hostile feelings and impulses.

Finally, certain patients are characterized by their diminished ability to experience both pain and pleasure; they have neither a normal need for pleasure nor a normal need to avoid punishment. Another group of patients are also distinguished by a diminished ability to feel pleasurable reinforcers, but they are notably sensitive to pain; life is experienced as possessing few gratifications but much anguish. Both groups share a deficit capacity to sense pleasurable reinforcers, although one may be hyperreactive to pain. Both of these were described as "detached" patterns; unable to experience rewards from themselves or from others, they drifted increasingly into socially isolated and self-alienated behaviors.

Though the taxonomy of personality patterns to follow is combinatorially generated, the personologic consequences of a single polar extreme should first be noted. A high standing on the pain pole—a position typically associated with a disposition to experience anxiety—will be used for this purpose. The upshot of this singular sensitivity takes different forms depending on a variety of factors that lead to the learning of diverse styles of anxiety coping. For example, "avoidants" learn to deal with their pervasively experienced anxiety sensitivity by removing themselves "across the board," that is, actively withdrawing from most relationships unless strong assurances of acceptance are given. The "compulsive," often equally prone to experience anxiety, has learned that there are sanctioned but limited spheres of acceptable conduct; the compulsive reduces anxiety by restricting activities only to those that are permitted by more powerful and potentially rejecting others, as well as to adhere carefully to rules so that unacceptable boundaries will not be transgressed. And the anxiety-prone "paranoid" has learned to neutralize pain by constructing a semidelusional pseudocommunity (Cameron, 1963), one in which environmental realities are transformed to make them more tolerable and less threatening, albeit not very successfully. In sum, a high standing at the pain pole leads not to one, but to diverse personality outcomes.

Another of the polar extremes will be selected to illustrate the diversity of forms that coping styles may take as a function of covariant polarity positions; in this case, reference will be made to a shared position on the passivity pole. Five primary Axis II disorders demonstrate the passive style, but their passivity derives from and is expressed in appreciably different ways that reflect disparate polarity combinations. "Schizoids," for example, are passive as a result of their relative incapacity to experience pleasure and pain; without the rewards these emotional valences normally activate, they will be devoid of the drive to acquire rewards, leading them to become rather indifferent and passive observers. "Dependents" typically are average on the pleasure and pain polarity, yet they are usually no less passive than schizoids. Strongly oriented to "others," they are notably weak with regard to "self." Passivity for them stems from deficits in self-confidence and competence, leading to deficits in initiative and autonomous skills, as well as a tendency to wait passively while others assume leadership and guide them. Passivity among "compulsives" stems from their fear of acting independently, resulting from intrapsychic resolutions they have made to quell hidden thoughts and emotions generated by their intense self–other ambivalence. Dreading the possibility of making mistakes or engaging in disapproved behaviors, they become indecisive, immobilized, restrained, and passive. High on pain, and low on both pleasure and self, the "self-defeating" personalities operate on the assumption that they dare not expect, nor do they deserve to have, life go their way; giving up any efforts to achieve a life that accords with their "true" desires, they passively submit to others' wishes, acquiescently accepting their fate. Finally, "narcissists," especially high on self and low on others, benignly assume that "good things" will come their way with little or no effort on their part; this passive exploitation of others is a consequence of the unexplored confidence that underlies their self-centered presumptions.

To turn to slightly more complex cases, there are individuals with appreciably different personality disorders who are often characterized by highly similar clinical features. To illustrate: to be correctly judged as "humorless and emotionally restricted" may be the result of diverse polarity combinations. "Schizoids," as noted previously, are typically at the low end of both dimensions of the pleasure–pain bipolarity, experiencing little joy, sadness, or anger, they are quite humorless and though not restricted emotionally, do lack emotional expressiveness and spontaneity. By contrast, "avoidants" are notably high at the pain polar extreme; whatever their other traits may be, they are disposed to chance neither interpersonal humor nor an emotional openness. Finally, the self–other conflicted "compulsive" has learned to deny "self" expression as a means of assuring the approval of others; rarely will the compulsive permit his/her guard down, lest any true "oppositional" feelings be betrayed; a compulsive rarely is relaxed sufficiently to engage in easy humor, nor willing to expose any contained emotions. All three personalities are humorless and emotionally restricted but from rather different polarity combinations.

The seeming theoretical fertility of the polarities secures but a first step toward a systematic personality nosology. Convincing professionals of the validity of the schema requires detailed explications, on the one hand, and unequivocal evidence of utility, on the other. We must not only clarify what is meant by each term comprising the polarities— for example, identify or illustrate their empirical referents—but also specify ways in which they combine and manifest themselves clinically. The following paragraphs are addressed to this end. Specifically, each of the DSM disorders will be described and, in part, interpreted in terms of the polarity model.

Schizoid Personalities

On what basis can pathology in the level or capacity of either the pain and pleasure polarities be seen as relevant to personality disorders? Several possibilities present themselves. Schizoid patients are those in whom both polarity systems are deficient, that is, they lack the capacity, relatively speaking, to experience life's events either as painful or pleasurable. They tend to be apathetic, listless, distant, and asocial. Affectionate needs and emotional feelings are minimal, and the individual functions as a passive observer detached from the rewards and affections as well as from the demands of human relationships. Schizoid patients who are characterized by a diminished capacity to experience *both* pleasure and pain seem neither interested in personal enjoyment or social satisfaction, nor do they evidence much discomfort with personal difficulties or social discord. Deficits such as these across the entire pleasure–pain polarity underlie what is termed the "passive-detached" style.

Aspects of the developmental background and clinical features of these personalities may provide the reader with a sense of how abstract concepts such as pain and pleasure can be conceived as relevant etiological attributes. Schizoid patients neither strive for rewards nor seek to avoid punishment (relatively speaking). Deficiencies such as these may arise from several etiological sources. Some may lack the constitutional makeup requisite for seeking, sensing, or discriminating pleasurable or painful events. Others may have been deprived of the stimulus nourishment necessary for the maturation of motivational or emotional capacities. A third group may have been exposed to irrational and confusing family communications or to contradictory patterns of learning, both of which may result in cognitive perplexities or motivational apathies. Whatever the complex of causes may have been, schizoid patients acquire little or no body of either pleasurable or painful objects to motivate their behaviors.

Avoidant Personalities

The second clinically meaningful combination based on problems in the pleasure–pain polarity comprises patients with a diminished ability to experience pleasure but with a foreboding anticipation and responsiveness to psychic pain. To them, life is vexatious, possessing few rewards and much anxiety. This imbalance of heightened anxious pain and diminished pleasure lies at the heart of the DSM avoidant personality. Schizoids, avoidants, and depressives share a minimal sense of joy and contentment; only one, the avoidant, is disposed also to feel apprehensively tormented. The theory groups the first two personalities as detached patterns, the former, schizoid, noted as the passive–detached, the latter, avoidant, as the active–detached. Unable to experience pleasures either from self or others, both detached types tend to drift into isolating circumstances and self-alienated behaviors.

Avoidants experience few pleasures in life, but they do expect and react strongly to discomfort and punishment. Perhaps their neurological or physiochemical makeup may dispose them maximally to "foresee" and overrespond to psychic pain; for example, centers of the limbic system may be unequally dense or may be disadvantageously wired to other brain regions. Equally possible, if not more probable, a history of harsh and rejecting early experiences may have oversensitized these individuals to anticipate anxiety and alarm. Exposed repeatedly to such events, avoidants may have learned not only to expect omnipresent threat, but to devise a widespread protective strategy of avoidance to minimize its recurrence. Experientially, avoidants often have been deprived of relationships that strengthen their feelings of competence and self-worth. Having a low self-opinion complicates matters further; they cannot turn to themselves as a worthy source of fantasized positive reinforcement. Ultimately, they learn to seek rewards neither from themselves nor from others. Many seem perpetually "on guard," oriented solely to the avoidance of painful rejection and humiliation, ever-ready to distance themselves from a disquieting anticipation of life's negatively reinforcing experiences. Reflecting fear and mistrust of others, they maintain a constant vigil lest their longing for affection result in a repetition of the pain they previously experienced with others. Despite desires to relate, they have learned that it is best to deny these feelings and maintain their interpersonal distance.

Depressive Personalities

Akin to both the schizoid and avoidant personalities, as well as the soon-to-be discussed self-defeating (masochistic) type, is the newly introduced DSM depressive personality disorder. All four disorders share the inability to experience pleasure. Avoidants, depressives, and self-defeating types also share an overreactivity to pain. The avoidant, however, actively eschews pain, anticipates it, and, as best as possible, attempts to distance from its occurrence. Avoidant personalities display a vigorous effort to elude and circumvent the pain they envisage, resulting in their perennial state of anguished expectation. By contrast, the depressive's difficulty reflects hopeless resignation, a giving up, a sense that something of significance has been lost and can no longer be retrieved. Depressives are passive rather than active, accepting as inevitable the pain they have experienced, torturing themselves for their deficiencies and failures, and exhibiting the mood and outlook of those who have been vanquished and humbled. Conquered by circumstance and subdued in their abilities to remedy matters, they will quietly or agitatedly deplore what has happened to them, but will, in contrast to the avoidant, neither try to undo, redeem, or overcome it, nor to take action to prevent its repetition. Theirs is a somber helplessness, a gloomy pessimism, one unrelieved by an occasional redemptive effort or a momentarily bright future prospect. (Not to be overlooked among depressive personalities is the likelihood of a biological vulnerability to one or the other mood disorders. The interplay of such biogenic factors throughout development is a complex one whose course should be explored.) In contrast to the self-defeating personalities, depressive personalities usually show a sluggish torpor, insomnia or hypersomnia, persistent feelings of subjective sadness, as well as a turning inward of acts of self-torture, including recurrent thoughts of death or suicidal ideation. Those who are self-defeating will put themselves repeatedly in abject and compromising relationships, which depressives do not. Similarly, self-defeating personalities appear to provoke or recreate experiences of pain and disappointment, seemingly gaining a measure of comfort in their usually discomforting circumstances.

Self-Defeating (Masochistic) Personalities

This disorder stems largely from a reversal of the pain–pleasure polarity. These persons interpret events and engage in relationships in a manner that is not only at variance with this deeply rooted polarity but is contrary to the associations these life-promoting emotions usually acquire through learning. To the self-defeating personality, pain may be a preferred experience, tolerantly accepted if not encouraged in intimate relationships. It is often intensified by purposeful self-denial and blame acceptance may be aggravated, and by acts that engender difficulties, as well as by thoughts that exaggerate past misfortunes and anticipate future ones. Relating to others in an obsequious and self-sacrificing manner, these persons allow, if not encourage others to exploit or take advantage of them. Focusing on their very worst features, many assert that they deserve being shamed and humbled. To compound their pain and anguish, they actively and repetitively recall their past misfortunes as well as transform otherwise fortunate circumstances into problematic outcomes. Typically acting in an unpresuming and self-effacing way, they often intensify their deficits and place themselves in an inferior light or abject position.

The background of the self-defeating personality has been a topic of considerable speculation for decades, most prominently in the psychoanalytic literature on masochism. This chapter is not the place to summarize this body of hypotheses. The role of biological anomalies in the inherent wiring of these personalities is a domain of speculation that cannot be totally dismissed, but it does stretch imagination beyond the usual range of plausibility. Not so incredulous are hypotheses of a social-learning or developmental nature. For example, by virtue of circumstantial association, elements normally evocative of pain and pleasure could very well become transposed or interconnected; thus, among future self-defeatists the pain of physical brutality or the anguish of verbal conflict may have been followed repetitively by love and intimacy, leading to the learned assumption that fractious provocations are a necessary precursor to ultimate acceptance and tenderness. In a more complicated sequence, guilt absolution may have been successfully achieved by repeated self-abasement acts that, generalized over time into a broad pattern of self-denial and servility, preventively "undo" negative future consequences.

Aggressive (Sadistic) Personalities

There are other patients in which the usual properties associated with pain and pleasure are conflicted or reversed. As with the self-defeating, these patients not only seek or create objectively "painful" events, but experience them as "pleasurable." This second variant of pain–pleasure reversal, what we term the "aggressive" personality (DSM-III-R sadistic, deleted from DSM-IV), considers pain (stress, fear, cruelty) rather than pleasure to be the preferred mode of relating to others; in contrast to the self-defeating, this individual assumes an active role in controlling, dominating, and abusing others. Acts that humiliate, demean, if not brutalize, are experienced as pleasurable. We have grouped the self-defeating and aggressive personalities under the label "discordant patterns" to reflect, on the one hand, the dissonant structure of their pain–pleasure systems and, on the other, the conflictive character of their interpersonal relations. The self-defeating type, being on the receiving end of these fractious relationships, is referred to as the "passive–discordant," whereas the latter, more expressive aggressive type, is termed the "active-discordant."

Depending on social class and other moderating factors, they may parallel the clinical features of what is known in the psychoanalytic literature as the sadistic character. They are generally hostile, pervasively combative, and appear indifferent to, if not pleased, by the destructive consequences of their contentious, if not abusive and brutal behaviors. Although many cloak their more malicious and power-oriented tendencies in publicly approved roles and vocations, they give themselves away in their dominating, antagonistic, and frequent persecutory actions. As is all too well known, competitive ambition and social brutality may readily be reinforced as a means to security, status, and pleasure in our society by demonstrably resulting in personal achievement and dominance over others.

Dependent Personalities

Following the polarity model, one must ask whether particular clinical consequences occur among individuals who are markedly imbalanced by virtue of turning almost exclusively either toward others or toward themselves as a means of experiencing pleasure and avoiding pain. Such persons differ from the two detached and the two discordant types discussed previously; for example, neither detached type experiences pleasure from self or others. Personalities whose difficulties are traceable to the pathology of choosing one or the other polar end of the self–other dimension do experience both pain and pleasure, and do experience them in a consonant, nonreversed manner; their pathology arises from the fact that they are tied almost exclusively either to others or to themselves as the source of these experiences. The distinction between these two contrasting reproductive strategies underlies what is termed the "dependent" and "independent" personality orientations. In later paragraphs we describe the ambivalent orientation, those who are in conflict between turning toward self (maximizing propagation) or toward others (maximizing nurturance) as their replication styles. For the present, however, those termed as the dependent types will be described clinically.

Those with a dependency pathology have learned that feeling good, secure, confident, and so on—that is, those feelings associated with pleasure or the avoidance of pain—is provided almost exclusively in their relationship with others. Behaviorally, these persons display a strong need for external support and attention; should they be deprived of affection and nurturance, they will experience marked discomfort, if not sadness and anxiety. Any number of early experiences may set the stage for this dependency imbalance. In the dependent personality, we often see individuals who have been exposed to an overprotective training regimen and who thereby fail to acquire competencies for autonomy and initiative; experiencing peer failures and low self-esteem leads them to forego attempts at self-assertion and self-gratification. They learn early that rewarding experiences are not readily achieved by themselves but are secured better by leaning on others. They learn not only to turn to others as their source of nurturance and security but to wait *passively* for others to take the initiative in providing safety and sustenance. Clinically, most are characterized by a search for relationships in which others will reliably furnish affection, protection, and leadership. Lacking both initiative and autonomy, they assume a passive role in interpersonal relationships, accepting what kindness and support they may find and willingly submitting to the wishes of others in order to maintain nurturance and security.

Histrionic Personalities

Also turning to others as their primary strategy are a group of personalities that take an "active" dependency stance. They achieve their goal of maximizing protection, nurturance, and reproductive success by engaging busily in a series of manipulative, seductive, gregarious, and attention-getting maneuvers. This active dependency *imbalance* in particular characterizes the behavior of the DSM histrionic personality.

Although histrionics turn toward others to no less extent than do passive-dependents, these individuals appear on the surface to be quite dissimilar from their passive counterparts; this difference in overt style owes to the active-dependent's facile and enterprising manipulation of events, which maximizes the receipt of attention and favors as well as avoids social disinterest and disapproval. These patients often show an insatiable, if not indiscriminate search for stimulation and affection. Their clever and often artful social behaviors give the appearance of an inner confidence and independent self-assurance; beneath this guise, however, lies a fear of genuine autonomy and a need for repeated signs of acceptance and approval. Tribute and affection must constantly be replenished and are sought from every interpersonal source in most social contexts.

Narcissistic Personalities

Patients falling into the "independent" personality pattern also exhibit an *imbalance* in their replication strategy; in this case, however, there is a primary reliance on self rather than others. These individuals have learned that reproductive success, as well as maximum pleasure and minimum pain, are achieved by turning exclusively to themselves. The tendency to focus on self follows two major lines of development. In the first, the narcissistic personality, it reflects the acquisition of a self-image of superior worth learned largely in response to admiring and doting parents. Providing self-rewards are highly gratifying if one values oneself or possesses either a real or inflated sense of self-worth. Displaying manifest confidence, arrogance, and an exploitive egocentricity in social contexts, this self-orientation is termed the "passive–independent'" style in the theory, since the individual "already" has all that is important—him/herself.

Narcissistic individuals are noted by their egotistical self-involvement, experiencing primary pleasure simply by passively being or attending to themselves. Early experience has taught them to overvalue their self-worth; this confidence and superiority, perhaps founded on false premises, may be unsustainable by real or mature achievements. Nevertheless, they blithely assume that others will recognize their specialness. Hence, they maintain an air of arrogant self-assurance and without much thought or even conscious intent, they benignly exploit others to their own advantage. Although the tributes of others are both welcome and encouraged, their air of snobbish and pretentious superiority requires little confirmation either through genuine accomplishment or social approval and provides them with little incentive to engage in the reciprocal give and take of social life.

Antisocial Personalities

Those whom we characterize as exhibiting the active–independent orientation resemble the outlook, temperament, and socially unacceptable behaviors of the DSM antisocial personality disorder. They act to counter the expectation of pain at the hand of others; this is done by actively engaging in duplicitous or illegal behaviors in which they seek to exploit others for self-gain. Skeptical when regarding the motives of others, they desire autonomy, and wish revenge for what are felt as past injustices. Many are irresponsible and impulsive, actions they see as justified because they judge others to be unreliable and disloyal. Insensitivity and ruthlessness with others are the primary means they have learned to head off abuse and victimization.

In contrast to the narcissistic personality, this second pattern of self-orientation develops as a form of protection and counteraction. These types turn to themselves, first to avoid the depredation they anticipate and, second, to compensate by furnishing self-generated rewards in their stead. Learning that they cannot depend on others, these patients counterbalance this loss not only by trusting themselves alone but also by actively seeking retribution for what they see as past humiliations. Turning to self and seeking actively to gain strength, power, and revenge, they act irresponsibly, exploiting and usurping what others possess as sweet reprisal. Their security is never fully "assured," even when they have aggrandized themselves beyond their lesser origins.

Negativistic (Passive—Aggressive) Personalities

In both dependent and independent orientations, patients demonstrate pathology in that the strategy of being oriented either toward others or toward themselves is unbalanced, grossly one-sided. An imbalance toward self or other is not the only pattern seen in this polarity. "Normal" individuals, of course, exhibit a comfortable intermediary position within the bipolarities of self and others. Certain pathological personalities, those whom we shall speak of as "ambivalent," also are oriented both toward self and others, but they are in intense conflict between one or the other. A number of these patients, those represented in the DSM negativistic personality, vacillate between others and self, behaving obediently one time and reacting defiantly the next. Feeling intensely, yet unable to resolve their ambivalence, they weave an erratic course from voicing their self-depreciation and guilt for failing to meet the expectations of others to expressing stubborn negativism and resistance over having submitted to the wishes of others rather than their own. Patients whose conflicts are overt, worn on their sleeves, so to speak, are characterized in the theory as actively ambivalent, a richer and more varied lot than the early DSM portrayals of the passive–aggressive.

The struggle between following the rewards offered by others as opposed to those desired by self represents a conflict similar to those of the passive–ambivalent (obsessive–compulsives); however, the conflicts of actively ambivalent personalities remain close to consciousness and intrude into everyday life. These patients get themselves into end-

less wrangles and disappointments as they fluctuate between deference and obedience one time, and defiance and aggressive negativism
the next. Their behavior displays an erratic pattern of explosive anger
or stubbornness intermingled with periods of guilt and shame.

Obsessive–Compulsive Personalities

Another major conflicted pattern, the DSM obsessive–compulsive personality disorder, displays a picture of distinct other-directedness, a
consistency in social compliance and interpersonal respect: their histories usually indicate their having been subjected to constraint and
discipline, but only when they transgressed parental strictures and expectations. Beneath the conforming other-oriented veneer they exhibit
are intense desires to rebel and assert their own self-oriented feelings
and impulses. They are trapped in an ambivalence to avoid intimida-
tion and punishment, having learned to deny the validity of their own
wishes and emotions and, in their stead, adopting as "true" the values
and precepts set forth by others. The disparity they sense between their
own urges and the behaviors they must display to avoid condemna-
tion often leads to omnipresent physical tensions and rigid psychological controls.

Etiologically, obsessive–compulsives are likely to have been intimi-
dated and coerced into accepting standards imposed on them by others.
As noted, their prudent, controlled, and perfectionistic ways derive
from a conflict between hostility toward others and a fear of social disapproval. They resolve this ambivalence not only by suppressing
resentment but by overconforming and by placing high demands on
both themselves and others. Their disciplined self-restraint serves to
control intense, though hidden oppositional and self-centered feelings,
resulting in their characteristic hesitation, doubt, passivity, and public compliance. Behind their front of propriety and restraint lurks intense angry feelings that occasionally break through their controls.

A visual schema illustrating the coordination of the personality patterns with their evolutionary polarities is portrayed in Table 5.1

LEVELS OF PERSONALITY SEVERITY

How are severity levels gauged; that is, what criteria are employed
to determine whether one personality disorder is typically more severe than another? Two classification systems in current use pay special attention to criteria differentiating personality disorders along the
dimension of severity, those of Kernberg (1967) and of Millon (1969;

TABLE 5.1. Polarity Model and Its Personality Disorder Derivatives

	Existential aims		Replication strategy		
	Life enhancement	Life preservation	Reproductive propagation		Reproductive nurturance
Polarity	Pleasure–Pain		Self–Other		
Deficiency, imbalance, or conflict	Pleasure – Pain +	Pain ↔ pleasure (reversal)	Self – Other +	Self + Other –	Other ↔ self (reversal)
Adaptation mode	DSM personality disorder				
Passive: Accommodation	Schizoid	Self-defeating (masochistic)	Dependent	Narcissistic	Obsessive–compulsive
	Depressive				
Active: Modification	Avoidant	Aggressive (sadistic)	Histrionic	Antisocial	Negativistic (passive–aggressive)
Dysfunctional	Schizotypal	Borderline/paranoid	Borderline	Paranoid	Borderline/paranoid

Millon & Davis, 1995). A direct comparison is not feasible, since the character types presented by Kernberg only marginally correspond to the DSM personality disorders. Nevertheless, it will be useful to put aside DSM comparability and consider the conceptual distinctions that differentiate Kernberg's views from our own. The major distinction is not found in the clinical signs included to gauge severity but, rather, in the signs given emphasis. For Kernberg, primary attention is given to the *internal* structural characteristics of the personality, whereas for the author, the *external* social system and interpersonal dynamics are given a status equal that of internal organization.

A Systems Perspective on Severity

The construct of a borderline personality organization as a level or quantitative degree of psychic cohesion that cuts across all personality patterns is a valid one. The truth of this proposition is seen by relating the borderline personality back to the root metaphor of the personality construct, integration. Whereas the moderately severe personality patterns are predominately differentiated according to their stylistic qualities, the striking feature of the borderline personality, when the label is justified, is its level of disintegration. In this way, the borderline is the obverse of the personality construct and is inherently disjoined and dysregulated rather than cohesive and regulated. Accordingly, the borderline personality resembles more a hodge-podge of primitive cognitive–affective–behavioral modules, any one of which may assume control of the individual on contextual prompting, given the borderline's absence of higher-order controls. Kernberg's language, of course, is focused dynamically on ''nonspecific manifestations of ego weakness,'' as illustrated in shifts toward primary process thinking, defensive operations characterized as ''splitting,'' increasingly primitive idealizations, and early forms of projection and omnipotence. As illustrated amply in this chapter, our own view is that personality is a multireferential construct anchored to multiple personologic domains.

In addition, our own stress is on a systems perspective that interprets the internal structure as being functional or dysfunctional depending on its efficacy and stability within the context of interpersonal, familial, and other social dynamics. Thus, there exist such severity criteria as deficits in social competence, checkered personal relationships, digressions from early aspirations, and repetitive interpersonal quandaries and disappointments. From this view, severity is conceived as a person–field interaction that includes not only intrapsychic dynamics but interpersonal dynamics as well. Although Kernberg recognizes the importance of internalized object relations, the authors assign them a major role by stressing both "internalized" past and contemporary "real" social relationships. In this way, the boundaries of both structure and dynamics are expanded such that internal structural features are placed within a context or system of external social dynamics, which are, consistent with evolutionary notions, considered in terms of their adaptability for the individual organism.

A positive consequence of broadening the criteria of severity is that personality pathology need no longer be traced exclusively to intrapsychic origins in conflict and defense. By enlarging our vista so as to include interpersonal efficacy within a social context, our reference base for conceptualizing disordered personality has been expanded. A shift from the view that all pathogenic sources derive from internal conflicts is consistent with Fenichel's (1945) notion of "sublimation" character types and reinforces the ego analysts' assertion of conflict-free spheres of development and learning. No longer restricted by the limiting intrapsychic outlook, personality disorders can now be conceived best as any behavior pattern that is consistently inappropriate, maladaptive, or deficient in the social and familial system within which the individual operates. And, in accord with this broader systems perspective, several personality syndromes described by the authors and formulated for DSM-III are recognized as having developed "conflict-free"—that is, they are products of inadequate or misguided learning; others, of course, are conceived more traditionally as primarily "reactive"—that is, they are consequences of conflict resolutions. For example, some dependent personalities unfold in large measure as a result of simple parental overprotection and insufficiently learned autonomous behaviors and not from instinctual conflicts and regressive adaptations.

The logic for broadening the criteria of severity to include the interplay of both individual and social systems seems especially appropriate when we consider personality syndromes. Not only do personality traits express themselves primarily within group and familial environments, but the patient's style of communication, interpersonal competency, and social skill will, in great measure, elicit reactions that feed back to shape the future course of whatever impairments the person may already have. Thus, the behavior and attitudes that individuals exhibit with others will evoke reciprocal reactions that influence whether their problems will improve, stabilize, or intensify. Internal organization or structure is significant, of course, but the character or style of relating interpersonally may have as much to do with whether the sequence of social dynamics will prove rewarding or destructive. It is not only the structural ego capacity, therefore, but also the particular features of social and familial behavior that will dispose the patient to relate to others in a manner that will prove increasingly adaptive or maladaptive. Utilizing a systems perspective that includes the interplay of both internal and external dynamics groups the personality disorders of DSM-IV into three broad categories.

The first group includes the dependent, histrionic, narcissistic, and antisocial personality disorders. These four personality patterns are either dependent or independent in their style of interpersonal functioning. Their intrapsychic structures enable them to conceive of themselves and to deal with others in a relatively coherent, "nonsplit," or nonconflictful manner—that is, in a reasonably consistent and focused rather than a diffused or divided way. Moreover, because the needs and traits that underlie their coping styles dispose them to seek out others and to relate socially, they are able either to adapt to or to control their interpersonal environment so as to be sustained and nourished emotionally and thereby maintain their psychic cohesion.

The second group, that viewed at a midlevel of personality severity, includes the compulsive, negativistic (passive–aggressive), aggressive (sadistic), self-defeating (masochistic), depressive, schizoid, and avoidant personality disorders. These represent a lower level of functioning than the first group for several reasons. In the two ambivalent types, the compulsive and negativistic personalities, there is a split within both their interpersonal and their intrapsychic orientations; they are unable to find a coherent or consistent direction to focus either their personal relationships or their defensive operations. They are in conflict, split between assuming an independent or dependent stance; hence, they often undo or reverse their social behaviors and frequently feel internally divided. The second group of this midlevel set, the two detached types—the schizoid and avoidant—as well as the depressive personality are judged at a moderate level of severity because they are or feel characteristically isolated or estranged from external support systems. As a consequence, they are likely to have few subliminatory channels and fewer still interpersonal sources of nurturance and stability, the lack of which will dispose them to increasingly dysphoric moods, autistic preoccupations, and behavioral regressions.

Structurally Defective Personality Pathologies

The key dimensions of the polarity model were both useful and feasible in making the clinical features of the basic patterns of personality functioning more explicit, from the actively pain-sensitive avoidant to the passively self-centered narcissist, from the actively other-oriented histrionic to the self–other conflicted negativistic. These distinctions were made on the basis of coupling contents, in the form of polarities, to boundaries derived from the formal characteristics of systems functioning—the system itself, the system embedded in its environment, and the system as propagating itself across time—thus attaining both content and structural validity within the integrative world view.

The third group consists of three personality syndromes which, though not derived directly from the polarity framework (pain–pleasure, active–passive, self–other) of the evolutionary model, are no less theoretically based, because they follow from the integrative root-metaphor itself. We speak of the borderline, the paranoid, and the schizotypal. In each of these patterns, the part–whole relationships necessary for the functioning of an integrative totality are pathological in some way (see Figure 5.2).

Borderline Personalities

Although the borderline personality has been referred to previously, it may be helpful to discuss the construct here in order to describe it further. The cardinal feature of this pattern is that its hierarchical control structures are poorly differentiated and modular rather than integrated. In the relative absence of higher self-regulatory processes wrought by a consistent view of the world and self, there is intense lability between competing cognitive–affective–behavioral structures as one and then another co-opts control of the personality system on the basis of fleeting and idiosyncratic associations with the current environment.

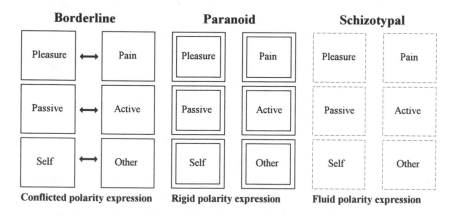

FIGURE 5.2. Structurally severe personality disorders.

Some personality patterns tend to possess lower levels of integration and confused self-regulation than others. Accordingly, this personality pattern corresponds to the theory's emotionally dysfunctional and maladaptively ambivalent polarity orientation. Conflicts exist across the board, between pleasure and pain, active and passive, and self and other. They seem unable to take a consistent, neutral, or balanced position among these polar extremes, tending to fluctuate from one end to the other. Each of these persons experiences intense endogenous moods, with recurring periods of dejection and apathy, often interspersed with spells of anger, anxiety, or euphoria. Among the features that distinguish them from their less severe personality covariants is the dysregulation of their affects, seen most clearly in the instability and lability of their moods. Additionally, many express, if not enact, recurring self-mutilating and suicidal thoughts. Some appear overly preoccupied with securing affection. Many have difficulty maintaining a consistent sense of identity. Interpersonally, most display a cognitive–affective ambivalence, evident in simultaneous feelings of rage, love, and guilt toward others. These features represent a low level of structural cohesion in their psychic organization. For many there is a split within both their interpersonal and their intrapsychic orientations. Unable to build inner structural coherence, they are unable to maintain a nonconflictual direction in their personal relationships, or a consistency in their defensive operations. There are fundamental intrapsychic dissensions, core splits between taking an independent *or* taking a dependent stance, between acting out impulsively *or* withdrawing into passive disengagement, following the wishes of others or damning them and doing the opposite of what they wish. They repeatedly undo or reverse the actions they previously took, thereby embedding further the reality of being internally divided.

Schizotypal Personalities

This personality disorder represents a cognitively dysfunctional and maladaptively detached orientation in the polarity theory. Schizotypal personalities experience minimal pleasure, have difficulty consistently differentiating between self and other strategies, as well as active and passive modes of adaptation. Most prefer social isolation with minimal personal attachments and obligations. Inclined to be either autistic or confused cognitively, they think tangentially and often appear self-absorbed and ruminative. Behavioral eccentricities are notable and the individual is often perceived by others as strange or different. Depending on whether their pattern is basically more active or more passive, there will be either an anxious wariness and hypersensitivity or an emotional flattening and deficiency of affect. Estranged from external support systems, they are likely to have few subliminatory channels and fewer still sources for emotional nurturance and cognitive stability, the lack of which disposes them to social regressions and autistic preoccupations.

Paranoid Personalities

Here are seen a vigilant mistrust of others and an edgy defensiveness against anticipated criticism and deception. Driven by a high sensitivity to pain (rejection–humiliation) and oriented strongly to the self polarity, these patients exhibit a touchy irritability, a need to assert themselves, not necessarily in action, but in an inner world of self-determined beliefs and assumptions. They are "prepared" to provoke social conflicts and fractious circumstances as a means of gratifying their confused mix of pain–sensitivity and self-assertion. The interplay of these polarities perpetuates their pathology: not only is it sustained, but it is increased as in a vicious circle. There is an ever-present abrasive irritability and a tendency to precipitate exasperation and anger in others. Expressed often is a fear of losing self-autonomy, leading the patient to vigorously resist external influence and control. Whereas borderline patterns are noted by the instability of their polarity positions, paranoids are distinctive by virtue of the immutability and inflexibility of their respective positions.

These severe dysfunctional levels differ from the basic patterns by several criteria, notably deficits in social competence and frequent (but readily reversible) psychotic episodes. Moreover, they almost invariably coexist with and are more intense variants of the basic eleven personality disorders discussed in the previous pages—for example, schizotypals tend to exhibit more problematic features also seen among schizoids and/or avoidants. Less integrated in terms of their personality organization and less effective in coping than their milder counterparts, they are especially vulnerable to decompensate when faced with the everyday strains of life. All three of the most severe disorders are adaptively problematic, difficult to relate to socially, and often isolated, hostile, or confused: Hence, they are not likely to elicit the interpersonal support that could bolster their flagging defenses and orient them to a more effective and satisfying lifestyle. Moreover, a clear breakdown in the cohesion of personality organization is seen in the first two of these disorders: The converse is evident in the third, where there is an overly rigid and narrow focus to the personality structure. In the former pair, there has been a dissolution or diffusion of ego capacities; in the latter pattern, there is an inelasticity and constriction of personality, giving rise to a fragility and inadaptability of adaptive functions.

PERSONOLOGIC ASSESSMENT

Personality may be usefully conceptualized and measured with a variety of approaches and methodologies. Six instruments—the Millon Clinical Multiaxial Inventory (MCMI), the Millon Adolescent Clinical Inventory (MACI), the Millon Adolescent Personality Inventory (MAPI), the Millon Behavioral Health Inventory (MBHI), the Millon Personality Diagnostic Checklist (MPDC), and the Millon Index of Personality Styles (MIPS)—have been created to operationalize the constructs of the theoretical model presented herein. These instruments vary according to their intended populations, and all but one, the MPDC, follow the self-report format. Three of these are briefly discussed, the MCMI, the MPDC, and the MIPS. First, however, a few philosophically oriented notations.

Paradoxically, the methodology through which assessment instruments are created is in spirit opposed to the goal that directs their use. In tapping dimensions of individual differences, we abstract from persons only those dimensions we take as being common to all. Yet in using our instruments, we seek to build up again as a reconstructive process the very individuality we had previously distilled, so that the circle completes itself as a kind of synthesis: From rich idiographic individuality, to nomothetic commonalities, and finally, to what might be called nomothetic individuality. Apparently, the assessment is itself somewhat of a self-regulatory process, the validity of which depends on our first giving up the person in order to ultimately understand him/her.

Integrative assessment is concerned with the last two links of this process. The fractionated person, the person who has been dispersed across scales and instruments must be put back together again as the organic whole he/she once was. How is such a venture to be achieved? First and foremost, we argue that assessment is an eminently theoretical process, indeed, an evolutionary process that requires a weighing of this and a disqualifying of that across the idiosyncrasies and commonalities of methods and data sources through multiple iterations of hypothesis generation and testing. Much as we have sought an integrative theory of personality and psychopathology, the end goal of the assessment process is *the* theory of the patient. Ideally, every loose end should be tied up in a theory, a theory so compelling one gets the feeling that things could not be otherwise than the assessment supposes them to be. Only such an eminently integrative theory allows the referral question to be addressed with confident words and concrete suggestions.

Implicit in this description is the idea that not all patients with the same personality diagnosis should be viewed as possessing the same problem. Platitudinous though this statement may be, care must be taken not to force patients into the procrustean beds of our theoretical models and nosological entities. Whether they are derived from mathematical analyses, clinical observations, or a systematic theory, all taxonomies are essentially composed of prototypal classes, classes that may cause clinicians to exaggerate within-group homogeneity (Cantor & Genero, 1986). Instead, clinical categories must be conceived as flexible and dimensionally quantitative, permitting the full and distinctive configuration of characteristics of patients to be displayed (Millon, 1987a). The multiaxial schema of the DSM structure is a step in the right direction: Its structural format encourages multidimensional and contextual considerations (Axes I, II, and IV) as well as multidiagnoses that approximate the natural heterogeneity of patients, such as portrayed in personality profiles.

To return to definitions offered at the beginning of this chapter, "personality" is a system with referents across multiple clinical domains. In attempting to arrive at a content-valid assessment of the patient, clinicians should beware of approaching these domains as concretized, independent entities. Rather, these domains are all part of a single, integrated whole. Nevertheless, although every domain is necessary in order to maintain functional–structural integrity of the organism, individuals differ with respect to the domains they enact most frequently, and even more so, diverge in which of the expressive variations of these functions they typically manifest. If personality is conceptualized as a system, we might say that the constraints (traits) on the states the system may assume (adaptive behaviors) inhere in different parts of the system for different individuals. In this sense, the goal of an assessment is to illuminate those constraints that perpetuate the system's narrow, rigid functioning and consequent adaptive inflexibility. Thus identified, the purpose of therapy should be to relax these constraints, allowing the system to assume a greater variety of states or adaptive behaviors across situations than before. Another way of saying this is by noting that each patient displays the durability and pervasiveness of his/her personality only in certain characteristics: That is, each possesses a limited number of attributes that are resistant to changing times and situational influences, whereas other attributes are readily modified. The features exhibiting this consistency and stability in one patient may not be the same features exhibited by others. These core qualities of persistence and extensiveness appear only in characteristics that have become crucial in maintaining the patient's polarity balance and functional style. As noted previously, the "interpersonal" attribute of significance for one patient is being totally other-oriented, never differing or having conflict (dependent); for another, it may be interpersonally critical to keep one's distance from people so as to avoid the pain of rejection or humiliation (avoidant); for a third, the influential interpersonal characteristic may be that of asserting one's will and inflicting pain on others (sadistic). Each personality disorder comprises a small and distinct group of primary attributes that persist over time and exhibit a high degree of consistency across situations (Mischel, 1984). These enduring (stable) and pervasive (consistent) characteristics or constraints are what we search for when "diagnose" personality.

Millon Personality Diagnostic Checklist: Clinical Assessment of Personality Disorders

Heterogeneous characteristics are especially problematical in classically structured syndromes, that is, those requiring singly necessary or jointly sufficient diagnostic criteria. Personality categories, by contrast, are composed intentionally in a heterogeneous manner, that is, they accept the legitimacy of syndromic diversity and overlap. Nevertheless, there is still need to reduce the "fuzziness" between boundaries so as to eliminate excessive numbers of unclassifiable and borderline cases, of which Axis II has been notoriously deficient. Consistent with the multidomain model put forward in this chapter, one step toward the goal of sharpening diagnostic discriminations is to spell out a distinctive criterion for every diagnostically relevant clinical attribute aligned with every personality pattern in a domain by pattern matrix. By composing a taxonomic schema that includes all relevant clinical attributes (e.g., behavior, affect, cognition), and specifies a defining feature on every attribute for each of the personality disorders, the proposed descriptions would be both fully comprehensive in their clinical scope and possess parallel and directly comparable criteria among all Axis II categories, thus optimizing the content and construct validity of the classification system.

The issue of construct validity requires a special note. Because the root metaphor of Axis II personality construct is organizational or integrative, the question of interest is: How do the characteristics or traits vary across the types or patterns? However, the format of the DSM model is listwise—each pattern is operationalized simply as a list of traits or characteristics. Clinicians, then, see not the intrinsic holism of each personality pattern but, instead, only a list of uncoordinated characteristics. Such a list encourages the view that personality patterns can be decomposed into atomistic units without any loss in their organizational quality. This diagnostic methodology checks the presence of certain parts without regard for the organization through which the parts derive their meaning, a procedure inconsistent with the epistemology of the personality construct. What is to be known is inconsistent with the means to knowing it. A traits-by-patterns table gives clinicians the kind of appreciation for the organizational integrity of each personality pattern impossible for a list to convey. A format of this nature will furnish logic, symmetry, and content validity to the DSM taxonomy. These two issues, content and organization, may be taken as critiques of the DSM-IV operationalization of the personality disorders.

As a system, personality may be assessed and quantified in any of several domains. Because the emphasis of this chapter is on integrative foundations, multiple criteria were used to select and develop the domains that comprise the current schema: (1) that each domain be varied in the features its embodies; that is, not be limited just to behaviors or cognitions, but to encompass a full range of personality-relevant characteristics; (2) that it parallel, if not correspond, to many of our profession's current traditions and therapeutic modalities (e.g., self-oriented analytic methods for altering dysfunctional cognitions; procedures for modifying interpersonal conduct); and (3) that it not only be coordinated with the guiding model of evolutionary polarities but also that each personality be characterized by a distinctive feature within each personologic domain.

Many signs, symptoms, and characteristics of patients can usefully be categorized and dimensionalized for purposes of clinical analysis. As portrayed in Table 5.2, one basis for organizing diagnostic features would be to distinguish them in accord with the data levels they represent (e.g., biophysical, intrapsychic, phenomenological, and behavioral). This differentiation reflects the four historic approaches that characterize the study of psychopathology, namely, the biological, the psychoanalytic, the cognitive, and the behavioral (Millon, 1967).

These clinical domains can be further grouped in a manner similar to distinctions drawn in the biological realm, that is, by dividing them into structural and functional attributes, a conception again consistent with general systems theory. The basic sciences of anatomy and physiology, respectively, investigate embedded and essentially permanent structures, which serve, for example, as substrates for mood and memory, and processes that underlie functions that regulate internal dynamics and external transactions. Such a division is, of course,

TABLE 5.2 Functional (F) and Structural (S) Domains of Personality

Behavioral level

(F) Expressive acts
(F) Interpersonal conduct

Phenomenological level

(F) Cognitive style
(S) Object representations
(S) Self-image

Intrapsychic level

(F) Regulatory mechanisms
(S) Morphological organization

Biophysical level

(S) Mood/temperament

by no means a novel notion. Psychoanalytic theory has dealt since its inception with topographic constructs such as conscious, preconscious, and unconscious, and later with structural concepts such as id, ego, and superego. Likewise, a host of quasistationary functional processes, such as the so-called ego apparatuses, have been posited and studied (Gill, 1963; Rapaport, 1959).

Functional Characteristics

"Functional characteristics" represent dynamic processes that transpire within the intrapsychic world and between the individual's self and psychosocial environment. For definitional purposes, we might say that functional domains represent "expressive modes of regulatory action," that is, behaviors, social conduct, cognitive processes, and unconscious mechanisms that manage, adjust, transform, coordinate, balance, discharge, and control the give and take of inner and outer life in a self-regulatory manner.

Not only are there several realms of regulatory action (e.g., interpersonal, cognitive, unconscious), but there are numerous variations in the way each of these functional modalities is manifested or expressed (e.g., interpersonally aloof, interpersonally submissive, interpersonally exploitive). Although every individual employs every modality in a lifetime to maintain its functional–structural unity, individuals differ with respect to the domains they enact most frequently, and even more so, they diverge in which of the expressive variations of these functions they typically manifest. Particular domains and expressive variations characterize certain personalities best.

Four *functional* domains relevant to the personality system are briefly described.

Expressive Acts.   These attributes relate to the observables seen at the "behavioral level" of data, and they are usually recorded by noting what and how the patient acts. Through inference, observations of overt behavior enable us to deduce either what the patient unknowingly reveals about him- or herself or, often conversely, what he/she wishes others to think or to know about him/her. The range and character of expressive actions are not only wide and diverse, but they convey both distinctive and worthwhile information about personality, from communicating a sense of personal incompetence to exhibiting general defensiveness to demonstrating a disciplined self-control, and so on. This domain of personality data is likely to be especially productive in differentiating patients on the passive–active polarity of the theoretical model.

Interpersonal Conduct.   A patient's style of relating to others also is noted essentially at the "behavioral" data level; it may be captured in a number of ways, such as how his/her actions impact on others, intended or otherwise, the attitudes that underlie, prompt, and give shape to these actions, the methods by which he/she engage others to meet his/her needs, or his/her way of coping with social tensions and conflicts. Extrapolating from these observations, the clinician may construct an image of how the person functions in relation to others, be it antagonistically, respectfully, aversively, secretively, and so on. Among the most fruitful attributes, interpersonal conduct may provide useful data on all three polarities, but especially on that of self–other.

Cognitive Style.   How the patient perceives events, focuses attention, processes information, organizes thoughts, and communicates reactions and ideas to others represent data at the "phenomenological" level and are among the most useful indices to the clinician of the patient's distinctive way of functioning. By synthesizing these signs and symptoms, it may be possible to identify indications of what may be termed an impoverished style, or distracted thinking, or cognitive flightiness, or constricted thought, and so on. As with interpersonal conduct, cognitive style may be productive in uncovering data on all three polarities; the passive–active dimension may be especially well identified by analyses of this attribute.

Regulatory Mechanism. Although "mechanisms" of self-protection, need gratification, and conflict resolution are consciously recognized at times, they represent data derived primarily at the "intrapsychic" level and thereby avoid reflective appraisal. As such, they serve a protective function but may at times begin a sequence of events that intensifies the very problems they were intended to circumvent. Mechanisms usually represent internal processes and, hence, are more difficult to discern and describe than processes anchored closer to the observable world. Despite the methodological problems they present, the task of identifying which mechanisms are chosen (e.g., rationalization, displacement, reaction formation) and the extent to which they are employed is extremely useful in a comprehensive personality assessment. Inferences pertaining to this attribute are likely to be effective in yielding distinctions along both the passive–active and pleasure–pain polarities.

Structural Attributes

"Structural attributes" represent a deeply embedded and relatively enduring template of imprinted memories, attitudes, needs, fears, conflicts, and so on, which guide the experience and transform the nature of ongoing life events. Psychic structures have an orienting and preemptive effect in that they alter the character of action and the impact of subsequent experiences in line with preformed inclinations and expectancies. By selectively lowering thresholds for transactions that are consonant with either constitutional proclivities or early learnings, future events are often experienced as variations of the past. The following describes both the character and persistence of these structural residues of early experience (Millon, 1969):

> Significant experiences of early life many never recur again, but their effects remain and leave their mark. Physiologically, we may say they have etched a neurochemical change; psychologically, they are registered as memories, a permanent trace and an embedded internal stimulus. In contrast to the fleeting stimuli of the external world, these memory traces become part and parcel of every stimulus complex which activates behavior. Once registered, the effects of the past are indelible, incessant, and inescapable. They now are intrinsic elements of the individual's makeup; they latch on and intrude into the current events of life, coloring, transform-

ing and distorting the passing scene. Although the residuals of subsequent experiences may override them, becoming more dominant internal stimuli, the presence of earlier memory traces remains in one form or another. In every thought and action, the individual cannot help but carry these remnants into the present. Every current behavior is a perpetuation, then, of the past, a continuation and intrusion of these inner stimulus traces.

The residuals of the past do more than passively contribute their share to the present. By temporal precedence, if nothing else, they guide. shape or distort the character of current events. Not only are they ever present, then, but they operate insidiously to transform new stimulus experiences in line with the past. (p. 200)

For purposes of definition, "structural domains" may be conceived as substrates and action dispositions of a quasipermanent nature. Possessing a network of interconnecting pathways, these structures contain the internalized residues of the past in the form of memories and affects that are associated intrapsychically with conceptions of self and others. We now briefly describe four *structural* domains relevant to personality.

Self-Image. As the inner world of symbols is mastered through development, the "swirl" of events that buffet the young child gives way to a growing sense of order and continuity. One major configuration emerges to impose a measure of sameness on an otherwise fluid environment, the perception of self-as-object, a distinct, ever-present, and identifiable "I" or "me." Self-identity stems largely from conceptions drawn at the "phenomenological" level of analysis; it is especially significant in that it provides a stable anchor to serve as a guidepost and to give continuity to changing experience. Most persons have an implicit sense of who they are, but they differ greatly in the clarity and accuracy of their self-introspections. Few can articulate the psychic elements that comprise this image, such as stating knowingly whether they view themselves as primarily alienated, or inept, or complacent, or conscientious, and so on. As should be evident, this attribute is closely oriented to provide data on the "self'" pole of the self–other polarity; also likely to be clarified are features relevant to the pleasure–pain polarity.

Object Representations. As noted previously, significant experiences from the past leave an inner imprint, a structural residue composed of memories, attitudes, and affects that serve as a substrate of dispositions for perceiving and reacting to life's ongoing events. As such, these representations inhere within the "phenomenological realm." Analogous to the various organ systems of which the body is composed, both the character and substance of these internalized representations of significant figures and relationships of the past can be differentiated and analyzed for personality purposes. Variations in the nature and content of this inner world can be associated with one or another personality and lead us to employ descriptive terms to represent them, such as shallow, vexatious, undifferentiated, concealed, and irreconcilable. Balancing the preceding attribute on self–other polarity, the focus of this attribute is clearly oriented to provide information on the "other" pole; the pleasure–pain aspects of other may also be usefully generated.

Morphological Organization. The overall architecture that serves as a framework for an individual's psychic interior may display weakness in its structural cohesion, exhibit deficient coordination among its components, and possess few mechanisms to maintain balance and harmony, regulate internal conflicts, or mediate external pressures. The concept of "morphological organization" refers to the structural strength, interior congruity, and functional efficacy of the personality system. "Organization" of the mind is almost exclusively derived from inferences at the "intrapsychic level" of analysis. The concept is akin to and employed in conjunction with current psychoanalytic notions such as borderline and psychotic levels, but this usage tends to be limited, relating essentially to quantitative degrees of integrative pathology, not to variations either in integrative character or configuration. Although impossible to observe directly and difficult to infer, nevertheless this important clinical attribute relates most directly to the structural character of "self" in the self–other polarity.

Mood–Temperament. Few observables are clinically more relevant from the "biophysical" level of data analysis than the predominant character of an individual's affect and the intensity and frequency with which he/she expresses it. The "meaning" of extreme emotions is easy to decode. This is not so with the more subtle moods and feelings that insidiously and repetitively pervade the patient's ongoing relationships and experiences. Not only are the expressive features of mood and drive conveyed by terms such as distraught, labile, fickle, or hostile communicated via self-report, but they are revealed as well, albeit indirectly, in the patient's level of activity, speech quality, and physical appearance. Clearly, the most useful aspect of this attribute as it relates to the theory is its utility in appraising features relevant to the pleasure–pain and active–passive polarities.

Accordingly, in the MPDC each specific domain is given a prototypal standard for each personality. Thus, it is the diagnostic *criterion* that is conceived to be prototypal, not the personality as a whole. These "prototypal domain traits" synthesize the categorical and dimensional elements in a personologic classification. To illustrate: if the clinical attribute "interpersonal conduct" was deemed of value in assessing personality, then a specific prototypal criterion would be identified to represent the characteristic or distinctive manner in which each personality ostensibly conducts its interpersonal life. Not only does MPDC (Millon, Tringone, Bockian, Green, & Sandberg, in press) not suffer from criterial asymmetry, its diagnostic attributes have, unlike DSM, been constructed to maintain such psychometric standards as internal consistency. Nevertheless, it allows the clinician to make personality diagnoses in accord with DSM types, including the new depressive personality, offering an opportunity for diagnosticians to systematically assess patients across a wide range of clinical domains. However, as a result of the noninferential character of DSM criteria, this form of MPDC encompasses only the domains of expressive acts, interpersonal conduct, cognitive style, self-image, and mood-temperament. This is a narrower scope of attributes than desirable—some domains are perhaps so inferential in nature they cannot be readily calibrated without special training—but one sufficient to provide a reasonably comprehensive picture of a patient's personality system, one sufficient to serve as a basis for intervention efforts.

The prototypal domain model illustrates that "categorical" (qualitative distinction) and "dimensional" (quantitative distinction) approaches need not be framed in opposition, no less be considered mutually exclusive. Assessments can be formulated, first, to recognize qualitative (categorical) distinctions in what prototypal features best characterize a person, permitting the multiple listing of several such features and second, to differentiate these features quantitatively (dimensionally) so as to represent their relative degrees of clinical prominence or pervasiveness. The prototypal domain approach includes the specification and use of categorical attributes in the form of distinct prototypal characteristics, yet it allows for a result that permits the diversity and heterogeneity of a dimensional schema.

Moreover, the prototype construct would appear epistemically sound; it is based on an interactional paradigm that operationalizes diagnostic constructs not as they exist "in reality" but as they exist in thought (Cantor & Genero, 1986). The perennial categories–dimensions controversy can be compared to the wave–particle controversy in physics, which flourished from the 1700s until recent times. Specifically, the progression from "classical" physics to the "new" physics entailed overcoming reifications of various kinds—absolute particles and absolute waves (quantum physics) and absolute space and absolute time (general relativity)—inherent to the ''flat earth'' perceptual processes of middle-level objects. Observations that showed the limited generality of classical physics had to await advances in instrumentation—advances that eventually revealed the indeterminate structure of the very large and the very small and the essential role of the observer in the construction of what is taken to be ''real.''

Millon Clinical Multiaxial Inventory: Self-Report Assessment of Personality Disorders

A 175-item true–false self-report inventory, the MCMI and its subsequent revisions, MCMI-II (Millon, 1987b), and MCMI-III (Millon, Millon, & Davis, 1994), include 14 personality disorder scales (all the personality disorders in both the main texts and appendices of DSM-III, DSM-III-R, and DSM-IV), nine clinical syndrome scales, as well as three ''modifying indices'' to appraise problematic response tendencies.

Within the restrictions on validity set by the limits of the self-report mode, the narrow frontiers of psychometric technology, as well as the slender range of consensually shared diagnostic knowledge, all steps were taken to maximize the MCMI's concordance with its generative theory and the official classification system. Pragmatic and philosophical compromises were made where valued objectives could not be simultaneously achieved (e.g., instrument brevity versus item independence; representative national patient norms versus local base-rate specificity; theoretical criterion considerations versus empirical data).

A major goal in constructing the MCMI was to keep the total number of items comprising the inventory small enough to encourage use in all types of diagnostic and treatment settings, yet large enough to permit the assessment of a wide range of clinically relevant behaviors. At 175 items, the final form is much shorter than comparable instruments. Potentially objectionable statements were screened out, and terminology was geared to an eighth-grade reading level. As a result, the great majority of patients can complete MCMI in 20 to 30 minutes.

Unfortunately, as many have noted (Butcher, 1972), assessment techniques and personality theorizing have developed almost independently. As a result, few diagnostic measures have either been based on or have evolved from clinical theory. MCMI is different: Each of its personality disorder and clinical syndrome scales was constructed as an operational measure of a syndrome derived from a theory of personality and psychopathology (Millon, 1969, 1981, 1990).

No less important than its link to theory is an instrument's coordination with the official diagnostic system and its syndromal categories. With the advent of the various recent editions of DSM (American Psychiatric Association, 1980, 1987, 1994), diagnostic categories and labels have been precisely specified and defined operationally. Few diagnostic instruments currently available are as consonant with the nosological format and conceptual terminology of this official system as MCMI.

Separate scales of MCMI have been constructed in line with DSM to distinguish the more enduring personality characteristics of patients (Axis II) from the acute clinical disorders they display (Axis I), a distinction judged to be of considerable use by both test developers and clinicians (Dahlstrom, 1972). This distinction should enable the clinician to separate those syndrome features of psychopathological functioning that are persistent and pervasive from those that are transient or circumscribed. Moreover, profiles based on all 23 clinical scales illuminate the interplay between long-standing characterological patterns and the distinctive clinical symptomatology a patient manifests under psychic stress.

Similarly, it seemed useful to construct scales that distinguish syndromes in terms of their levels of psychopathological severity. For example, the premorbid characterological pattern of a patient is assessed independently of its degree of pathology. To achieve this, separate scales are used to determine the style of traits comprising the basic personality structure—schizoid, avoidant, depressive, dependent, histrionic, narcissistic, antisocial, aggressive (sadistic), compulsive, negativistic (passive–aggressive), and self-defeating—and the greater level of pathology of that structure—schizotypal, borderline, and paranoid. In like manner, moderately severe clinical syndromes—anxiety, somatoform, hypomania, dysthymia, alcohol abuse, drug abuse, and posttraumatic distress disorder (PTSD)—are separated and independently assessed from those with parallel features but more of a "psychotic" nature—thought disorder, major depression, and delusional disorder.

Cross-validation data gathered with nondevelopment samples supported the measure's generalizability, dependability, and accuracy of diagnostic scale cutting lines and profile interpretations. Large and diverse samples have been studied with MCMI, but it is still necessary to achieve full domain coverage and engage in ongoing cross-validation studies. Moreover, local base rates and cutting lines must be developed for special settings. Nevertheless, validation data with a variety of populations (e.g., outpatients and inpatients; alcohol and drug centers) suggest that MCMI can be used with a reasonable level of confidence in most clinical settings. Its recognition as one of only four assessment instruments (the others being the Rorschach, TAT, and MMPI), and the only one developed in the last five decades, to be considered necessary tools by more than half of those who train PhD and PsyD psychologists, attests to its level of acceptance and utility.

As should be evident, MCMI is not a general personality instrument to be used for "normal" populations or for purposes other than diagnostic screening or clinical assessment. Hence it contrasts with other, more broadly applied, inventories whose presumed utility for diverse populations is often highly questionable. Normative data and transformation scores for MCMI are based on presumed clinical samples and are applicable therefore only to persons who evince psychological symptoms or are engaged in a program of professional psychotherapy or psychodiagnostic evaluation. As should also be noted, there are distinct boundaries to the accuracy of the self-report method of clinical data collection; by no means is it a perfect data source. The inherent psychometric limits of the tools, the tendency of similar patients to interpret questions differently, the effect of current affective states on trait measures, the effort of patients to effect certain false appearances and impressions, all narrow the upper boundaries of this method's potential accuracy. However, by constructing a self-report instrument in line with accepted techniques of validation (Loevinger, 1957), an inventory should begin to approach these upper boundaries.

Millon Index of Personality Styles: Self-Report Assessment of Normal Personality

Beyond breaking down the theory's manifest personality types into their constituent latent constructs, the theory as described in previous pages has been expanded substantially. Whereas the three polarities of the theory are crucial elements of the model as a gauge of personality pathology, they are now judged to be insufficient as a scaffold for encompassing the many varieties of normal personality styles. This is not the chapter to elaborate both the full rationale and specifics of the expanded model; a recent essay on this theme may be found in the MIPS manual (Millon, Weiss, Millon, & Davis, 1994).

Briefly, we should note that cognitive differences among individuals and the manner in which they are expressed have not been a sufficiently appreciated domain for generating personality traits. We have added a set of four polarities that reflect different "modes" of cognitive style to MIPS. These follow the initial three polarities (e.g., self–

other), which may be termed "motivational aims." Similarly, we have added a third domain of polarities to those of "motivation" and "cognition," that of "interpersonal behavior." Although we do not share the view of many who give the manifest forms of the interpersonal dimensions (e.g., FFM) primacy in their personality gauges, we do judge them no less significant than either the motivational or cognitive, especially if they are organized in terms of the latent or fundamental polarities they express. Thus a third domain, comprising five relating polarities, concludes the MIPS test form. The following précis of the tripartite structure of the MIPS scales divides the test in the manner in which organisms function in their environment, one which we believe may be a useful theory-based schema for purposes of normal personologic analysis.

As noted, we have termed the first segment in this tripartite sequence "motivating aims," to signify that the behaviors of organisms are prompted, energized, and directed by particular purposes and goals they wish to achieve. The second component of the sequence is labeled "cognitive modes" to indicate the manner in which human organisms seek out, regulate, internalize, and transform information about their environment and themselves, a step necessary if organisms are to achieve their aims effectively. The third segment in the sequence, referred to as "interpersonal behaviors," represents the different ways in which human organisms relate to and negotiate with other humans in their social environment in light of the aims that motivate them and the cognitions they have formed. To capture personality more or less fully, we must find ways to characterize all three components of the sequence: the deeper motives that orient individuals, the characteristic sources they utilize to construct and to transform their cognitions, and the particular behaviors they have learned to relate to others interpersonally. By dimensionalizing and quantifying these three elements, we should be able to represent individual differences in accord with the major features that characterize normal personality styles.

1. "Motivating aims" are most closely akin to concepts such as need, drive, affect, and emotion in that they pertain to the strivings and goals that spur and guide the organism, that is, the purposes and ends that stir them into one or another course of behavior. The aims of motivation reflect strivings for survival, seen as composed of three elements, referred to earlier as "existence," "adaptation," and "replication." These three elements are organized as polarities, each of which comprises two contrasting scales. At one extreme of the first bipolarity is a motivation-based scale pertaining to the existential aim of strengthening one's life or reinforcing one's capacity to survive by en-

gaging in "pleasurable" behaviors (phrased as "enhancing"); at the other extreme is an emotion-based scale that reflects the need to protect one's survival against "pain" or life-threatening events (referred to as "preserving"). The second of the motivating aim bipolarities relates to adaptation, that is, methods by which one operates in one's environment to enhance and preserve life. One end of this bipolarity represents tendencies to alter actively and energetically the conditions of one's life, (termed "modifying"); the other end represents the inclination to accept passively in a neutral and nonresponsive manner one's life circumstances as they are given (referred to as "accommodating"). The third bipolarity comprising the motivating domain also differentiates two scales; one scale represents those who seek to realize and fulfill their self-potentials and possibilities before those of others (spoken of as "individuating"), as contrasted to those who are disposed to value the fortunes and potentials of relatives and companions to a greater degree than their own (called "nurturing").

2. The second group of bipolarity scales relate to the fourth phase of evolution, that of "abstraction." Termed "cognitive modes," they incorporate both the sources employed to gather knowledge about life and the manner in which this information is transformed. Four bipolarities, the constructs they reflect, and the eight scales developed to represent them comprise this section of the MIPS. Here we are looking at contrasting "styles of cognizing," differences among people, first, in what they attend to in order to experience and learn about life and, second, what they habitually do to make this knowledge meaningful and useful to themselves. The first two of these bipolarities refer to the "information sources" to which attention and perception are drawn to provide cognitions. One pair of scales contrasts individuals who are disposed to look outward or external-to-self for information, inspiration, and guidance (termed "extraversing"), versus those inclined to turn inward or internal-to-self (referred to as "introversing"). The second pair of scales contrasts predilections for direct observational experiences of a tangible, material, and concrete nature (labeled "sensing") with those geared more toward inferences regarding phenomena of an intangible, ambiguous, symbolic, and abstract character (named "intuiting"). The second set of cognitive mode bipolarities relate to "processes of transformation," that is, ways in which information and experiences, once apprehended and incorporated, are subsequently evaluated and reconstructed mentally. The first pair of the transformation scales differentiates processes based essentially on intellect, logic, reason, and objectivity (entitled "thinking") from those that depend on affective empathy, personal values, sentiment, and subjectivity (designated "feeling"). The second of the transformational

scales are likewise divided into a bipolar pairing. At one end are reconstruction modes that transform new information so as to make it con-
serve and assimilate to preconceived formal, tradition-bound,
well-standardized, and conventionally structured schemas (called "systematizing"); at the other bipolar scale are represented inclinations to
avoid cognitive preconceptions, to distance from what is already known
and to originate new ideas in an informal, open-minded, spontaneous, individualistic, and often imaginative manner (termed *innovating*).

3. The third group of bipolar scales represent "interpersonal ways
of relating," reflecting how individuals prefer to conduct their transactions with others. These styles of social behavior derive in part from
the interplay of the person's distinctive pattern of motivating aims and
cognitive modes. Five bipolarities have been constructed to represent
contrasting styles of relating behaviors; in a broader context these styles
of behavior may be considered to be located at the lower end of a continuum that shades progressively into the moderately severe personality disorders of DSM-IV, Axis II. The first pair of scales in this, the third
section of MIPS, pertains to a bipolar dimension characterized by contrasting degrees of sociability. At one bipolar end are those persons
whose high scale scores suggest that they relate to others in a socially
distant, disengaged, affectless, and coolly indifferent manner (termed
"retiring"); on the other high scale end are those who seek to be engaged, are lively, talkative, and interpersonally gregarious (called "out-
going"). The second polarity pair relates to one's comfort and poise
in social settings; it contrasts those who tend to be uncertain and fearful, are unsure of their personal worth, and are inclined to feel insecure and to withdraw socially (named "hesitating"), with those who
are socially confident and self-possessed as well as bold and decisive
in their relationships (entitled "asserting"). The third pairing relates
to contrasting degrees of conventionality and social deference; it
differentiates those who are disinclined more than most to adhere to
public standards, cultural mores, and organizational regulations, act
autonomously, and insist on functioning socially on their own terms
(labeled "dissenting"), as compared to those who are notably tradition-
bound, socially compliant and responsible, respectful of authority, as
well as appropriately diligent and dutiful (termed "conforming").
Facets of the interpersonal dimension of dominance–submission are
tapped in the fourth polarity. High on one polar scale are those who
are not only submissive, but also self-demeaning, diffident, overly
modest, and self-depriving (designated "yielding"), as compared to
those who, beyond being merely domineering, are also willful, ambitious, forceful, and power-seeking (termed "controlling"). The fifth
and final set of polarities pertains to features of a dimension of social

negativism versus social agreeableness. The former is seen among those who are dissatisfied with both themselves and others, who are generally displeased with the status quo, and tend to be resentful and oppositional (designated ''complaining''); they contrast with those who are cooperative and compromising, not only considerate of others, but highly obliging, and willingly adapting their behaviors to accord with the wishes of others (named ''agreeing'').

SYNERGISTIC PERSONOLOGIC THERAPY

This chapter has advocated integrative and organizational conceptions, not only of the personality construct, but also of clinical science itself. We have noted that the polarity schema and clinical domains serve as useful points of focus for corresponding modalities of therapy, the fourth and final element of a mature clinical science. In a way, everything that went before was done in order to arrive at this *summum bonum* of an applied clinical science. A good theory allows us not only to appreciate nature in is aesthetic glory but also as a basis on which to *do* something; a good theory is a theory of action. If the constraints are where they have been assumed to be, then the theory should allow us to address the constraints in order to create more flexible functioning, if the technologies to do so exist.

Ideally, of course, patients would be ''pure'' prototypes, and all polarities prototypally and invariably manifest. Were this so, each diagnosis would automatically match with its polarity configuration and corresponding therapeutic mode. Unfortunately, real patients rarely are pure textbook prototypes; most, by far, are complex mixtures, exhibiting, for example, the deficient pain and pleasure polarities that typify the schizoid prototype, the interpersonal conduct and cognitive style features of the avoidant prototype, the self-image qualities that characterize the schizotypal, and so on. Further, the polarity configurations and their expressive domains are not likely to be of equal clinical relevance or prominence in a particular case. Thus, interpersonal characteristics may be especially troublesome for one patient, whereas cognitive processes, though problematic, may be of lesser significance for another. Which domains and which polarities should be selected for therapeutic intervention is not, therefore, merely a matter of making a diagnosis but requires a comprehensive assessment, one that appraises not only the overall configuration of polarities and domains but also differentiates their balance and degrees of salience.

In a world of overriding contextualism, every construct is informed by many others in a complex network of direct and mediated nomological linkages and circular causal pathways. In such a world as this, diagnosis and therapy cannot be deterministically coupled so that the first specifies the second. As Reich (1945) said, the therapeutic plan must be derived from the logic of the individual case. Determining what this logic is (characterizing the patient), however, requires the use of reference points. To restate what was noted above, we abstract from persons only those dimensions we take as being common to all in order to create our reference points, yet we use these points in a reconstructive process the very individuality we had previously distilled: From rich idiographic individuality, to nomothetic commonalities, and finally, to what might be called nomothetic individuality. To interpret a psychological test profile is to seek to return to a contextual understanding of the individual as an integrative network of personality variables existing at a particular point in historical time. Though it is an effort to understand the individual on his/her own terms, beyond this it is an effort to understand how the terms themselves have been mutually informed each by the others in their crystallization as a single individual. Accordingly, the whole process of creating a theoretical basis to undergird the science of personology, of deriving therefrom a nosology of personality patterns, of constructing the instrumentation coordinated with these nosological constructs, ends back at the beginning, in a highly individuated understanding of the patient.

Before we turn to substantive therapeutic matters, a brief comment on a few philosophical issues is necessary. These issues bear on a rationale for developing theory-based treatment techniques and methods, that is, methods that transcend the merely empirical (e.g., electroconvulsive therapy for depressives). We should also note, albeit briefly, an epistemologically spurious issue found in its most obtuse form in debates concerning which treatment orientation (cognitive-behavioral, biological, intrapsychic) is "closer to the truth," or which therapeutic method is intrinsically the most efficacious.

What differentiates these treatment orientations has little to do with either their theoretical underpinnings or their empirical support. Although personality is an integrative construct, what differentiates the behavioral, cognitive, psychodynamic, and biological orientations is merely the fact that they limit their attention to different clinical domains. Imagine physicists, chemists, and biologists arguing over which field was a truer representation of nature! Because personality is an integrated system, intervention of sufficient magnitude at any point in the system is likely to set off reverberations that will be somewhat effectual (unless they are totally misguided to begin with). Thus, efforts to establish the inherent efficacy of one approach over another will likely be thwarted by holism of personality, a hypothesis that has been borne out through the history of psychotherapy research.

Eclectic versus Integrative Psychotherapy

To the credit of those of an eclectic persuasion, they have recognized the arbitrary if not illogical character of such contentions, as well as the need to bridge schisms that have been constructed less by philosophical considerations, theoretical logic, or pragmatic goals than by the accidents of history and professional rivalries. Much of what travels under the "eclectic" or "integrative" banner, however, sounds like the talk of a "goody two shoes," a desire to be nice to all sides, and to say that everybody is right. These terms have degenerated to the point that they have become platitudinous buzzwords, philosophies with which open-minded people certainly would wish to ally themselves.

But integrative psychotherapy, at least as it should be applied to the personality disorders, must make specifications of both form and substance. First, integrative therapy is more than eclecticism; perhaps it should be termed posteclecticism, if we may borrow a characterization from the art world. Eclecticism, of course, is not a matter of choice. We all must be eclectics, engaging in differential (Frances, Clarkin, & Perry, 1984) and multimodal (Lazarus, 1981) therapeutics, selecting the techniques that are empirically the most efficacious for the problems at hand. Second, integration is more than the coexistence of two or three previously discordant orientations or techniques. We cannot piece together the odds and ends of several theoretical schemas, each internally consistent and oriented to different data domains, and expect them to cohere. Such a hodgepodge will lead only to illusory syntheses that cannot long hold together. Efforts such as these, meritorious as they may be in some regards, represent the work of peacemakers, not innovators and not therapeutic integrationists.

The integration labeled "personologic psychotherapy" (Millon, 1988) insists on the primacy of an overarching gestalt that gives coherence, provides an interactive framework, and creates an organic order among otherwise discrete polarities and attributes. Although it is eclectic in the sense that it pulls from here and there, it does so to create a coherent picture of the patient; it is synthesized from a substantive theory whose overall utility and orientation derive from that old chestnut, "The whole is greater than the sum of its parts." As we know well, the personality problems our patients bring to us are an inextricably linked nexus of interpersonal behaviors, cognitive styles, regulatory processes, and so on. They flow through a tangle of feedback loops and serially unfolding concatenations that emerge at different times in dynamic and changing configurations. Each component of these configurations has its role and significance altered by virtue of its place in these continually evolving constellations. In parallel form, so should personologic psychotherapy be conceived as an integrated configuration of strategies and tactics in which each intervention technique is selected not *only* for its efficacy in resolving particular pathological attributes but also for its contribution to the overall constellation of treatment procedures of which it is but one.

At the center of all therapies, whether we work with "part functions" that focus on behaviors, or cognitions, or unconscious processes, defects, and the like, or whether we address contextual systems that focus on the psychosocial environment, the family, the group, or the socioeconomic conditions of life, the point of dynamic synthesis, the place that links parts to contexts, is the person, the individual, the intersecting medium in which influences from diverse levels of organization are organically integrated. Moreover, persons are the *only* organically integrated system in the psychological domain, inherently created from birth as natural entities. Persons lie at the heart of the psychotherapeutic experience as the substantive beings that give meaning and coherence to symptoms and traits—be they behaviors, affects, or mechanisms—and experience and express what transpires in family interactions and social processes.

The new breed of integrative and eclectic therapists should take cognizance of the person from the start, for the parts and the contexts take on different meanings, and call for different interventions in terms of the person to whom they are anchored. To focus on one social structure or one psychic form of expression, that is, to advocate a "variable-centered" approach without understanding the embeddedness of even nosological constructs in substantive persons, is to engage in potentially misguided, if not random, therapeutic techniques. Although the admonition that we should not employ the same therapeutic approach with all patients is self-evident, it appears that therapeutic approaches accord more with where training occurred than with the nature of the patients' pathologies. To paraphrase (Millon, 1969), there continues to be a disinclination among clinical practitioners to submit their cherished techniques to detailed study or to revise them in line with critical empirical findings. Despite the fact that most of our therapeutic research leaves much to be desired in the way of proper controls, sampling, and evaluative criteria, one overriding fact comes through repeatedly: Therapeutic techniques must be suited to the patient's problem. Simple and obvious though this statement is, it is repeatedly neglected by therapists who persist in utilizing and argue heatedly in favor of a particular approach to *all* variants of psychopathology. No "school" of therapy is exempt from this notorious attitude.

The Form of Synergistic Personologic Therapy

Why should we formulate a synergistic therapeutic strategy with the personality disorders? The short answer to this question is that the form of the intervention should be consonant with the nature of that which the intervention endeavors to change. The methodology of the intervention must be consistent with the epistemology of the personality construct. The answer may perhaps be best grasped if we think of the polarities of personality as analogous to the sections of an orchestra and the clinical attributes of a patient as a clustering of discordant instruments that exhibit imbalances, deficiencies, or conflicts within these sections. To extend this analogy, therapists may be seen as conductors whose task is to bring forth a harmonious balance among all the sections, as well as their specifically discordant instruments, muting some here, accentuating others there, all to the end of fulfilling the conductor's knowledge of how "the overall composition" can best be made consonant. The task is not that of altering one instrument, but of all, *in concert*. What is sought in music, then, is a balanced score, one composed of harmonic counterpoints, rhythmic patterns, and melodic combinations. What is needed in therapy is a likewise balanced program, a coordinated strategy of counterpoised techniques designed to optimize synergistically sequential and combinatorial treatment effects.

In eclectic psychotherapy, there is merely a separateness among techniques, just a wise selectivity of what works best. In synergistic therapy there are psychologically designed composites and progressions among diverse techniques. Just as the person is a hierarchically integrated system, these composites and progressions must also be hierarchized according to the needs of the individual case. If the therapy is to be a success, some issues must be remedied before others. Not everything can be worked on simultaneously. As a rule, each issue must be dealt with in the order of its severity and urgency, and its capacity to undermine and confound the treatment of other issues. Terms such as "catalytic sequences" and "potentiating pairings" (Millon, 1988) are employed to represent the synergistic nature of these polarity-oriented and attribute-focused treatment plans. In essence, they comprise therapeutic arrangements and timing series that promote polarity balances and effect attribute changes that would otherwise not occur by the use of only one technique.

A defining feature of personality disorders is that they are themselves pathogenic. Millon (1969) described this process as "self-perpetuation"; Horney (1937) characterized it earlier in her use of the concept of "vicious circles"; Wachtel (1977) has suggested the term "cyclical psychodynamics." All of these terms refer to the reflexive unfolding of the person as a system-in-time. Such ceaseless and entangled sequences of repetitive cognitions, interpersonal behaviors, and unconscious mechanisms call for the use of simultaneous or alternately focused methods. The enhancement of therapeutic efficacy produced by such catalytic and potentiating processes are what comprise genuine synergistic strategies. In a "catalytic sequence," for example, one might seek first to alter a patient's humiliating and painful stuttering by direct modification procedures, which, if achieved, may facilitate the use of cognitive methods in producing *self-image* changes in confidence that may, in turn, foster the utility of interpersonal techniques in effecting improvements in relationships with others. In "potentiated pairing" one may simultaneously combine, as is commonly done these days, both behavioral and cognitive methods synergistically to overcome problematic interactions with others and conceptions of self that might be refractory to either technique alone.

As a general philosophy then, we should select our specific treatment techniques as synergistic tactics to achieve our goals. These goals should be hierarchized according to the personologic domains believed by the therapist to represent the greatest constraints on system functioning. Depending on the pathological polarity and domains to be modified, and the overall treatment sequence one has in mind, the goals of therapy should be oriented toward the improvement of imbalanced or deficient polarities by the use of techniques that are optimally suited to modify their expression in those clinical domains that are problematic.

Table 5.3 provides a synopsis of what may be considered the primary goals of personologic therapy according to the polarity model. Therapeutic efforts responsive to problems in the pain–pleasure polarity would, for example, have as their essential aim the enhancement of pleasure among schizoid and avoidant personalities (+ pleasure). Given the probability of intrinsic deficits in this area, schizoids might require the use of pharmacological agents designed to activate their "flat" mood–temperament. Increments in pleasure for avoidants, however, are likely to depend more on cognitive techniques designed to alter their alienated self-image, and behavioral methods oriented to counter their aversive interpersonal inclinations. Equally important for avoidants is reducing their hypersensitivities especially to social rejection (− pain); this may be achieved by coordinating the use of medications for their characteristic "anguished" mood–temperament with cognitive methods geared to desensitization. In the passive–active polarity, increments in the capacity and skills to take a less reactive and more proactive role in dealing with the affairs of their lives (− passive; + active) would be a major goal of treatment for schizoids, dependents, narcissists, self-defeatists, and compulsives. Turning to the

TABLE 5.3. Polarity-Oriented Personologic Therapy

Modifying the pain–pleasure polarity

+ Pleasure (schizoid, avoidant, depressive)
- Pain (avoidant, depressive)
Pain ↔ pleasure (self-defeating, sadistic)

Balancing the passive–active polarity

+ Passive − active (avoidant, histrionic, antisocial, sadistic, negativistic)
- Passive + active (schizoid, depressive, dependent, narcissistic, self-defeating, compulsive)

Altering the other–self polarity

- Other + self (dependent, histrionic)
+ Other − self (narcissistic, antisocial)
Other ↔ self (compulsive, negativistic)

Rebuilding the personality structure

+ Cognitive, interpersonal cohesion (schizotypal)
+ Affective, self-cohesion (borderline)
- Cognitive, affective rigidity (paranoid)

other–self polarity, imbalances found among narcissists and antisocials, for example, suggest that major aims of their treatment would be a reduction in their predominant self-focus and a corresponding augmentation of their sensitivity to the needs of others (+ other; − self).

To make unbalanced or deficient polarities the primary aim of therapy is a new focus and a goal as yet untested. In contrast, the clinical domains in which problems are expressed lend themselves to a wide variety of therapeutic techniques, the efficacy of which must, of course, continue to be gauged by ongoing experience and future systematic research. Nevertheless, our repertoire here is a rich one. For example, there are numerous behavior modification techniques (Bandura, 1969; Goldfried & Davison, 1976), such as assertiveness training, that may fruitfully be employed to establish a greater sense of self-autonomy or an active rather than a passive stance with regard to life. Similarly, pharmaceuticals are notably efficacious in reducing the intensity of pain (anxiety, depression) when the pleasure–pain polarity is in marked imbalance.

Turning to the specific domains in which clinical problems exhibit themselves, we can address dysfunctions in the realm of "interpersonal conduct" by employing any number of family (Gurman & Kniskern, 1981) or group (Yalom, 1986) therapeutic methods, as well as a series of recently evolved and explicitly formulated interpersonal techniques (Anchin & Kiesler, 1982). Methods of classical analysis or its more contemporary schools may be especially suited to the realm of "object representations," as the methods of Beck (1976, Ellis, 1970), and Meichenbaum (1977) would be well chosen to modify difficulties of "cognitive style" and "self-image." The goals, as well as the strategies and modes of action, for when and how one might practice synergistic therapy have only begun to be specified (Millon & Davis, in press).

CONCLUDING COMMENT

Our goals in this chapter were as follows: first to connect the conceptual structure of both normal and abnormal personalities to their latent and common foundations in the natural world, a theoretical ambition; second, to connect the explicated theory to a deductively derived taxonomy; third, to link this taxonomy to the development of assessment instruments; and finally, to comment briefly on some prescriptions the integrative root metaphor offers for psychotherapy.

What was proposed is akin to Freud's unfulfilled *Project for a Scientific Psychology* (1895), an endeavor to advance our understanding of human behavior by exploring interconnections among seemingly diverse but related disciplines. It is also akin to Jung's effort to explicate the foundations of personality with reference to deeply rooted or latent polarities. A new "science" that explores the interface between human social functioning and evolutionary biology has recently emerged (Wilson, 1975, 1978). Our formulations, as briefly summarized here, have likewise proposed that substantial progress may be achieved by applying evolutionary notions to the study of both normal and abnormal personality.

REFERENCES

Ainsworth, M. D. S. (1967). *Infancy in Uganda*. Baltimore: Johns Hopkins University Press.

Ainsworth, M. D. S., Behar, M., Waters, E., & Wall, S. (1978). *Patterns of attachment: A psychological study of the strange situation*. Hillsdale, NJ: Erlbaum.

Allport, G. (1961). *Pattern and growth in personality*. New York: Holt, Rinehart & Winston.

American Psychiatric Association. (1980). *Diagnostic and statistical manual of mental disorders* (3rd ed.). Washington, DC: Author.

American Psychiatric Association. (1987). *Diagnostic and statistical manual of mental disorders* (3rd ed., rev.). Washington, DC: Author.

American Psychiatric Association. (1994). *Diagnostic and statistical manual of mental disorders* (4th ed.). Washington, DC: Author.

Anchin, J. C., & Kiesler, D. J. (Eds.). (1982). *Handbook of interpersonal psychotherapy*. New York: Pergamon.

Bandura, A. (1969). *Principles of behavior modification*. New York: Holt, Rinehart & Winston.

Bandura, A. (1982). The psychology of change encounters and life paths. *American Psychologist, 7,* 747–755.

Bartholomew, K., & Horowitz, L. M. (1991). Attachment styles among young adults: A test of a four-category model. *Journal of Personality and Social Psychology, 61,* 226–244.

Beach, F., & Jaynes, J. (1954). Effects of early experience upon the behavior of animals. *Psychological Bulletin, 51,* 239–262.

Beck, A. T. (1976). *Cognitive therapy and the emotional disorders*. New York: International Universities Press.

Benjamin, L. S. (1993). *Interpersonal diagnosis and treatment of personality disorders*. New York: Guilford Press.

Bowers, K. S. (1977). There's more to Iago than meets the eye: A clinical account of personality consistency. In D. Magnusson & N. S. Endler (Eds.), *Personality at the crossroads*. Hillsdale, NJ: Erlbaum.

Bowlby, J. (1952). *Maternal care and mental health*. Geneva: World Health Organization.

Bowlby, J. (1960). Grief and mourning in infancy and early childhood. *Psychoanalytic Study of the Child, 15,* 9–52.

Bowlby, J. (1969). *Attachment and loss: Vol 1. Attachment*. New York: Basic Books, 1982.

Bowlby, J. (1973). *Attachment and loss: Vol 2: Separation*. New York: Basic Books.

Bretherton, I. (1985). Attachment theory: Retrospect and prospect. *Monographs of the Society for Research in Child Development, 50*(Serial No. 209), 3–35.

Buss, A., & Plomin, R. (1975). *A temperament theory of personality development*. New York: Wiley.

Buss, A., & Plomin, R. (1984). *Temperament: Early developing personality traits*. Hillsdale, NJ: Erlbaum.

Buss, D. M (1984). Evolutionary biology and personality psychology. *American Psychologist, 39,* 1135–1147.

Butcher, J. N. (Ed.). (1972). *Objective personality assessment*. New York: Academic Press.

Butler, J. M., & Rice, L. N. (1963). Adience, self-actualization, and drive theory. In J. L. Wepman & R. Heine (Eds.), *Concepts of personality*. Chicago: Aldine.

Cameron, N. (1963). *Personality development and psychopathology*. New York: Houghton-Mifflin.

Cantor, N., & Genero, N. (1986). Psychiatric diagnosis and natural categorization: A close analogy. In T. Millon & G. L. Klerman (Eds.), *Contemporary directions in psychopathology: Toward the DSM-IV* (pp. 233–256). New York: Guilford Press.

Carson, R. (1993). Can the big-five help salvage the DSM? *Psychological Inquiry, 4,* 98–100.

Cattell, R. B. (1970). The integration of function and psychometric requirements in a quantitative and computerized diagnostic system. In A. R. Mahrer

(Ed.), *New approaches to personality classification* (pp. 9–52). New York: Columbia University Press.

Clark, L., & Watson, D. (1988). Mood and the mundane: Relations between daily life events and self-reported mood. *Journal of Personality and Social Psychology, 54,* 296–308.

Cloninger, C. R. (1986). A unified biosocial theory of personality and its role in the development of anxiety states. *Psychiatric Developments, 3,* 167–226.

Cloninger, C. R. (1987). A systematic method for clinical description and classification of personality variants. *Archives of General Psychiary, 44,* 573–588.

Cole, L. C. (1954). The population consequences of life history phenomena. *Quarterly Review of Biology, 29,* 103–137.

Costa, P. T., & McCrae, R. R. (1990). Personality disorders and the five-factor model of personality. *Journal of Personality Disorders, 4,* 362–371.

Crittenden, P. M. (1990). Internal representational models of attachment. *Infant Mental Health Journal, 11,* 259–277.

Dahlstrom, W. G. (1972). Whither the MMPI? In J. N. Butcher (Ed.), *Objective personality assessment* (pp. 85–116). New York: Academic Press.

Davis, R. D., & Millon, T. (1993). The five-factor model for personality disorders: Apt or misguided? *Psychological Inquiry, 4,* 104–109.

de Charms, R. (1968). *Personal causation: The internal affective determinants of behavior.* New York: Academic Press.

Digman, J. M. (1990). Personality structure: Emergence of the five-factor model. *Annual Review of Psychology, 41,* 417–440.

Ellis, A. (1970). *The essence of rational psychotherapy: A comprehensive approach to treatment.* New York: Institute for Rational Living.

Erikson, E. (1950). *Childhood and society.* New York: Norton.

Erikson, E. (1959). Growth and crises of the healthy personality. In G. S. Klein (Ed.), *Psychological issues.* New York: International Universities Press.

Eysenck, H. (1960). *The structure of human personality.* London: Routledge and Kegan Paul.

Fenichel, O. (1945). *The psychoanalytic theory of the neurosis.* New York: Norton.

Fox, N. A., Kimmerly, N. L., & Schafer, W. D. (1991). Attachment to mother/ attachment to father: A meta-analysis. *Child Development, 62,* 210–225.

Frances, A., Clarkin, J., & Perry, S. (1984). *Differential therapeutics in psychiatry.* New York: Brunner/Mazel.

Freud, S. (1895). Project for a scientific psychology. In *Standard Edition* (Vol. 1). London: Hogarth Press, 1950.

Freud, S. (1908). Character and anal eroticism. In *Collected Papers* (Vol. 2). London: Hogarth Press, 1925.

Freud, S. (1915). The instincts and their vicissitudes. In *Collected Papers* (Vol. 4). London: Hogarth Press, 1925.

Freud, S. (1940). *An outline of psychoanalysis.* New York: Liveright.

Fromm, E. (1955). *The sane society.* New York: Holt, Rinehart & Winston.

Fromm, E. (1968). *The revolution of hope: Toward a humanized technology.* New York: Harper & Row.

Gewirtz, J. L. (1963). A learning analysis of the effects of normal stimulation upon social and exploratory behavior in the human infant. In B. M. Foss (Ed.), *Determinants of infant behavior II.* New York: Wiley.

Gill, M. M. (1963). *Topography and systems in psychoanalytic theory.* New York: International Universities Press.

Gilligan, C. (1982). *In a different voice.* Cambridge, MA. Harvard University Press.

Goldberg, L. R. (1990). An alternative "description of personality": The big-five factor structure. *Journal of Personality and Social Psychology, 59,* 1216–1229.

Goldfarb, W. (1955). Emotional and intellectual consequences of psychologic deprivation in infancy: A reevaluation. In P. Hoch & J. Zubin (Eds.), *Psychopathology of childhood.* New York: Grune & Stratton.

Goldfried, M., & Davison, G. (1976). *Clinical behavior therapy.* New York: Holt, Rinehart & Winston.

Goldstein, K. (1939). *The organism.* New York: American Books.

Goldstein, K. (1940). *Human nature in the light of psychopathology.* Cambridge, MA: Harvard University Press.

Gray, J. A. (Ed.). (1964). *Pavlov's typology.* New York: Pergamon.

Gray, J. A. (1973). Causal theories of personality and how to test them. In J. R. Royce (Ed.), *Multivariate analysis and psychological theory.* New York: Academic Press.

Grove, W. M., & Tellegen, A. (1991). Problems with classification of personality disorders. *Journal of Personality Disorders, 5,* 31–41.

Gurman, A. S., & Kniskern, D. (Eds.). (1981). *The handbook of family therapy.* New York: Brunner/Mazel.

Hall, G. S. (1916). *Adolescence.* New York: Appleton.

Hartmann, H. (1939). *Ego psychology and the problem of adaptation.* New York: International Universities Press.

Hempel, C. G. (1965). *Aspects of scientific explanation.* New York: Free Press.

Hinde, R. A. (1982). Attachment: Some conceptual issues. In J. Stevenson-Hinde (Ed.), *The place of attachment.* New York: Basic Books.

Horney, K. (1937). *The neurotic personality of our time.* New York: Norton.

Jahoda, M. (1958). *Current concepts of positive mental health.* New York: Basic Books.

John, O. P. (1990). The "big five" factor taxonomy: Dimensions of personality in the natural language and in questionnaires. In L. A. Pervin (Ed.), *Handbook of personality: Theory and research* (pp. 66–100). New York: Guilford Press.

Jung, C. G. (1921). *Psychological types.* Zurich: Rasher Verlag.

Jung, C. G. (1961). *Memories, dreams, reflections.* New York: Vintage Books.

Kendall, R. E. (1975). *The role of diagnosis in psychiatry.* Oxford: Blackwell.

Kernberg, O. (1967). Borderline personality organization. *Journal of the American Psychoanalytic Association, 15,* 641–685.

Killackey, H. P. (1990). Neocortical expansion: An attempt toward relating phylogeny and ontogeny. *Journal of Cognitive Neuroscience, 2,* 1–17.

Kline, P., & Barrett, P. (1983). The factors in personality disorders: Ideal types, prototypes, or dimensions? *Journal of Personality Disorders, 5,* 52–59.

Lamb, M. E., Thompson, R. A., & Gardner, W., & Estes, D. (1985). *Infant-mother attachment.* Hillsdale, NJ: Erlbaum.

Lazarus, A. A. (1981). *The practice of multimodal therapy.* New York: McGraw-Hill.

Lipton, S. A., & Kater, S. B. (1989). Neurotransmitter regulation of neuronal outgrowth, plasticity, and survival. *Trends in Neuroscience, 12,* 265–269.

Loevinger, J. (1957). Objective tests as instruments of psychological theory. *Psychological Reports, 3,* 635–694.

Maslow, A. H. (1968). *Toward a psychology of being* (2nd ed.). New York: Van Nostrand.

Maslow, A. H. (1970). *Motivation and personality* (2nd. ed.). New York: Harper & Row.

Meehl, P. E. (1978). Theoretical risks and tabular asterisks: Sir Karl, Sir Ronald, and the slow progress of soft psychology. *Journal of Consulting and Clinical Psychology, 46,* 806–834.

Meichenbaum, D. (1977). *Cognitive-behavior modification.* New York: Plenum Press.

Melzack, R. (1965). Effects of early experience upon behavior: Experimental and conceptual considerations. In P. Hoch & J. Zubin (Eds.), *Psychopathology of perception.* New York: Grune & Stratton.

Menninger, K. (1963). *The vital balance.* New York: Viking.

Millon, T. (1967). (Ed.). *Theories of psychopathology.* Philadelphia: Saunders.

Millon, T. (1969). *Modern psychopathology: A biosocial approach to maladaptive learning and functioning.* Philadelphia: Saunders.

Millon, T. (1977). *Millon Clinical Multiaxial Inventory manual.* Minneapolis: National Computer Systems.

Millon, T. (1981). *Disorders of personality: DSM-III, Axis II.* New York: Wiley–Interscience.

Millon, T. (1983). The DSM-III: An insider's perspective. *American Psychologist, 38,* 804–814.

Millon, T. (1986). A theoretical derivation of pathological personalities. In T. Millon & G. L. Klerman (Eds.), *Contemporary directions in psychopathology: Toward the DSM-IV* (pp. 639–670). New York: Guilford Press.

Millon, T. (1987a). On the nature of taxonomy in psychopathology. In C. Last & M. Hersen (Eds.), *Issues in diagnostic research* (pp. 3–85). New York: Plenum Press.

Millon, T. (1987b). *Millon Clinical Multiaxial Inventory—II.* Minneapolis: National Computer Systems.

Millon, T. (1988). Personologic psychotherapy: Ten commandments for a posteclectic approach to integrative treatment. *Psychotherapy, 25,* 209–219.

Millon, T. (1990). *Toward a new personology: An evolutionary model.* New York: Wiley–Interscience.

Millon, T., & Davis, R. D. (1995). *Disorders of personality: DSM-IV and beyond.* New York: Wiley–Interscience.

Millon, T., & Davis, R. D. (in press). *Synergistic psychotherapy: Integrative syndromic and personologic treatment.* New York: Wiley–Interscience.

Millon, T., Millon, C., & Davis, R. D. (1994). *Millon Chemical Multiaxial Inventory—III.* Minneapolis: National Computer Systems.

Millon, T., Tringone, R., Bockian, N., Green, C., & Sandberg, M. (in press). *The Millon Personality Diagnostic Checklist.* Minneapolis: National Computer Systems.

Millon, T., Weiss, L., Millon, C., & Davis, R. D. (1994). *MIPS: Millon Index of Personality Styles manual.* San Antonio, TX: Psychological Corporation.

Murphy, G. (1947). *Personality: A biosocial approach to origins and structures.* New York: Harper.

Norman, W. (1963). Toward an adequate taxonomy of personality attributes: Replicated factor structure in peer nomination personality ratings. *Journal of Abnormal and Social Psychology, 66,* 574–583.

Offer, D., & Sabshin, M. (Eds). (1974). *Normality.* New York: Basic Books.

Offer, D., & Sabshin, M. (Eds.). (1991). *The diversity of normality.* New York: Basic Books.

Pap, A. (1953). Reduction-sentences and open concepts. *Methods, 5,* 3–30.

Piaget, J. (1952). *The origins of intelligence in children.* New York: International Universities Press.

Purves, D., & Lichtman, J. W. (1985). *Principles of neural development.* Sunderland, MA: Sinauer.

Quine, W. V. O. (1961). *From a logical point of view* (2nd ed.). New York: Harper & Row.

Quine, W. V. O. (1977). Natural kinds. In S. P. Schwartz (Ed.), *Naming, necessity, and natural groups.* Ithaca, NY: Cornell University Press.

Rakic, P. (1985). Limits of neurogenesis in primates. *Science, 227,* 154–156.

Rakic, P. (1988). Specification of cerebral cortical areas. *Science, 241,* 170–176.

Rapaport, D. (1958). The theory of ego-autonomy: A generalization. *Bulletin of the Menninger Clinic, 22,* 13–35.

Rapaport, D. (1959). The structure of psychoanalytic theory: A systematizing attempt. In S. Koch (Ed.), *Psychology: A study of a science.* New York: McGraw-Hill.

Reich, W. (1945). *Character analysis* (3rd ed.). New York: Simon & Schuster, 1972.

Ribble, M. A. (1943). *The rights of infants.* New York: Columbia University Press.

Riesen, A. H. (1961). Stimulation as a requirement for growth and function in behavioral development. In D. Fiske & S. Maddi (Eds.), *Functions of varied experience* (pp. 57–80). Homewood, IL: Dorsey.

Rogers, C. R. (1963). Toward a science of the person. *Journal of Humanistic Psychology, 3,* 79–92.

Rosenzweig, M. R., et al. (1962). Effect of environmental complexity and training on brain chemistry and anatomy: A replication and extension. *Journal of Comparative Physiological Psychology, 55,* 429–437.

Rushton, J.P. (1985). Differential K theory: The sociobiology of individual and group differences. *Personality and Individual Differences, 6,* 441–452.

Russell, J. A. (1980). A circumplex model of affect. *Journal of Personality and Social Psychology, 39,* 1161–1178.

Scott, J. P. (1968). *Early experience and the organization of behavior.* Belmont, CA: Brooks-Cole.

Skinner, B. F. (1938). *The behavior of organisms: An experimental analysis.* New York: Appleton.

Skinner, B. F. (1953). *Science and human behavior.* New York: Macmillan.

Smith, E. E., & Medin, D. L. (1981). *Categories and concepts.* Cambridge, MA: Harvard University Press.

Spencer, H. (1870). *The principles of psychology.* London: Williams & Norgate.

Spitz, R. A. (1965). *The first year of life.* New York: International University Press.

Sprock, J., & Blashfield, R. K. (1984). Classification and nosology. In M. Hersen, A. Kazdin, & A. Bellack (Eds.), *The clinical psychology handbook.* New York: Pergamon Press.

Sroufe, L. A., & Fleeson, J. (1986). Attachment and the construction of relationships. In W. Hartup & Z. Rubin. (Eds.), *Relationships and development* (pp. 51–71). Hillsdale, NJ: Erlbaum.

Tellegen, A. (1985). Structures of mood and personality and relevance to assessing anxiety, with an emphasis on self-report. In A. H. Tuma & J. Maser (Eds.), *Anxiety and the anxiety disorders.* Hillsdale, NJ: Erlbaum.

Thompson, W. R., & Schaefer, T. (1961). Early environmental stimulation. In D. Fiske & S. Maddi (Eds.), *Functions of varied experience* (pp. 81–105). Homewood, IL: Dorsey.

Trivers, R. L. (1974). Parental investment and sexual selection. In B. Campbell (Ed.), *Sexual selection and the descent of man 1871–1971.* Chicago: Aldine.

Tversky, A. (1977). Features of similarity. *Psychological Review, 84,* 327–352.

Volkmar, F., & Provence, S. (1990). *Disorders of affect* (Yale Child Study Center Working Paper). New Haven, CT: Yale Child Study Center.

Wachtel. P. (1977). *Psychoanalysis and behavior therapy: Toward an integration.* New York: Basic Books.

Watson, D., & Clark, L. (1984). Negative affectivity: The disposition to experience aversive emotional states. *Psychological Bulletin, 96,* 465–490.

Watson, D., & Tellegen, A. (1985). Toward a consensual structure of mood. *Psychological Bulletin, 98,* 219–235.

Werner, H. (1940). *Comparative Psychology of Mental Development.* New York: Follett.

White, R. W. (1960). Competence and the psychosexual stages of development. In M. R. Jones (Ed.), *Nebraska Symposium on Motivation.* Lincoln: University of Nebraska Press.

Wilson, E. O. (1975). *Sociobiology: The new synthesis.* Cambridge: Harvard University Press.

Wilson, E. O. (1978). *On human nature.* Cambridge: Harvard University Press.

Yalom, I. D. (1986). *The theory and practice of group psychotherapy* (3rd ed.). New York: Basic Books.

Yarrow, L. J. (1961). Maternal deprivation: Toward and empirical and conceptual reevaluation. *Psychological Bulletin, 58,* 459–490.

6

A Neurobiological Framework for the Structure of Personality and Emotion: Implications for Personality Disorders

RICHARD A. DEPUE

Most psychological research in personality has focused on structure, that is, on the smallest number of higher-order traits derived factor analytically that best account for the larger array of lower-order variables. Although this approach has at times been based on theoretical notions (Eysenck, 1981), the bulk of the work has been characterized by either no, or only loosely formulated, theory (Digman, 1990). Whereas empirical structural analysis in this domain may not require detailed, a priori theoretical foundations, we believe that attempts to relate the structure of central nervous system neurobiology and neurochemistry to the structure of personality, thereby doubling the complexity of the problem, require a clear conceptual framework. The reason for this is that the vast number of potentially relevant central neurobiological variables, and of divergent methods of studying those variables, do not allow, simply on grounds of expense, an empirical structural analysis of many concurrently measured variables, as is common practice in the structure of personality area. Thus, a theoretical strategy is needed to guide selection of the neurobiological and personality variables hypothesized to relate. Unfortunately, the neurobiology of personality area has not evidenced strong theoretical or empirical development since it was initiated by the remarkably insightful ideas of Gray (1973) 20 years ago, creating a paucity of well-recognized, alternative models in the area. Therefore, in order to provide a broad context for a neurobiological analysis of the structure of personality, our theoretical approach to the neurobiology of personality is first explicated.

Recognizing that personality has a reliable structure that appears to be stable across the lifespan, we began by broadening our understanding of this structure by assessing the structure of behavioral systems as defined by ethology and psychology. These domains often utilize an evolutionary biology perspective and, accordingly, suggest that behavioral response patterns evolved as a means of adapting to stimuli that are critical to the organism's survival and to species preservation (Fonberg, 1986; Fowles, 1980; Gray, 1973, 1982; MacLean, 1986, 1990; Panksepp, 1986; Rolls, 1986; Schneirla, 1959). Within this framework, defensive aggression, for instance, serves as an adaptive behavioral response to pain and potential destruction, whereas, in the case of appetitive behaviors, specific olfactory cues serve as critical stimuli in signaling a suitable mate or appropriate food and in eliciting sexual and feeding behavior, respectively. The importance of delineating such systems at the behavioral level is that the behavior provides an observable indicator for discovering the neurobiological networks that mediate the interface between classes of stimulus and specific response patterns.

The fact that the development of behavioral systems has been tightly linked to critical stimulus conditions indicates that the underlying neurobiology of such systems must be closely integrated with brain networks responsible for the recognition of stimulus significance, on the one hand, and the activation of effector systems in addition to locomotor behavior (e.g., hormonal, autonomic, facial, vocal), on the other. Collectively, this group of interrelated brain functions has been referred to as emotion, or emotional evaluation and emotional expression, respectively (LeDoux, 1987). Thus, it is possible to view behavioral systems more generally as emotional systems. This distinction is important, because, the term emotion, derived from the Latin verb *emovere* (to move, to push), not only implies elicitation of behavior in response to critical stimuli but also elicitation of a motivational state and subjective emotional experience that is concordant with the affective nature or reinforcement properties of critical stimuli (Fonberg, 1986; Gray, 1973, 1982; MacLean, 1986; Rolls, 1986). In the broadest sense, then, the structure of behavior reflects the existence of neurobehavioral–emotional systems that elicit and motivate certain subjective emotional experiences and overt patterns of behavior to particular *classes* of stimulus. Thus, a particular class of stimulus, the emotional feelings and motivation generated, and the behavior patterns expressed all form integral components of a coherent emotional system.

ANALOGOUS STRUCTURE OF NEUROBEHAVIORAL–EMOTIONAL SYSTEMS AND PERSONALITY

Types and Organization of Neurobehavioral Systems

As a group, neurobehavioral systems can be conceived as lying along a dimension of increasing generality in all components of a system, including eliciting stimuli, motivational–emotional feelings, and response patterns (Fonberg, 1986; Gray, 1973; MacLean, 1986; Panksepp, 1986). At the highest level of the dimension, there are a limited number of *general* neurobehavioral systems (Blackburn, Phillips, Jakubovic, & Fibiger, 1989; MacLean, 1986; Ploog, 1986). They are general because none of the components of the system, such as eliciting stimuli, motivational–emotional feelings, or overt response patterns, is highly specialized for direct interaction with specific stimulus contexts. Rather, general neurobehavioral systems are elicited by a broad *class* of unconditioned and conditioned stimuli (Collins & Depue, 1992; Depue, in press; Gray, 1973; Rolls, 1986). In turn, these systems provide the emotional, motivational, and behavioral components that comprise a general emotional–behavioral disposition, such as desire–approach or anxiety–constraint–inhibition. This general disposition can be viewed as modulatory rather than mediating in nature. That is, the disposition serves to affectively modulate goal-directed activity according to internal conditions and to a changing external context of reinforcement.

It is this type of neurobehavioral system that is associated with the more generalized subjective experiences typically referred to as *emotion* (or emotional experience; LeDoux, 1987). This is not to imply, however, that the emotion is not specific to a particular system. Indeed, analyses of the basic types of emotion (Levi, 1975; Plutchik, 1980; Plutchik & Kellerman, 1986), combined with ethological descriptions of mammalian behavioral systems (MacLean, 1969, 1970, 1990), suggest that the emotions of desire, anger, fear, sorrow, joy, and affection are elicited by particular classes of stimulus and subsequently motivate six generalized forms of behavior including searching, aggressive, protective, dejected, gratulant, and caressive, respectively (MacLean, 1986). Gray (1973, 1982) has added to this list a system of behavioral inhibition that is associated with anxiety and that is activated by conditioned signals of punishment, nonreward, and novelty.

It is the *general* neurobehavioral–emotional systems that greatly influence the structure of mammalian behavior. The reason for this relates to frequency of elicitation: The general systems, which provide the relatively small number of behavioral–emotional dispositions supporting all goal-directed activity, are frequently activated by broad classes of stimulus that are almost always present in a widespread array of goal contexts. In reference to the stucture of *human* behavior, the contribution of general neurobehavioral systems in determining an enduring emotional–motivational disposition is magnified because of the predominant influence of symbolic (conditioned) processes in guiding human behavior in the absence of unconditioned stimuli (Fowles, 1987; Gray, 1973). Hence, in humans, the general neurobehavioral systems would be subject to highly frequent stimulus elicitation, arousing an affective dispositional tone to ongoing behavior.

The Structure of a General Neurobehavioral–Emotional System

Defining the basic structure of a general neurobehavioral–emotional system per se is of great importance if it is to guide an analogy to the structure of personality traits. An example, which will provide a focus of our discussion below, will help to reveal this structure. One general neurobehavioral–emotional system that has been consistently described in all animals across phylogeny (Hebb, 1949; Schneirla, 1959) has been referred to variously as a search system (MacLean, 1986), a foraging–expectancy system (Panksepp, 1986), an approach system (Gray 1973; Schneirla, 1959), a preparatory system (Blackburn et al., 1989), and a behavioral activation system (Fowles, 1980). For reasons that become evident later, we integrate these terms into one notion of a "behavioral facilitation system" (BFS). All of these descriptions, with minor variations, converge on the same basic theme: The BFS is an emotional system characterized by incentive–reward motivation and subjective feelings of desire and positivity that activate forward locomotion and search behavior as a means of satisfying an animal's need for food, a sex partner, social interaction, a nesting place, and so forth. That is, the BFS is elicited by, and serves to bring the animal into contact with, the broad class of unconditioned and conditioned incentive stimuli connoting reward (Collins & Depue, 1992; Gray, 1973; Panksepp, 1986).

As illustrated in Figure 6.1A, the BFS (in shaded box) can be modeled as a construct having a hierarchical structure. At the bottom of

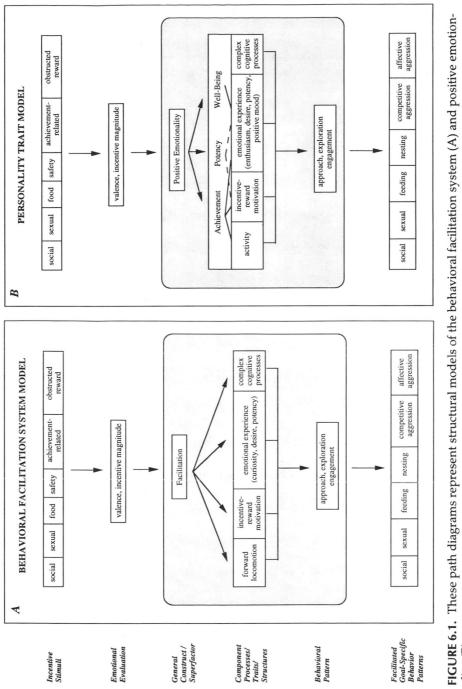

FIGURE 6.1. These path diagrams represent structural models of the behavioral facilitation system (A) and positive emotionality (B).

the hierarchy, interaction with specific rewarding stimuli (e.g., social, sexual, achievement-related) is mediated by *goal-specific* neurobehavioral systems that have evolved as behavioral patterns that are appropriate to a particular rewarding stimulus context (e.g., social). At an intermediate level of the hierarchy, hypothetical intervening processes comprise major BFS components that operate *jointly* in each of the different interactional contexts in order to provide a general modulation of the *specific* neurobehavioral systems. As indicated in Figure 6.1A, this modulation is comprised of motivational (incentive–reward motivation), emotional (desire and positive feelings), locomotor, and cognitive processes. The highest level of the hierarchy represents the higher-order or general behavioral construct of facilitation that orchestrates, via various neurobiological networks, an activation of the BFS components that jointly modulate each of the specific behavioral interactions.

The structure of this model illustrates the common, broad, affective modulatory influence that general neurobehavioral–emotional systems may potentially exert. It also suggests that the putative neurobiology of the higher-order, general neurobehavioral system in the model is likely to be one that can achieve widely dispersed, generalized neurobiological influence across several neurobiological networks that are all aimed at eliciting, motivating, and guiding various forms of goal-directed behavior.

The Structure of Personality and Its Superfactors

The importance of a neurobehavioral systems perspective for understanding the structure of *human* behavior has not been generally recognized. However, as Gray (1973) and others (Fonberg, 1986; MacLean, 1986, 1990; Panksepp, 1986) have argued, behavioral systems that are closely linked to emotional mechanisms are likely to be largely unchanged along the pathway of mammalian evolution and, hence, may be subject to strong genetic influence in our own species. Such systems, therefore, may provide a foundation for individual differences in human emotional patterns (Plutchik, 1980). When viewed from a broad temporal perspective, emotional systems may be conceptualized not simply as phasic response patterns but, rather, as emotional dispositions with respect to particular classes of stimulus. That is to say that humans may have individual differences in their sensitivity to particular classes of stimulus (Gray, 1973) and that these differences are evident as trait variation both in subjective emotional experience and in overt patterns of emotional expression. Thus, it is possible to view emotional systems as major structural components of stable patterns of human behavior—or, put simply, of personality (Ervin & Martin, 1986; Fowles, 1980; Gray, 1973; Plutchik, 1980; Tellegen & Waller, in press; Zuckerman, 1983).

Human personality can be characterized as having an organizational structure that is analogous to that of neurobehavioral systems (see personality reviews by Digman, 1990; Eysenck & Eysenck, 1985; Tellegen, 1985; Tellegen & Waller, in press; Zuckerman, Kuhlman, Thornquist, & Kiers, 1991). As appears to be the case for the general neurobehavioral systems, a limited number, typically varying between three and five, of higher-order personality superfactors have been repeatedly confirmed in recent years. One of the most robust structural approaches defines a three-factor model (Eysenck & Eysenck, 1985; Tellegen, 1985; Tellegen & Waller, in press; Zuckerman et al., 1991) where, in both the Eysenck and Tellegen models, as well as in the three-factor solution of Zuckerman et al. (1991), the three superfactors (extraversion or positive emotionality, neuroticism or negative emotionality, psychoticism or constraint, respectively) are quite similar in nature. Of particular importance to our discussion is that at least two of the three superfactors in three-factor models of personality have been conceived as representing major emotional–motivational dispositional traits, one characterized by positive emotionality based on an incentive–reward system, the other by negative emotionality based on a fear–anxiety system (Eysenck, 1981; Fowles, 1980, 1987; Gray, 1973, 1982; Tellegen, 1985; Tellegen & Waller, in press; Watson & Tellegen, 1985; Zuckerman, 1983; Zuckerman et al., 1991).

Importantly, each of the superfactors, like the general neurobehavioral systems, is conceived as having a hierarchical structure. That is, the three superfactors, as illustrated in the example of a personality trait model in Figure 6.1B, can be subdivided into a larger number of lower-order traits, and each of these may, in turn, be subdivided further into even narrower, or what is referred to as *surface,* traits. As in the structural model of a general neurobehavioral system, the superfactor represents a general emotional–behavioral (affective) disposition with respect to the class of stimulus relevant to the superfactor, whereas lower-order traits comprising major components of the superfactor (achievement, potency, well-being) exert their influence *jointly* on each of a variety of goal-specific behavior patterns, which represent self-reported behavior in specific stimulus contexts. For instance, as shown in Figure 6.1B, Tellegen's superfactor construct of positive emotionality (PEM, which I suggest is the personality construct analogous to the animal construct of the BFS) represents the general tendency to experience feelings of incentive, effectance motivation, excitement, ambition, potency, positive affect, and well-being—that is, subjective characteristics associated with the BFS construct (Collins & Depue, 1992). The traits comprising PEM (achievement, potency, well-being) reflect this same general disposition (incentive, locomotor activity, well-being), which, in turn, jointly motivate goal-specific behavior patterns (Tellegen & Waller, in press).

If this structural analysis is correct, then the hierarchical structures of personality superfactors and general neurobehavioral–emotional systems may be more than descriptively similar, as suggested in Figure 6.1. Particularly at the highest level of the hierarchical structure, the emotional–motivational disposition associated with *general* neurobehavioral system constructs and with personality *superfactor* constructs may share a common neurobiology and neurochemistry (Depue, in press). The power of this conceptual approach to personality is that the nature of neurobehavioral systems can be informed by basic animal research in behavioral neurobiology, thereby providing a guiding framework for *exploring* the nature of the neurobiology of personality. This means that the goal of human research comparing the concordance of neurobehavioral and personality structures represents an attempt to specify the psychometrically based "open" concepts (such as PEM in Figure 6.1) with neurobehavioral systems.

PUTATIVE NEUROBIOLOGY OF THREE PERSONALITY SUPERFACTORS

Positive Emotionality

It has been proposed (Depue, in press) that the BFS, and its underlying neurobiology, forms a central component of a major superfactor of personality structure, that is, positive emotionality. Similar to theoretical accounts of PEM, the BFS is activated by a broad array of stimulus contexts, where these contexts share in common an incentive–reward component. All of these stimulus conditons could be viewed as initiating at least three core BFS processes: (1) incentive–reward motivation, (2) forward locomotion as a means of supporting goal acquisition, and (3) cognitive processes, since active goal seeking facilitated by the BFS will increase interaction with, and hence the need to evaluate, the environment. As we have reviewed previously, these core processes are mediated by activity in two major ascending dopamine (DA) projection systems (Collins & Depue, 1992; Depue, in press; Depue & Iacono, 1989; Depue, Luciana, Arbisi, Collins, & Leon, 1994): (1) the mesolimbic system, arising from A-10 DA cells in the ventral tegmental area (VTA) of the midbrain and projecting to limbic structures such as the amygdala, hippocampus, and nucleus accumbens (NAS, included here as part of the limbic striatum; Oades & Halladay, 1987); and (2) the mesocortical system, also originating in the VTA and projecting to all areas of the cerebral cortex.

A Motivational–Emotional Role for the Mesolimbic System

A vast literature on the behavioral effects of DA manipulations indicates that mesolimbic DA projections play a critical role in motivational and emotional aspects of the BFS (see reviews of Depue, in press; Depue et al., 1994; Kalivas & Barnes, 1993; Le Moal & Simon, 1991; Oades, 1985). The nature of this role has been the subject of several recent reviews that are concordant in their conclusions that VTA DA projections appear to have the general function of facilitating neural processes in brain regions subserving motivational–emotional behavior (Cools, 1980; Kalivas & Barnes, 1993; Le Moal & Simon, 1991; Louilot, Taghzouti, Deminiere, Simon, & Le Moal, 1987; Oades, 1985; Robbins & Everitt, 1982). The general effects of DA agonists in rats and monkeys are to facilitate locomotor activity, incentive–reward motivation, exploratory behavior, aggressive behavior, an increased number of behavioral strategies, and acquisition and maintenance of approach and active avoidance behavior. Conversely, bilateral 6-hydroxydopamine (6-OHDA) lesions in rats and monkeys resulting in DA reductions of 90% or more in the VTA or NAS produce major deficits in the initiation of behavior associated with incentive motivation, including social interaction, sexual behavior, food-hoarding, behavior, maternal nursing behavior, approach and active avoidance responses, exploratory activity in novel environments, and locomotor activity. These deficits are not motor per se, because diurnal locomotor patterns remain unchanged, and animals perform various tasks normally once they are moved or pushed by the experimenter to do so (Oades, 1985). Moreover, the deficit is not evident in nonvolitional behavior, such as escape behavior. It is precisely the incentive-motivational influence that is lost with DA lesions (Beninger, 1983; Bozarth, 1987; Le Moal & Simon, 1991; Stein, 1983), such that volitional behavior elicited by incentive stimuli cannot be initiated or facilitated. On the basis of such findings, Stein (1983) concluded that DA activity mediates the incentive type of reward that activates goal acquisition, rather than the gratifying type of reward that terminates behavior.

The *initiation* of forward locomotion relates to the facilitation of emotion, because the initiation process is closely tied to affective-motivational input to the motor system (Mogenson, Brudzynski, Wu, Yang, & Yim, 1980). There is a vast literature demonstrating that DA, but not norepinephrine (NE), is the primary neurotransmitter in the initiation of locomotion (see reviews by Fishman, Feigenbaum, Yanaiz, & Klawans, 1983; Le Moal & Simon, 1991; Oades, 1985). Importantly, locomotion initiation occurs via the action of DA and its agonists in the mesolimbic DA projections to the NAS in particular (Fishman et al., 1983). Other mesolimbic DA projections do not account in a significant way for initiation of locomotion (Oades, 1985; Oades, Taghzouti, Rivet, Simon, & Le Moal, 1986).

The fact that a facilitation function is observed in an array of different neural structures and different behavioral functions suggests that DA does not *mediate* specific functions but rather provides a facilitatory *modulation* of behavioral processes integrated within different areas of the brain. This has been demonstrated by examining the behavioral consequences of selective lesions of DA neurons both at the level of the cell bodies (Simon, Scatton, & Le Moal, 1980) and at the level of the terminals in the prefrontal cortex (Simon et al., 1980), in the NAS (Taghzouti, Le Moal, & Simon, 1985; Taghzouti, Louilot, Herman, Le Moal, & Simon, 1985), and in the lateral septum (Taghzouti, Simon, Louilot, Herman, & Le Moal, 1985; Taghzouti, Simon, Tazi, Dantzer, & Le Moal, 1985; Taghzouti, Simon, & Le Moal, 1986). This interpretation is also suggested by the fact that selective DA lesions in these various projection areas create behavioral deficits that are similar to deficits produced by electrolytic lesions of those same areas (Le Moal & Simon, 1991; Louilot et al., 1987; Taghzouti, Louilot, et al., 1985; Taghzouti et al., 1986).

Cognitive Processes and the Mesocortical System

To ensure that approach behavior is adaptively related to stimulus events, there will be an increased need to construct maps of extrapersonal space, to identify objects in space, to organize behavioral strategies, and to evaluate the emotional significance of objects and the outcome of those behavioral strategies. These are complex cognitive functions. Their functional integrity requires the passage of information among distinct brain regions that serve as processing nodes in neural networks devoted to cognitive functions (Goldman-Rakic, 1987, 1988; Kosslyn, 1988; Mesulam, 1990; Posner, Petersen, Fox, & Raichle, 1988). Mesocortical DA projections appear to facilitate neocortical processes that underlie cognitive functions necessary for behavioral flexibility. This evidence is reviewed elsewhere (Depue, Luciana, & Collins, 1995; Luciana, Depue, Arbisi, & Leon, 1992; Oades, 1985) but can be summarized briefly. First, mesocortical–prefrontal, as compared to mesolimbic, neurons show markedly enhanced DA utilization to perturbations of environmental conditions that require adaptive responding (such as in a range of mild stressors; Deutch, Bourdelais, & Zahm, 1993). From an evolutionary biology perspective, the relatively higher reactivity to variation in environmental challenge by the prefrontal mesocortical, compared to the mesolimbic, DA system may be advantageous: It would be appropriate to cognitively evaluate environmental conditions through cognitive processing *prior* to the facilitation of overt emotional responding. Second, mesocortical DA projections play a critical role in spatial working memory processes of the principal sulcal (PS) region of the dorsolateral prefrontal cortex (DLPFC) (Goldman-Rakic, 1987, 1988). Neurochemical DA lesion of the DLPFC (Brown, Crane, & Goldman, 1979) and pharmacological blockade of D_1 receptors in the PS region of monkeys (Sawaguchi & Goldman-Rakic, 1991) impairs, and D_2 receptor agonists in humans facilitate (Luciana et al., 1992), visuospatial delayed response performance. Finally, DA enhances the activity of PS neurons of monkeys that show activity associated with mnemonic processes, including the spatial visual cue, the delay, and/or the response during delayed response tasks (Sawaguchi, Matsumura, & Kubota, 1990).

In sum, then, the BFS, via its underlying VTA DA ascending projection systems, (1) facilitates cognitive processes required in the construction and evaluation of the environment, (2) provides an interface between neural structures communicating the emotional state of incentive motivation to the initiatory structures of the motor system, and (3) initiates emotional response patterns that support goal acquisition.

A Functional Model of VTA DA Response Facilitation

Models of behavioral facilitation typically define the minimum threshold for response facilitation as being a joint function of two main variables: level of DA postsynaptic receptor activation and amplitude of stimulation (Blackburn et al., 1989; Cools, 1980; Oades, 1985; White, 1986). Because at least two variables determine the minimum threshold for response facilitation, independent variation in either one of the variables not only modifies the probability of response facilitation, but it also simultaneously modifies the value of the other variable that is required to reach a minimum threshold for facilitation. The relationship between these two variables is represented in Figure 6.2 as a trade-off function (White, 1986) where the set of values of the two input variables (DA activation and stimulus amplitude) required to produce a minimum threshold value for response facilitation is described. The trade-off function can be thought of as a central nervous system weighting of

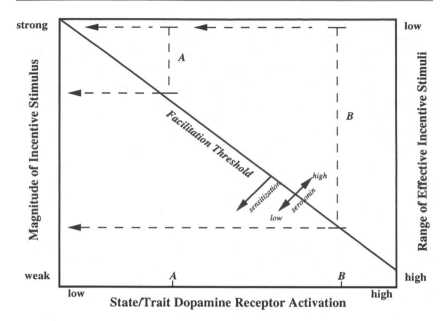

FIGURE 6.2. The threshold for behavioral facilitation is illustrated as a trade-off function between incentive stimulus magnitude (left vertical axis) and DA postsynaptic receptor activation (horizontal axis). Range of effective (facilitating) incentive stimuli is illustrated on the right vertical axis as a function of level of DA activation. Two hypothetical individuals with low and high trait DA postsynaptic receptor activation (demarcated on the horizontal axis as A and B, respectively) are shown to have narrow (A) and broad (B) ranges of effective incentive stimuli, respectively. The effects of variation in serotonin functioning and of sensitization of VTA DA functioning on the threshold for behavioral facilitation is illustrated as well.

the external and internal factors that contribute to response facilitation (White, 1986).

As discussed above, there is a large body of evidence demonstrating that modulation of VTA DA projection systems markedly influences the probability of response facilitation. Moreover, enduring alterations of VTA DA functioning, particularly in DA release in the NAS, are associated with long-term or permanent changes in the threshold for response facilitation. For instance, the number of DA neurons in the VTA cell group, the relative density of innervation of DA terminals in target fields, and the DA content in the NAS in inbred mouse strains are positively related to the degree of facilitation of spontaneous exploratory and amphetamine-induced locomotion, effects perhaps related to the proportionately greater synthesis and release of DA in high-DA neuron strains (Fink & Reis, 1981; Oades, 1985; Sved, Baker,

& Reis, 1984, 1985). It also appears to be the case that the effective value of stimulation with respect to the threshold for response facilitation is modified by alterations in DA activity: Increased DA activity has been found to enhance responding to conditioned reinforcers (Beninger, 1983; Beninger, Hanson, & Phillips, 1980; Hill, 1970; Robbins, 1975). To the extent that the incentive value of these stimuli are then encoded in an enduring manner, thus becoming valenced central affective representations of the stimulus (Mishkin, 1982), the learning of incentive value will vary depending on current DA activity level and, hence, may represent one form of state-dependent learning.

Stable Individual Differences in DA Functioning

The trade-off function between stimulus amplitude and DA activation would predict that individual differences in DA reactivity to incentive stimuli may have marked effects on the probability of behavioral facilitation. There is a broad range of stable individual differences in animals in DA-mediated behaviors that support the importance of individual differences in DA responsiveness for behavioral facilitation processes (Le Moal & Simon, 1991; Piazza, Deminere, Le Moal, & Simon, 1989). For instance, an inbred mouse strain that has a significantly increased number of neurons in all DA cell groups examined (including the VTA) reliably shows markedly facilitated behavior, including higher levels of spontaneous exploratory locomotion in novel but not frightening environments, and a greater locomotor activity response to DA agonist challenge (Oades, 1985). That this increased behavioral facilitation in high-DA-neuron strains results from DA activation is suggested by a greater density of innervation of DA terminals in target fields, proportionately greater synthesis and release of DA, greater inhibition of prolactin secretion by a DA agonist, and, importantly in terms of locomotor facilitation, an increased DA content in the NAS. Furthermore, Piazza et al. (1989) found that rats selected for highly facilitated locomotor activity in novel environments also showed a significantly greater locomotor response to a DA agonist (amphetamine) challenge and a more rapid acquisition, as well as a higher final level, of self-administration of amphetamine than rats selected for low locomotor responses to novelty.

The effective value of stimulation with respect to the threshold for response facilitation is modified by alterations in DA activity: Increased DA activity has been found to enhance responding to conditioned reinforcers (Beninger, 1983; Beninger et al., 1980; Hill, 1970; Robbins, 1975). This implies that stable individual differences in DA activity may have the effect of modulating the emotional evaluation of incentive stimuli (i.e., their perceived intensity) as well as the threshold for stimulus elicitation of subsequent responses. This relation of DA to stimulus effective value is illustrated in Figure 6.2 as creating variation in the *range* of effective stimuli: With increasing levels of trait DA activity, the effective facilitatory value of stimuli increases in that an increasing number of weaker stimuli, that may even be normally of subthreshold facilitatory efficacy, now have the capacity to facilitate responses. This suggests that the range of effective stimuli increases with increasing DA activity, a relationship that is illustrated by narrow (A) and broad (B) ranges in Figure 6.2 as a function of low- and high-DA activity, respectively. Since the number of DA cells in the VTA also displays substantial variation in humans (Oades & Halliday, 1987), if the positive relationship between DA cell number and behavioral facilitation found in animals holds in humans, stable individual differences in DA activity in humans may bear a relationship to differences in behavioral facilitation thresholds, or, according to our model, in trait levels of PEM.

Constraint

One of the three superfactors in three-factor models of personality structure has many names, including psychoticism (Eysenck, 1981; Zuckerman et al., 1991) and constraint (Tellegen & Waller, in press), but together they convey a core construct of affective and cognitive impulsivity. Moreover, generally, and for Tellegen in particular, this trait is not associated with any particular affective system, that is, it is a nonaffective dimension of behavior reflecting the ease at which behavior is elicited by controlling stimuli. Inventory measures of constraint are heterogeneous in subdomains: for instance, Tellegen's Multidimensional Personality Questionnaire (MPQ) Constraint scale includes three subscales: control (impulsivity), harm avoidance (fear of unconditioned stimulus [UCS] contexts), and traditionalism (uneasiness with novelty). We propose, and present data below, that constraint—specifically the *impulsivity* subdomain—is related to functional activity in central nervous system serotonin (5-HT) projections (see reviews by Depue & Spoont, 1986; Depue & Zald, 1993; Spoont, 1992).

A Functional Principle of 5-HT in Interaction with DA Activity

Animal research helps to clarify the role of 5-HT in behavioral processes. Anatomical features of ascending 5-HT neurons suggest a tonic modulatory, usually inhibitory, influence on the flow of information in the brain. 5-HT terminals provide a widespread, diffuse pattern of innervation in the brain (Spoont, 1992; Tork, 1990). Moreover, 5-HT neurons display slow regular firing, have a long latency of exerting postsynaptic effects, have a long temporal postsynaptic effect, and manifest nonspecific changes in unit activity to a variety of afferent inputs arising from the cortex, and limbic, reticular, motor, and arousal structures (Azmitia & Gannon, 1986). Thus, the 5-HT signal appears to be a tonic inhibitory one that lacks differentiation as to the information being conveyed.

Behavioral neurobiology research with animals has demonstrated repeatedly that 5-HT provides a tonic inhibitory influence over DA-mediated facilitatory effects on initiation of locomotor activity, exploratory activity to novelty, reactivity to reward, aggression, and general emotional reactivity (Depue & Spoont, 1986; Spoont, 1992). Indeed, low 5-HT animals and humans are consistently described as emotionally hyperreactive or emotionally labile to most incentive–reward contexts. Moreover, 5-HT plays a crucial role in neurobiological reactivity to stimulation. For instance, 5-HT exerts a tonic inhibitory influence on (1) sensitization to auditory and tactile startle stimuli, (2) nociceptive sensitivity, and (3) escape latencies following periacquiductal gray stimulation (Depue & Zald, 1993). Investigators have consistently noted an exaggerated reactivity in animals and humans with low 5-HT functioning to all forms of stimulation, even stimulation of relatively low intensity. It is as if the individual has exquisite sensitivity to sensory input, and finds this sensitivity to be aversive, resulting in a rather *chronic irritability*.

Thus, the low 5-HT animal could be viewed as one that has a low threshold to the facilitation of behavioral or emotional responding, whereas the high 5-HT animal would require a much stronger stimulus input to overide the higher 5-HT threshold effect and, thus, to facilitate a behavioral response. This effect on the threshold for behavioral facilitation is shown in interaction with DA in Figure 6.2 above. This interaction is also illustrated in Figure 6.3 within a *hypothetical* personality framework, where the affectively unipolar dimension of PEM (DA facilitation) is seen in interaction with the nonaffective dimension of constraint (5-HT threshold for facilitation). The interaction of these two traits creates, along the diagonal, a dimension of behavioral stability in terms of affective, cognitive, interpersonal, motor, and incentive processes. This diagonal represents the line of greatest variance in stability, from lability in the upper-left quadrant of the two-space (low 5-HT, high DA) to rigidity in the lower-right quadrant (high 5-HT, low DA). Thus, in this model, the ease with which an individual expresses emotional responses, and the extent to which emotional responding alternates between different behavioral responses (stability), are joint functions of the relative strength of DA- and 5-HT-

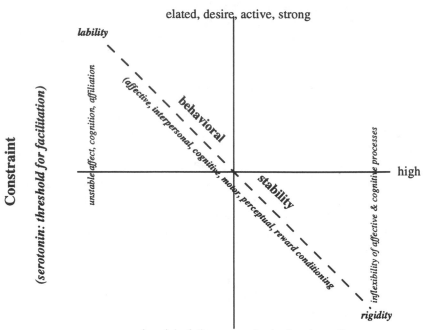

FIGURE 6.3. A hypothetical personality framework illustrating the interaction of two personality superfactors: positive emotionality and constraint.

modulatory influences on the threshold for behavioral–emotional facilitation.

Low 5-HT Activity and Behavioral Instability in Humans

This work has been reviewed previously (Coccaro & Siever, 1991; Depue & Spoont, 1986; Depue & Zald, 1993; Spoont, 1992). It began with Brown's (Brown, Goodwin, Ballenger, Goyer, & Major, 1979) inventive studies on military recruits who had committed aggressive acts that led to discharge. Brown found that most of these men had personality disorders characterized by emotional instability and impulsivity, including impulsive, explosive, borderline, and antisocial personality disorders. That is, they had what now would be referred to as the unstable group of personality disorders. Quantitative estimates of aggressive life history derived from interview correlated highly ($r = -.78$) with the major metabolite of 5-HT measured in cerebrospinal fluid (CSF), CSF 5-hydroxyindoleacetic acid (5-HIAA), as did the Minnesota Multiphasic Personality Inventory (MMPI) Psychopathic deviancy (Pd) scale ($r = -.77$). Other patterns of correlation among different scales helped to define the trait underlying the 5-HT–aggression association. The aggressive life history index correlated highly ($r = .77$) with the overall Buss–Durkee Hostility Inventory (BDHI), whereas the Pd scale correlated with the life history index only at $r = .57$. Thus, although both BDHI and Pd measures contain a domain related to 5-HT functioning, these domains may not be identical. Interestingly, the Pd scale does not relate significantly to the behavioral aggression subscale of BDHI, but it does relate ($r = .64$) to the irritability subscale, indicating that irritable aggression may be accounting for the Pd–5-HIAA correlation.

Numerous studies have since documented a strong relationship between irritable, assaultive aggression and various indicators of low 5-HT. For instance, in one of the most carefully performed investigations, Coccaro et al. (1989) found that the maximum increase in prolactin stimulated by the 5-HT agonist fenfluramine was most highly correlated with the Irritability plus Assault scales of BDHI ($r = -.77$), and this was particularly the case in patients with unstable types of personality disorders, including borderline disorder. This confirms previous work (see Coccaro & Siever, 1991) showing that reduced levels of CSF 5-HIAA are inversely related to impulsive violence, impulsive homicide, impulsive arson, and outwardly directed hostility, as well as Eysenck's Psychoticism scale, in normal volunteers (Coccaro et al., 1989). Moreover, a 2-year prospective follow-up study of children and adolescents with disruptive behavior disorders at time 1 found that baseline CSF 5-HIAA significantly predicted severity of physical aggression during follow-up. And a significant inverse correlation between CSF 5-HIAA and ranking of aggression was found for rhesus monkeys in their natural habitat. Thus, one of the strongest, most consistent findings in the human behavioral neurobiology area is between aggression of an impulsive type, rather than planned or attitudinal hostility forms, and reduced 5-HT functioning.

Low indices of 5-HT functioning have also been robustly related to suicidal behavior (including both attempters and completers) (Coccaro & Siever, 1991; Depue & Spoont, 1986). Reduced 5-HT in this case does not appear to be a marker of depressed state, depressive disorder, or suicide in general. It is particularly related to what is referred to as "violent" suicidal behavior, where the means of suicide include jumping off high places, gun shots, stabbing, gas poisoning, and multiple longitudinal wrist cuts (as opposed to drug overdose). This appears to be an impulsive suicidal behavior in that, on Beck's suicide scale, the only difference between high and low CSF 5-HIAA suicide attempters (besides violence of method) was that the latter had a shorter period of planning for the attempt (Depue & Spoont, 1986). The relationship of suicidal behavior and low 5-HT functioning appears to be unrelated to type of psychopathology, having been found for depression, nondepressed schizophrenics, nondepressed alcoholics and personality disorder subjects, obsessive–compulsive patients, schizoaffective subjects, and anxiety disorders (Coccaro & Siever, 1991). When reduced 5-HT has been related to depression, it appears to bear a closer, inverse relationship to frequency of episode as opposed to depressive disorder per se (van Praag, 1984).

It is possible that suicidal behavior and impulsive aggression represent two different indicators of a central (behavioral and biochemical) trait, such as a low threshold for emotional facilitation. This is supported by the fact that both indicators often co-occur, and by the fact that this co-occurrence is associated with the most extreme quantitative values of the trait (i.e., the lowest CSF 5-HIAA values) (Depue & Spoont, 1986). Moreover, other forms of disorder appear to be associated with reduced 5-HT functioning, and these have a high incentive–reward sensitivity component. For instance, there is initial evidence that sufferers of so-called type B alcoholism (Babor et al., 1992), which is characterized by childhood risk factors, early onset of alcohol-related problems, polydrug use, a more chronic treatment history, greater psychopathological dysfunction, and poorer treatment outcome, have reduced 5-HT functioning that may serve as a vulnerability factor.

Taking the human work together with the animal behavioral research on 5-HT and with our model on the interaction of 5-HT and DA in Figures 6.2 and 6.3 above, at least three broad characteristics of low 5-HT functioning are indicated:

1. *Emotional instability.* A 5-HT-produced low threshold for emotional expression should result in (a) easier elicitation of an emotional response by a relatively low intensity stimulus, (b) an increased magnitude of the emotional response due to more slowly engaged negative feedback mechanisms, and (c) emotional lability, that is, an increased propensity to experience a variety of emotions per unit time. This would reflect a reduced threshold to emotionally eliciting stimuli gaining access to, and coming to dominate, output neural circuits, even when the circuits are currently engaged in expression of another emotional response (Spoont, 1992). Emotions that are accompanied by strong BFS (and DA) activity as a means of supporting the behavioral

components of the emotional pattern may be expressed with particularly high frequency and intensity. For instance, this would be true of "affective aggression," which is strongly enhanced by DA administration (Dupue & Spoont, 1986). Affective aggression is a goal-oriented response pattern that follows many principles of incentive–reward–elicited behavior. An attack program must be facilitated in order to be effective. Therefore, low 5-HT conditions in man, as in animals, are accompanied by a history of frequent, intense, impulsive affective aggression and assault.

2. *Exaggerated response to stimulus conditions eliciting DA facilitation.* A 5-HT-produced low threshold to DA facilitation of behavior (i.e., to BFS reactivity) should result in an exaggerated response to stimulus conditions of incentive reward. If the animal literature can be taken as a model here, this exaggeration should be greatest in conflict situations that can be resolved by engaging the reward option or by actively avoiding punishment by engaging the reward of safety. The effects of this condition are at least fourfold:

a. The person's sensitivity to current reward stimuli would be greater than the person's sensitivity to imagined, expected future rewards and to cues of future, potential aversive outcomes (i.e., conditioned stimuli of future punishment). This would seem devastating for adult levels of behavior, because it implies that the human ability to guide extensively delayed, long-term behavior programs, such as in obtaining a Bachelor's degree at the end of completing 4 years of college, by repeatedly bringing and holding on-line rewarding expected outcomes of the program and aversive expected outcomes if the program is not followed, is compromised. Behavior would be oriented to "chasing" short-term rewards at the expense of achieving more enduring life goals.

b. An increased reactivity to the reward of safety—or in daily life circumstances, sanctuary from stress and conflict—may become manifest as strong active avoidance. When the conflict is intense, and no other means of dealing with it are apparent, active avoidance may be engaged in rather impulsively, as a means of gaining relief. Therefore, low-5-HT conditions in humans may be associated with active avoidance at its most tragic level, that is, *suicidal behavior.*

c. The combination of overreactivity to reward and of performance of active avoidance when conflict becomes unbearable suggests that low-5-HT conditions in humans may be characterized by a general tendency to *impulsive behavior,* that is, a propensity to respond to reward when withholding or delaying a response may produce a more favorable long-term outcome.

d. A low-5-HT condition may be accompanied by frequent, varied attempts to experience the increased magnitude and frequency of DA facilitation—or rather, DA-related incentive reward. Thus, it may be expected that use and *abuse of DA-activating agents* would be a strong correlate of low 5-HT conditions. This has been found to be the case in animal research (Depue & Spoont, 1986; Spoont, 1992), where there is increased self-administration of DA-active drugs and an increased preference and tolerance for alcohol, whose initial incentive effects result from increased DA release (Depue & Iacono, 1989). This also seems to be the case in humans (Babor et al., 1992; Coccaro & Siever, 1991).

3. *Irritability–hypersensitivity.* Low-5-HT animals are excessively irritable to any environmental purturbation. They are described as hypersensitive and hyperreactive to stimulation in several sensory modalities, including tactile, auditory, and visual. This may be caused in part, by reduced sensory modulation at several levels of the brain (see Depue & Zald, 1993), as well as by reduced 5-HT inhibition of the lateral hypothalamic region that activates autonomic reactivity under stressful conditions. Thus, it is not surprising that irritability is a central feature of low-5-HT conditions in humans (Coccaro et al., 1989).

Negative Emotionality

Tellegen (Tellegen & Waller, in press; Watson & Tellegen, 1985) has demonstrated that one of the three major superfactors consistently discovered in factor analytic studies of personality structure is the trait of negative emotionality (NEM), which is highly related to Eysenck's trait of neuroticism. NEM is composed of lower-order traits that evoke a subjective experience of a variety of negative emotions, including anger and hostility, depression, anxiety, alienation, and feeling easily distressed by life circumstances. Tellegen conceives of negative emotionality, which has substantial genetic influence when considered as a trait (Tellegen et al., 1988), as a warning-alarm system that produces a diffuse state of negative affect that serves to motivate the directing of attention under conditions of environmental uncertainty. For example, a deer at the threshold of a meadow must, for survival sake, inhibit forward locomotion (hence, Gray's association of negative emotion with a behavioral inhibition system) and attend to the environment for sources of potential threat before entering. Negative affect would be activated by uncertainty and alarm the deer as to potential danger, and it would motivate a directed attentional scanning process. When environmental uncertainty is reduced (in this case, when no threat is perceived), negative affect would decrease, and forward locomotion and incentive motivation as a means of supporting exploratory behavior would ensue.

The neurobiology of NEM is virtually unknown in humans, although several points raise the hypothesis that NE activity in the locus ceruleus (LC) may *modulate* this affective system (Blizzard, 1988). The LC is composed of 20,000 neurons in humans. This small number of neurons, nevertheless, projects to many diverse brain regions, accounting for 80% of forebrain NE and providing the only source of NE to neocortical regions except for the orbital area. This diverse innervation is accomplished with few cells, because each NE fiber displays an extensive pattern of collateralization (or network), where no cortical cell is further than 30 µm from an NE-containing bouton. This type of nonspecific innervation pattern suggests that the LC does not convey specialized information to different brain regions but, rather, that it widely transmits a uniform message.

This role for the LC is supported by the fact that the afferents reaching the LC come mainly from two large nuclei (n. prepositus hypoglossi, n. paragigantocellularis) located in the rostral medulla. The functions of these latter two nuclei are not well understood, but they are thought to be crossroads for circuitry pertaining to autonomic neuron integration as well as polymodal extero- and interoceptive stimuli. Both of these nuclei have cells using 5-HT, enkephalins, substance P, acetylcholine, neurotensin, corticotropin-releasing hormone, somatostatin, and epinephrine as transmitter. Hence, input to the LC is comprised of a host of transmitter systems.

Functions of LC NE Activity

This form of configuration of input to the LC has implications for LC function. The LC receives information via these nuclei on diverse sensory and behavioral events, to which the LC is responsive. However, the signals reaching the LC are apparently highly preprocessed in the cortex and by these medullary nuclei. Thus, the LC receives undifferentiated, homogeneous information, and perhaps, in turn, it weighs input from these two nuclei in distributing a uniform message. This means that the LC may be under greater influence or control from the medulla than the forebrain and, therefore, is not likely to be required *in a primary way* in processes associated with the forebrain, such as learning, memory, emotion, and so forth. That is, the LC may be seen as modulating such processes as part of a more global function, such as behavioral orientation and directed attention.

Behavioral Orientation and Alertness. Studies of LC activity in behaving animals indicate that the LC displays slow spontaneous activity, which is more in keeping with a phasic rather than tonic neural system. Indeed, LC discharge rates correlate with spontaneous changes in levels of vigilance and alertness, where rates are very low in states of inattentive waking and during slow-wave sleep, but are increased in states of behavioral orientation and alertness. The greatest increases in rates of discharge occur when surveillance of the external environment was suddenly and dramatically increased, such as during sensory-evoked increases in behavioral arousal to unexpected or preferred stimuli. Intense LC reactivity occurs, in general, when stimuli disrupt any behavioral state and require increased vigilance and behavioral re-orienting. The most intense reactivity occurred in monkeys in response to human imitations of primate agonistic social signals. This reactivity showed no evidence of habituation, and during long-term, highly significant exteroceptive stimulation, LC activity can be tonically enhanced. The type of stimulation seems to be less important: LC reactivity has been observed in response to simple (low-intensity tone, light flash, touch, 100-dB tone) and complex (food, but not when it is unaccessible and hence requires no attention; restraint, novel objects, entrance or exit of experimenters; signals of noxious stimulation) stimuli. Moreover, LC activity increases dramatically in response to threatening environmental stimuli (Grant & Redmond, 1984; Jacobs, 1986; Rassmussen, Morilak, & Jacobs, 1986). But in most of these cases, LC reactivity is homogeneous to some extent, where groups of LC cells increase and decrease in concert.

Of course, the LC is composed of subgroups of cells that may be grouped by termination region. It is known that LC turnover rates due to psychological stress are regionally specific (Tsuda & Tanaka, 1985). For instance, in rats, psychological stress induced by exposure to other rats being shocked causes marked elevations of turnover in the hypothalamus, amygdala, and LC but not in other regions (Tsuda et al., 1986). Furthermore, reexposure to an environment in which the animal has been shocked, or had observed other animals being shocked, caused significant elevations in NE turnover in the hypothalamus and amygdala.

Interoceptive Stimuli, Physiological Arousal, and Fear–Alarm Responses. The LC dramatically increases firing in response to peripheral somatosensory and autonomic stimuli (Elam, Yao, Thoren, & Svensson, 1981; Elam, Svensson, & Thoren, 1986; Svensson, 1987). The importance of reactivity of the LC to interoceptive stimuli may stem from two factors. First, it is likely that such input to the LC serves as a means of "judging" the magnitude of the psychological significance of the situation at hand (Mesulam, 1990). As significance (coded by level of interoceptive input) increases, LC activity may react in kind and, hence, induce equivalent levels of alertness and orientation to the environment via its projections to the forebrain and neocortex. Second, the ventral aspect of the LC issues descending projections to the spinal cord and, thereby, influences in an inhibitory manner autonomic nervous system activity. Thus, interoceptive input would aid the LC in modulating autonomic arousal (Blizzard, 1988).

The interaction of the LC with autonomic processes may be important with respect to the experience of fear or alarm (Mason, 1981). Although bilateral lesions or pharmacological inhibition of the LC do not affect response to primary negative reinforcers, such as the efficacy of shock in the acquisition of an avoidance task, the amplitude of the fear or alarm responses in monkeys to social group situations, threatening confrontations with humans, lights, sounds, and rubber snakes is greatly reduced (Huang, Redmond, & Snyder, 1976; Redmond, Huang, & Snyder, 1972; Uhde et al., 1984). In these studies, the fear response was not eliminated, as indicated by the lack of effect on defecation and grooming; and, concordantly, LC lesions or chemical destruction of NE terminals in rats does not block conditioned emotional responses or active or passive avoidance performance. Only the amplitude of fear responding appears to be affected. Thus, it is not surprising that electrical stimulation or pharmacological activation of the LC enhances naturally occurring or experimentally induced fear states in monkeys (Redmond & Huang, 1979).

Clarification of the role of NE and epinephrine in the periphery is important in discussions of LC NE and arousal. The "fight–flight" system described by Cannon (1929) involves the sympathoadrenomedullary system, which reacts in emergency situations by releasing epinephrine and NE into the bloodstream. Cannon theorized that this system enabled the organism to prepare rapidly for emergency responses in crisis situations. These include tachycardia, hyperventilation, sweating, inhibition of the gastrointestinal tract, and changes in vasoconstriction and dilation. The LC appears to act as a central analogue to the peripheral sympathoadrenomedullary system, preparing the organism to react in threatening situations. In fact, LC activity correlates highly with peripheral sympathoadrenal activation (Abercrombie & Jacobs, 1987). In threatening situations, then, central NE may serve the function of adaptively increasing vigilance, accuracy of directed attention, and emotional evaluation, whereas the sympathoadrenal system prepares the organism to respond physically.

Stimulus Relevancy and Selective Attention. Mason (1981) and Jacobs (1986) have provided extensive reviews of the evidence on the effects of NE manipulations on behavior, and we shall only briefly summarize their conclusions. Reductions in NE most consistently result in an increased resistance to extinction, but only when the reductions are effected during the acquisition phase of learning. The results hold equally for positive and negative reinforcement tasks. Mason showed that this effect is due to NE's ability to increase the salience of relevant to irrelevant stimuli. Thus, reductions in NE result in poor selective attention to the most task-relevant stimuli, and, hence, many irrelevant stimuli become associated with reward during the phase of acquisition. That is, many irrelevant stimuli in the environment become associated with increased DA activity during goal acquisition and, thereby, become effective incentive stimuli (Beninger, 1983). In the extinction phase, more incentive stimuli need to be extinguished, leading to the overall effect of increased resistance to extinction. This explanation would apply to why partial reinforcement, where the relevant stimuli are more difficult to discriminate, also leads to increased resistance to extinction.

In view of a selective attention function for LC NE projections, it seems concordant that the LC is particularly reactive whenever environmental conditions require close scrutiny, such as when sudden changes occur, or when the animal is more alert and actively exploring the environment, or when interoceptive cues indicate an aroused state induced by environmental change or threat.

A Functional Principle of NE

Oades (1985) has provided an extensive review of the role of NE in many different functions and has concluded that what underlies the selective attention to relevant stimuli is NE's ability to tune neural information. Tuning occurs by NE's enhancement of the signal-to-noise ratio, which involves a reduction in spontaneous firing rates of neurons, accompanied by an increased response of the neuron when a stimulus of sufficient strength evokes an action potential. Conceptually, NE hyperpolarizes a field of cells, making them more difficult to respond to general (i.e., irrelevant) stimulus input. However, strong (i.e., relevant) stimuli will evoke a particularly large response in the neurons receiving stimulation. Thus, the relevant stimuli evoke a response, while the irrelevant stimuli have diminished effects. And this effect would likely occur for signals derived from both external (environmental) and internal (memory retrieval, corticocortical input, interoceptive stimuli) sources.

Although the subject is well beyond the scope of this chapter, it is worth noting briefly that there is anatomical support for the LC NE system's role in directed attention. In the visual system, LC NE projections preferentially innervate structures associated with spatial analysis (e.g., medial pulvinar, inferior parietal lobe, and dorsolateral convexity of prefrontal cortex) and visuomotor (posterior parietal and primary motor cortices) response rather than feature extraction and pattern analysis (e.g., occipital and inferior temporal lobe). Sensory information coursing through the sensory nuclei of the thalamus must pass the gatelets of the reticular nucleus of the thalamus, which then passes the information to other thalamic nuclei having the function of directing the information to specific cortical areas (Stuss & Benson, 1986). LC NE projections densely innervate the reticular nuclei gatelets, hyperpolarizing them. Thus, in the case of visual sensory information, visual signals converging on the gatelets are generally constrained from passing when LC NE activity is high; only the strongest or most relevant stimuli will pass the gatelets. The information that does pass will go to the medial pulvinar, which will then direct it to the appropriate cortical areas, such as the inferior parietal lobe for mapping of extrapersonal space. The important point here is that NE has helped to select the visual information that is from the relevant part of extrapersonal space that now requires mapping. Thus, in this example, the LC NE system plays a critical role, via its influence on reticular gatelets, in directing attention to the relevant regions of extrapersonal space or, put simply, to the relevant stimuli in space.

The LC NE System and Negative Emotionality

Blizzard (1988) has, on the basis of a large pharmacological, behavioral, and genetic literature, proposed an association between LC NE activity and negative emotionality (NEM) in animals. Blizzard hypothesizes that high trait negative emotionality may be related to traitwise low LC activity. According to our understanding of Blizzard's hypothesis, traitwise low LC activity would have two main effects. First, low LC NE activity in ascending projections would result in reduced signal-to-noise ratios and, thus, in chronic inability to detect relevant from irrelevant, or threatening from nonthreatening, stimuli. That is, environmental *uncertainty* would be chronically high, overactivating the NE system. The NE system would, in turn, continually generate a subjective sense of negative affect, accompanied by cognitions of worry, vague threat, and anticipatory fear. Second, the above process would be aggravated by low activity in the ventral LC NE descending projections that provide inhibitory modulation over autonomic reactivity.

Thus, low LC functioning would result in elevated physiological activity that normally accompanies arousal and alarm.

If we extend Blizzard's hypothesis to humans, the source of the negative affect, physiological arousal, and environmental uncertainty created by low LC NE activity would not be clear to the individual characterized by high trait levels of NEM, since the problem would not be located externally in the environment, but, rather, would be located internally within NE's signal-to-noise ratio function. Over time, assessment of such an individual's subjective emotional state would produce a picture consistent with a trait of elevated NEM, as defined by Tellegen and Waller (in press). The extent to which elevated levels of NEM are associated with central NE reactivity is, unfortunately, completely untested and remains an area in need of empirical attention.

As with the PEM system, hypothetically the NEM system would also likely be modified by constraint (i.e., 5-HT functioning). As shown in Figure 6.4, we suggest that the interaction of NEM and constraint will give rise to a dimension of behavioral stability, as was the prediction for PEM × constraint in Figure 6.3. The effects of low constraint are predicted to increase the stress reactiveness of the NEM system in that the threshold for the elicitation of negative affect by environmental uncertainty and threat (signals of punishment) will be reduced.

A Caveat

Models of personality traits based on only one neurotransmitter are clearly too simplistic and will require the addition of other modulating factors. There is, however, good reason to entertain such models when the biogenic amines (DA, 5-HT, NE) are involved. None of the amines appears to serve primarily a *mediating* role in the central nervous system. Rather, each has a particular *modulatory* role in influencing the flow of information in neural networks (Depue, in press; Depue & Zald, 1993; Le Moal & Simon, 1991; Mesulam, 1990; Oades, 1985). This fact, taken together with their broad distribution patterns in the brain (Oades & Halliday, 1987; Tork, 1990), indicates that variation in a single amine can have widespread effects on behavior, as animal research clearly shows (Le Moal & Simon, 1991). Thus, variation in the biogenic amines may come to provide a powerful predictor of behavioral variation. And because the amines are very old from a phylogenetic perspective, they modulate brain structures associated with very basic forms of behavior relevant to personality, including emotions, incentive reward, and motor propensity, as well as important cognitive functions (Le Moal & Simon, 1991; Luciana et al., 1992). Therefore, simplistic amine models of behavior may be viewed as im-

Negative Emotionality

(increased discrimination of signals of punishment)

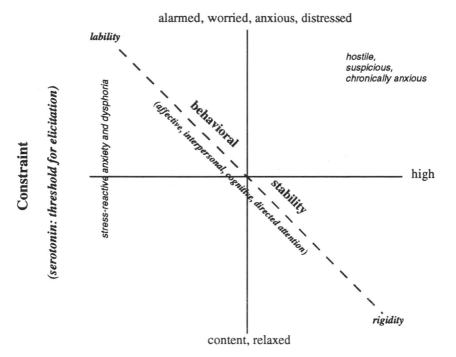

alarmed, worried, anxious, distressed

FIGURE 6.4. A hypothetical personality framework illustrating the interaction of two personality superfactors: negative emotionality and constraint.

portant building blocks for more complex future modeling of personality traits.

STUDIES OF THE RELATIONSHIP OF DA TO POSITIVE EMOTIONALITY AND 5-HT TO CONSTRAINT

We have recently begun testing these theoretical notions in male and female young adults. Because the full explanation of our empirical strategy is presented elsewhere, results are only briefly presented here (Depue et al., 1994, 1995; Depue & Zald, 1993; Luciana et al., 1992). In this work, we have employed a pharmacological challenge protocol, where agonists of DA (bromocriptine, methylphenidate) and 5-HT (fenfluramine) are administered in order to assess individual differences in the reactivity of DA and 5-HT indicators. The indicators are hormonal, cognitive, motor (spontaneous eye-blinking), and affective, although the present discussion will focus on prolactin (PRL) secretion only (DA inhibits, whereas 5-HT elevates, PRL secretion). PEM and NEM are measured using Tellegen's Multidimensional Personality Questionnaire (Tellegen & Waller, in press), although a battery of other personality inventories are also administered. The typical protocol on any given day involves drug administration at 12 noon, followed by blood sampling at 30-minute intervals via an indwelling cannula.

Our initial study (Depue et al., 1994) demonstrated that PRL reactivity to a DA agonist was strongly and *specifically* related to MPQ PEM ($r = .75$, $p < .008$), but not to MPQ NEM ($r = .39$, $p < .25$) or MPQ Constraint (Con) ($r = .02$, $p > .50$). We refined and extended this initial study by assessing 80 subjects in a randomized crossover design under double-blind conditions, not only the relationship of DA to personality structure, but also that of 5-HT and monoamine oxidase activity (MAO-B) (Depue, 1995). MAO-B may be viewed as a trait *modifier* of monoamine function, particularly DA (Depue et al., 1995). From a trait perspective in the general population, low MAO levels have been conceptualized as increasing the probability of impulsivity and sensation-seeking behavior and of various manifestations of affective instability or lability (Haier, Buchabaum, Murphy, Gottesman, & Coursey, 1980). High MAO values also may relate to affective dysfunction and personality disorder. Not all results of this study are available as yet since subject running was completed only recently and because of the large-scale nature of the data generated.

Table 6.1 shows the relationship of maximum DA (1.25 mg bromocriptine)- and 5HT (60 mg fenfluramine)- induced inhibition and activation, respectively, of PRL secretion to MPQ and Eysenck Personality Questionnaire (EPQ) superfactors. DA-PRL is very specifically associated with an *unmodified* MPQ PEM ($r = .52$, $p < .05$), where the correlations with Con and NEM are near zero. Although DA-PRL correlations with PEM first-order traits (well-being, achievement, and social potency) were of similar magnitude, the correlation with the short version of well-being ($r = .63$, $p < .01$) is substantially higher than with the long version ($r = .40$, $p > .05$), possibly because of the former having more of an element of motivation than mere contentment (e.g., excitement about, as opposed to simply pleased with, life). Similarly, the correlation with the subset of achievement items assessing incentive motivation ($r = .59$, $p < .01$) rather than mere persistence (.33) was substantially higher. Thus, when a *modified* MPQ PEM is derived using the short version of well-being and the motivational subset of achievement items, the correlation between DA-PRL increased to $r = .60$ ($p < .01$). DA-PRL was only related highly to one other MPQ trait: harm avoidance (fear of unconditioned stimulus contexts) ($r = -.47$, $p < .05$), suggesting that the subjective state generated by DA activity may reduce the subjective sense of fear to naturally aversive stimuli. By contrast, EPQ correlations with DA-PRL are not significant and are split evenly between extraversion (E) ($r = .31$) and psychoticism (P) ($r = -.39$). MAO-B activity is also significantly, inversely ($r = -.50$, $p < .05$), and specifically related to MPQ PEM (see Table 6.1). This is consistent with the experimental literature indicating that MAO-B activity is negatively related to DA effects on behavioral facilitation (Depue & Iacono, 1989). Table 6.1 also shows that 5-HT-PRL, on the other hand, has a different pattern of relations with MPQ traits. Whereas 5-HT-PRL relates to PEM at near-zero magnitude, it relates moderately but insignificantly to Con ($r = .31$) and NEM ($r = -.27$) but with opposite signs. Also, as was the case with DA-PRL, EPQ E and P are similarly related to 5-HT-PRL ($r = -.37$, $r = -.31$, respectively).

Closer inspection of the first-order traits in MPQ Con and NEM superfactors clarifies the lack of specificity for MPQ-5-HT relations. As shown in Table 6.2, 5-HT-PRL is significantly related only to the control–impulsivity ($r = -.44$, $p < .05$) scale of Con and only to the aggression scale ($r = -.43$, $p < .05$) of NEM. These are the two primary personality traits that have been consistently related highly to indices of 5-HT in unstable personality disorder subjects, where low-5-HT functioning characterizes the more impulsive, explosive, and aggressive disorders (Coccaro & Siever, 1991). Thus, 5-HT-PRL does not appear to be related to a nonimpulsive type of constrained behavior, such as MPQ harm avoidance ($r = .01$) and traditionalism ($r = .04$), where the low extreme of these traits is probably not impulsivity but, rather, a relative absence of fear to negative unconditional stimuli (harm avoidance) and to novelty (traditionalism) (Tellegen & Waller, in press).

TABLE 6.1. Correlations of DA- and 5-HT-Induced PRL and MAO Activity with Telegen's MPQ (PEM, Con, NEM) and Eysenck's EPQ (E, P, N) Superfactors

	PEM	(E)	Con	(P)	NEM	(N)
DA-PRL	.60[a]	(.31)	.09	(−.39)	.06	(.14)
5-HT-PRL	.01	(−.37)	.31	(−.31)	−.27	(−.19)
MAO	−.50		−.16		.03	

Note. Underscores indicate significant correlations.
[a]Modified PEM (see text).

TABLE 6.2. Correlations of 5-HT-Induced PRL with MPQ Constraint and NEM Subscales

	Constraint			NEM		
	Harm-avoidance	Traditionalism	Control	Aggression	Stress reaction	Alienation
5-HT-PRL	.01	.04	$-.44$	$-.43$	$-.21$	$-.12$

Note. Underscores indicate significant correlations.

Table 6.3 assesses more extensively the correlation between 5-HT-PRL and *aggression* on the BHDI (BDHI total score: $r = -.63$, $p < .01$). As seen in Table 6.3, the quantitatively similar significant correlations of 5-HT-PRL with several forms of aggression measured on different inventories (i.e., MPQ NEM Aggression and BDHI) suggest convergent validity for a 5-HT–aggression relationship. On the BDHI, the irritability, as well as the assault (impulsive aggressive acts), subscales are both components of the type of aggression related to 5-HT-PRL, which is in line with extensive work on animals and personality disorders (Coccaro & Siever, 1991; Depue & Spoont, 1986; Spoont, 1992). For instance, Coccaro et al. (1989) found that BDHI irritability was the best correlate of fenfluramine-PRL values in personality disordered subjects. Moreover, as shown in Table 6.3, DA-PRL relates only weakly to these forms of aggression, providing an initial form of discriminant validity for a 5-HT–aggression relationship. More passive, cognitive forms of aggression, such as measured on the resentment, suspiciousness, and negative feelings subscales of the BDHI (correlations with 5-HT-PRL = $-.29$, $-.31$, $-.24$, respectively, p's $> .05$), are less strongly associated with 5-HT activity than impulsive, action-related (but not necessarily goal-oriented, as in irritative) aggression.

Table 6.4 assesses the relationship between 5-HT-PRL and *impulsivity* more extensively. Examining the DA- and 5-HT-PRL correlations in Table 6.4 confirms what others have noted (Depue, Krauss, &

TABLE 6.3. Correlations of DA- and 5-HT-Induced PRL with Aggression Scales

	MPQ NEM Aggression	Buss–Durkee Hostility Inventory		
		Total	Irritability	Assault
5-HT-PRL	$-.43$	$-.63$	$-.51$	$-.49$
DA-PRL	$-.02$	$-.22$	$-.33$	$-.19$

Note. Underscores indicate significant correlations.

TABLE 6.4. Correlations of DA- and 5-HT-Induced PRL
with Impulsivity—Sensation Seeking Scales

| | MPQ control | EPQ P | Sensation seeking scales | | Barratt | Eysenck | |
			Soc. Dis.	Boredom		Ven.	Risk.
5-HT-PRL	−.44	−.39	−.44	−.44	−.51	−.13	−.10
DA-PRL	−.13	−.39	−.12	−.06	−.27	.40	.33

Note. Underscores indicate significant correlations. Soc. Dis., Social Disinhibition; Boredom, Boredom Susceptibility; Ven., Venturesomeness; Risk., Risk Taking.

Spoont, 1987; Eysenck, 1981): Impulsivity is a heterogeneous construct incorporating several forms of behavior. In Table 6.4, 5-HT-PRL is consistently and significantly (p's $< .05$) related to five different scales assessing impulsivity and sensation seeking, and DA-PRL is not significantly related to these same scales. On the other hand, DA-PRL is related more highly than 5-HT-PRL to scales of venturesomeness and risk taking. The DA-PRL correlations suggest that DA may be related to a behavioral impulsivity that incorporates a positive affective state, where there is a strong component of desire and incentive motivation to succeed in reaching a goal. 5-HT is much less related to this aspect of impulsivity and to the seeking of contexts that generate positive affect, although the animal literature is clear that under low 5-HT conditions, DA-facilitated behaviors are enhanced. Perhaps 5-HT relates to the DA-type of impulsivity only at low levels of 5-HT functioning (i.e., where there is a substantial disinhibition of DA facilitation), thereby limiting correlations derived from the full range of 5-HT functioning. 5-HT may be broadly related to cognitive, motor, and social impulsivity. For instance, 5-HT-PRL was related consistently and significantly to scales tapping a cognitive impulsivity, including nonplanning (Eysenck's [1981] $r = -.49$, $p < .05$; Barratt's [1983] $r = -.42$, $p < .05$), doing things without due consideration (Eysenck's [1981] narrow $r = -.52$, $p < .01$), and Barratt's (1983) cognitive subscale of impulsivity ($r = -.38$, $p < .05$). Moreover, Barratt's (1983) subscale of motor-behavior impulsivity was substantially related to 5-HT-PRL ($r = -.54$, $p < .01$).

Thus, the type of impulsivity associated with 5-HT activity appears to affect overt expression of behavioral acts when those acts are associated with particularly strong motivational imperative, such as in affective aggression and in the impulsive suicidal behavior strongly associated with psychological states of distress and reactive depression. Behavioral acts associated with incentive motivational states may also be influenced by 5-HT, but that relationship seems to be more complex and requires more detailed examination than we have done thus far. It also seems clear that low 5-HT functioning is related to non-action- oriented behavioral processes, such as cognitive decision making and planning, and fine-motor control.

What is intriguing is that PRL, reflecting the action of DA in hypothalamic DA systems, was so strongly related to a set of behaviors (PEM) that most likely reflect DA function in ascending projections arising from VTA DA cells (Depue, in press; Le Moal & Simon, 1991; Louilot et al., 1987; Oades, 1985). Coccaro et al. (1989) also demonstrated strong correlation between *inventory* trait measures of irritability ($r = -.68$, $p < .002$) and impulsive aggressive behavior ($r = -.65$, $p < .002$) (BDHI) and the magnitude of PRL response to the 5-HT agonist fenfluramine (60 mg). Since the 5-HT influence on PRL secretion is thought to arise from ascending projections from dorsal raphe neurons to the hypothalamus (Coccaro et al., 1989), and since the dorsal raphe projections to the limbic forebrain also appear to influence affective behavior (Depue & Spoont, 1986), it is possible that characteristics of dorsal raphe function are manifested in both PRL and behavioral variables, as suggested for the VTA above. It appears, then, that the PRL system holds considerable promise in the study of the relation among DA, 5-HT, and emotional behavior. The reason that the PRL system relates strongly to certain personality traits is not completely clear. As noted above, DA cell groups, including those in the substantia nigra, VTA, and hypothalamus, can manifest a common genetic influence that is reflected in their functional properties. For instance, DA agonist effects are correlated across PRL secretion, exploratory behavior, and locomotor activity in inbred strains of mice that differ in DA neuron number in all DA cell groups (Fink & Reis, 1981; Oades, 1985; Sved et al., 1984, 1985). It is possible, therefore, that the heritability of MPQ PEM and Con (Tellegen et al., 1988) is related to genetic influences on DA and 5-HT cell groups and that unmeasured genetic variance in our subjects contributed substantially to the observed correlations between MPQ PEM and Con, and PRL response.

IMPLICATIONS FOR PERSONALITY DISORDERS

It has been estimated that the overall prevalence for any diagnosable personality disorder in community samples is in the range of 10–13%. Currently, DSM-IV (American Psychiatric Association, 1994) defines 11 personality disorders that may be clustered into three conceptual groups. The "odd/eccentric" group of personality disorders includes paranoid, schizoid, and schizotypal personality disorders; the "impulsive/erratic" cluster consists of the antisocial, borderline, narcissistic, and histrionic personality disorders; and the "anxious/avoidant" cluster contains avoidant, dependent, passive–aggressive, and compulsive personality disorder. A major focus of current research in personality disorders concerns their continuity versus discontinuity in relation to normal personality. Although it is unrealistic to conceive of precise one-to-one correspondences between personality disorder symptoms and normative personality traits, it is reasonable to expect that some correspondences will be observed between several of the major dimensions underlying normal personality and personality disorder symptomatology. The meaning of such correspondences represents a substantive challenge, because an implicit assumption of the work has been that an association between such variables suggests a causal *continuity* between the phenomena. However, just as a correlation does not imply causation, it also does not imply continuity in biological, psychological, or social processes. It could quite conceivably be that in some instances no genuine connection between a dimension of personality and a personality disorder exists, even though a statistically significant correlation may exist between them.

At this time, it is completely unclear if the same neurobiological processes thought to underlie normal personality are functionally and structurally similar to those involved in personality pathology. The personality–neurobiology model outlined above has clear implications and hypotheses regarding the placement of personality disorders in relation to PEM and DA, NEM, and constraint and 5-HT. (I am grateful for the ideas contributed to this conceptualization by my colleague Mark Lenzenweger.) These are depicted in Figure 6.5, which shows how Cluster B ("erratic/impulsive"), Cluster C ("anxious avoidant"), and schizoid personality disorders would be placed within the theoretical model; paranoid and schizotypal personality disorders are less likely to fit within the model, given the growing body of evidence linking them with schizophrenia. Figure 6.5 illustrates the type of affective experience expected at the extremes of the interaction of the three personality superfactors. The horizontal axis is comprised of values represented by the interaction of PEM and NEM, and placement along this dimension determines the type of affective experience to predominate in interactions with environmental cues. The vertical axis is represented by constraint, where increasingly low values at the top are associated with increasing affective instability of a type determined by one's position on the horizontal axis.

Thus, interaction of the three superfactor traits produces a "cloud" of affective experience around the perimeter of Figure 6.5. The personality disorders, as typological entities, emerge within this "cloud,"

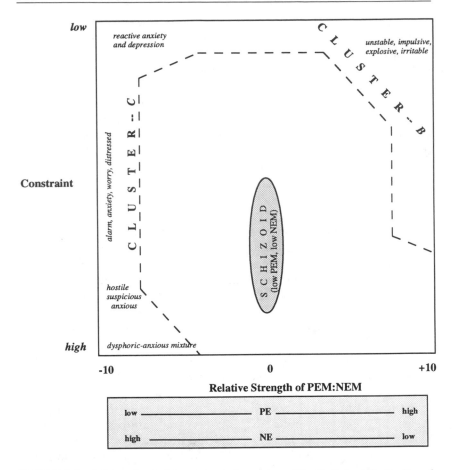

FIGURE 6.5. A hypothetical framework for personality disorder Cluster B and C and schizoid personality as a function of the interaction of the three major personality superfactors: positive emotionality, negative emotionality, and constraint.

although they are probably better conceptualized in this model as prototypes that blend or mix at the end of their affective range with other prototypes. For example, Cluster C and Cluster B would merge and become mixed in the extreme upper center of the figure. Schizoid disorder is represented within the central, lower two-space as a low-PEM–low-NEM condition that does not extend to the low extremes of constraint.

Interaction of Neurobiological–Personality Systems in Personality Disorders

Human disorders of impulsive and irritable aggression, impulsive suicidal behavior, unstable personality, certain types of alcohol abuse, pharmacological substance abuse, and impulse-related homocide are likely best understood as interactions of neurobiological–personality systems. The potential usefulness of considering the three superfactor traits jointly can be illustrated by considering the Cluster B personality disorders. Although reduced 5-HT functioning appears to be related, in general, to instability of emotional behavior and, formally, to the unstable group of personality disorders (Cluster B), the phenotype of the unstable, Cluster B personality disorders varies substantially. In the model represented in Figure 6.5, phenotypic variation in the Cluster B group would be due to other modifying traits that contribute to the behavioral profile. One such modifying trait may be the level of PEM (or trait level of DA activity) or, behaviorally, level of facilitation to incentive reward. For instance, the depressive patients who have a history of impulsive suicidal behavior, often referred to historically as neurotic depression, not only display reduced 5-HT functioning but also reduced CSF levels of the major DA metabolite, homovanillic acid (HVA), when depressed (Roy, Pickar, Linnoila, Doran, & Paul, 1986; Roy, Karoum, & Pollack, 1992; Traskman, Asberg, Bertilsson, & Sjostrand, 1981) and at 5-year follow-up (Roy, Lamponski, De Jong, Moore, & Linnoila, 1989). However, it seems more difficult to imagine that other forms of unstable, Cluster B personality disorders, such as histrionic and antisocial personality disorders, would also have low HVA accompanying low 5-HT. Thus, antisocial and histrionic personality, for example, may naturally fall at the high end of DA-PEM trait functioning, whereas borderline personality with strong depressive features may fall lower on the DA-PEM trait dimension. Furthermore, the role of sensitization of the DA system, described below in relation to substance abuse, may also be worth considering in Cluster B disorders. To the extent that DA may modify Cluster B phenotypes as just discussed, the low 5-HT conditions associated with this cluster could, according to our model, render the DA system more liable to sensitization. This could have implications for several aspects of Cluster B disorders, including their intensity, variation in or severity of expression over time, and in the susceptibility to abuse of substances that are DA agonists.

In a similar way, 5-HT-constraint and MAO-B may be considered as modifying traits in personality disorders that involve extreme values in the DA-PEM or NEM systems. For instance, 5-HT could be viewed as modifying the frequency of periods of distress and dysphoria in some forms of personality disorders: Low serotonin has been associated with an increased frequency of so-called neurotic depression with personality disorder, and low levels of DA functioning may contribute to such depressions (Depue & Iacono, 1989; Depue & Zald, 1993). Furthermore, natural trait variation in MAO-B activity may similarly modify the role of DA in modifying Cluster B phenotypes, as discussed above.

Implications for the Development of Substance Abuse

One of the reasons that substance abuse may be elevated in Cluster B personality disorders may be related to the framework being discussed here. Because the basic principle underlying the DA foundation of the BFS is sensitivity to incentive–reward stimuli, one way in which the BFS may serve as the foundation for one component of Cluster B disorders is as a susceptibility to self-administration behavior. That is, the BFS could serve as a liability factor to abuse of substances that are DA agonists. Such substances would naturally have incentive–reward effects, and individuals with extremely reactive DA systems and/or extremely low 5-HT modulation of DA reactivity could learn to self-administer the substance in order to create a strong subjective state of incentive reward. Substances that have been implicated as DA agonists that may lead to abuse, or excessive self-administration, include psychostimulant drugs (such as amphetamine and cocaine; Koob & Bloom, 1988); alcohol, whose initial excitatory effects involve the activation of DA release in the NAS (Depue & Iacono, 1989); and, most recently, certain sweet substances, such as chocolate, thereby contributing to obesity. Because the role of DA in substance abuse would, according to our model, be modulated by 5-HT functional levels as well (Depue & Spoont, 1986), DA and 5-HT may both contribute to a liability to substance abuse in Cluster B disorders.

One other aspect of substance abuse may be relevant here. Self-administration behavior is a learned behavior that is subject to a process of sensitization with repeated experience—that is, where the self-administration behavior increases dramatically with repeated experience of the same dose of DA agonist. Piazza et al. (1989) demonstrated that rats could be inbred for extreme trait levels of locomotor reactivity to the incentive condition of novelty. Not only were these two extreme groups substantially different in their locomotor response to a single injection of the DA agonist amphetamine (the high-locomotor group responded much more vigorously to amphetamine), but the groups also showed differential sensitization when the same dose of amphetamine was repeatedly injected at a constant temporal interval of days. The high-locomotor trait group quickly sensitized, whereas the low-locomotor trait group sensitized much more slowly and achieved a less exaggerated level of sensitization. Moreover, the two groups also differed with respect to their acquisition performance of self-administration of amphetamine: The high-locomotor group quickly learned to self-administer amphetamine and showed a sensitization effect over time, whereas the low-locomotor group *did not acquire* self-administration. Put differently, the high-trait group was more susceptible to acquiring self-administration of a DA agonist, whereas the low-trait group apparently experienced such low incentive reward effects from the self-administration of amphetamine that they were resistant to acquiring this behavior.

The Piazza et al. study (1989) also demonstrated the probabilistic nature of susceptibility, a probability that was modifiable with experience. After it was demonstrated that the low-locomotor group could not acquire self-administration of amphetamine, the low-trait group was first sensitized to amphetamine and then tested for acquisition of self-administration of amphetamine. Subsequent to the sensitization manipulation, the low-locomotor group was able to acquire self-administration of amphetamine at a comparable rate to the nonsensitized high-locomotor group. The liability or susceptibility to self-administration of a DA agonist had apparently been increased in the low-locomotor group as a function of the experience-dependent processes involved in sensitization of the mesolimbic DA projection system (Piazza et al., 1989).

In summary, then, it seems quite reasonable to expect that consideration of normative personality traits and their underlying neurobiology will help to clarify basic etiological or modifying processes involved in personality disorder. This may be most likely in forms of personality disorders that appear to be related to PEM and NEM in interaction with constraint.

ACKNOWLEDGMENTS

This work was supported by NIMH Research Grant Nos. MH37195 and MH48114 and NIMH Research Training Grant No. MH 17069 awarded to Richard A. Depue.

REFERENCES

Abercrombie, E. D., & Jacobs, B. L. (1987). Single-unit response of noradrenergic neurons in the locus coeruleus of freely moving cats: I. Acutely presented stressful and nonstressful stimuli. *Journal of Neuroscience, 7,* 2837–2843.

Azmitia, E. C., & Gannon, P. J. (1986). The primate serotonergic system: A review of human and animal studies and a report on *Macaca fascicularis.* In S. Fahn (Ed.), *Advances in neurology: Vol. 43. Myoclonus* (pp. 407–468). New York: Raven Press.

Babor, T., Hofmann, M., Del Boca, F., Hesselbrock, V., Meyer, R., Dolinsky, Z., & Rounsaville, B. (1992). Types of alcoholics I. *Archives of General Psychiatry, 49,* 599–608.

Barratt, E. (1983). Impulsivity: Cognitive, behavioral, and psychphysiological correlates. In M. Zuckerman (Ed.), *Biolgical basis of sensation seeking, impulsivity, & anxiety.* Hillsdale, NJ: Earlbaum.

Beninger, R. J. (1983). The role of dopamine in locomotor activity and learning. *Brain Research Reviews, 6,* 173–196.

Beninger, R. J., Hanson, D. R., & Phillips, A. G. (1980). The effects of pipradrol on the acquisition of responding with conditioned reinforcement: A role for sensory preconditioning. *Psychopharmacology, 69,* 235–242.

Blackburn, J. R., Phillips, A. G., Jakubovic, A., & Fibiger, H. C. (1989). Dopamine and preparatory behavior: II. A neurochemical analysis. *Behavioral Neuroscience, 103,* 15–23.

Blizzard, D. (1988). The locus coeruleus: A possible neural focus for genetic differences in emotionality. *Experientia, 44,* 491–495.

Bozarth, M. A. (1987). Ventral tegmental reward system. In J. Engel & L. Oreland (Eds.), *Brain reward systems and abuse* (pp. 1–17). New York: Raven Press.

Brown, G., Goodwin, F., Ballenger, J., Goyer, P., & Major, L. (1979). Aggression in humans correlates with cerebrospinal fluid metabolites. *Psychiatric Research, 1,* 131–139.

Brown, R. M., Crane, A. M., & Goldman, P. S. (1979). Regional distribution of monoamines in the cerebral cortex and subcortical structures of the rhesus monkey: Concentrations and in vitro synthesis rates. *Brain Research, 168,* 133–150.

Buss, A., & Durkee, A. (1957). An inventory for assessing different kinds of hostility. *Journal of Consulting Psychology, 21,* 343–348.

Cannon, W. B. (1929). *Bodily changes in pain, hunger, fear and rage: An account of recent researches into the functions of emotional excitement* (2nd ed.). New York: Appleton-Century-Crofts.

Coccaro, E., & Siever, L. (1991). *Serotonin and psychiatric disorders.* Washington, DC: American Psychiatric Press.

Coccaro, E., Siever, L., Klar, H., Maurer, G., Cochrane, K., Cooper, T., Mohs, R., & Davis, K. (1989). Serotonergic studies in patients with affective and personality disorders. *Archives of General Psychiatry, 46,* 587–599.

Collins, P., & Depue, R. (1992). A neurobehavioral systems approach to developmental psychopathology: Implications for disorders of affect. In D.

Cicchetti (Ed.), *Developmental psychopathology* (Vol. 4, pp. 46–98). Rochester, NY: University of Rochester Press.

Cools, A. R. (1980). The role of neostriatal dopaminergic activity in sequencing and selecting behavioral strategies: Facilitation of processes involved in selecting the best strategy in a stressful situation. *Behavioral Brain Research, 1,* 361–374.

Depue, R. A. (in press). *Neurobehavioral systems, personality, and psychopathology.* New York: Springer-Verlag.

Depue, R. A. (1995). [Neurobiology correlates of personality]. Unpublished raw data.

Depue, R. A., & Iacono, W. G. (1989). Neurobehavioral aspects of affective disorders. *Annual Review of Psychology, 40,* 457–492.

Depue, R. A., Krauss, S., & Spoont, M. R. (1987). A two-dimensional threshold model of seasonal bipolar affective disorder. In D. Magnusson & A. Ohman (Eds.), *Psychopathology: An interactional perspective* (pp. 95–123). New York: Academic Press.

Depue, R. A., Luciana, M., Arbisi, P., Collins, P. F., & Leon, A. (1994). Relation of agonist-induced dopamine activity to personality. *Journal of Personality and Social Psychology, 67,* 485–498.

Depue, R., Luciana, M., & Collins, P. (1995). A neurobiology–experience interaction model for developmental psychopathology. In M. Lenzenweger & J. Haugaard (Eds.), *Frontiers in developmental psychopathology.* New York: Oxford University Press.

Depue, R. A., & Spoont, M. R. (1986). Conceptualizing a serotonin trait: A behavioral dimension of constraint. *Annals of the New York Academy of Sciences, 487,* 47–62.

Depue, R. A., & Zald, D. H. (1993). Biological and environmental processes in nonpsychotic psychopathology: A neurobehavioral perspective. In C. G. Costello (Ed.), *Basic issues in psychopathology* (pp. 127–237). New York: Guilford Press.

Deutch, A., Bourdelais, A., & Zahm, D. (1993). In P. Kalivas & C. Barnes (Eds.), *Limbic motor circuits and neuropsychiatry.* Boca Raton, FL: CRC Press.

Digman, J. (1990). Personality structure: Emergence of the five-factor model. *Annual Review of Psychology, 41,* 417–440.

Elam, M., Svensson, T. H., & Thoren, P. (1986). Locus coeruleus neurons and sympathetic nerves: Activation by cutaneous sensory afferents. *Brain Research,, 366,* 254–261.

Elam, M., Yao, T., Thoren, P., & Svensson, T. H. (1981). Hypercapnia and hypoxia: Chemoreceptor-mediated control of locus coeruleus neurons and splanchnic, sympathetic nerves. *Brain Research, 222,* 281–287.

Ervin, F. R., & Martin, J. (1986). Neurophysiological bases of the primary emotions. In E. Plutchik, & H. Kellerman (Eds.), *Emotion: Theory, research, and experience: Vol. 3. Biological foundations of emotion* (pp. 145–170). New York: Academic Press.

Eysenck, H. J. (1981). *A model for personality.* New York: Springer-Verlag.

Eysenck, H. J., & Eysenck, M. W. (1985). *Personality and individual differences: A natural science approach.* New York: Plenum Press.

Fink, J. S., & Reis, D. J. (1981). Genetic variations in midbrain dopamine cell number: Parallel with differences in responses to dopaminergic agonists and in naturalistic behaviors mediated by dopaminergic systems. *Brain Research, 222,* 335–349.

Fishman, R., Feigenbaum, J., Yanaiz, J., & Klawans, H. (1983). The relative importance of dopamine and norepinephrine in mediating locomotor activity. *Progress in Neurobiology, 20,* 55–88.

Fonberg, E. (1986). Amygdala, emotions, motivation, and depressive states. In E. Plutchik & H. Kellerman (Eds.), *Emotion: Theory, research, and experience—Vol. 3: Biological foundations of emotion* (pp. 301–331). New York: Academic Press.

Fowles, D. C. (1980). The three arousal model: Implications of Gray's two-factor learning theory for heart rate, electrodermal activity, and psychopathy. *Pyschophysiology, 17,* 87–104.

Fowles, D. C. (1987). Application of a behavioral theory of motivation to the concepts of anxiety and impulsivity. *Journal of Research in Personality, 21,* 417–435.

Goldman-Rakic, P. S. (1987). Circuitry of the prefrontal cortex and the regulation of behavior by representational memory. In V. Mountcastle, F. Plum, & S. Geiger (Eds.), *Handbook of physiology* (Vol. 1, pp. 373–417). New York: Oxford University Press.

Goldman-Rakic, P. S. (1988). Topography of cognition: Parallel distributed networks in primate association cortex. *Annual Review of Neuroscience, 11,* 137–156.

Grant, S. J., & Redmond, D. E., Jr. (1984). Neuronal activity of the locus coeruleus in awake *Macaca arctoids. Experimental Neurology, 84,* 701–708.

Gray, J. A. (1973). Causal theories of personality and how to test them. In J. R. Royce (Ed.), *Multivariate analysis and psychological theory* (pp. 409–462). New York: Academic Press.

Gray, J. A. (1982). *The neuropsychology of anxiety.* New York: Oxford University Press.

Haier, R., Buchsbaum, M., Murphy, D., Gottesman, I., & Coursey, R. (1980). Psychiatric vulnerability, monoamine oxidase and the average evoked potential. *Archives of General Psychiatry, 37,* 340–346.

Hebb, D. O. (1949). *The organization of behavior.* New York: Wiley.

Hill, R. T. (1970). Facilitation of conditioned reinforcement as a mechanism of psychomotorstimulants. In E. Costa & S. Garattini (Eds.), *Amphetamines and related compounds* (pp. 781–795). New York: Raven Press.

Huang, Y. H., Redmond, D. E., Jr., & Snyder D. R. (1976). Loss of fear following bilateral lesions in the locus coeruleus in the *Macaca arctoides. Neuroscience Abstract, 2,* 573.

Jacobs, B. L. (1986). Single unit activity of the locus coeruleus neurons in behaving animals. *Progress in Neurobiology, 27,* 83–194.

Kalivas, P., & Barnes, C. (1993). *Limbic motor circuits and neuropsychiatry.* New York: CRC Press.

Koob, G. F., & Bloom, F. E. (1988). Cellular and molecular mechanisms of drug dependence. *Science, 242,* 715–723.

Kosslyn, S. (1988). Aspects of a cognitive neuroscience of mental imagery. *Science, 240,* 1621–1626.

LeDoux, J. E. (1987). Emotion. In V. Mountcastle, F. Plum, & S. Geiger (Eds.), *Handbook of physiology* (Vol. 1, pp. 419–459). New York: Oxford University Press.

Le Moal, M., & Simon, H. (1991). Mesocorticolimbic dopaminergic network: Functional and regulatory roles. *Physiological Reviews, 71,* 155–234.

Levi, L. (1975). *Emotions—Their parameters and measurement.* New York: Raven Press.

Louilot, A., Taghzouti, K., Deminiere, J. M., Simon, H., & Le Moal, M. (1987). Dopamine and behavior: Functional and theoretical considerations. In M. Sandler (Ed.), *Neurotransmitter interactions in the basal ganglia.* New York: Raven Press.

Luciana, M., Depue, R. A., Arbisi, P., & Leon, A. (1992). Facilitation of working memory in humans by a D_2 dopamine receptor agonist. *Journal of Cognitive Neuroscience, 4,* 58–68.

MacLean, P. D. (1969). The hypothalamus and emotional behavior. In W. Haymaker, E. Anderson, & W. J. H. Nauta (Eds.), *The hypothalamus* (pp. 72–89). Springfield, IL: Charles C. Thomas.

MacLean, P. D. (1970). The triune concept of the brain and behavior. In F. O. Schmitt (Ed.), *The neurosciences second study program* (pp. 117–182). New York: Rockefeller University Press.

MacLean, P. D. (1986). Ictal symptoms relating to the nature of affects and their cerebral substrate. In E. Plutchik & H. Kellerman (Eds.), *Emotion: Theory, research, and experience: Vol. 3. Biological foundations of emotion* (pp. 61–90). New York: Academic Press.

MacLean, P. D. (1990). *The triune brain in evolution: Role in paleocerebral functions.* New York: Plenum Press.

Mason, S. T. (1981). Noradrenaline in the brain: Progress in theories of behavioral function. *Progress in Neurobiology, 16,* 263–303.

Mesulam, M.-M. (1990). Large-scale neurocognitive networks and distributed processing for attention, language, and memory. *Annals of Neurology, 28,* 597–613.

Mishkin, M. (1982). A memory system in the monkey. *Philosophical Transactions of the Royal Society, B298,* 85–95.

Mogenson, G., Brudqynski, S., Wu, M., Yang, C., & Yim, C. (1993). From motivation to action. In P. Kalivas & C. Barnes (Eds.), *Limbic motor circuits and neuropsychiatry* (pp. 193–236). Ann Arbor MI: CRC Press.

Oades, R. D. (1985). The role of noradrenaline in tuning and dopamine in switching between signals in the CNS. *Neuroscience and Biobehavioral Reviews, 9,* 261–282.

Oades, R. D., & Halliday, G. M. (1987). Ventral tegmental (A10) system: Neurobiology. 1. Anatomy and connectivity. *Brain Research Reviews, 12,* 117–165.

Oades, R. D., Taghzouti, K., Rivet, J-M., Simon, H., & Le Moal, M. (1986). Locomotor activity in relation to dopamine and noradrenaline in the nucleus accumbens, septal and frontal areas: A 6-hydroxydopamine study. *Neuropsychobiology, 16,* 37–43.

Panksepp, J. (1986). The anatomy of emotions. In E. Plutchik & H. Kellerman (Eds.), *Emotion: Theory, research, and experience: Vol. 3. Biological foundations of emotion* (pp. 91–124). New York: Academic Press.

Piazza, P. Deminiere, J., Le Moal, M., & Simon, H. (1989). Factors that predict individual vulnerability to amphetamine self-administration. *Science, 245,* 1511–1513.

Ploog, D. (1986). Biological foundations of the vocal expressions of emotions. In E. Plutchik & H. Kellerman (Eds.), *Emotion: Theory, research, and experience—Vol. 3: Biological foundations of emotion* (pp. 173–197). New York: Academic Press.

Plutchik, R. (1980). *Emotion: A psychoevolutionary synthesis.* New York: Harper & Row.

Plutchik, E., & Kellerman, H. (Eds.). (1986). *Emotion: Theory, research, and experience: Vol. 3. Biological foundations of emotion.* New York: Academic Press.

Posner, M. I., Petersen, S. E., Fox, P. T., & Raichle, M. E. (1988). Localization of cognitive operations in the human brain. *Science, 240,* 1627–1631.

Rasmussen, K., Morilak, D. A., & Jacobs, B. L. (1986). Single unit actibity of locus coeruleus neurons in the freely moving cat: I. During naturalistic behaviors and in response to simple and complex stimuli. *Brain Research, 371,* 324–334.

Redmond, D. E., Jr., & Huang, Y. H. (1979). New evidence for a locus coeruleus-norepinephrine connection with anxiety. *Life Sciences, 25,* 2149–2162.

Redmond, D. E., Jr., Huang, Y. H., & Snyder, D. R. (1972). Behavioral changes following lesions of the locus coeruleus in the monkey. *Neuroscience Abstracts, 1,* 472.

Robbins, T. W. (1975). The potentiation of conditioned reinforcement by psychomotorstimulant drugs: A test of Hill's hypothesis. *Psychopharmacology, 45,* 103–114.

Robbins, T. W., & Everitt, B. J. (1982). Functional studies of the central catecholamines. *International Review Neurobiology, 23,* 245–261.

Rolls, E. T. (1986). Neural systems involved in emotion in primates. In E. Plutchik & H. Kellerman (Eds.), *Emotion: Theory, research, and experience: Vol. 3. Biological foundations of emotion* (pp. 125–143). New York: Academic Press.

Roy, A., Karoum, F., & Pollack, S. (1992). Marked reduction in indexes of dopamine metabolism among patients with depression who attempt suicide. *Archives of General Psychiatry, 49,* 447–450.

Roy, A., Lamponski, D., De Jong, J., Moore, V., & Linnoila, M. (1989). Characteristics of alcoholics who attempt suicide. *American Journal of Psychiatry, 147,* 761–765.

Roy, A., Pickar, D., Linnoila, M., Doran, A., & Paul, S. (1986). Cerebrospinal fluid monoamine and monamine metabolite levels and the dexanethasone suppression test in depression. *Archives of General Psychiatry, 43,* 356–360.

Sawaguchi, T., & Goldman-Rakic, P. S. (1991). D_1 dopamine receptors in prefrontal cortex: Involvement in working memory. *Science, 251,* 947–950.

Sawaguchi, T., Matsumura, M., & Kubota, K. (1990). Effects of dopamine antagonists on neuronal activity related to a delayed response task in monkey prefrontal cortex. *Journal of Neurophysiology, 63,* 1401-1412.

Schneirla, T. (1959). An evolutionary and developmental theory of biphasic processes underlying approach and withdrawal. In M. Jones (Ed.), *Nebraska symposium on motivation* (pp. 27-58). Lincoln: University of Nebraska Press,

Simon, H., Scatton, B., & Le Moal, M. &1980). Dopaminergic A10 neuroses are involved in cognitive functions. *Nature, 286,* 150-151.

Spoont, M. (1992). Modulatory role of serotonin in neural information processing: Implications for human psychopathology. *Psychological Bulletin, 112,* 330-350.

Stein, L. (1983). The chemistry of positive reward. In M. Zuckerman (Ed.), *The biological bases of sensation seeking, impulsivity, and anxiety* (pp. 56-64). Hillsdale, NJ: Erlbaum.

Stuss, D. T., & Benson, D. F. (1986). *The frontal lobes.* New York: Raven Press.

Sved, A. F., Baker, H. A., & Reis, D. J. (1984). Dopamine synthesis in inbred mouse strains which differ in numbers of dopamine neurons. *Brain Research, 303,* 261-266.

Sved, A. F., Baker, H. A., & Reis, D. J. (1985). Number of dopamine neurons predicts prolactin levels in two inbred mouse strains. *Experientia, 41,* 644-646.

Svensson, T. H. (1987). Peripheral, autonomic regulation of locus coeruleus neoradrenergic neurons in brain: Putative implications for psychiatry and psychopharmacology. *Psychopharmacology, 92,* 1-7.

Taghzouti, K., LeMoal, M., & Simon, H. (1985). Enhanced frustrative nonreward effect following 6-OHDA lesions of the lateral septum in the rat. *Behavioral Neuroscience, 99,* 1066-1073.

Taghzouti, K., Louilot, A., Herman, J. P., Le Moal, M., & Simon, H. (1985). Alternation behavior, spatial discrimination, and reversal disturbances following 6-hydroxydopamine lesions in the nucleus accumbens of the rat. *Behavioral and Neural Biolology, 44,* 354-363.

Taghzouti, K., Simon, H., & Le Moal, M. (1986). Disturbances in exploratory behavior and functional recovery in the Y and radial mazes following dopamine depletion of the lateral septum. *Behavioral and Neural Biology, 45,* 48-56.

Taghzouti, K., Simon, H., Louilot, A., Herman, J. P., & Le Moal, M. (1985). Behavioral study after 6-hydroxydopamine lesions of the nucleus accumbens. *Brain Research, 344,* 9-20.

Taghzouti, K., Simon, H., Tazi, A., Dantzer, R., & Le Moal, M. (1985). The effect of 6-OHDA lesions of the lateral septum on schedule-induced polydipsia. *Behavioral Brain Research, 15,* 1-8.

Tellegen, A. (1985). Structures of mood and personality and their relevance to assessing anxiety, with an emphasis on self-report. In A. H. Tuma & J. D. Maser (Eds.), *Anxiety and the anxiety disorders* (pp. 681-706). Hillsdale, NJ: Erlbaum.

Tellegen, A., Lykken, D. T., Bouchard, T. J., Wilcox, K. J., Segal, N. L., & Rich, S. (1988). Personality similarity in twins reared apart and together. *Journal of Personality and Social Psychology, 54,* 1031-1039.

Tellegen, A., & Waller, N. G. (in press). Exploring personality through test construction: Development of the multidimensional personality question-naire. In S. R. Briggs & J. M. Cheek (Eds.), *Personality measures: Development and evaluation* (Vol. 1). Greenwich, CT: JAI Press.

Tork, I. (1990). Anatomy of the serotenergic system. *Annals of the New York Acadamy of Science, 600,* 9–31.

Traskman, L., Asberg, M., Bertilason, L., & Sjostrand, L. (1981). Monoamine metabolites in CSF and suicidal behavior. *Archives of General Psychiatry, 38,* 631–636.

Tsuda, A., & Tanaka, M. (1985). Differential changes in noradrenaline turnover in specific regions of rat brain produced by controllable and uncontrollable shocks. *Behavioral Neuroscience, 99,* 802–817.

Tsuda, A. Tanaka, M., Yoshishige, I., Tsujimaru, S., Ushijima, I., & Nagasaki, N. (1986). Effects of preshock experience on enhancement of rat brain noradrenergic turnover induced by psychological stress. *Pharmacology, Biochemistry and Behavior, 24,* 115–119.

Uhde, T. W., Boulenger, J.-P. , Post, R. M., Siever, L. J., Vittone, B. J., Jimerson, D. C., & Roy-Byrne, P. P. (1984). Fear and anxiety: Relationship to noradrenergic function. *Psychopathology, 17*(Suppl. 3), 8–23.

Van Praag, H. (1984). Serotonin and depression. In R. Post & J. Bollengen (Eds.), *Neurobiology of mood disorders* (pp. 91–117). Baltimore, MD: Williams & Wilkins.

Watson, D., & Tellegen, A. (1985). Toward a consensual structure of mood. *Psychological Bulletin, 92,* 426–457.

White, N. (1986). Control of sensorimotor function by dopaminergic nigrostriatal neurons: Influence on eating and drinking. *Neuroscience and Biobehavioral Reviews, 10,* 15–36.

Zuckerman, M. (1983). *Biological bases of sensation seeking, impulsivity, and anxiety.* Hillsdale, NJ: Erlbaum.

Zuckerman, M., Kuhlman, M., Thornquist, M., & Kiers, H. (1991). Five (or three) robust questionnaire scale factors of personality without culture. *Personality and Individual Differences, 12,* 929–941.

Index